AF365186

Advanced
UNIX Programming

Second Revised Edition

Advanced UNIX Programming

Second Revised Edition

Prof. N. B Venkateswarlu

B.Tech (SVUCE), M.Tech(IIT-K), Ph.d(BITS, Pilani), PDF(Univ of Leeds, UK)
AITAM, TEKKALI, A.P
&

Director

RITCH CENTER

Opp TSR Complex, 47-15-6, Ratna Arcade, Visakhapatnam – 530016

Tel: 0891-2598705

Email: venkat_ritch@yahoo.com, Web Site:www.ritchcenter.com/nbv

BS Publications

An unit of **BSP Books Pvt., Ltd.**

4-4-309/316, Giriraj Lane, Sultan Bazar,
Hyderabad - 500 095 - A.P.
Phone : 040 - 23445605, 23445688

Published by :

BS Publications

An unit of **BSP Books Pvt., Ltd.**

4-4-309/316, Giriraj Lane, Sultan Bazar,
Hyderabad - 500 095 - A.P.
Phone : 040 - 23445605, 23445688
e-mail : info@bspbooks.net

ISBN : 978-93-52300-54-9 (HB)

<u>*Dedicated to*</u>

My Beloved Parents

Preface

Since early 1970, Unix Operating System has gone through many metamorphosis. As of now many variants of Unix systems are available and some of them are commercial and whereas the others are freely available. In the recent years, Linux, a public domain, freely available. Unix variant has attracted the people very much. Till today, Unix is believed to be bread and butter of Computer Science intern's. However, because of this freely available Unix variant, many people are becoming Unix enthusiasts, especially in India.

Hundreds of books had been written in the past which explores various facets of Unix such as user commands, shell programming. However, there are very few books which detail Unix internals (leave out on device drivers, kernel development). This book is an attempt to explain Unix system calls (internals) in a lucid and problem oriented manner. The examples which are discussed are the result of the author's lectures at RITCH center and also from the suggestions (answers) made by thousands of Unix enthusiasts in USENET groups on Unix, and personnel web pages of many Linux enthusiasts.

This book assumes that the prosperous reader has no hands on exposure to Unix Operating System. However, it assumes that he has good exposure to theoretical aspects of Operating Systems Design and 'C' programming.

First nine chapters deal with "how to get hands on exposure to Unix Operating System". Subsequent chapters explain "Unix internal programming". All the examples given are tested under Linux environment. Examples given in Processes are very illustrative and concept oriented. Simple examples are taken to explain the concepts in thorough manner. Chapter on Signals explains the reliable and unreliable way of handling signals while introducing the basic concepts from scratch. Chapters such as pipes, message queues, shared memory, semaphores and memory mapping are dealt in detail with vivid examples such that the users can immediately correlate their theoretical concepts learnt in Operating Systems courses with practical programming examples, explained in this book.

In this edition, we have added a new chapter on network programming under unix. It introduces the reader to elements of network programming using TCP/IP relate system calls. Simple and easy examples are included which are tested under Linux.

- Author

Acknowledgement

There are many people, to whom I profoundly indebted while bringing out this book. Especially, those thousands of Linux enthusiasts who actively participate in mailing lists, USENET groups are the ones who shoud be thanked by me first.

I shall also thank my wife Dr. Sarada and the little Appu, my daughter for bearing me while preparing this manuscript and sacrificing their marvelous Sunday evenings also.

I would like to express my sincere thanks to Prof PS Rao, Principal, Prof BR Gandhi, Prof. B. Kantha Rao, Prof P Soma Raju, Secretary, and the Computer Science & IT Departments staff and students of GVP Engg College, Visakhapatnam. Also, I shall express my sincere thanks to staff and students of RITCH center, Visakhapatnam.

Also, I am thankful to prof. V.V. Nageswara Rao, prof. Dharmaje, prof. Ramesh of AITAM, Tekkali; prof EV Prasad, prof. JVR Murthy, prof. E.V. Prasad, Dr. Krishna Prasad of JNTU, Kakinada.

Prof. PSVSK Raju, KLC, Vijayawada, Prof. N Patel, BIT Ranchi, Dr. MN Reddy, APAU, Hyderabad deserve to recollect them for their consistent and constant encouragment.

I would like express my thanks to hundreads of those students who expressed their views on our first edition. This is improvement of first edition using Their feedback.

Lastly, I would like to express my thanks to Mr. Nikhil Shah, BS Publications for bringing this book.

- Author

Contents

CHAPTER 1

Introduction to Unix system

CHAPTER 2

Vi Editor

CHAPTER 3

Redirection Operators

CHAPTER 4

Filters

CHAPTER 5

Pipes

CHAPTER 6

Awk Command

CHAPTER 7

Backup Commands

CHAPTER 8

Internet Related Commands

CHAPTER 9

Shell Programming

CHAPTER 10

Unix System Calls

CHAPTER 11

Unix File System Calls API

CHAPTER 12

Unix System Calls API for Directory Operations

CHAPTER 13

Standard Library Functions

CHAPTER 14

Process

CHAPTER 15

Process Timers

CHAPTER 16

Signals

CHAPTER 17

Unix Memory Management

CHAPTER 18

File Locking

CHAPTER 19

Pipes

CHAPTER 20

Message Queues

CHAPTER 21

Shared Memory

CHAPTER 22

Semaphores

CHAPTER 23

Memory Mapped Files

CHAPTER 24

Network Programming: A Brief Introduction

1 Introduction to UNIX System

Simple View of an Operating System

In the developments of computers most commendable developments can be mentioned as the development of operating systems with the help of which a lay man is also in a position to avail the services of computers without joining computer science majors! An Operating System is the SW layer between the hardware and user as shown in the following figure and gives clean and easy interface to the user.

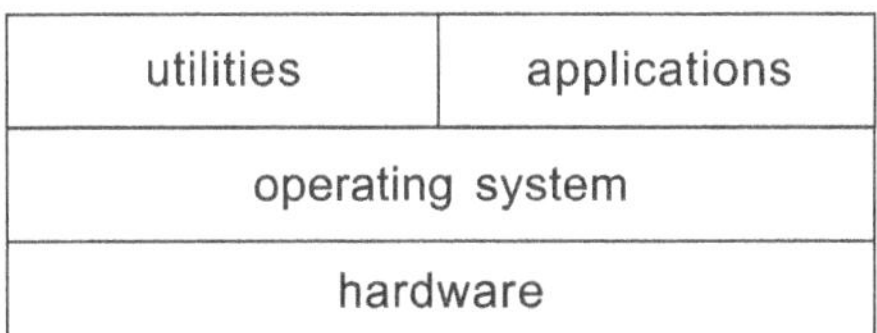

Figure 1.1

An Operating System is responsible for the following functions :

- device management using device drivers,
- process management using processes and threads,
- inter-process communication,
- memory management,
- file systems.

In addition, all operating systems come with a set of standard utilities. The utilities allow common tasks to be performed such as :

▸ being able to start and stop processes,

▸ being able to organize the set of available applications,

▸ organize files into sets such as directories,

▸ view files and sets of files,

▸ edit files,

▸ rename, copy, delete files and

▸ communicate between processes.

Kernel

The *kernel* of an operating system is the part responsible for all other operations. When a computer boots up, it goes through some initialization functions, such as checking memory. It then loads the kernel and switches control to it. The kernel then starts up all the processes needed to communicate with the user and the rest of the environment (e.g. the LAN).

The kernel is always loaded into memory, and kernel functions always run, handling processes, memory, files and devices.

The traditional structure of a kernel is a *layered* system, such as Unix. In this, all layers are part of the kernel, and each layer can talk to only a few other layers. Application programs and utilities live above the kernel.

The Unix kernel looks like (Fig. 1.2).

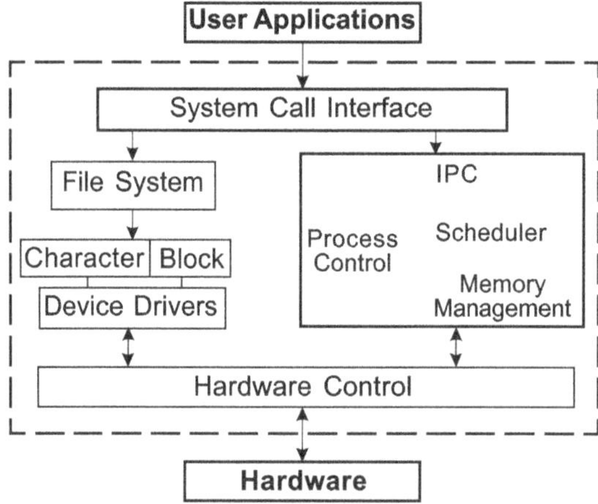

Figure 1.2 UNIX Kernel

Most of the Operating Systems being built now use instead a micro kernel, which minimizes the size of the kernel. Many traditional services are made into user level services. Communication being services is often by an explicit *message passing* mechanism.

The major micro-kernel Operating System is Mach. Many others use the concepts of Mach (*see* Fig. 1.3).

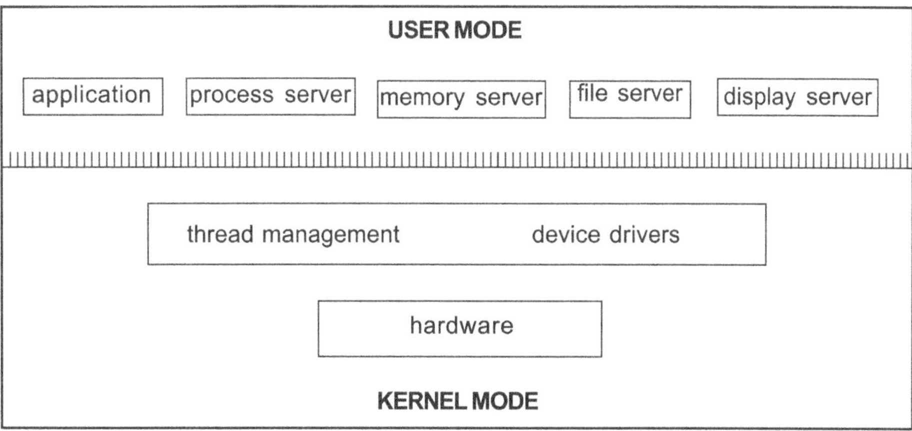

Figure 1.3 Micro Kernel Architecture

Some systems, such as Windows NT use a mixed approach (Fig. 1.4).

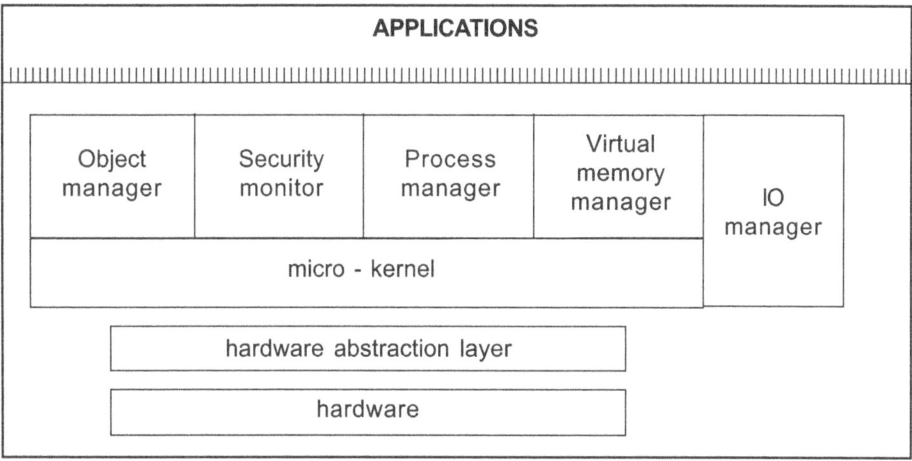

Figure 1.4

Distinguished Applications

An Operating System has been described as an *"application with no top"* (B. Meyer, *"Object-oriented Software Construction"*). *Other* applications interact with it, through a large variety of entry points. In order to use an OS, you need to be supplied with at least some applications that already use these entry points.

All Operating Systems come bundled with a set of *"utilities"* which do this. For example :

- Windows95 has a shell that allows programs to be started from the Start button. There is a standard set of applications supplied.
- MSDOS starts up with COMMAND.COM to supply a command line prompt, and a set of utilities.
- Unix has a set of command line shells and a huge variety of command line utilities.
- X-Windows supplies a login shell (xdm). Others supply file managers, session managers, etc which can be used to provide a variety of interfaces to the underlying Unix/POSIX system.

Command Interpreter

When a user interacts with an Operating System they always do so through the intermediary of a command interpreter. This responds to user input in the following ways :

- it starts applications,
- it stops applications,
- it allows the user to switch control between applications and
- it may allow control over communication between an application and other applications or the user.

The command interpreter may be character based, as in the MSDOS COMMAND.COM or the Unix shells. It may be a GUI shell, such as the Windows 3.1 Program Manager.

The interpreter may be simple, or can have the power of a full programming language. It may be imperative (as in the Unix shells), use message passing (as in AppleScript) or use visual programming metaphors such as drag-and-drop for object embedding (as in Microsoft's OLE).

It is important to distinguish between the command interpreter and the underlying Operating System. The command interpreter may only use a subset of the capabilities offered by the Operating System; it may offer them in a clumsy or sophisticated way; it may require complex skills or be intended for novice.

Introduction to Unix File System

Files are stored on devices such as hard and floppy disks. OS defines a *file system* on the devices. Many OS use a *hierarchical* file system.

A directory is a file that keeps a list of other files. This list is the set of children of that directory node in the file system. A directory cannot hold any other kind of data.

On MSDOS a file system resides on each floppy or partition of the hard disk. The device name forms part of the file name.

On Unix there is a single file system. Devices are *mounted* into this file system. (Use the command mount to see this.)

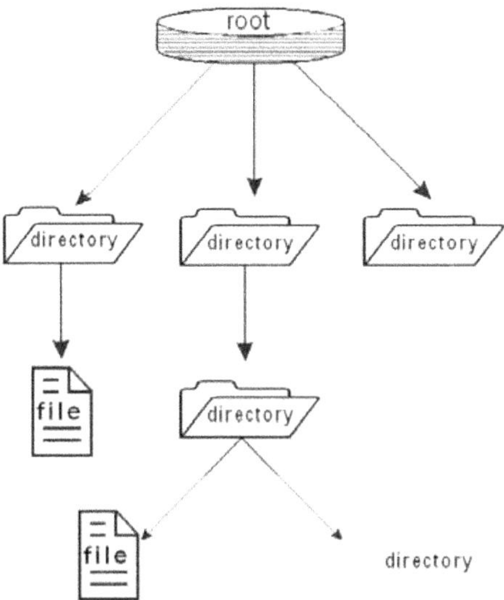

Figure 1.5 Hierarchical File Systems

File and Directory Naming

An individual node of the file system has its own name. Naming conventions differ between operating systems. In MSDOS, a name is constructed of upto 8+3 characters. Windows95 uses tricks on top of the MSDOS file system to give "long file names" of upto 255 characters. In "*standard Unix*" (POSIX) a name may consist of upto 256 characters.

The full file names are constructed by concatenating the directory names from the root down to the file, with some special separator between names. This is known as absolute path naming. In MSDOS, the full path name also includes the drive name.

Example : **MSDOS**

```
C : \expsys\lectures\search.txt
```

Example : **Unix**

```
/usr/usrs/os
```

```
/usr/usrs/os/myfile
```

Relative naming means that files are named from some special directory :

```
.  current directory (Unix and MSDOS)
.. parent directory (Unix and MSDOS)
~  home directory (some Unix shells)
~  user home directory of user (some shells)
```

Example : Unix

```
~fred/../bill/dir1/./../file1
```

If just the name itself is given without any special prefixes (such as /, ., .., ~) then it refers to the file in the current working directory.

Command `history`

Bash has a command `history` for convenience. The list of previous commands may be obtained by executing the following command.

```
history
!n
```

(n is an integer) will re-execute the nth command.

```
!!
```

This executes the most recent command

```
!cp
```

This executes the most recent command which starts with cp.

Up arrow, down arrows can be used in some shells to recollect the commands from command `history` buffer.

`man` **Pages**

All the Unix command information are organized in a special fashion like the following :

  ▸   The user-level commands are all in Section One.
  ▸   Section Two is the Unix Application Programmer's Interface, API (i.e., C functions directly supported by Unix).
  ▸   Section Three is library extensions to these.
  ▸   Section Four defines devices known to Unix.
  ▸   Section Five defines common file formats.
  ▸   Sections Local and New are for stuff we have added to our local system.

If we run man command with a name first it will check for commands with that name.

Example

```
man sleep

man 2 sleep
```

This displays details of sleep library function if available

```
man 3 sleep
```

This displays details of sleep system call if exists any.

`apropos` command can be used to displays names of all the commands whose manual page contains a search pattern.

Example

```
apropos TERM
```

This displays names of the Unix commands, system calls or library functions whose manual page contains the search pattern TERM.

`cat` **Command**

This is used to create files.

Example

```
cat > ABC
```

This is a test file.

I wish you find happy to create first file.

```
^d
```

This is also used to see the file(s) content. If the file contains more lines then it simply scrolls the matter of that file.

Example

```
cat ABC
```

This command is also used to create duplicate of a file.

Example

```
cat ABC >XYZ
or
cat <ABC >XYZ
```

XYZ becomes duplicate copy of file ABC.

This `cat` command can be used to see the content of more than one file.

Example

```
cat ABC XYZ
```

This `cat` command can be used to join the content of two or more files and create another file.

Example

```
cat ABC XYZ > MNO
```

Now MNO file contains the contents of both file XYZ and ABC.

While joining two or more files and creating a combined file we can add interactive input also.

Example

```
cat ABC - XYZ > PPP
```

You type what ever you want followed by CTRL d at the end.

```
^d
```

Now file PPP contains content of ABC, the interactive input and the content of file XYZ in the same order. By changing the location of –, we can add interactive input between any two files.

2 The vi Editor

This is the popular editor in Unix since last 30 years. This is a screen editor which is based on another editor known as elvis. It has three modes: **Input Mode** in which what ever user typed will be written into the document. **Command Mode** is the one in which the user can enter commands. To move from Input mode to command mode, we have to press ESC key. If you are already in command mode and when we press ESC key we will get beep sound. This command mode is also called as ESC mode. The third mode is called as **colon mode** in which also users can run commands to do some editing on the document content. Ofcourse, there are some people who debate that this is not a separate mode!! In a nutshell, the following commands are summarized to immediately work under Unix.

1. **vi filename** Opens vi editor with the given filename.

2. When the editor opens a screen will be opened with the command mode.

3. To enter text press **i** then input mode will be displayed at bottom right part of the screen.

4. To stop typing, press **Esc** key. Then command mode comes. Press

    : w   to save the matter and resume editing.

    : wq   to save the matter and quit the vi editor.

    : q!   to quit the editor without saving.

5. Three modes are present in `vi` editor namingly

    (i)   Command mode,

    (ii) Input mode,

    (iii) Colon mode.

6. In command mode commands can be entered. By pressing **Esc** key one can go to command mode from other modes.

    (a)   press **i** to insert text before the current cursor position.

    (b) press **I** to insert text at the beginning of the line.

    (c) press **a** to insert text after the cursor position.

    (d) press **A** to insert text at the end of the current line.

    (e) press **o** to open a new line below the current line.

    (f) press **O** to open a new line above the current line.

    (g) press **r** to replace the present character with a character.

    (h) press **R** to replace a group of characters from current cursor position.

    (i)   press **x** to delete present character.

    (j)   press **J** to join the next line to the end of the current line.

    (k) press **dd** to delete the current line.

    (l)   press **4dd** to delete 4 lines from the current line.

   (m) press **dw** to delete the current word.

    (n) press **7dw** to delete 7 words from the current word onwards.

    (o) press **30i*Esc** (invisible command) to insert 30 *'s at the cursor position.

    (p) press **u** to undo the effect of the previous command on the document.

    (q) press **.** to repeat the previous command.

    (r) press **yy** to copy the entire line in to the buffer.

    (s) press **yw** to copy the entire word in to buffer.

    (t) press **p** to place the copied or deleted information below the cursor.

    (u) press **P** to place the copied or deleted information above the cursor.

7. **Colon mode commands**

    (a) Search and substitute commands

        1. **:/raja** searches for the string "raja" in the forward direction. press **n** to repeat the search.

        2. **:?raja** search for the string in the backward direction press **n** to repeat the above search.

3. **:s/raja/rama** replaces the first occurrence of "raja" with "rama".

4. **:s/raja/rama/g** replaces all "raja"'s with rama in the present line.

5. **:g/raja/s/raja/rama/g** replaces all "raja"'s by "rama" in whole file.

(b) *Block delete commands*

1. **:1d** delete the line 1.

2. **:1,5d** deletes the lines from 1 to 5.
   $ Means last line of the file.
   .Means present line (i.e) present line.

3. **:10,$d** deletes lines from 10th line to the last line of the file.

4. **:1,$d** deletes lines from 1 to last line of the file.

5. **:.,$d** deletes lines from present line to the last line.

6. **:.–3,.d** deletes the lines from present line and above 2 lines (deletes 3 lines including the cursor line).

7. **:.,.+4d** deletes the lines from the present cursor line followed 3 lines (total 4 lines).

8. **:–1,.+3d** deletes the lines one above the cursor line followed by it 3 lines.

9. **:18** cursor goes to 18th line of the file.

(c) *Block copy commands*

1. **:1,5 co 10** copies the lines from 1 to 5 after 10th line.

2. **:1,$ co $** copies the lines from 1 to last line after last line.

3. **:.,.+5 co 8** copies lines from present line to 5 lines after 8th line.

4. **:–3,. co 10** copies the lines from present cursor line and above 3 lines after 10th line.

(d) *Block moving commands*

1. **:1,5 mo 9** moves lines from 1 to 5 after 9th line.

2. **:1,$ mo $** moves lines from 1 to $ after last line.

3. **:.,.+5 mo 10** moves lines from present line and next 5 lines after 10th line onwards.

4. **:.–3,.mo 10** moves present line and above 3 lines after 10th line.

Importing & Exporting the files

1. **:1,5 w filename** writes lines 1 to 5 in the specified filename.

2. **:1,5 w! filename** overwrites lines 1 to 5 in the specified filename.

3. **:r filename** adds the content of filename after   the current line.

8. Book mark command

Bookmarks (markers) are not visible and are useful to jump from one line to another quickly. Markers should be in lower case. To have the marker on a specified line press **m** followed by a lower case alphabet (say a) then marker for that line is set as a. To go to the marked line press '**a** ('back quote) followed a. eg: go to 500 th line, press mb (b is the marker). To go to the 500th line from anywhere in the document press '**b**. Then the cursor goes to the 500th line.

3 Redirection Operators

Standard Input, Output Redirection Operators

Unix supports input, output redirection. We can send output of any command to file by using > operator.

Example

```
command>aaa
```

Output of the given `command` is sent to the file. First, file `aaa` is created if not existing, otherwise its content is erased and then output of the command is written.

```
cat aa>aaaa
```

Here, `aaaa` file contains the content of the file `aa`.

We can let a command to take necessary input from a file with < operator (standard input operator).

```
cat<aa
```

This displays output of file `aa` on the screen.

```
cat aa aa1 aa3>aa12
```

This creates the file `aa12` which contains the content of all the files `aa, aa1` and `aa3` in order.

```
cat <aa >as
```

This makes `cat` command to take input from the file `aa` and write its output to the file `as`. That is, it work like a `cp` command.

Unix has a nice (intelligent) command line interface. Thus, all the following commands work in the same manner.

```
cat <aa >as
cat >as <aa
<aa cat >as
<aa >as cat
>as cat <aa
>as <aa cat
```

This discussion is meaningful with any command. For example, consider the following C program which takes these integers and writes their values.

```c
#include <stdio.h>
void main()
{
    int x,y,z;
    scanf("%d%d%d", &x, &y, &z);
    printf("%d\n%d\n%d\n", x, y, z);
}
```

Let the file name be `a.c` and by using the either of the following commands, its machine language file `a` is created.

```
gcc-o a a.c
cc-o a a.c
```

When we start this program `a` by simply typing `a` at the dollar prompt, it takes 3 values and displays given values on the screen.

```
a>res
```

This program takes these values interactively and writes the same into file `res`. You can check by typing `cat res`.

```
a<res
cat <aa >as
cat >as <aa
<aa cat >as
<aa >as cat
>as cat <aa
>as <aa cat
```

This command takes necessary input from the file `res` and displays the results on the screen.

```
a <res >as
a >as <res
<res a >as
<res >as a
>as a <res
>as <res a
```

Each of these commands takes three values from the file `res` and write the same in the file `as`.

Similarly, `>>` operator can be used to append standard output of a command to a file.

Example

```
command>>aaa
```

This makes, output of the given command to be appended to the file `aaa`. If the file `aaa` is not existing, it will be created a fresh and then standard output is written.

Here the document operator (`<<`)

This is used with shell programs. This signifies that the data here is rather in a separate file.

Example

```
grep Rao<<end
I like PP Reddy
I know Mr. PN Rao since 1987
I wanted to see Raj today
Mr. Rao, please see me today
end
```

The above sequence of commands when executed at the dollar prompt, we will get those lines having `Rao` as output of `grep` command. Here, by using `<<` operator we are mentioning that the data is directly available here.

`more` **Command**

This command is used to see the content of the files page by page or screen by screen fashion. This is very useful if the file contains more number of lines.

Example

```
more filenames(s)
```

```
more file1 file2
```

This displays content of the files `file1` and `file2` one after another.

```
more <file1
```

This also displays the content of the `file1` in screen by screen fashion.

```
more file1 file2  ... filen > XXX
```

This command creates file XXX such that it contains the content of all the given files in the strictly same order.

```
more +/rao  filename
```

This command displays the content of the given file starting from the line which contains the string "rao".

```
more +10 filename
```

This command displays the content of the file from 10th line.

`pg` command

This command is also used to see the content of the files in page by page fashion. However, this is not available in recent versions. Rather `more` command is in wide use and is more flexible.

`nl` command

This command is used to display the content of the file along with line numbers.

Example

```
nl filename
```

`tail` command

```
tail filename(s)
```

This command displays last 10 lines of the given file(s).

```
tail -1 filename(s)
```

This command displays last 1 line of the given file(s).

```
tail  +2 filename(s)
```

This command displays second line to last line of the given file(s)

head **command**

```
head filename(s)
```

This command displays first 10 lines of the given file(s).

```
head -2 filename(s)
```

This command displays first 2 lines of the given file(s)

mkdir **command**

This is used to create a new directory.

```
mkdir rao
```

This creates rao directory in the current directory.

```
mkdir /tmp/rao
```

This creates rao directory in /tmp directory.

```
mkdir /bin/rao
```

This fails for normal users because of permissions (/bin belongs to super user).

rmdir **command**

This is used to remove empty directory only.

```
rmdir rao
```

This removes rao directory of current working directory.

```
rmdir /tmp/rao
```

This removes rao diretcory in /tmp directory.

pwd **command** displays where currently we are located.

cd **directoryname**

This changes the current working directory to the given directory.

```
cd
```

This command takes you to your home directory.

`ls` **command**

This command displays names of the files and directories of current directory.

```
al
a2
a3
a4
a5
```

The following command displays names of files and directories of current directory in long fashion. That is, file permissions, owner name, group, links, time stamps, size and names.

```
ls - l
total 4
-rw-r--r--      1 root      root          0 Feb 13 23:55 a1
-rw-r--r--      1 root      root          0 Feb 13 23:55 a2
-rw-r--r--      1 root      root          0 Feb 13 23:56 a3
-rw-r--r--      1 root      root          0 Feb 13 23:55 a4
-rw-r--r--      1 root      root        290 Feb 13 23:59 a5
```

In Unix, files whose names start with . are called as hidden files. If we want to see their details also, then we have to use –a option (ofcourse either alone or with other options).

For example, the following command displays other files also whose names starts with '.'.

```
ls - al
total 12
drwxr-xr--x     2 root      root       4096 Feb 14 00:01 .
drwxr-x--      29 root      root       4096 Feb 14 00:01 ..
-rw-r--r--      1 root      root          0 Feb 13 23:55 a1
-rw-r--r--      1 root      root          0 Feb 13 23:55 a2
-rw-r--r--      1 root      root          0 Feb 13 23:56 a3
-rw-r--r--      1 root      root          0 Feb 13 23:55 a4
-rw-r--r--      1 root      root        882 Feb 14 00:01 a5
-rw-r--r--      1 root      root          0 Feb 14 00:01 .aa1
```

The following command displays details of the files in chronological order.

```
ls -alt
total 12
drwxr-xr--x     2 root      root       4096 Feb 14 00:03 .
drwxr-x--      29 root      root       4096 Feb 14 00:03 ..
-rw-r--r--      1 root      root       1451 Feb 14 00:03 a5
-rw-r--r--      1 root      root          0 Feb 14 00:01 .aa1
-rw-r--r--      1 root      root          0 Feb 13 23:56 a3
-rw-r--r--      1 root      root          0 Feb 13 23:55 a2
-rw-r--r--      1 root      root          0 Feb 13 23:55 a1
-rw-r--r--      1 root      root          0 Feb 13 23:55 a4
```

```
ls -l filename
```

It displays only that file details if it exists.

```
ls -l directoryname
```

It displays the files and directory detials in the given directory.

All the options –a, –t etc can be also used. Moreover, Unix commands will be having excellant command line interface. Thus, all the following commands are equivalent.

```
ls -a -l -t
ls -alt
ls -a -t -l
ls -atl
ls -l -a -t
ls -lat
ls -l -t -a
ls -lta
ls -t -l -a
ls -tla
ls -t -a -l
ls -tal
```

–R option with ls command displays details of files and subdiretcories recursively.

Example

`ls –alR /` (ofcourse, you can go for a cup of coffee and come back before you see the prompt again!!)

This command displays all the files in Unix system.

`cp` **command**

cp command is used to duplicate a file(s).

Syntax
   cp source destination

cp a1.c /tmp	Creates a1.c file in /tmp directory which contains same content as that of file a1.c of current working directory.
cp /bin/ls /tmp/AA	Creates a new file AA in /tmp directory with the content of /bin/ls
cp /tmp/a1.c	Creates a1.c file in current working directory with the content of file /tmp/a1.c

Contd... Table

cp a1.c a2.c	Creates a2.c in current working directory with the content of a1.c
cp *.c /tmp	Copies all files with extension c in current directory to /tmp directory
cp /tmp/*.c	Copies all files with extension c in /tmp directory to current working directory
cp /bin/* /tmp	Copies all files of /bin directory to /tmp
cp –r sourcedirectory destinationdirectory	Copies all files, subdirectories and files in them of the source directory to destination directory.
cp *.c /bin	This command will fail if you are a normal user as we do not have permissions usually on /bin directory. However, it will work for super (root) user.

mv **command**

mv command is used to move file(s) from one directory to another directory or to rename the file.

The options include

```
-i   interactive confirmation of overwrites
-f   force a copy
-R   recursively copy to a directory
```

Syntax

 mv source destination

mv a1.c /tmp	*Creates a1.c file in /tmp directory while file a1.c of current working directory is removed.*
mv a1.c a2.c	*Creates a2.c in current working directory with the content of a1.c while a1.c is disappered*
mv *.c /tmp	*Moves all files with extension c in current directory to /tmp directory*
mv /tmp/*.c	*Moves all files with extension c in /tmp directory to current working directory*
mv /bin/* /tmp	*Moves all files of /bin directory to /tmp*

The options include

```
-i interactive confirmation of overwrites
-f force a move
```

wc **command**

wc filename or wc<filename

This command displays number of lines, words and characters in the given file.

```
wc -l filename
```

This displays number lines in the given file.

```
wc -w filename
```

This displays number words in the given file.

```
wc -c filename
```

This displays number characters in the given file.

`find` **command**

This command is used to locate files in the Unix directory tree.

Find directoryname-name filename to be found

Example

```
find / -name core
```

This command displays all the occurrences of the file named core under / directory.

```
find. -ctime 2 -name
```

This command displays names of those files which are created in the last two days and are in the current directory.

```
find . -mtime 2 -name
```

This command displays names of those files which are modified in the last two days and are in the current directory.

```
find . -size 10 -name
```

This command displays names of those files whose size is greater than 10 blocks of `size` 512 bytes and are in the current directory.

```
find . -type d -name
```

This command displays names of directories in the current directory.

Link Files

Unix supports two types of links (shortcuts) for files and directories namingly hard links and symbolic links.

Example

```
ln a1 a6
```

Here, a6 becomes hard link to the file a1. Whatever operations we do on a6 is really seen from a1 also. The reverse also is true. In fact, a6 will not take extra disk space. If we delete a1 (or a6) yet the file content is accessible through other name.

Hard links cannot be created to directories. Moreover, they cannot be created to the files of other partitions.

ls -l a1 a6 gave the following result

```
-rw-r—r—     2 root      root    20 Feb 14 00:13 a1
-rw-r—r—     2 root      root    20 Feb 14 00:13 a6

ln a1 a7
```

ls -al a1 a6 a7 gave the following result

```
-rw-r—r—     3 root      root    20 Feb 14 00:13 a1
-rw-r—r—     3 root      root    20 Feb 14 00:13 a6
-rw-r—r—     3 root      root    20 Feb 14 00:13 a7
```

We can observe that link count is increasing whenever a new hardlink is created for a file. Similarly, whenever we remove a hardlink file link count is reduced.

```
rm a6
```

ls -l a1 a7 gives results

```
-rw-r—r—     2 root      root    20 Feb 14 00:13 a1
-rw-r—r—     2 root      root    20 Feb 14 00:13 a7
```

I–node numbers or hardlink and original files are same.

ls -li a1 a7

```
264826 -rw-r—r— 2 root    root 20 Feb 14 00:13 a1
264826 -rw-r—r— 2 root    root 20 Feb 14 00:13 a7
```

Symbolic Links

```
ln -s a1 a8
ls -l a1 a8
-rw-r—r—             1 root   root  20 Feb 14 00:13 a1
lrwxrwxrwx           1 root   root   2 Feb 14 00:20 a8 -> a1
```

We can see the difference. Though, whatever operations we do on symbolic link really takes place on the original file yet if we delete original file the information of the file cannot be accessible through symbolic link unlike hardlink files. Ofcourse, if we delete symbolic link yet the information is accessible through original name. Moreover, i-node numbers or orginal file and symbolic link files are different. In fact, symbolic link file will take seperate disk block in which path of the original file is saved.

```
ls -li a1 a8
264826 -rw-r—r—   3 root   root   20 Feb 14 00:13 a1
264831 lrwxrwxrwx 1 root   root    2 Feb 14 00:20 a8 -> a1
```

Main advantage of symbolic link files is that they can be used to create links for directories and also to the files of other partitions. In fact, symbolic links are used for SW fine tuning. For example check for file 'x' in Linux system, which is normally symbolic link to the appropriate X server (Check in `/usr/X11R6/bin`).

`ls -l /usr/X11R6/bin/X` gave me the following results

```
lrwxrwxrwx  1 root   root 7 Feb 7 06:31 /usr/X11R6/bin/X -> XFree86
```

If we want to change to some other X server, simply we change X to point to that and start the X server.

4 Filters

uniq command

This command displays uniq lines of the given files. That is if successive lines of a file are same then they will be removed. By default, the output will be on to the screen. This can be used to remove sucessive empty lines from the given file.

```
cat list-1 list-2 list-3 | sort | uniq final.list
```

Concatenates the list files, sorts them, removes duplicate lines, and finally writes the result to an output file.

The useful –c option prefixes each line of the input file with its number of occurrences.

Let the file "testfile" contains the following lines.

```
This line occurs only once.
This line occurs twice.
This line occurs twice.
This line occurs three times.
This line occurs three times.
This line occurs three times.
```

Then, the following command is executed the result is as displayed below.

```
uniq -c testfile
```

```
1 This line occurs only once.
2 This line occurs twice.
3 This line occurs three times.
```

Similarly, when the following command is executed the result is displayed as below.

```
sort testfile | uniq -c | sort -nr
```

```
3 This line occurs three times.
2 This line occurs twice.
1 This line occurs only once.
```

`grep` **command**

This command is used to select lines from a file having some specified string.

```
grep "rao"  xyz
```

This displays those lines of the file `xyz` having string `rao`.

```
grep "[rR]ao"  xyz
```

This displays those lines of the file `xyz` having strings either "`Rao`", or "`rao`".

```
grep "[rR]a[uo]"  xyz
```

This displays those lines of the file `xyz` having strings either "`Rao`", or "`Rau`", or "`rao`", or "`rau`".

```
grep "^rao"  xyz
```

This displays those lines of the file `xyz` which starts with string "`rao`"

```
grep "rao$"  xyz
```

This displays those lines of the file `xyz` which ends with string "`rao`".

```
grep "^rao$"  xyz
```

This displays those lines of the file `xyz` which contains the string "`rao`" only. No more characters in the line.

```
grep "^$"  xyz
```

This displays empty lines of the file `xyz`.

```
grep "^[rR]ao" xyz
```

This displays those lines of the file xyz which starts with either "Rao" or "rao".

```
grep "[rR]ao$" xyz
```

This displays those lines of the file xyz which ends with "Rao" or "rao".

-n option if we use with grep command it displays line numbers also.

```
grep -n "rao" xyz
```

This displays those lines of file xyz which are having the string "rao" along with their line numbers.

-v option if we use with grep command it displays those lines which does not have the given search pattern.

```
grep -v "rao" xyz
```

This displays those lines of the file xyz which does not contain the string "rao".

fgrep **(fixed grep) and** egrep **(extended grep) commands**

fgrep is used to search for a group of strings. One string has to be seperated from the other by a newline.

```
$fgrep 'rao
>ram
>raju' filename
```

This command displays those lines having either rao or ram or raju.

fgrep will not accept regular expressions.

egrep is little more different. It also takes a group of strings. While specifying strings piping (|) can be used as seperator.

Example

```
egrep 'rao|ram|raju' filename
```

In addition, it accepts regular expressions also.

cut **command**

```
cut -f1,3 filename
```

This displays 1st and 3rd words of each line of the given file. Between word to word TAB should be available.

```
cut -d":"  -f1,3 /etc/passwd
```

This displays username, UID of each legal user of the machine. Here, with `-d` option we are specifying that : is the field seperator between word to word.

Cut command cannot change the natural order of the fields. That is, the following command also gives same result as that of the above command.

```
cut -d":"  -f3,1 /etc/passwd
```

```
cut -d":"  -f1-3 filename
```

This displays 1st word to third word from each line of the given file.

```
cut -f":" -f3- filename
```

This displays 3rd word to till last word of each line of the given file.

```
cut -c3-5 filename
```

This displays 3rd character to 5th character of each line of the given file.

```
cut -d":" -f1 /etc/passwd > a1
```

File `a1` contains usernames of legal users of the machine.

```
cut -d":"  -f3 /etc/passwd > a3
```

File `a3` contains UID's of each legal user of the machine.

`paste` **command**

This is used to join files vertically.

```
paste a3 a1 >a31
```

```
cat a31
```

This displays

```
0    root
1    bin
2    daemon
3    adm
4    lp
5    sync
6    shutdown
7    halt
8    mail
```

```
9   news
10  uucp
11  operator
12  games
13  gopher
14  ftp
99  nobody
38  ntp
32  rpc
69  vcsa
28  nscd
74  sshd
37  rpm
47  mailnull
51  smmsp
25  named
42  gdm
80  desktop
101 rao
39  canna
78  fax
57  nut

paste -d"|" a3 a1 >a13
```

This command places the given field seperator while joining the files contents vertically.

```
cat a13

   0|root
   1|bin
   2|daemon
   3|adm
   4|lp
   5|sync
   6|shutdown
   7|halt
   8|mail
   9|news
  10|uucp
  11|operator
  12|games
  13|gopher
```

```
14|ftp
99|nobody
43|xfs
25|named
42|gdm
39|canna
49|wnn
78|fax
57|nut
```

`join` command

This is used to join files. Unlike paste it works similar to join operation of DBMS.

Let the files content are :

```
File aa1 contains
111|NBV Rao
121|PP Raj
116|Teja
119|Rani

File aa2 contains
111|Prof
112|Asst Prof
121|lecturer
116|Prof


join -t"|" -j 1 1 aa1 aa2
```

This command produces the following result :

```
111|NBV Rao|Prof
121|PP Raj|lecturer
116|Teja|Prof

join -t"|" -j 1 1 -o 1.1 2.2 aa1 aa2
```

This command produces output such as the following. That is, first field from the first file and second field from the second file is displayed.

```
111|Prof
121|lecturer
116|Prof

join -t"|" -a1 -o 1.1 2.2 aa1 aa2
```

This command gives the following results.

```
111|Prof
121|lecturer
116|Prof
119|

join -t"|"  -a2 -o 1.1 2.2 aa1 aa2
```

This command gives the following results.

```
111|Prof
   |Asst Prof
121|lecturer
116|Prof
```

`tr` command

This command can be used for transliteration. That is replacing a character with another chracter. It accepts standard input and gives standard output.

```
tr '*' '-' <xyz
```

This command replaces all the occurrences of character * with – in the given file `xyz`.

```
tr '*/' '-?' <xyz
```

This command replaces all the occurrences of * with - and / with ? in the given file. In both the situations output appears on the screen. By standard redirection operator output can be stored in a file.

Example

```
tr '*' '-' <xyz >pqr

tr '[a-z]' '[A-Z]' < xyz
```

This command replaces all lower case characters of the file `xyz` to uppercase.

```
tr -d '*' <xyz
```

This command removes all occurrences of * in the given file `xyz`.

```
tr -s '*' <xyz
```

This command replaces multiple consequtive *'s with a single * in the given file.

`df` **command**

This command displays details about the each of the mounted partition, percentage of free-ness, percentage of occupation etc.

```
Filesystem   1K-blocks  Used Available  Use% Mounted on
/dev/hdb5    6048288    5163420  577632 90%  /
none         62520            0   62520  0%  /dev/shm
```

`du` **command**

This command displays disk usage(usually in multiples of 1K blocks).

`du` command without any argument displays disk usage of all files, subdirectories of current working directory.

```
du  directoryname
```

This displays disk usage of all files, sub-directories of the given directory.

Please note that `du` command will not display the actual size of the file in bytes. Rather, number of 1K blocks assigned for the file. Try the following and find out the difference.

```
du filename
ls -l filename
du -b filename
```

`who` **command**

This displays details about the users such as user name, terminal on which working and since when they are working.

```
root    :0      Feb  9 00:22
root    pts/0   Feb  9 00:25(:0.0)
root    pts/1   Feb  9 20:25(:0.0)
```

`w` **command**

This displays details about the users in addition to what command they are working now.

```
w
```

Presents who the users are and what they are doing in the following fashion.

```
USER  TTY     FROM  LOGIN@    IDLE  JCPU  PCPU     WHAT
root   :0      -     12:22am   ?     0.00s 1.66s /usr/bin/gnome-
root  pts/0  :0.0  12:25am  0.00s 0.81s 0.03s     w
```

```
w username
```

Displays what that user is doing.

```
w -i
```

Displays details sorted by idle time.

`rm` command

This is used to remove file(s)

Example

```
rm xyz
```

This command removes file `xyz` (If it is not write protected).

Only legal owner of the file can remove file (Exception for super user).

```
rm f1 f2 f3 .... fn
```

Removes all files `f1, f2, ... fn`.

```
rm a*.c
```

Removes all files with extension c and primary name starts with a.

```
rm a?.c
```

Removes all files with extension c and primary is two characters length with first character as a.

```
rm a[0-9]*.c
```

Removes all files with extension c and primary name starting with a and second character as digit.

```
rm a[!a-zA-Z0-9]*.c
```

Removes all files with extension c and primary name starting with a and second character is other than alphanumeric.

```
rm -R directoryname
```

Removes all files, sub-directories of the given directory recursively.

```
rm -i file(s)
```

Interactive deletion. That is, it prompts before deleting the file(s).

```
rm -F file(s)
```

File(s) are deleted forcibly (ignoring permissions).

unlink filename

This command also removes the given file.

`ulimit` **command**

Unix system has resource limits such as limits on number of processes, maximum allowed file size, etc.

Example

```
ulimit -a

core file size          (blocks, -c) 0
data seg size           (kbytes, -d) 231122
file size               (blocks, -f) 231122
max locked memory       (kbytes, -l) unlimited
max memory size         (kbytes, -m) unlimited
open files                      (-n) 1024
pipe size            (512 bytes, -p) 8
stack size              (kbytes, -s) 8192
cpu time               (seconds, -t) unlimited
max user processes              (-u) 1016
virtual memory          (kbytes, -v) unlimited

ulimit
```

This command displays file size limit on the system currently.

```
ulimit -f 121212
```

This changes file size limit to `121212`.

Similarly, we can change resource limits such as max data, text segment sizes etc.

`umask` **command**

This command when executed without any argument it displays the current value of the umask.

This `umask` value is used to change the default permissions of any file or directory created.

By changing the umask value we can change default permissions of a file or directory created.

Example

```
cat>p1
add
adjda
^d
ls -l p1
```

```
-rw-r—r—    1 root   root    4 Feb 10 00:32 p1
umask 000
cat>p3
ads
sad
sdsd
^d
ls -l p3

-rw-rw-rw-  1 root   root    9 Feb 10 00:35 p3
```

We can see that permissions of files p1 and p3 are different.

Unix Kernel uses a mask known as file creation mask (octal 666). While a file is created this mask and umask combinedly plays role in deciding the permissions of a file. Default umask value is 022. Thus, when file p1 is created this is used. Whereas while p3 is created umask value is taken as 000, which we have specified.

```
                           P1                  P3
File Mask (Binary)  110110110           110110110
Umask               000010010 (022)     000000000 (000)
Exclusive-OR        110100100           110110110
Permissions         rw-r—r—             rw-rw-rw-
```

The same is applicable to default directory permissions also. Unix Kernel uses default directory creation mask as 777.

Directory 11 is created after changing the umask where as directory 12 is created before changing. We can see the difference in the permissions.

```
drwxrwxrwx   2 root    root    4096 Feb 10 00:43 11
drwxr-xr-x   2 root    root    4096 Feb 10 00:44 12
```

diff **command**

This is used to compare the contents of two files in general.

Example

```
diff p1 p2
```

If the content of p1 and p2 are exactly same it displays nothing. Otherwise it displays the difference information in a special format such as the following:

```
1c1
< ass
—-
> add
3d2
< ass
```

Software Patching

Normally SW products are supplied either as binary distribution or source distribution. In source distribution, all the source program files are supplied to the curstomer and the customer is required to compile on his target machine to get binary or executable code of the SW. Moreover, it is common that SW systems are released in incremental fashion. When a new release is made, a patch file (difference file) is prepared by comparing with the previous release files. This can be downloaded by the customer who is having previous release and by applying the SW patching he can get recent version of the SW source which he can compile to get updated version of SW running on his machine.

Example

```
diff p1 p2>p3
```

Here p3 can be called as patch file.

```
patch p1 <p3 will change the content of the file p1 as p2.
patch p2 <p3 will change the p2 file content as p1.
```

5 Pipes

Pipes

Unix operating system supports a unique approach through which we can join two commands and generate new command with the help of pipe concept.

Example

```
command1 | command2
```

Here, whatever the output that the first command generates becomes standard input for the second command. We can develop complex unix command sequences by joining many commands while maintaining this input output relation ships. Whenever left hand side of piping symbol does not generate we may get broken pipe error.

Example

```
ls -l | grep "^d"
```

This command displays details of only the directories of the current working directory. That is output of ls -l command becomes input to `grep` command which displays only those lines which starts with d (they are nothing but details of files).

```
ls -l | grep "^d" | wc -l
```

This command displays number of directories in the given file.

```
grep "bash$" /etc/passwd|wc -l
```

This command displays number of users of the machine whose default shell is bash.

```
cut -t":" -f 3 /etc/passwd|sort -n|tail -1
```

This command displays a number which is largest used UID number in the system. Here, `cut` command first extract UID's of all the users in the system from the `/etc/passwd` file, and the same becomes input to `sort`; which sorts these numbers in numerical order and sends to `tail` command as input which in turn displays the largest number (last one).

`tee` **command**

`tee` command is used to save intermediate results in a piping sequence. It accepts a set of filenames as arguments and sends its standard input to all these files while giving the same as standard output. Thus, use of this in piping sequence will not break the pipe.

For example if you want to save details of the directories of current working directory while knowing their using the above piping sequence we can use `tee` as follows. Here, the file `xyz` will have the details of directories saved.

```
ls -l|grep "^d"|tee xyz|wc -l
```

The following piping sequence writes the number of directories into the file `pqr` while displaying the same on the screen.

```
ls -l|grep "^d"|tee xyz|wc -l|tee pqr
```

`cmp` **command**

The `cmp` utility compares two files of any type and writes the results to the standard output. By default, `cmp` is silent if the files are the same; if they differ, the byte and line number at which the first difference occurred is reported.

Bytes and lines are numbered beginning with one.

Example

```
cmp file1 file2
```

`comm` **command**

`comm` - compare two sorted files line by line

Compare sorted files LEFT_FILE and RIGHT_FILE line by line.

```
-1 suppress lines unique to left file
-2 suppress lines unique to right file
-3 suppress lines that appear in both files
```

Example

```
comm p1 p2
```

6 awk Command

awk **command**

This facility is very much useful for small scale database applications requiring no precision.

Syntax of awk command

```
awk option 'BEGIN{}
                  {
                  }
              END{}' filename
```

awk command considers the given file as database file; each line of the file is considered as a record, each word of a line is taken as field. Whatever operations we wanted to execute, we have to write in the BEGIN section which are really executed before processing any record. The operations which are required to be executed after processing all the records has to be written in END section. Instructions which are required to be executed on every record has to be written in the middle block. It is not necessary that every awk command to have all the three blocks. However, opening curly braces should immediately follow the BEGIN and END words and should be on the same line as that of BEGIN, END words. awk supports a limited amount of C style programming constructs. However, we cannot say that it can be used in place of C though! While running, instructions in the BEGIN block are executed, then instructions in the middle block are executed on every record and the instructions in END block are executed at the last.

Normally, awk assumed space or TAB as the field separator between word to word. However, if a file contains some other character as field separator, the same can be informed through -d option.

awk uses the following things :

```
NF = number of fields
NR = number of records
OFS = output field seperator
$0 = current record as a whole
$1,$2,$3…=first,second,third etc.,fieldsofcurrentrecord

awk '{ print $0} 'filename
awk '{ printf "%s", $0 }'  filename
```

These commands display the content of the file

```
awk -F":" '{ print $3, $1}'  /etc/passwd
awk -F":" '{ printf "%3d %s", $3, $1 }' /etc/passwd
```

These commands display UID's and usernames of the users of the machine.

```
awk '{ printf "%3d  %s", NR, $0}' filename
```

This command displays file content along with line numbers. Here, NR value refers to the record number.

Like "grep", find string "fleece" (the {print} command is the default if nothing is specified)

```
awk '/fleece/' file
```

Select lines 14 through 30 of file

```
awk 'NR==14, NR==30' file
```

Select just one line of a file

```
awk 'NR==12' file
awk "NR==$1" file
```

Rrearrange fields 1 and 2 and put colon in between

```
awk '{print $2 ":" $1}' file
```

All lines between BEGIN and END lines (you can substitute any strings for BEGIN and END, but they must be between slashes)

```
awk '/BEGIN/,/END/' file
```

Print number of lines in file (of course wc -1 does this, too)

```
awk 'END{print NR}' file
```

We can use variables in awk wherever we wanted and their initial value will be taken as 0.

The following prints no. of lines, words, characters.

```
awk '{w+ = NF c+ = length($0)} END{print NR, w, c}'filename
```

Substitute *every* occurrence of a string XYZ by the new string ABC: Requires nawk.

```
nawk '{gsub(/XYZ/,"ABC"); print}' file
```

Print 3rd field from each line, but the colon is the field separator

```
awk -F: '{print $3}' file
```

Print out the last field in each line, regardless of how many fields:

```
awk '{print $NF}' file
```

To print out a file with line numbers at the edge :

```
awk '{print NR, $0}' somefile
```

This is less than optimal because as the line number gets longer in digits, the lines get shifted over. Thus, use printf:

```
awk '{printf "%3d %s", NR, $0}' somefile
```

Print out lengths of lines in the file

```
awk '{print length($0)}' somefile
   or
awk '{print length}' somefile
```

Print out lines and line numbers that are longer than 80 characters

```
awk 'length 80 {printf "%3d. %s\n", NR, $0}' somefile
```

Total up the lengths of files in characters that results from "ls -1"

```
ls -1 | awk 'BEGIN{total=0} {total += $4} END{print total}'
```

Print out the longest line in a file

```
awk 'BEGIN {maxlength = 0} \
   { \ if (length($0) maxlength) { \
   maxlength = length($0) \
   longest = $0 \
   } \
   } \
END {print longest}' somefile
```

How many entirely blank lines are in a file?

```
awk '/^$/ {x++} END {print x}' somefile
```

Print out last character of field 1 of every line

```
awk '{print substr($1,length($1),1)}' somefile
```

Comment out only #include statements in a C file. This is useful if you want to run "cxref" which will follow the include links.

```
awk '/#include/{printf "/* %s */\n", $0; next}
            {print}'file.c | cxref -c $*
```

If the last character of a line is a colon, print out the line. This would be useful in getting the pathname from output of ls -lR:

```
awk '{ \
lastchar = substr($0,length($0),1) \
if (lastchar == ":") \
print $0 \
}' somefile
```

Here is the complete thing....Note that it even sorts the final output

```
ls -lR | awk '{ \
lastchar = substr($0,length($0),1) \
if (lastchar == ":") \
dirname = substr($0,1,length($0)-1) \
else \
if ($4 20000) \
printf "%10d %25s %s\n", $4, dirname, $8 \
}' | sort -r
```

The following is used to break all long lines of a file into chunks of length 80:

```
awk '{ line = $0
while (length(line) 80)
{
print substr(line,1,80)line=substr(line,81,length(line)-80)
}
 if (length(line) 0) print line
}' somefile.with.long.lines>whatever
```

If you want to use `awk` as a programming language, you can do so by not processing any file, but by enclosing a bunch of `awk` commands in curly braces, activated upon end of file. To use a standard UNIX "file" that has no lines, use `/dev/null`.

Here's a simple example :

```
awk 'END{print "hi there everyone"}' < /dev/null
```

Here's an example of using this to print out the ASCII characters:

```
awk ' { for(i=32; i<127; i++) \
printf "%3d %3o %c\n", i,i,i \
}' </dev/null
```

Sometimes you wish to find a field which has some identifying tag, like $X=$ in front. Suppose your file (playfile1) looked like :

```
50 30 X=10 Y=100 Z=-2
X=12 89 100 32 Y=900
1 2 3 4 5 6 X=1000
```

Then to select out the $X=$ numbers from each do

```
awk '{ for (i=1; i <=NF; i++) \
if ($i ~ /X=.*/) \
print substr($i,3) \
}' playfile1
```

Note that we used a regular expression to find the initial part: `/X=.*/`

Pull an abbreviation out of a file of abbreviations and their translation. Actually, this can be used to translate anything, where the first field is the thing you are looking up and the 2nd field is what you want to output as the translation.

```
nawk '$1 == abbrev{print $2}' abbrev=$1 translate.file
```

Join lines in a file that end in a dash. That is, if any line ends in -, join it to the next line. This only joins 2 lines at a time. The dash is removed.

```
awk '/-$/ {oldline = $0 \
getline \
print substr(oldline,1,length(oldline)-1) $0 \
next} \
{print}' somefile
```

Function in nawk to round : function round(n) `{return int(n+0.5)}`

If you have a file of addresses with empty lines between the sections, you can use the following to search for strings in a section, and print out the whole section. Put the following into a file called "`section.awk`":

```
BEGIN {FS = "\n"; RS = ""; OFS = "\n"} $0 ~ searchstring {print}
```

Assume your names are in a file called "`rolodex`". Then use the following nawk command when you want to find a section that contains a string. In this example, it is a person's name:

```
nawk -f section.awk searchstring=Wolf rolodex
```

We assume the following data in the file EMPLOYEE having employee ID, name, designation, department, salary, no. of dependents and age in each line.

```
111|NB Venkateswarlu|Professor|CSE|27000|2|42
121|GV Saradamba|Professor|CHEM|32000|2|46
122|PN Rao|Assistant Professor|Civil|26000|3|54

awk -F"|"  '{ printf "%s %d", $2 , $1}' EMPLOYEE
```

This command displays names of the employees and their ID's in a tabular fashion.

```
awk -F"|" ' $2 ~ /Rao/{ printf "%s %d", $2 , $1}' EMPLOYEE
```

This command displays names of the employees and their ID's whose name contains the string "Rao".

```
awk -F"|" '$2 ~ /Ra[ou]/{ printf "%s %d", $2 , $1}' EMPLOYEE
```

This command displays names of the employees and their ID's whose name contains the string "Rao" or "Rau".

```
awk -F"|" ' $2 ~ /^Rao/{printf "%s %d", $2 , $1}' EMPLOYEE
```

This command displays names of the employees and their ID's whose name starts with the string "Rao".

```
awk -F"|" '$2 ~ /^Ra[ou]/{ printf "%s %d", $2 , $1}' EMPLOYEE
```

This command displays names of the employees and their ID's whose name starts with the string "Rao" or "Rau".

```
awk -F"|"  ' $2 ~ /Rao$/{ printf "%s %d", $2 , $1}' EMPLOYEE
```

This command displays names of the employees and their ID's whose name ends with the string "Rao".

```
awk -F"|" '$2 ~ /Ra[ou]$/{ printf "%s %d", $2 , $1}' EMPLOYEE
```

This command displays names of the employees and their ID's whose name ends with the string "Rao" or "Rau".

```
awk -F"|" '$2 ~ /^Ra[ou]$/{printf "%s %d", $2, $1}' EMPLOYEE
```

This command displays names of the employees and their ID's whose name contains the strings "Rao" or "Rau".

```
awk -F"|" '$2 ~ /^[rR]a[ou]$/{printf "%s %d", $2, $1}' EMPLOYEE
```

This command displays names of the employees and their ID's whose name contains the strings "Rao", "rao", "Rau" or "rau".

```
awk -F"|" ' $4 >10000 { printf "%s %d", $2 , $1}' EMPLOYEE
```

This command displays names of the employees and their ID's whose salary is more than 10000.

```
awk -F"|" '{s+=$4p+=$6}END{printf "%d%d", s/NR, p/NR}' EMPLOYEE
```

This command displays average salary and average number of dependents of the `employees`.

```
awk -F"|" '$4<5000{s+=$4 p+=$6}END{printf"%d %d",s/NR,p/NR}' EMPLOYEE
```

This command displays average salary and average number of dependents of the `employees` whose salary is less than 5000.

```
awk -F"|" '$6<5000{s+=$4  p+=$6}END{printf"%d %d",s/NR,p/NR}' EMPLOYEE
```

This command displays average salary and average number of dependents of the `employees` whose age is more than 5000.

```
awk -F"|" ' {
If ($4 >5000)  n1++
Else n2++
}END{ printf "%d %d", n1, n2 }' EMPLOYEE
```

This command displays no. of employees whose salary is greater than `5000` and less than `5000`.

```
awk -F"|" ` {
   If ($4 >5000)
   {
   n1++
   s1+=$4
   }
   else
   {
   n2++
   s2+=$4
   }
   }END{ printf "%d %d", s1/n1, s2/n2 }' EMPLOYEE
```

This command displays average salary of `employees` whose salary is greater than `5000` and less than `5000` .

We can use arrays also. Their initial values also taken as zeros.

```
awk -F"|" ` {
if ($4 >5000)
{
s[1]++
s[2]+=$4
}
else
{
s[3]++
s[4]+=$4
}
}END{ printf "%d %d", s[2]/s[1], s[4]/s[3] }' EMPLOYEE
```

This command displays average salary of `employees` whose salary is greater than `5000` and less than `5000` .

We can use content addressable arrays. That is, the element indexes for these arrays can be strings rather than usual integers.

```
awk -F"|" `{ s[$3]++} END{for(desig in s) printf "%s %d",
desig, s[desig] }' EMPLOYEE
```

The above command displays designation and number of people having that designation.

```
awk '{ l=(80-length($0))/2
I=0;
While(I<l)
{
printf "%s", " "
I++;
}
printf "%s", $0 }'  filename
```

This program prints every line of the program centered on the screen.

```
awk '{ l=(80-length($0))/2
for(I=0;I<l; I++)
{
printf "%s", " "
}
printf "%s", $0 }' filename
```

This program prints every line of the program centered on the screen.

7 Backup Commands

`tar` **command**

This command is used to join a group of files and prepare an archive file.

```
tar -cvf  a.tar directoryname(s)orfilename(s)
```

This command creates an archive file `a.tar` by joining the given file or files in the given directories.

```
tar -cvZf a.tZ  directoryname(s)orfilename(s)
```

This command creates compressed `tar` archive.

```
tar -cvzf a.tgz  directoryname(s)orfilename(s)
```

This command creates gzipped `tar` archive.

```
tar -xvf a.tar
```

This command extracts all files from the archive.

```
tar -xvZf a.tZ
```

This command extracts all files from the compressed archive.

```
tar -xvzf a.tgz
```

This command extracts all files from the gzipped archive.

```
tar -xvf a.tar fileordirectoryname
```

This extracts the given file or directory from the archive.

```
tar -xvZf a.tZ fileordirectoryname
```

This extracts the given file or directory from the archive.

```
tar -xvzf a.tgz fileordirectoryname
```

This extracts the given file or directory from the archive.

cpio **command**

This is also used for backup purpose. Normally this command requires list of filenames as input and the result is archive file which appears on the standard output.

```
ls|cpio -o > archivefilename
```

The above command creates archive having all the files of current directory.

```
cpio -i <archivefilename
```

This command restores all the files from the archive file.

```
cpio -i abc <archivefilename
```

This command restored the file abc from the given archive file.

```
cpio -i "*.c" <archivefilename
```

This command restores all the files with extension c from the archive file.

We can create the archive on the tapes or other devices also.

```
find . -ctime 2 -print |cpio -ov > /dev/rmt0
```

This command creates backup file on magnetic tape rmt0 and stores all the files which are created in the recent 2 days.

8 Internet Related Commands

`finger` **command**

This command is used to know the information about the user such as when he has logged into the machine, when did he/she see their email, etc in addition to content of .plan (and other files) of his home directory.

Example

finger root gave the following result.

```
Login: root          Name: root
Directory: /root      Shell: /bin/bash
On since Tue Feb 12 09:55 (IST) on :0 (messages off)
On since Tue Feb 12 09:59 (IST) on pts/0 from :0.0
New mail received Tue Feb 12 10:01 2002 (IST)
Unread since Sun Feb 10 00:03 2002 (IST)
```

Plan

```
I have class at  9.00AM
                10.00AM
          4.30 to 9.00PM
```

If any user wants to convey any thing to the people who fingers his account he can write in his .plan file. Best thing we can write is our schedule today. Such that, other people can see and accordingly they can start interatctive sessions such as talk, chat, or calling by phone etc.

If this command is executed without any arguments then displays details of all currently logged in users (similar to who command) such as:

```
Login  Name   Tty    Idle     Login Time  Office  Office Phone
rao           pts/2  Feb 12   10:37 (localhost)
root   root   *:0    Feb 12   09:55
root   root   pts/0  Feb 12   10:33 (:0.0)
root   root   pts/1  Feb 12   10:36
```

Remote Login Services

```
rlogin
```

With the help of this command it is possible to login to remote machine if we happend to have legal username and password on that machine. When we do so, the current machine becomes terminal to that remote machines. After that whatever file we create it will be stored in that remote machine. When we run a command that remote machine's processor and RAM is used for running the same.

Example

```
rlogin IPaddressormachinename -l username
```

It will prompt the password and after entering valid password we will see that remote machines prompt. For proper functioning TERM environment variable on local machine should be set appropriately such that it matches with that remote machine. Usually, rlogin is used for GUI based remote login service unlike telnet service.

telnet **command**

```
telnet IPaddressormachinename
```

The following output appear on the screen

```
Trying 127.0.0.1...
Connected to localhost.localdomain (127.0.0.1).
Escape character is '^]'.
Red Hat Linux release 9 (Shrike)
Kernel 2.4.20-8 on an i686
login:
Login incorrect
```

Login

When we enter legal username and password then we will be logging into that remote machine and we will see its prompt. Here also the local machine becomes dumb terminal for the remote machine.

Unlike rlogin service this supports only character based remote login service.

`ftp` **command**

This command is used to transfer from files from one machine to another machine.

```
ftp Ipaddressormachiename
```

This command gives a prompt namingly `ftp>` after we enter legal user name and password of that remote machine. Once we have logged in, we can download files with command **get filename**. We can use commands such as `ls`, `cd` etc on remote machine directory while `mls`, `mcd` commands can be used on local machine. We can set transfer as ascii or binary by simply typing ascii or binary commands at `ftp>` prompt.

We can put files of the local directory using **put filename** command. On some `ftp` servers we can download files using `mget` and upload files using `mput` command.

If we execute `ftp` command without any argument then we will see `ftp>` prompt. Using `open Ipaddressormachinename` we can connect to remote machine for file transfer. By type ! symbol at the `ftp>` prompt we can exit from the `ftp` program.

There are many `ftp` servers are available in the internet for free download. While logging into those servers we can login with anonymous as username and our email address as password. Thus these servers are often called as anonymous servers. From these servers we can download only. If we have some SW is available and want to be available freely to others we have to contact these servers administrators who can give permission temporarily to upload our SW into their servers.

`arp` **command**

This command is used to manipulate `arp` cache. That is, we can see the `arp` cache, remove a host's entry from the `arp` cache, etc. In a networked system when a packet arrives at router machine (often a UNIX machine) then the IP address to Ethernet address mapping is needed. This is achieved by `arp` protocol. These mappings are stored in `arp` cache such that next time another packet arrives the same IP address then its Ethernet or physical address is calculated by carrying out a lookup opertion on this `arp` cache. With `arp` command we can modify, view, delete the entries of this cache.

arp –a	All entries are displayed
arp –a hostname	Displays entry of the given host
arp –d hostname	Removes the entry of the specified host
arp –s hostname HW_addr	Creates manually ARP entry for the host with the given hardware address (HW address has to be given in hexadecimal seperated by colons)

Wildcards

Unix has special meaning for some chracters such as `*`, `?`, `.`, `/`, `[,]`. Words in the commands that contain these characters are treated as patterns (model) for filenames. The word is expanded into a list of file names, according to the type of pattern. If we want that the shell not to expand these characters then we have to pre-pend \ before them. This way we can make these characters to get escape from shells normal interpretation and is known as escaping and thus these characters are called as escape characters.

The following expansions are made by most shells, including bash :

```
* matches any string (including null)
? matches any single character As a special case, any .
  beginning a word must be matched explicitly.
/ root diretcory
. any charcater
```

Example : The directory contains the files

```
tmp
tmp1
tmp2
tmp10
tmpx
```

The pattern *1* matches the files tmp1 and tmp10.

The pattern t??? matches tmp1 and tmp2

The pattern tmp[0-9] matches with tmp1 and tmp2

The pattern tmp[!0-9] matches with tmpx only

The pattern tmp[a-z] matches with tmpx only

The pattern tmp* matches with all files.

This models can be used with any command.

Example

```
ls -l tmp[0-9] displays details of files tmp1 and tmp2 only
rm tmp*  deletes all files whose names starts with tmp.
```

Printing a file

```
lpr [options] files...
lpr -#2 filename   prints two copies of the given file
lpq                prints the printer queue status along with
                   printer process job id.
Lprm  jobid        removes specified printer job id from
                   printer queue (only legal owner can do
                   this. Exception for super user).
```

9   Shell Programming

Shell Programming

Why Shell Programming ? A working knowledge of shell scripting is essential to everyone wishing to become reasonably adept at system administration, even if they do not anticipate ever having to actually write a script. Consider that as a Linux machine boots up, `init` process is initiated first then it executes the shell scripts in `/etc/rc.d` to restore the system configuration and set up services. A detailed understanding of these startup scripts is important for analyzing the behavior of a system, and possibly modifying it.

Writing shell scripts is not hard to learn, since the scripts can be built in bite-sized sections and there is only a fairly small set of shell-specific operators and options to learn. The syntax is simple and straightforward, similar to that of invoking and chaining together utilities at the command line, and there are only a few "rules" to learn. Most short scripts work right the first time, and debugging even the longer ones is straightforward. A shell script is a "quick and dirty" method of prototyping a complex application. Getting even a limited subset of the functionality to work in a shell script, even if slowly, is often a useful first stage in project development. This way, the structure of the application can be tested and played with, and the major pitfalls found before proceeding to the final coding in C, C++, Java, or Perl. Shell scripting hearkens back to the classical UNIX philosophy of breaking complex projects into simpler subtasks, of chaining together components and utilities. Many consider this a better, or at least more esthetically pleasing approach to problem solving than using one of the new generation of high powered all-in-one languages, such as Perl, which attempt to be all things to all people, but at the cost of forcing you to alter your thinking processes to fit the tool.

When we want to execute some set of commands one after another without users physical intervention and presence (batch operations), shell scripts are very handy.

Moreover, for small scale database applications where precision, speed and security is little botheration, shell scripts are very preferable and SW project cost may tremendously reduces.

Shell scripts are very much employed in developing automatic SW installation scripts and for fine tuning the SW's installed.

When not to use shell scripts

- resource-intensive tasks, especially where speed is a factor (sorting, hashing, etc.)
- procedures involving heavy-duty math operations, especially floating point arithmetic, arbitrary precision calculations, or complex numbers (use C++ or FORTRAN instead)
- cross-platform portability required (use C instead)
- complex applications, where structured programming is a necessity (need typechecking of variables, function prototypes, etc.)
- mission-critical applications upon which you are betting the ranch, or the future of the company
- situations where security is important, where you need to guarantee the integrity of your system and protect against intrusion, cracking, and vandalism
- project consists of subcomponents with interlocking dependencies
- extensive file operations required (Bash is limited to serial file access, and that only in a particularly clumsy and inefficient line-by-line fashion)
- need multi-dimensional arrays
- need data structures, such as linked lists or trees
- need to generate or manipulate graphics or GUIs
- need direct access to system hardware
- need port or socket I/O
- need to use libraries or interface with legacy code
- proprietary, closed-source applications (shell scripts are necessarily Open Source)

If any of the above applies, consider a more powerful scripting language, perhaps Perl, Tcl, Python, or possibly a high-level compiled language such as C, C++, or Java. Even then, prototyping the application as a shell script might still be a useful development step.

Shell programs also called as shell scripts. In the simplest case, a script is nothing more than a list of system commands stored in a file. If we want to execute a set of commands many times repeatedly, we can write the same in a file and execute which saves the effort of retyping that particular sequence of commands each time they are needed.

Invoking the script

Having written the script, you can invoke it by `sh` scriptname, or alternately `bash` scriptname. (Not recommended is using `sh <` scriptname as this effectively disables reading from `stdin` within the script.)

Much more convenient is to make the script itself directly executable with a `chmod`.

Either

```
chmod 555 scriptname (gives everyone read/execute permission)
or
chmod +rx scriptname (gives everyone read/execute permission)
chmod u+rx scriptname (gives only the script
                       owner read/execute permission)
```

Having made the script executable, you may now test it by `./scriptname`.

As a final step, after testing and debugging, you would likely want to move it to `/usr/local/bin` (as root, of course), to make the script available to yourself and all other users as a system-wide executable. The script could then be invoked by simply typing scriptname [ENTER] from the command line.

It is shell programming practice in which line starting with # ! at the head of a script tells your system that this file is a set of commands to be fed to the command interpreter indicated. The # ! is actually a two-byte "magic number", a special marker that designates a file type, or in this case an executable shell script . Immediately following the # ! is a path name. This is the path to the program that interprets the commands in the script, whether it be a shell, a programming language, or a utility. This command interpreter then executes the commands in the script, starting at the top (line 1 of the script), ignoring comments.

```
#!/bin/sh
#!/bin/bash
#!/usr/bin/perl
#!/usr/bin/tcl
#!/bin/sed -f
#!/usr/awk -f
```

Each of the above script header lines calls a different command interpreter, be it /bin/sh, the default shell (bash in a Linux system) or otherwise. Using #!/bin/sh, the default Bourne Shell in most commercial variants of UNIX, makes the script portable to non-Linux machines, though you may have to sacrifice a few Bash-specific features (the script will conform to the POSIX sh standard).

#! can be omitted if the script consists only of a set of generic system commands, using no internal shell directives.

Variables are at the heart of every programming and scripting language. They appear in arithmetic operations and manipulation of quantities, string parsing, and are indispensable for working in the abstract with symbols - tokens that represent something else. A variable is nothing more than a location or set of locations in computer memory holding an item of data.

Unlike many other programming languages, Bash does not segregate its variables by "type". Essentially, Bash variables are character strings, but, depending on context, Bash permits integer operations and comparisons on variables. The determining factor is whether the value of a variable contains only digits.

Shell programming supports prominently the following type of variables :

▶ Shell Variables

▶ Environment Variables

▶ Positional Variables

Shell Variables

```
X=Hello    (no spaces before and after = )
```

The above statement at the bash prompt defines a shell variable X and assigns a value for it. Anywhere, $X indicates the value of the variable X.

Very often shell variables are used to reduce typing burden. For example, in the following examples after defining shell variable DIR the same can be used wherever we need to type /usr/lib.

```
DIR=/usr/lib

ls  $DIR            displays listing of /usr/lib directory
cd $DIR             moves to /usr/lib directory
ls $DIR/libm*.so    displays all files /usr/lib which
                    satifies libm*.so   model
```

Environment Variables

Variables that affect the behavior of the shell and user interface. In a more general context, each process has an "environment", that is, a group of variables that hold information that the process may reference. In this sense, the shell behaves like any other process.

Every time a shell starts, it creates shell variables that correspond to its own environmental variables. Updating or adding new shell variables causes the shell to update its environment, and all the shell's child processes (the commands it executes) inherit this environment; Caution the space allotted to the environment is limited. Creating too many environmental variables or ones that use up excessive space may cause problems.

If we execute "env" command at the dollar prompt we may find the details of all the environment variables defined in our current shell. The output may look like

```
PATH=/bin:/sbin:/usr/local/bin
MANPATH=/usr/man:/usr/man/man1:/usr/man/man2
IFS=
TERM=VT100
HOST=darkstar
USER=guest
HOME=/usr/guest
MAIL=/var/spool/mail/guest
MAILCHECK=300
```

Environment variables are used by shell and other application programs. For example, the value of MAILCHECK, i.e 300 indicates that the mailer has to check for every 300 seconds for new arrivals and intimate the same to the user. A dynamic business user can set this variable value to a low value such that the mailer informs the user within the specified time period it will indicate the user about new mails arrival.

Similarly, PATH environment variable is used by shell in locating the executable file of the commands typed by the user. System will check for the executable files in the directories of the PATH variable and if found it will be loaded and executed. Otherwise, we may get error "bad command or file not found".

Let the following C language file named "a.c" :

```
#include<stdio.h>
main()
{
printf("Hello\n");
}
```

To compile :

```
gcc -o aa  a.c
```

The file a.c is the C language source file and "aa" will become executable file.

Very often (if PATH is set properly) by simply typing "aa" at the $ prompt we can run the above program. If in the value of PATH variable dot (".") is not available then we may get error "bad command or file not found" as the system is not in position to identify the file "aa". By typing ./aa we can run program (this problem is very much seen Redhat Linux distributions).

Similarly, if we created executable file name as "test" (normally, new users behaviour) then if we type "test" at the dollor prompt the above program may not. This is because, there exists a "test" unix command. Thus when you try to start "test" command instead of running our developed program, Unix command test runs. This may be also attributed to PATH problem only. When we type test, the system will check first say in /bin or /usr/bin then system first checks there and the same is executed. Thus, never our can run. Thus, we can add . (dot) to PATH in the following manner such that the above problem is not seen.

```
PATH=.:$PATH
```

If a script sets environmental variables, they need to be "exported", that is, reported to the environment local to the script. This is the function of the export command.

Main difference between shell variables and environment variables is that the latter are inheritable to sub-shells. Environment variables defined in a shell or modified in a shell are visible in its sub-shells only. That is, parent shells do not see the environment variables defined in its sub-shell or the modifications done to environment variables in the sub-shells. Please note that when you see $ prompt, you are in bash shell.

```
X=Hello
Y=How
echo $PATH      // displays value of PATH environment variable
echo $X         // displays value of X shell variable
echo $Y         // displays value of Y shell variable
export Y         // makes Y as environment variable

bash            // a sub-shell bash is created run ps -Al
                   in other terminal to see
echo $PATH      // displays value of PATH environment
                   variable which is same as above
echo $X         // displays nothing as X shell variable is
                   not inherited
echo $Y    // displays How as Y is environment variable value
Z=Raj
export Z
echo $Z         // displays Z variable value

csh             // another sub shell is initiated
echo $PATH      // displays value of PATH environment
                   variable which is same as above
echo $X         // displays nothing as X shell variable is
                   not inherited
```

```
echo $Y         // displays how as Y is environment variable
Z=Raj
export Z
echo $Z         // displays Z variable value
exit  or ^c     // to come out from C shell

^d              // to come out from bash sub-shell
echo $PATH      // displays value of PATH environment
                   variable which is same as above
echo $X         // displays  X shell variable value
echo $Y         // displays how as Y is environment variable
Z=Raj
export Z
echo $Z         // displays nothing as Z is not visible
```

Note : A script can export variables only to child processes, that is, only to commands or processes which that particular script initiates. A script invoked from the command line cannot export variables back to the command line environment. Child processes cannot export variables back to the parent processes that spawned them.

Positional Parameters

These parameters are arguments passed to the script from the command line - $0, $1, $2, $3... Here, $0 is the name of the script itself, $1 is the first argument, $2 the second, $3 the third, and so forth. After $9, the arguments must be enclosed in brackets, for example, ${10}, ${11}, ${12}.

Also, the following parameters can be also used in shell scripts

```
$#   number of command line arguments
$*   list of command line arguments
$@   list of command line arguments
$$   PID of the current shell
$?   Exit status of most recent command. Usually it is
     zero if the command is succesful.
$!   PID of most recent background job
```

if - then - else - fi condition

Like high level languages Shell supports if condition. The syntax is as follows :

```
•  if [ expr ]
   then
      statements
   fi
```

```
• if [ expr ]
  then
     statements
  else
     statements
  fi


• if [ expr ]
  then
     statements
  elif [ expr ]
  then
     statements
  elif [expr]
  then
     statements
  else
     statements
  fi
```

The expressions can be using the variables as described or numbers or filenames and relational operators. Any number of `elif` clauses can be used in third style which is commonly called as nested `if` statement. However, it has to terminate with an `else` block.

```
if [ $1 -gt $2 ]
then
   echo $1
else
   echo $2
fi
```

The above program takes two numbers along the command line and displays the maximum of them.

Similar to `-gt` we can also use `-ge`, `-lt`, `-le`, `-ne`, and `-eq` to compare numeric values of two arguments.

File Testing Opertions

Some times, we may required to find out whether given file is having reading permissions or writing permissions, etc or we may required to check whether given name is a file or a directory etc. The following can be used if conditions expression with the argument.

```
-r  true if the file/directory is having reading permissions
-w  true if the file/directory is having writing permissions
-x  true if the file/directory is having execution permissions
```

```
-f   true if the given argument is file
-d   true if the given argument is directory
-c   true if the argument is character special file
-b   true if the given argument is block special file

if [-f $1]
then
   echo Regular file
elif [ -d $1 ]
then
   echo Directory
elif [ -c $1 ]
then
   echo character special file
elif [ -b $1 ]
then
   echo Block special file
else
   echo others
fi
```

For the above shell script if we give /etc/passwd as argument we will get message "Regular file". If we give /etc as argument we will get message "Directory". If we give /dev/ttyS0 as argument we will get message "character special file". If we give /dev/hda1 as argument we will get message "block special file".

String comparison

```
= is equal to
```

Example : if ["$a" = "$b"]

```
== is equal to
```

Example : if ["$a" == "$b"] This is a synonym for =.

Example : [[$a == z*]] # true if $a starts with an "z" (pattern matching)

Example : [[$a == "z*"]] # true if $a is equal to z*

Example : ["$a" == "z*"] # true if $a is equal to z*

```
!= is not equal to
```

Example : if ["$a" != "$b"] #true if both the strings are different

This operator uses pattern matching within a [[...]] construct.

-z string is "null", that is, has zero length

Example : if [-z "$1"]   #true if $1 is null

-n string is not "null".

Example : if [-n "$1"]   # true if $1 is not null

- Write a shell program which takes two file names and if their contents are same then second one will be deleted.

Ans :

```
   if diff $1 $2
then
     rm $2
   fi
```

- Write a shell script which says Good Morning, Good Evening, Good Afternoon depending on the present time.

```
   x=`date|awk `{ print $4 }' |awk -F: `{ print $1 }''

   if [ $x -lt 3 ]
   then
      echo "Good Night"
   elif [ $x -lt 12 ]
   then
      echo "Good Morning"
   elif [ $x -lt 16 ]
   then
      echo "Good Evening"
   else
      echo "Good Night"
   fi
```

Case construct

- The following lines in file abc and is having world permissions and its name is entered in /etc/profile file. What happens?

```
   case $LOGNAME in
   guest)  echo "It is common directory. don't disturb files" ; ;
   root)   echo "Don't be Biased"; ;
      *)   echo "Don't waste your time on internet" ; ;
   esac
```

Ans :

If the username is guest first message will display at the login time, whereas root user logs in, the second message is displayed otherwise the third one is displayed.

- Explain what happen if you run this shell script?.

```
#!/bin/sh
usage="usage:
  -help   display help
  -opt    display options"
case $# in
  1)
    case "$1" in
      --help) echo "$usage"; exit 0; ;
      --opt) echo "1 for kill"; ;
        exit 0;;
      *) echo "$usage"; exit 0; ;
esac              S
```

Ans :

If the above shell program name is assumed as XX, if you enter XX at command line without arguments or with option `--help` it will display the following message.

```
--help   display help
--opt    display options
```

otherwise it will display the following message.

```
1 for kill
```

While loop

Like any other high level language, shell also supports loops which can be used to execute some set of instructions repeatedly, probably in given number of times.

The following styles of while loop are used to execute a group of statements eternally.

```
while:
do
  --
  -
done

while true
do
  --
  -
done
```

The following while loop structure is used to execute a group of statements as long as the expression is true.

```
while [expr]
do
--
-
done
```

Here, the `expr` can be having relational or string comparison operations between command line arguments, environment variables, shell variables or literals both numbers or strings. As long as the expr is true the statements between do and done will be executed.

```
while  command
do
--
-
done
```

The above style of while loop execute the group of statements as long as given command is executed successfully.

```
while test command
do
--
-
done
```

This version of while loop also behaves similar to the above while loop.

- Write a shell program which informs as soon as a specified user whose name is given along the command line is logged into the system.

```
while :
do
     if  who|grep $1 >/dev/null
     then
           echo $1 is logged in
           exit
else
           sleep 6
fi
done
```

- Write a shell program which takes a source file name and other duplicate file names as command line arguments and creates the duplicate copies of the first file with the names given as subsequent command line arguments.

Solution 1 :

```
while [ "$2" ]
do
   cp $1 $2
   shift
done
```

Solution 2 :

```
X=$1
shift
while [ "$1" ]
do
   cp $X $1
   shift
done
```

Solution 3 :

```
X=$1
shift
while [ $# -ne 0 ]
do
   cp $X $1
   shift
done
```

- Write a shell program which takes a source file name and directories names as command line arguments and prints message yes if the file is found in any of the given directories.

Solution 1 :

```
X=$1
shift
while [ "$1" ]
do
if [  -f   $1/$X ]
            then
                  echo Yes
                  exit
```

```
   else
      shift
   fi
done
echo No
```

- The following program takes primary name of a C language program and it executes the same if it compiles successfully otherwise automatically it brings the vi editor to edit the C language program. This repeats till the program is corrected to have no compile time errors.

```
while true
gcc -o $1  $1.c
case "$?" in
0)echo executing
     $1
     exit ;;
*)vi $1.c ;;
esac
done
```

- Write a shell script to lock your terminal till you enter a password.

```
trap "  "1 2 3
echo terminal locked
read key
pw=xxxxxx
while [  "$pw"  = "xxxxxx"  ]
do
echo Enter password
stty -echo
read pw
stty sane
done
```

Untill loop

```
until [ expr ]
do
--

-
done
```

Here, the expr can be having relational or string comparison operations between command line arguments, environment variables, shell variables or literals both numbers or strings. As long as the expr is false the statements between do and done will be executed.

```
until command
do
--

-

done
```

The group of statements between do and done will be executed as long the command is failure.

- Write a shell program which informs as soon as a specified user whose name is given along the command line is logged into the system.

```
until if     who|grep $1 >/dev/null
do
   sleep 60
   done
echo $1 is logged in
```

- Write a shell program which takes a source file name and other duplicate file names as command line arguments and creates the duplicate copies of the first file with the names given as subsequent command line arguments.

Solution 1 :

```
until [ $# -eq 1 ]
do
   cp $1 $2
   shift
done
```

Solution 2 :

```
X=$1
shift
until [ $# -eq 0  ]
do
   cp $X $1
   shift
done
```

- Write a shell program which takes a source file name and directories names as command line arguments and prints message yes if the file is found in any of the given directories.

```
X=$1
shift
until [ $# -ne 0 ]
do
```

```
if [-f $1/$X]
        then
                echo Yes
                exit
    else
       shift
    fi
done
echo No
```

- The following program takes primary name of a C language program and it executes the same if it compiles successfully otherwise automatically it brings the vi editor to edit the C language program. This repeats till the program is corrected to have no compile time errors.

```
until gcc -o $1  $1.c
vi $1.c
done
echo executing
$1
```

For loop

```
for var in list
do
___

___

done
```

- What is the **output** of

```
for x in .
   do
     ls $x
done
```

Ans : lists all file names in P.W.D.

- What is the output of

```
for x in *
   do
     ls $x
done
```

Ans : lists all file names in P. W. D.

- What is the output of

```
for x in ..
   do
      ls $x
done
```

Ans : lists all file names of parent directory of P.W.D..

- What is the output of the following program

```
IFS=#
for x in .#..
   do
      ls $x
done
```

Ans : lists file names in P.W.D and its parent directory.

- Write a shell program which takes a source file name and other duplicate file names as command line arguments and creates the duplicate copies of the first file with the names given as subsequent command line arguments.

```
X=$1
shift
for Y in $*
do
      cp $X $Y
      shift
done
```

- Write a shell program which takes a source file name and directories names as command line arguments and prints message yes if the file is found in any of the given directories else prints no.

```
X=$1
shift
for Y in $*
do
if [  -f   $Y/$X ]
                then
                    echo Yes
                    exit
   fi
done
echo No
```

- What does the following script does?.

```
a="$1"
shift
readonly a
for I in  $*
do
   cp $a $I
   shift
done
```

Ans : makes the first command line argument as readonly. Then duplicates of the same
will be created with the names $2 $3 . . . and so on.

- What is the output of following shell script.

```
set `who am i`
for in i *
do
   mv $i  $i.$1
done
```

Ans : it adds username as extension to files of **P.W.D.**

- What does the following shell script.

```
for x in `ls`
do
chmod  u=rwx  $x
done.
```

Ans : changes permissions of files in **P.W.D** as **rwx** for users.

- What does the following shell script does.

```
for x in *.ps
do
compress $x
mv $x.ps.Z/backup
done
```

Ans : It compresses all postscript files in P.W.D and moves to /backup directory.

- What does the following shell script does.

```
for i in  $*
do
cc -C  $i.c
done
```

Ans : Creates object files for those c program files whose primary names are given along
the command line to the above shell script.

- What does the following shell script does.

```
for i in *.dvi
   do
dvips $i.dvi | lpr
done
```

Ans : It converts all dvi files in P.W.D and converts to postscript and redirects to printer.

- Explain what happens if you run the following shell script.

```
I=1
for i in $*
do
J=I
for j in $*
if [  $I -ne $J  ]
then
   if diff $i $j
      then
          rm $j
      else
        J=`expr $J + 1`
      fi
fi
done
I=`expr $I + 1`
done
echo $I
```

Ans :   Takes a set of file names along the command line removes if there exists duplicate files.

- Write a shell program such that files (only) of P.W.D will contain PID of the current shell (in which shell script is running) as their extension.

```
for x in `ls`
   do
     if [  !  -d  $x  ]
         then
             mv  $x  $x.$$
     fi
done
```

- Two files contains a list of words to be searched and list of filenames respectively. Write a shell script which display search word and its no. of occurrences over all the files as a tabular fashion.

```
echo "Word Filename Ocurrences"
for  x  in  `cat $file1`
   do
      for y in `cat $file2`
        do
           I=0
        for z in `cat $y`
           do
              if [ "$x" == "$y" ]
                 then
                    I=`expr $I + 1`
                 fi
              done
      echo $x    $y $I
   done
```

- Write a shell script which accepts in command line usersname and informs you as soon as he/she log into system.

```
uname=$1
while :
do
who | grep "$uname">/dev/null
if [ $? -eq 0 ]
   then
        echo $uname is logged in
        exit
      else
        sleep 60
   done
```

- Write a shell script which lists the filenames of a directory (reading permissions are assumed to be available) which contains more than specified no. of characters.

```
read size
foreach x
do
y=`wc -c $x`
if [ $y -gt $size ]
echo $x
fi
done
```

- Write a shell script which displays names of c programs which uses a specified function.

```
read functname
for prog in *.c
do
if grep $functname $prog
then
echo $prog
fi
done
```

- Write a shell script which displays names of the directories in PATH in one line each.

Ans :

```
IFS=:
set`echo $PATH`
for i in $*
do
   echo $i
done

IFS=:
for i in $PATH
do
   echo $i
done
```

- A file (ABC) having a list of search words. Write a program that takes a file name as command line argument and print's success if atleast one line of the file contains all the search words of ABC otherwise display failure.

```
cat $1 |
while read xx
do
FLAG=1
for y in `cat ABC`
do
if ! grep $y $xx
then
FLAG=0
break
fi
done
if $FLAG -eq 1
```

```
then
echo "SUCCESS"
exit
fi
done
echo "FAILURE"
```

- Write a shell script which removes empty files from PWD and changes other files time stamps to current time.

```
for x in .
do
if [ -f $x ]
then
  if [ -s  $x ]
    then
        touch $x
    else
      rm $x
    fi
  fi
done
```

- Write a program to calculate factorial value

```
#!/bin/sh

factorial()
{
  if [ "$1" -gt "1" ]; then
    i=`expr $1 - 1`
    j=`factorial $i`
    k=`expr $1 \* $j`
    echo $k
  else
    echo 1
  fi
}

while :
do
  echo "Enter a number:"
  read x
  factorial $x
done
```

- Write a program which reads a digit and prints its BCD code.

```
#!/bin/sh

convert_digit()
{
  case $1 in
  0) echo "0000 \c" ;;
  1) echo "0001 \c" ;;
  2) echo "0010 \c" ;;
  3) echo "0011 \c" ;;
  4) echo "0100 \c" ;;
  5) echo "0101 \c" ;;
  6) echo "0110 \c" ;;
  7) echo "0111 \c" ;;
  8) echo "1000 \c" ;;
  9) echo "1001 \c" ;;
  *) echo
     echo "Invalid input $1, expected decimal digit"
     ;;
  esac
}

decimal=$1
stringlength=`echo $decimal | wc -c`
char=1

while [ "${char}" -lt "${stringlength}" ]
do
     convert_digit `echo $decimal|cut -c ${char}`
     char=`expr ${char} + 1`
done
echo
```

- Write a program which reads a filename along the command line and prints frequency of the occurrence of words.

```
#!/bin/sh
# Count the frequency of words in a file.
# Syntax: frequency.sh textfile.txt
INFILE=$1
```

```
WORDS=/tmp/words.$$.txt
COUNT=/tmp/count.$$.txt

if [ -z "$INFILE" ]; then
  echo "Syntax: `basename $0` textfile.txt"
  echo "A utility to count frequency of words in a text file"
  exit 1
fi
if [ ! -r $INFILE ]; then
  echo "Error: Can't read input file $INFILE"
  exit 1
fi

> $WORDS
> $COUNT

# First, get each word onto its own line...
# Save this off to a temporary file ($WORDS)
# The "tr '\t' ' '" replaces tabs with spaces;
# The "tr -s ' '" removes duplicate spaces.
# The "tr ' ' '\n' replaces spaces with newlines.
# Note: The "tr "[:punct:]"" requires GNU tr, not UNIX tr.
  cat $INFILE | tr "[:punct:]" ' ' | tr '\t' ' ' | tr -s ' '
  | tr ' ' '\n' | while read f
do
echo $f >> $WORDS
done
# Now read in each line (word) from the temporary file
$WORDS ...
while read f
do

    #  Have we already encountered this word?
      grep — " ${f}$" $COUNT > /dev/null 2>&1
      if [ "$?" -ne "0" ]; then
    # No, we haven't found this word before... count its
      frequency
      NUMBER=`grep -cw -- "${f}" $WORDS`
```

```
                # Store the frequency in the $COUNT file
                echo "$NUMBER $f" >> $COUNT
            fi
        done < $WORDS

        # Now we have $COUNT which has a tally of every word found,
          and how
        # often it was encountered. Sort it numerically for legibil-
          ity.
        # We can use head to limit the number of results - using 20
          as an example.
        echo "20 most frequently enountered words:"
        sort -rn $COUNT | head -20

        # Now remove the temporary files.
          rm -f $WORDS $COUNT
```

Arrays

A useful facility in the C-shell is the ability to make arrays out of strings and other variables. The round parentheses '(..)' do this. For example, look at the following commands.

```
        set array = ( a b c d )
        echo $array[1]
        a
        echo $array[2]
        b
        echo $array[$#array]
        d

        set noarray = ( "a b c d" )
        echo $noarray[1]
        a b c d
        echo $noarray[$#noarray]
        a b c d
```

The first command defines an array containing the elements 'a b c d'. The elements of the array are referred to using square brackets '[..]' and the first element is '$array[1]'. The last element is '$array[4]'.

Nfote : This is not the same as in C or C++ where the first element of the array is the zeroth element!

The special operator '$#' returns the number of elements in an array. This gives us a simple way of finding the end of the array. For example

```
echo $#path
23

echo "The last element in path is $path[$#path]"
```

The last element in path is .

Bash arrays

The original Bourne shell does not have arrays. Bash version 2.x does have arrays, however. An array can be assigned from a string of words separated by whitespaces or the individual elements of the array can be set individually.

```
colours=(red white green)
colours[3]="yellow"
```

An element of the array must be referred to using curly braces.

```
echo ${colours[1]}
white
```

Note that the first element of the array has index 0. The set of all elements is referred to by ${colours[*]}.

```
echo ${colours[*]}
red white green yellow
echo ${#colours[*]}
4
```

As seen the number of elements in an array is given by ${#colours[*]}.

10   Unix System Calls

A system call is a request for the operating system to do something on behalf of the user's program. The system calls are functions used in the kernel itself. To the programmer, the system call appears as a normal C function call. However, since a system call executes code in the kernel, there is a mechanism which change the mode of a process from user mode to kernel mode. The C compiler uses a predefined library of functions (the C library) that have the names of the system calls. The library functions typically invoke an instruction that changes the process execution mode to kernel mode and causes the kernel to start executing code for system calls. The instruction that causes the mode change is often referred to as an "operating system trap" which is a software generated interrupt. The library routines execute in user mode, but the system call interface is a special case of an interrupt handler. The library functions pass the kernel a unique number per system call in a machine dependent way – either as a parameter to the operating system trap, in a particular register, or on the stack – and the kernel thus determines the specific system call the user is invoking. In handling the operating system trap, the kernel looks up the system call number in a table to find the address of the appropriate kernel routine that is the entry point for the system call and to find the number of parameters the system call expects. The kernel calculates the (user) address of the first parameter to the system call by adding (or subtracting, depending on the direction of stack growth) an offset to the user stack pointer, corresponding to the number of the parameters to the system call. Finally, it copies the user parameters to the "u area" and call the appropriate system call routine. After executing the code for the system call, the kernel determines whether there was an error. If so, it adjusts register locations in the saved user register context, typically setting the "carry" bit for the PS (processor status) register and copying the error number into register 0 location. If there were no errors in the execution of the system call, the kernel clears the "carry" bit in the PS register and copies the appropriate return values from the system call into the locations for registers 0 and 1 in the saved user register context. When the kernel returns from the operating system trap to user mode, it returns to the library instruction after the trap instruction. The library interprets the return values from the kernel and returns a value to the user program.

UNIX system calls are used to manage the file system, control processes, and to provide interprocess communication. The UNIX system interface consists of about 80 system calls (as UNIX evolves this number will increase). The following table lists about 40 of the more important system call :

General class	Specific class	System call
File structure Related calls	Creating a Channel	creat() open() close()
	Input/Output	read() write()
	Random Access	lseek()
	Channel Duplication	dup()
	Aliasing and Removing Files	link() unlink()
	File Status	stat() fstat()
	Access Control	access() chmod() chown() umask()
	Device Control	ioctl()
Process related calls	Process Creation and Termination	exec() fork() wait() exit()
	Process Owner and Group	getuid() geteuid() getgid() getegid()
	Process Identity	getpid() getppid()
	Process Control	signal() kill() alarm()
	Change Working Directory	chdir()
Interprocess communication	Pipelines	pipe()
	Messages	msgget()

General class	Specific class	System call
		msgsnd()
		msgrcv()
		msgctl()
	Semaphores	semget()
		semop()
	Shared Memory	shmget()
		shmat()
		shmdt()

[***Note :*** The system call interface is that aspect of UNIX that has changed the most since the inception of the UNIX system. Therefore, when you write a software tool, you should protect that tool by putting system calls in other subroutines within your program and then calling only those subroutines. Should the next version of the UNIX system change the syntax and semantics of the system calls you've used, you need only change your interface routines.]

When a system call discovers an error, it returns `-1` and stores the reason the called failed in an external variable named "`errno`". The "`/usr/include/errno.h`" file maps these error numbers to manifest constants, and these constants you should use in your programs.

When a system call returns successfully, it returns something other than `-1`, but it does not clear "`errno`". The "`errno`" only has meaning directly after a system call that returns an error.

When you use system calls in your programs, you should check the value returned by those system calls. Furthermore, when a system call discovers an error, you should use the "`perror()`" subroutine to print a diagnostic message on the standard error file that describes why the system call failed. The syntax for "`perror()`" is :

```
void perror(string)
char string;
```

The function "`perror()`" displays the argument string, a colon, and then the error message, as directed by "errno", followed by a newline. The output of "`perror()`" is displayed on "standard error". Typically, the argument give to "`perror()`" is the name of the program that incurred the error, argv[0]. However, when using subroutines and system calls on files, the related file name might be passed to "`perror()`".

There are occasions where you the programmer might wish to maintain more control over the printing of error messages than "`perror()`" provides - such as with a formatted screen where the newline printed by "`perror()`" would destroy the formatting. In this case, you can directly access the same system external (global) variables that "`perror()`" uses. They are :

```
extern int errno;
extern char *sys_errlist[];
extern int sys_nerr;
```

The variable "errno" has been described above. "sys_errlist" is an array (table) of pointers to the error message strings. Each message string is null terminated and does not contain a newline. "sys_nerr" is the number of messages in the error message table and is the maximum value "errno" can assume. The "errno" is used as the index into the table of error messages. Following are two sample programs that display all of the system error messages on standard error.

Example 1

The program prints all system error messages using "perror()".

```c
#include <stdio.h>
 int main()
 {
   int i;
   extern int errno, sys_nerr;
   for (i = 0; i < sys_nerr; ++i)
     {
        fprintf(stderr, "%3d",i);
        errno = i;
        perror(" ");
 }
   exit (0);
 }
```

Example 2

This program prints all system error messages using the global error message table.

```c
#include <stdio.h>
 int main()
 {
   int i;
   extern int sys_nerr;
   extern char *sys_errlist[];
   fprintf(stderr,"Here are the current %d
                   error messages:\n\n",sys_nerr);
   for (i = 0; i < sys_nerr; ++i)
      fprintf(stderr,"%3d: %s\n", i, sys_errlist[i]);
 }
```

Example 3

This program prints out info about a known standard errors.

```c
#include <stdio.h>
#include <ctype.h>
#include <string.h>
#include <stdlib.h>
#include <errno.h>

struct err_t
{
  char *name;
  int val;
} errlist[] = {
  { "EPERM", EPERM },
  { "ENOENT", ENOENT },
  { "ESRCH", ESRCH },
  { "EINTR", EINTR },
  { "EIO", EIO },
  { "ENXIO", ENXIO },
  { "E2BIG", E2BIG },
  { "ENOEXEC", ENOEXEC },
  { "EBADF", EBADF },
  { "ECHILD", ECHILD },
  { "EAGAIN", EAGAIN },
  { "ENOMEM", ENOMEM },
  { "EACCES", EACCES },
  { "EFAULT", EFAULT },
  { "ENOTBLK", ENOTBLK },
  { "EBUSY", EBUSY },
  { "EEXIST", EEXIST },
  { "EXDEV", EXDEV },
  { "ENODEV", ENODEV },
  { "ENOTDIR", ENOTDIR },
  { "EISDIR", EISDIR },
  { "EINVAL", EINVAL },
  { "ENFILE", ENFILE },
  { "EMFILE", EMFILE },
  { "ENOTTY", ENOTTY },
  { "ETXTBSY", ETXTBSY },
  { "EFBIG", EFBIG },
  { "ENOSPC", ENOSPC },
  { "ESPIPE", ESPIPE },
```

```
            { "EROFS", EROFS },
            { "EMLINK", EMLINK },
            { "EPIPE", EPIPE },
            { "EDOM", EDOM },
            { "ERANGE", ERANGE },
            { "EDEADLK", EDEADLK },
            { "ENAMETOOLONG", ENAMETOOLONG },
            { "ENOLCK", ENOLCK },
            { "ENOSYS", ENOSYS },
            { "ENOTEMPTY", ENOTEMPTY },
            { "ELOOP", ELOOP },
            { "EWOULDBLOCK", EWOULDBLOCK },
            { "ENOMSG", ENOMSG },
            { "EIDRM", EIDRM },
            { "ECHRNG", ECHRNG },
            { "EL2NSYNC", EL2NSYNC },
            { "EL3HLT", EL3HLT },
            { "EL3RST", EL3RST },
            { "ELNRNG", ELNRNG },
            { "EUNATCH", EUNATCH },
            { "ENOCSI", ENOCSI },
            { "EL2HLT", EL2HLT },
            { "EBADE", EBADE },
            { "EBADR", EBADR },
            { "EXFULL", EXFULL },
            { "ENOANO", ENOANO },
            { "EBADRQC", EBADRQC },
            { "EBADSLT", EBADSLT },
            { "EDEADLOCK", EDEADLOCK },
            { "EBFONT", EBFONT },
            { "ENOSTR", ENOSTR },
            { "ENODATA", ENODATA },
            { "ETIME", ETIME },
            { "ENOSR", ENOSR },
            { "ENONET", ENONET },
            { "ENOPKG", ENOPKG },
            { "EREMOTE", EREMOTE },
            { "ENOLINK", ENOLINK },
            { "EADV", EADV },
            { "ESRMNT", ESRMNT },
            { "ECOMM", ECOMM },
            { "EPROTO", EPROTO },
            { "EMULTIHOP", EMULTIHOP },
```

```
{ "EDOTDOT", EDOTDOT },
{ "EBADMSG", EBADMSG },
{ "EOVERFLOW", EOVERFLOW },
{ "ENOTUNIQ", ENOTUNIQ },
{ "EBADFD", EBADFD },
{ "EREMCHG", EREMCHG },
{ "ELIBACC", ELIBACC },
{ "ELIBBAD", ELIBBAD },
{ "ELIBSCN", ELIBSCN },
{ "ELIBMAX", ELIBMAX },
{ "ELIBEXEC", ELIBEXEC },
{ "EILSEQ", EILSEQ },
{ "ERESTART", ERESTART },
{ "ESTRPIPE", ESTRPIPE },
{ "EUSERS", EUSERS },
{ "ENOTSOCK", ENOTSOCK },
{ "EDESTADDRREQ", EDESTADDRREQ },
{ "EMSGSIZE", EMSGSIZE },
{ "EPROTOTYPE", EPROTOTYPE },
{ "ENOPROTOOPT", ENOPROTOOPT },
{ "EPROTONOSUPPORT", EPROTONOSUPPORT },
{ "ESOCKTNOSUPPORT", ESOCKTNOSUPPORT },
{ "EOPNOTSUPP", EOPNOTSUPP },
{ "EPFNOSUPPORT", EPFNOSUPPORT },
{ "EAFNOSUPPORT", EAFNOSUPPORT },
{ "EADDRINUSE", EADDRINUSE },
{ "EADDRNOTAVAIL", EADDRNOTAVAIL },
{ "ENETDOWN", ENETDOWN },
{ "ENETUNREACH", ENETUNREACH },
{ "ENETRESET", ENETRESET },
{ "ECONNABORTED", ECONNABORTED },
{ "ECONNRESET", ECONNRESET },
{ "ENOBUFS", ENOBUFS },
{ "EISCONN", EISCONN },
{ "ENOTCONN", ENOTCONN },
{ "ESHUTDOWN", ESHUTDOWN },
{ "ETOOMANYREFS", ETOOMANYREFS },
{ "ETIMEDOUT", ETIMEDOUT },
{ "ECONNREFUSED", ECONNREFUSED },
{ "EHOSTDOWN", EHOSTDOWN },
{ "EHOSTUNREACH", EHOSTUNREACH },
{ "EALREADY", EALREADY },
{ "EINPROGRESS", EINPROGRESS },
```

```c
{ "ESTALE", ESTALE },
{ "EUCLEAN", EUCLEAN },
{ "ENOTNAM", ENOTNAM },
{ "ENAVAIL", ENAVAIL },
{ "EISNAM", EISNAM },
{ "EREMOTEIO", EREMOTEIO },
{ "EDQUOT", EDQUOT },
{ "ENOMEDIUM", ENOMEDIUM },
{ "EMEDIUMTYPE", EMEDIUMTYPE },
{ NULL, 0 }
};

char *lookuperrorname(int errnum)
{
  struct err_t * err = errlist;

  while(err->name != NULL)
  {
    if(err->val == errnum)
    {
      return(err->name);
    }
    err++;
  }
  // if we get here we didn't find it

  return("");
}

int errornumber(int errnum)
{
  printf("%4d, %-12s: %s\n", errnum, lookuperrorname(errnum),
  strerror(errnum));
  return(0);
}

int errorstr(char *str)
{
  int i;
  int retval = -1;
  char *lasterrstr = NULL;

  // As described earlier we can use sys_errlist[] but
  // that isn't portable
  for(i=0; i<2048; i++)
```

```c
{
  if(strncasecmp(str, strerror(i), strlen(str)) == 0)
  {
    printf("%4d, %-12s: %s\n", i, lookuperrorname(i),
    strerror(i));
    retval = 0;
  }
  // check if the same buffer is reused, if so we are at
  // the end of the
   error list

  if(lasterrstr && lasterrstr == strerror(i))
  {
    break;
  }
  lasterrstr = strerror(i);
}

return(retval);
}

int errorname(char *str)
{
  struct err_t * err = errlist;
  int retval = -1;

  while(err->name != NULL)
  {
    if(strncmp(err->name, str, strlen(str)) == 0)
    {
      printf("%4d, %-12s: %s\n", err->val, err->name,
      strerror(err->val));
      retval = 0;
    }
    err++;
  }

  return(retval);
}

int main(int argc, char **argv)
{
  int i;

  if(argc < 2)
```

```c
    {
      fprintf(stderr, "usage: %s <string> ...\n", argv[0]);
      fprintf(stderr, "\n");
      fprintf(stderr, "  string can be:\n");
      fprintf(stderr, "    an error number\n");
      fprintf(stderr, "    an error name\n");
      fprintf(stderr, "    an error description\n");
      fprintf(stderr, "\n");
    }

    for(i=1; i<argc; i++)
    {
      int res;

      if(isdigit(*argv[i]))
      {
        if(errornumber(strtol(argv[i], NULL, 0)) != 0)
          {
            fprintf(stderr, "%-18s: *** Not Found ***\n",
            argv[i]);
          }
      }
      else
      {
        res = 0;
        res += errorname(argv[i]);
        res += errorstr(argv[i]);

        if(res == -2)
        {
          fprintf(stderr, "%-18s: *** Not Found ***\n",
          argv[i]);
        }
      }
    }

    return 0;
}
```

Exit Status of Programs

The exit() system call ends a process and returns a value to its parent. The prototype for
the exit() system call is :

```c
void exit(status)
int status;
```

Where status is an integer and this number is returned to the parent as the exit status of the process. By convention, when a process exits with a status of zero that means it didn't encounter any problems; when a process exit with a non-zero value indicating it has encountered some problems.

The function exit() is actually not a system routine; it is a library routine that call the system routine_exit(). The exit() cleans up the standard I/O streams before calling _exit(), so any output that has been buffered but not yet actually written out is flushed. Calling _exit() instead of exit() will bypass this cleanup procedure. The exit() does not return.

Example 4

```
#include<stdio.h>
int main()
{
return 0;
}
```

When we execute the above program at the command prompt and then when execute echo $?. We will see zero which we call as the exit status of the above program. The same result we will get if we call exit(0) instead of `return 0`.

As mentioned earlier, exit system call cleans up the standard I/O, flushes the buffers and then exits from the program. To see their difference run the following program once and then replacing exit with _exit. We will see "Hello" message in the first instance whereas we see nothing in the second instance. This is because, the printf function uses line buffering principle. That is, when its buffer is full or when we write new line character its contents will be flushed. Thus, when we call exit function it will flush this buffer also unlike _exit function.

The basic difference between exit() and _exit() is that the former performs clean-up related to user-mode constructs in the library, and calls user-supplied cleanup functions, whereas the latter performs only the kernel cleanup for the process.

Example 5

```
#include<stdio.h>
int main()
{
printf("Hello");
exit(0)
}
```

Exit Handlers

Some times, we may need to execute some set of functions whenever we call exit system call from any part of the program. This is achieved with the help of `atexit()` system call. With the help of this system call we can register some functions at the kernel (thus known as exit handlers) and they will be automatically executed in accordance with their reverse order of their registration. That is, most recently registered function is executed first. The prototype of the function `atexit()` is as follows :

```
int atexit( void (*func)(void));
```

Example 6

```
#include<sdtio.h>
void xyz()
{
printf("Hello");
}

void pqr()
{
printf("How are you");
}

void ijk()
{
printf("My Dear");
}
int main()
{
atexit(ijk);
atexit(pqr);
atexit(xyz);

exit(0);
}
```

When we run this program, we may see the message "Hello How are you My Dear".

Check what happens if you replace_exit instead of exit in the above program.

Normally, the exit handlers are used to clean directory (i.e removing temporary files created by a program), to remove some core files automatically etc.,.

Conclusions

In this chapter, we have enumerated general system calls related to file operations, process management, signal handing, and IPC. We have explained with examples about error handling with system calles in a generalized manner. In addition, exit handlers are explained with lucid examples.

Questions

1. Write a program whenever it calls exit() system call in any function it removes files with name "core" in current working directory (Hint : see system call `system()`).

2. Write a program to find out the buffer size employed by `printf()` library function (Hint go on write characters through `printf ()` function till output appears on the screen).

11 Unix File System Call API

Unix has a variety of system calls for carrying out file operations. The standard I/O library in Unix which is also called as stdio library, which has a high-level interface for the file operations, such as printf, putchar, etc., is built from this lower-level interface. Typical system calls are :

```
int creat(char *path,  mode_t mode);
int unlink(char *path);
int rename(char *old, char *new);
int open(char *path,  int oflag,  ...);
int close(int fildes);
int read(int fildes, char *buf, unsigned nbyte);
int write(int fildes, char *buf, unsigned nbyte);
off_t lseek(int filedes, off_t offset, int whence);
int link(char *path1,char *path2);
int chmod(char *path, mode_t mode);
int stat(char *path, struct stat *buf);
int fstat(int fd, struct stat *buf);
int lstat(char *path, struct stat *buf);
```

Creat

This call, creat takes the pathname of a file and creates a new file, removing the contents if it already existed. The mode sets the access permissions. This is a bit-wise OR of the file permissions :

```
S_IRUSR   0400
S_IWUSR   0200
S_IXUSR   0100
S_IRGRP   040
S_IWGRP   020
S_IXGRP   010
S_IROTH   04
S_IWOTH   02
S_IXOTH   01
```

This follows the `rwx` for user, group and other that is shown by "`ls -l`".

Open

The open call opens the file in the mode given by oflag, and returns a file descriptor. This is an integer which the O/S uses to index into a per process file descriptor table, which is used to keep info about open files. Zero is always stdin, 1 is stdout, 2 is stderr. The oflag is a bit-wise OR of a number of constants

```
O_RDONLY
O_WRONLY
O_CREAT
O_TRUNC
```

When `O_CREAT` is one of these flags, an additional argument to open is the file permission mode.

Example 1

The following program checks and reports file descriptors of all the opened files.

```c
#include <stdio.h>
#include <stdlib.h>
#include <fcntl.h>

int checkForOpen(int h)
{
  int scratch;
  if(fcntl(h, F_GETFD, &scratch)< 0)
  {
    return 0;
  }
  else
  {
  return 1;
  }
}
```

```c
int main(int argc, char **argv)
{
  int i;
  for(i = 0; i< 128; i++)
  {
    if(checkForOpen(i))
    {
      printf("%4d found open\n", i);
    }
  }

  return 0;
}
```

Example 2

This program is to demonstrate the limitations on number of opened files. Usually every process will have limitations on number of opened files at any instant of time. The value of I when the program is terminated represents about this limitation.

```c
#include<stdio.h>
int main()
{
    FILE *fp;
    int I;  char x[20];
    for(I=0;I<128;I++)
    {
    sprintf(x,"test%d",I);
      fp = fopen(x,"w");
    if(fp==0)exit(-1);
      printf("%d\n",I);
    }
    return 0;
}
```

Example 3

To test, what happen when we close the file descriptor 1 and then open a new file and run some unix commands using system() system call.

```c
#include<unistd.h>
#include<fcntl.h>
#include<sys/stat.h>
```

```
int main()
{
    int fd,i;
    char x[20];
    close(1);
    fd = open(x,O_WRONLY|O_CREAT);
    printf("File: %d\n",fd);
    system("ls");
    return 0;
}
```

When we try to open a file, first empty (row) entry in the open file descriptor table is taken by searching this table always from first row, and is given to this new file to store this file's information. This row number is called as file descriptor of the file. For any program, by default three descriptors stdin(0), stdout(1) and stderr(2) are available.

Thus, in the above program after closing stdin i.e 1, when we call open() system call the file descriptor for the new file becomes 1 (under plain situations on most unix systems). Now, when we execute "ls" command, its output will be written into this file as by default "ls" commands output goes to standard output whose file descriptor is 1. Whereas now file descriptor 1 belongs to the file, thus "ls" command output goes to the file.

Read

The read call is a block read of a given number of bytes. This could be tuned to the physical characteristics of the device read from. For example, it may be much faster to do a block read of 1024 bytes from a hard disk than to do 1024 reads of 1 byte from the disk.

The value returned is the actual number of bytes read. This may be less than the number asked for. For example

- if you ask for 1024 bytes to be read from a file that only has 53 bytes in it, you will only get 53.
- input from the keyboard is normally line-buffered, so no matter how many you ask for, you will only get a line at a time.
- a pipeline is often implemented with a buffer size of 4k. Reads of more than that may cause the pipeline buffer to be filled and emptied several times.

The function "read" returns zero on EOF, and -1 on error. A while loop to read using this call should always test the return value for > 0:

```
while ((nread = read(...)) > 0)
...
if (nread == 0)
/* EOF code */
else
/* error code */
```

Write

The write call is also a block write of a number of bytes. It returns -1 if a write error occurs (such as no space left).

Example 4

This is a simple version of cp, using the low-level I/O ie read() and write.

```c
#include <stdio.h>
#include <sys/types.h>
#include <sys/stat.h>
#include <fcntl.h>

#define SIZE 1024
#define MODE (S_IRUSR | S_IWUSR |  S_IRGRP | S_IROTH)

int main(int argc, char *argv[])
{
  int src, dst;
  int in_count, out_count;
  char buf[SIZE];
  int nread;

  if (argc != 3) {
    printf("Usage: cp f1 f2\n");
    exit(1);
}

if ((src = open(argv[1], O_RDONLY)) == -1) {
  printf("Cant open \n", argv[1]);
exit(2);
}

if ((dst = creat(argv[2], MODE)) == -1) {
  printf( "cant create %s\n", argv[2]);
exit(3);
}

while ((nread = read(src, buf, SIZE)) > 0) {
if (write(dst, buf, nread) == -1) {
  printf( "cant write\n");
  exit(4);
}
}
}
exit(0);
}
```

Example 5

This program is to find what happens when a file is opened using file stream (i.e through standard I/O library function) and some things is written into it and also something is written into it through file descriptor.

```c
#include<unistd.h>
#include<fcntl.h>
#include<stdio.h>

int main()
{
   FILE *ip;
   int fd;
   char x[] = "Hello";
   fd = open("test2.dat", O_WRONLY|O_CREAT);
   ip = fdopen(fd, "w");
   write(fd,x,5);
   fprintf(ip,"%s",x);
   return 0;
}
```

Two times "Hello" will be written (confirm through file size). However, file is not readable. Why? Guess.

stat(): File status Information

The function stat() is used to get file status information. That is metadata information or statistics of the file can be accessed through this function call (also using fstat(), lstat()). All of these functions find out information about files (permissions, owner, filetype etc). The only difference between them is the way in which they treat symbolic links. If 'stat' is used on a symbolic link, it stats the file the link points to rather than the link itself. If 'lstat' is used, the data refer to the link. Thus, to detect a link, we must use 'lstat'.

All these functions use a data structure known as 'stat' which is defined in the file `/usr/include/sys/stat.h`. Here are the data members of the structure.

```c
struct stat
{
dev_t    st_dev;      /* device number*/
ino_t    st_ino;      /* file inode */
mode_t   st_mode;     /* permission */
short    st_nlink;    /* Number of hardlinks to file */
uid_t    st_uid;      /* user id */
gid_t    st_gid;      /* group id */
```

```
dev_t       st_rdev;
off_t       st_size;     /* size in bytes */
time_t      st_atime;    /* time file last accessed */
time_t      st_mtime;    /* time file contents last modified */
time_t      st_ctime;    /* time last attribute change */
long        st_blksize;
long        st_blocks;
};
```

The function 'stat()' treats symbolic links as though they were the files they point to. In other words, if we use 'stat()' to read a symbolic link, we end up reading the file the link points to and not the link itself— we never see symbolic links. As mentioned earlier, to avoid this problem, there is a different version of the stat function called 'lstat()' which is identical to 'stat()' except that it treats links as links and *not* as the files they point to. This means that we can test whether a file is a symbolic link, only if we use 'lstat()'. Once we have identified a file to be a symbolic link, we use the 'readlink()' function to obtain the name of the file the link points to.

```
#define bufsize 512
char buffer[bufsize];

readlink("/path/to/file",buffer,bufsize);
```

The result is returned in the string buffer.

Similarly, once the file is opened and its file descriptor is available then we can know its 'stat' information by calling fstat() system call.

The data member st_mode contains information about what permissions a file has, and also its most significant 4 bits describes the type of file - whether it is a directory or a link etc. There are ready made macros defined in UNIX to extract this information from the 'st_mode' member of the 'stat' structure. They are defined in the 'stat.h' headerfile and are given as :

```
#define S_ISBLK(m)     /* is block device */
#define S_ISCHR(m)     /* is character device */
#define S_ISDIR(m)     /* is directory */
#define S_ISFIFO(m)    /* is fifo pipe/socket */
#define S_ISREG(m)     /* is regular (normal) file */

#define S_ISLNK(m)     /* is symbolic link */  /* Not POSIX */
#define S_ISSOCK(m)    /* is a lock */
```

Also, permissions can be compared by using the following symbolic constants.

```
#define   S_IRWXU    /* rwx, owner */
#define   S_IRUSR    /* read permission, owner */
#define   S_IWUSR    /* write permission, owner */
#define   S_IXUSR    /* execute/search permission, owner */
#define   S_IRWXG    /* rwx, group */
#define   S_IRGRP    /* read permission, group */
#define   S_IWGRP    /* write permission, grougroup */
#define   S_IXGRP    /* execute/search permission, group */
#define   S_IRWXO    /* rwx, other */
#define   S_IROTH    /* read permission, other */
#define   S_IWOTH    /* write permission, other */
#define   S_IXOTH    /* execute/search permission, other */
```

A typical usage of the above macros can be summarized as:

```
struct stat statvar;

stat("file",&statvar);

/* test return values */

if (S_ISDIR(statvar.st_mode))
   {
   printf("Is a directory!");
   }
```

Example 6

This program prints UID of the file whose name is along the command line.

```
#include <sys/stat.h>
#include <stdio.h>
#include <unistd.h>
#include <limits.h>

int main(int argc, char *argv[])
{
   struct stat buff;

 char filename[NAME_MAX + 1];

 printf( "Enter file name: ");
 scanf("%s",filename);

 if (stat(filename, &buff) == -1)
 {
   perror(filename);
   exit(1);
 }
```

```
    else
    {
      printf("File owner: %d\n ", buff.st_uid );
    }
  exit(0);
  }
```

Example 7

Program takes a file name along the command line and prints its stat information using file descriptor. This program is given to demonstrate the use of fstat() function.

```
#include <unistd.h>
#include <sys/stat.h>
#include <fcntl.h>
#include <stdio.h>

int main(int argc, char **argv)
{
  struct stat X;
  int fd;
  if(argc == 1)
  {
    printf("Usage: %s [FILE]\n",argv[1]);
    return -1;
  }
  if((fd = open(argv[1], O_RDONLY)) < 0)
  {
    perror("Open");
    return -1;
  }

  if(fstat(fd, &X) < 0)
  {
    perror("fstat");
    return -1;
  }
  printf("Size :%ld\nInode :%ld\n",X.st_size,X.st_ino);
  return 0;
}
```

Example 8

Program to prints st_dev and st_rdev values and Major and Minor numbers of the file or directories whose names are given along the command line. Major number conveys the device driver which is to be used access the device on which the file is located. Whereas minor number of the file indicates the serial number of the device out of the devices which use this device driver.

```
#include <sys/types.h>
#include <sys/stat.h>
#include <unistd.h>

int main(int n, char *a[])
{
  int i;
  struct stat X;
  for (i = 1; i < n; i++)
{
  if(stat(a[i], &X) < 0)
  {
    perror("stat");
    continue;
  }
  printf("dev = %d/%d", major(X.st_dev), minor(X.st_dev));
  if (S_ISCHR(X.st_mode) || S_ISBLK(X.st_mode))
  //printf("(%s)rdev = %d/%d",(S_ISCHR(X.st_mode))
        ?"character": "block",major(X.st_rdev),
        minor(X.st_rdev));//
  printf("\n");
}
  return 0;
}
```

Example 9

The following example program demonstrates the use of the directory functions in
dirent and the stat function call (Please refer next chapeter for discussion on opendir(),
readdir(), etc,.).

```
#include <stdio.h>
#include <dirent.h>
#include <sys/types.h>
#include <sys/stat.h>

#define DIRNAME "/."
#define bufsize 255

main ()

{ DIR *dirh;
  struct dirent *dirp;
  struct stat statbuf;
  char *pathname[bufsize];
  char *linkname[bufsize];
```

```c
if ((dirh = opendir(DIRNAME)) == NULL)
  {
  perror("opendir");
  exit(1);
  }
for (dirp = readdir(dirh); dirp != NULL; dirp = readdir(dirh))
  {
if (strcmp(".",dirp->d_name) == 0 || strcmp("..",dirp->d_
                                            name) == 0)
{
continue;
}

if (strcmp("lost+found",dirp->d_name) == 0)
{
continue;
}

sprintf(pathname,"%s/%s",DIRNAME,dirp->d_name);

if (lstat(pathname,&statbuf) == -1) /* see man stat */
{
perror("stat");
continue;
}

if (S_ISREG(statbuf.st_mode))
{
printf("%s is a regular file\n",pathname);
}

if (S_ISDIR(statbuf.st_mode))
{
printf("%s is a directory\n",pathname);
}

if (S_ISLNK(statbuf.st_mode))
{
bzero(linkname,bufsize);   /* clear string */
readlink(pathname,linkname,bufsize);
printf("%s is a link to %s\n",pathname,linkname);
}
printf("The mode of %s is %o\n\n",
        pathname,statbuf.st_mode & 07777);
}

closedir(dirh);
}
```

Use of UNIX File API System Calls

When should you use these low-level (system calls) functions? Only when you have to. In general use the high-level functions. There will be many times when you need finer control.

Note that these functions are specific to the Unix API, and are not in Microsoft C, for example. So code written using these functions will only be portable across Unix, not to other Operating Systems.

Create, Open

These two functions control what happens when a file has to be created.

- The file permissions are set using the mode argument
- The functions may be used on things other than files (such as pipes)
- If the file is part of FIFO or is a device, then the function may be set to block or return immediately if the FIFO/device is not ready
- creat may be set to fail if the file exists, allowing a simple lock mechanism in addition
- The owner and group are set
- The file creation and modification times and the directory modification times are set
- The file is created in binary mode only, not in text or binary mode
- On failure, the global errno is set to a value that will give more information about the error such as
    - EMFILE - too many files are open by this process
    - EISDIR - write access was requested of a directory
    - EINTR - the request was interrupted

`lseek()`

The UNIX system file system treats an ordinary file as a sequence of bytes. No internal structure is imposed on a file by the operating system. Generally, a file is read or written sequentially - that is, from beginning to the end of the file. Sometimes sequential reading and writing is not appropriate. It may be inefficient, for instance, to read an entire file just to move to the end of the file to add characters. Fortunately, the UNIX system lets you read and write anywhere in the file. Known as "random access", this capability is made possible with the lseek() system call. During file I/O, the UNIX system uses a long integer, also called a File Pointer, to keep track of the next byte to read or write. This long integer represents the number of bytes from the beginning of the file to that next character. Random access I/O is achieved by changing the value of this file pointer using the lseek() system call. The prototype for lseek() is :

```
long lseek(file_descriptor, offset, whence)
int file_descriptor;
long offset;
int whence;
```

where file_descriptor identifies the I/O channel and offset and whence work together to describe how to change the file pointer according to the following table:

whence	new position
0	offset bytes into the file
1	current position in the file plus offset
2	current end-of-file position plus offset

If successful, `lseek()` returns a long integer that defines the new file pointer value measured in bytes from the beginning of the file. If unsuccessful, the file position does not change.

Certain devices are incapable of seeking, namely terminals and the character interface to a tape drive. lseek() does not change the file pointer to these devices.

Example 10

Following is an example using `lseek()`:

```
#include <stdio.h>
#include <fcntl.h>

int main()
{
  int fd;
  long position;

  fd = open("datafile.dat", O_RDONLY);
  if ( fd != -1)
    {
    position = lseek(fd, 0L, 2);  /* seek 0 bytes from
                                 end-of-file */
    if (position != -1)
      printf("The length of datafile.dat is %ld bytes.
                                 \n", position);
    else
      perror("lseek error");
    }
  else
      printf("can't open datafile.dat\n");
    close(fd);
  }
```

Many UNIX systems have defined manifest constants for use as the "whence" argument of `lseek()`. The definitions can be found in the "`file.h`" and/or "`unistd.h`" include files.

from `file.h` we have :

```
#define L_SET     0        /* absolute offset */
#define L_INCR    1        /* relative to current offset */
#define L_XTND     2       /* relative to end of file */
```

and from unistd.h we have:

```
#define SEEK_SET   0        /* Set file pointer to "offset" */
#define SEEK_CUR   1        /* Set file pointer to current
                               plus "offset" */
#define SEEK_END    2       /* Set file pointer to EOF
                               plus "offset" */
```

The definitions from unistd.h are the most "portable" across UNIX and MS-DOS C compilers.

Example 11

This program creates a File containing hole which is occupying some space but having nothing.

```
#include <unistd.h>
#include <fcntl.h>
#include <sys/stat.h>
#include <stdio.h>

int main()
{
   int fd,off;
   fd = open("Hole",O_WRONLY|O_CREAT,S_IRUSR);
   if((off = lseek(fd, 10000, SEEK_SET)) < 0)
   {
     perror("lseek");
     return -1;
   }
  return 0;
}
```

Run the above program and check the size of resulting file. In some appliction such as creation of **swap files** etc., this concept is used.

Example 12

Program to test if standard input is capable of seeking or not

```
#include <unistd.h>
#include <sys/types.h>

int main()
{
    if (lseek(STDIN_FILENO, 0 ,SEEK_CUR) == -1)
        printf("Cannot seek\n");
    else
        printf("Seek OK\n");
    return 0;
}
```

dup()

The dup() system call duplicates an open file descriptor and returns the new file descriptor. The new file descriptor has the following properties in common with the original file descriptor :

refers to the same open file or pipe.

has the same file pointer – that is, both file descriptors share one file pointer.

has the same access mode, whether read, write, or read and write.

The prototype for dup() is :

```
int dup(file_descriptor)

int file_descriptor;
```

where file_descriptor is the file descriptor describing the original I/O channel returned by creat(), open(), pipe(), or dup() system calls. Function dup() is guaranteed to return a file descriptor with the lowest integer value available. It is because of this feature of returning the lowest unused file descriptor available that processes accomplish I/O redirection. The following example shows standard output redirected to a file through the use of the dup() system call.

Example 13

This program demonstrate redirection of standard output to a file.

```c
#include <stdio.h>
#include <fcntl.h>
#include <sys/types.h>
#include <sys/stat.h>

int main()
{
   int fd;

   fd = open("foo.bar",O_WRONLY | O_CREAT, S_IREAD | S_IWRITE );
   if (fd == -1)
      {
      perror("foo.bar");
      exit (1);
      }
   close(1);        /* close standard output  */
   dup(fd); /* fd will be duplicated into standard out's slot */
   close(fd);          /* close the extra slot */
   printf("Hello, world!\n"); /* should go to file foo.bar */
   exit (0);          /* exit() will close the files */
}
```

Example 14

One more example to support above example.

```c
#include <unistd.h>
#include <fcntl.h>

int main()
{
   int fd, fd1;
   char x[] = "Hello";
   fd = open("xyz",O_WRONLY|O_CREAT);
   fd1 = dup(fd);
   write(fd, x, 5);
   write(fd1, x, 5);
   close(fd1);
   write(fd1, x, 5);
   return 0;
}
```

After executing the above program, if we check the content of file "xyz", we may find the word "Hello" two times. This supports, we are able to write into the file through both the descriptors.

dup2()

This system call syntax is :

```
int dup2(int fd, int newfd)
```

Example 15

Program to test, what happens to create a duplicate to 1 and write on that file

```c
#include <unistd.h>
#include <sys/stat.h>
#include <fcntl.h>
#include <stdlib.h>

int main()
{
   int fd, fd1;
   if(fd = open("OUT.dat",O_WRONLY|O_CREAT,S_IRWXU) < 0)
   {
      perror("open");
      return -1;
   }
   if ((fd1 = dup2(fd, 1)) < 0)
   {
      perror("dup2");
      return -1;
   }
   printf("The des is: %d\n",fd1);
   write(fd, "Hello How are you\n",20);
   system("ls -l");
   return 0;
}
```

Example 16

This program prints out the stat()'s of an inode.

```c
#include <stdio.h>
#include <sys/types.h>
#include <sys/stat.h>
#include <unistd.h>
#include <pwd.h>
```

```c
#include <grp.h>
#include <time.h>
#include <errno.h>

#define VERSION "1.0.0"

void print_usage(char *program_name)
{
  fprintf(stdout, "useage: ");
  fprintf(stdout,"%s[options]<file>[files...]\n",
                            program_name);
  fprintf(stdout, " options:\n");
  fprintf(stdout, "    -h —help\t\tthis message\n");
  fprintf(stdout, "    -v —version\tversion info\n");
  fprintf(stdout, "\n");
  fprintf(stdout, " note: the \"Blocks\" field is in
                            512k blocks\n");
}
  void print_version(void)
{
  fprintf(stdout, "stat\n");
  fprintf(stdout, "version %s\n", VERSION);
}
const char *filetype(struct stat *st)
{
  if(S_ISFIFO(st->st_mode))    { return("Pipe"); }
  else if(S_ISCHR(st->st_mode)){ return("Character Device"); }
  else if(S_ISDIR(st->st_mode)){ return("Directory"); }
  else if(S_ISBLK(st->st_mode)){ return("Blocks Device"); }
  else if(S_ISREG(st->st_mode)) { return("File"); }
  else if(S_ISLNK(st->st_mode)) { return("Link"); }
  else if(S_ISSOCK(st->st_mode)){ return("Socket"); }
#ifdef S_ISDOOR
  else if(S_ISDOOR(st->st_mode)) { return("Door"); }
#endif
  else             { return("Unknown"); }
}

const char *get_user(uid_t id)
{
  struct passwd *pw;
  static char buf[16];

  if((pw=getpwuid(id)) == NULL)
```

```c
{
  sprintf(buf, "%ld", id);
  return(buf);
}
  return(pw->pw_name);
}

const char *get_group(gid_t id)
{
  struct group *gr;
  static char buf[16];

if((gr=getgrgid(id)) == NULL)
{
  sprintf(buf, "%ld", id);
  return(buf);
}
return(gr->gr_name);
}
int format_mode(char *buf, size_t bufsize, const struct stat *st)
{
char *p;

if(buf == NULL || st == NULL)
{
  errno = EFAULT;
  return(-1);
}

p = buf;

// ensure that the buffer is big enough
if(p-buf >= bufsize) { goto OVERFLOW; }

// file type
if(S_ISREG(st->st_mode))        { *p = '-'; }
else if(S_ISDIR(st->st_mode))   { *p = 'd'; }
else if(S_ISLNK(st->st_mode))   { *p = 'l'; }
else if(S_ISCHR(st->st_mode))   { *p = 'c'; }
else if(S_ISBLK(st->st_mode))   { *p = 'b'; }
else if(S_ISFIFO(st->st_mode))  { *p = 'p'; }
else if(S_ISSOCK(st->st_mode))  { *p = 's'; }
else                            { *p = '-'; }

p++;
// check the buffer as we go, if it overflows then terminate
// the string and return
if(p-buf >= bufsize) {goto OVERFLOW;}
```

```c
// owner perms
if(st->st_mode & S_IRUSR)        { *p = 'r'; }
else                             { *p = '-'; }
p++;
if(p-buf >= bufsize) { goto OVERFLOW; }
if(st->st_mode & S_IWUSR)        { *p = 'w'; }
else                             { *p = '-'; }
p++;
if(p-buf >= bufsize) { goto OVERFLOW; }
if(st->st_mode & S_ISUID)        { *p = 's'; }
else if(st->st_mode & S_IXUSR)   { *p = 'x'; }
else                             { *p = '-'; }
p++;
if(p-buf >= bufsize) { goto OVERFLOW; }
// group perms
if(st->st_mode & S_IRGRP)        { *p = 'r'; }
else                             { *p = '-'; }
p++;
if(p-buf >= bufsize) { goto OVERFLOW; }
if(st->st_mode & S_IWGRP)        { *p = 'w'; }
else                             { *p = '-'; }
p++;
if(p-buf >= bufsize) { goto OVERFLOW; }
if(st->st_mode & S_ISGID)        { *p = 's'; }
else if(st->st_mode & S_IXGRP)   { *p = 'x'; }
else                             { *p = '-'; }
p++;
if(p-buf >= bufsize) { goto OVERFLOW; }
// other perms
if(st->st_mode & S_IROTH)        { *p = 'r'; }
else                             { *p = '-'; }
p++;
if(p-buf >= bufsize) { goto OVERFLOW; }
if(st->st_mode & S_IWOTH)        { *p = 'w'; }
else                             { *p = '-'; }
p++;
if(st->st_mode & S_ISVTX)        { *p = 't'; }
else if(st->st_mode & S_IXOTH)   { *p = 'x'; }
else                             { *p = '-'; }
p++;
if(p-buf >= bufsize) { goto OVERFLOW; }

*p = '\0';

return 0;
```

Overflow

```c
// terminate the buffer and return failure
if(p > buf)
{
   *(p-1) = '\0';
}
errno = EINVAL;
return(-1);
}

int do_stat(char *filename)
{
   struct stat st;
   struct tm *lt;
   char buf[64];

   if(stat(filename, &st) != 0)
   {
      perror(filename);
      return(-1);
   }

   printf(" File: \"%s\"\n", filename);
   printf(" Size: %-16ld  Block Size: %ld\n",
                        st.st_size, st.st_blksize);
   printf("Blocks: %-16ld Filetype: %s\n", st.st_blocks,
                                      filetype(&st));
   format_mode(buf, sizeof(buf), &st);
   printf(" Mode: (%04lo/%-10s) ", st.st_mode
                              & (~S_IFMT), buf);
   printf("UID: (%8lu/%s)  ", st.st_uid, get_user(st.st_uid));
   printf("GID: (%8lu/%s)\n", st.st_gid, get_group(st.st_gid));
   printf("Device: %-8ld  ", st.st_dev);
   printf("Inode: %-8ld  ", st.st_ino);
   printf("Links: %-8ld  ", st.st_nlink);
   printf("Device type: %-8ld\n", st.st_rdev);
   lt = localtime(&st.st_atime);
   strftime(buf, sizeof(buf), "%c", lt);
   printf("Access: %s (%ld)\n", buf, st.st_atime);
   lt = localtime(&st.st_mtime);
   strftime(buf, sizeof(buf), "%c", lt);
   printf("Modify: %s (%ld)\n", buf, st.st_mtime);
   lt = localtime(&st.st_ctime);
```

```c
strftime(buf, sizeof(buf), "%c", lt);
printf("Change: %s (%ld)\n", buf, st.st_ctime);

return 0;
}

int main(int argc, char **argv)
{
   char **filename;
   int skip_end_of_arg_marker = 1;
   int ret = 0;

   if(strcmp("-h", argv[1]) == 0 || strcmp("--help",
                                   argv[1]) == 0)
{
   print_usage(argv[0]);
   exit(0);
}

if(strcmp("-v", argv[1]) == 0 || strcmp("--version",
                                   argv[1]) == 0)
{
   print_version();
   exit(0);
}

for(filename=&(argv[1]); *filename; filename++)
{
   if(skip_end_of_arg_marker && strcmp("--", *filename) == 0)
   {
     skip_end_of_arg_marker = 0;
     continue;
   }
if(do_stat(*filename) != 0)
{
   // we failed
   ret = 1;
}
else if(ret == 1)
{
   // we partially failed
   ret = 2;
}
}

return(ret);
}
```

Example 17

Program which reads a source file name and destination file name along the command line and then converts into specified format (i.e. either from lower case to upper case or upper to lower case or inverse of each. This program is to explain how command line arguments can be used to define command line interface.

```c
#include <unistd.h>
#include <fcntl.h>
#include <ctype.h>
#include <stdio.h>
#include <string.h>
#include <sys/stat.h>

int main(int n, char **a)
{
   int fd1, fd2, f1=0, f2=0, i, len;
   char x[4096];
   if (n < 3)
   {
     printf("Usage: %s SOURCE DEST [OPTION]\n",a[0]);
     printf("[OPTION]\n-l  to lower case\n-u to upper case \
           \n-lu to interchange\n");
     return -1;
   }
if ((fd1 = open(a[1],O_RDONLY)) < 0)
{
     perror("Open for Read");
     return -1;
}
if ((fd2 = open(a[2],O_WRONLY|O_CREAT,S_IRUSR)) < 0)
{
     perror("Open for Write");
     return -1;
}
for (i = 3; i < n; i++)
{
   if((strcmp("-l",a[i])==0) || (strcmp("-L",a[i])==0))  f1=1;
   if((strcmp("-u",a[i])==0) || (strcmp("-U",a[i])==0))  f2=2;
}
```

```c
    printf("F1+F2: %d\n",f1+f2);
    while((len = read(fd1, x, 4092)) > 0)
    {
      for(i = 0; i < len; i++)
      {
        switch(f1+f2)
        {
          case 1:
            x[i] = tolower(x[i]);
            break;
          case 2:
            x[i] = toupper(x[i]);
            break;
          case 3:
            if(islower(x[i])) x[i] = toupper(x[i]);
            else  x[i] = tolower(x[i]);
            break;
        }
      }
      write(fd2, x, len);
    }
    return 0;
}
```

Example 18

Reads a set file names along the command line and then prints them according to their sizes

```c
#include<unistd.h>
#include<sys/types.h>
#include<sys/stat.h>
#include<stdlib.h>
#include<stdio.h>

int main(int argc, char **argv)
{
  struct stat X;
  int i, j;
```

```c
size_t *size, t;
char *tmp;
if (argc == 1)
{
  printf("Usage: [FILE]...\n\n");
  return -1;
}
size = (size_t*)malloc((argc-1) * sizeof(size_t));
for (i = 1; i < argc; i++)
{
  if (stat(argv[i], &X) < 0)
  {
    printf("%s\n",argv[i]);
    perror("stat");
    exit(-1);
  }
  size[i-1] = X.st_size;
}
for (i = 0; i < argc-2; i++)
  for (j = 0; j < argc-i-2; j++)
    if (size[j] < size[j+1])
    {
      t = size[j];
      size[j] = size[j+1];
      size[j+1] = t;
      tmp = argv[j+1];
      argv[j+1] = argv[j+2];
      argv[j+2] = tmp;
    }
  for (i = 0; i < argc-1; i++)
  printf("%s  %d\n",argv[i+1],size[i]);
  return 0;
}
```

Conclusions

We have explained various system calls related from file handling in Unix system such as read(), write(), open(), creat(). Also, we have explained about function such as stat(), fstat() from handle meta information of the files. Some live examples are given to manipulate file content.

Questions

1. Write a program which takes a file name along the command line and displays what permissions are there for the user (whoever is running this program) from this file.

2. Write a program from emulate touch command of unix.

3. Write a program which takes a set of filenames along the command line and prints them according from their sizes in bytes.

4. Write a program which takes a set of filenames along the command line and displays whether there are any files out of the given files which are hard links (Hint print those files whose I-node numbers are same).

5. Write a program from emulate cp command of unix. Make sure that you will be using read(), write() system calls and do read from input file and write into output file at 512 bytes at a time. Identify time required using time command.

12 Unix System Call API for Directory Operations

The following system calls are available for directory operations in Unix API.

```
int mkdir(char *path, mode_t mode);
int creat(char *path, mode_t mode);
int link(char *path1, char *path2);
int unlink(char *path);
int rmdir(char *path);
int chdir(char *path);
char *getcwd(char *buf, int size);
DIR *opendir(char *path);
struct dirent *readdir(DIR *dirp);
int closedir(DIR *dirp);
```

`mkdir`

This creates a new directory with no initial contents (apart from '.' and '..'). It returns
-1 on failure

`creat`

This creates a new file, using a new inode. It also creates a new entry in the directory.
Since this changes the directory (as a file), the last modified times of the directory
are updated.

`link`

link adds another name to an existing file. It does not make a new inode entry, but does make a new directory entry. The link count in the inode is increased.

`unlink`

This removes an entry from a directory. The link count in the inode is decreased. If the count falls to zero, the file can be removed once no process has it open. Removing a file from a directory changes the last modified time of the directory (it is a file with changed contents).

`rmdir`

Removing a directory will fail unless the directory is empty.

`chdir`

This will attempt to change directory. The types of patterns that will be accepted for directory names is not specified.

`getcwd`

This will fill in the buffer with the current directory. This call can actually fail if another process has succeeded in removing the current directory of a process.

Reading dirs

The call opendir() opens a directory for reading. The returned DIR value is opaque and is just passed to other functions. It is NULL on error.

Under Linux, the DIR structure is as follows. Please note this is implementation dependent.

```
typedef struct DIR
{
  /* file descriptor */
  int dd_fd;

  /* offset of the next dir entry in buffer */
  off_t dd_loc;

  /* bytes of valid entries in buffer */
  size_t dd_size;

  /* -> directory buffer */
  struct dirent *dd_buf;
} DIR;
```

The call `readdir()` returns a structure that you can use. It is specified to have one entry `char *d_name`. Under Linux it is defined as

```
struct dirent {
long            d_ino;
_kernel_off_t   d_off;
unsigned short  d_reclen;
char            d_name[256];
};
```

Example 1

This creates a directory, puts a file into it and then removes it.

```
#include <stdio.h>
#include <unistd.h>
#include <sys/stat.h>

int main(void)
{   int fd;

  if (mkdir("mydir", 0777) == -1)
    exit(1);
  if ((fd = creat("mydir/f1", 0777)) == -1)
    exit(2);

  close(fd);
  sleep(200); /* check from the other terminal for
              /the file created */
  unlink("mydir/f1");
  exit(0);
}
```

Example 2

This program is used to create a directory. Like mkdir –p <dir> in the shell

```
#include <string.h>
#include <stdio.h>
#include <unistd.h>
#include <stdlib.h>
#include <sys/stat.h>
#include <errno.h>
```

```c
int makedir(const char *path)
{
  char separator = '/';
  struct stat statBuf;
  char *copy;
  char *p;
  int done;

  if(path == NULL || *path == '\0')
  {
    return(-1);
  }
  // first check if it already exists, if so we are done
  if(stat(path, &statBuf) == 0)
  {
    if(S_ISDIR(statBuf.st_mode))
    {
  return 0;
    }
  }

copy = strdup(path);

p = copy;
done = 0;

while(!done)
{
  p = strchr(p, separator);
  if(p == NULL)
  {
    done = 1;
  }
  else
  {
  // temorarily place a null
  *p = '\0';
}
```

```c
// check for existing
if(stat(copy, &statBuf) == 0)
{
   if(!S_ISDIR(statBuf.st_mode))
   {
      goto makedir_ERR;
   }
}
else
{
   if(mkdir(copy, 0777) != 0)
   {
fprintf(stderr, "Error making direcotry \"%s\": %s\n",
        copy, strerror(errno));
 goto makedir_ERR;
}
}
}
if(!done)
{
// replace the separator and advance past it
*p++ = separator;
while(*p == separator) { p++; }
}
}

if(copy) { free(copy); }
return 0;

makedir_ERR:
if(copy) { free(copy); }
return(-1);
}

int main(int argc, char **argv)
{
   int i;
   int ret;
   int retval = 0;

   for(i=1; i<argc; i++)
   {
      ret = makedir(argv[i]);
      if(retval == 0)
      {
         retval = ret;
      }
   }
   return(retval);
}
```

Example 3

A program to scan the current directory, printing its contents is

```cpp
#include <iostream.h>
#include <dirent.h>

int main(int argc, char *argv[])
{
  DIR *dirp;
  struct dirent *dp;

  if ((dirp = opendir(".")) == NULL)
  {
    cerr << "Can't open .\n";
    exit(1);
  }

  for (dp = readdir(dirp); dp != NULL;  dp = readdir(dirp))
  printf("%s\n", dp->d_name );

 closedir(dirp);
  exit(0);
}
```

Example 4

A simple program that prints a directory structure.

```cpp
#include <stdio.h>
#include <sys/stat.h>
#include <stdlib.h>
#include <string.h>
#include <limits.h>
#include <unistd.h>
#include <sys/time.h>
#include <dirent.h>

#define MAX_DEPTH 128

typedef struct stat xpstat;

int recursfs(char *dirname, int level)
{
  DIR *d;
  struct dirent *e;
```

```c
    xpstat st;
    char *newpath = NULL;
    int dirlen;

if(level > MAX_DEPTH)
{
    fprintf(stderr, "too many directory levels (%d)\n",
                    MAX_DEPTH);
    return(-1);
}

dirlen = strlen(dirname);

// open the directory
if((d=opendir(dirname)) == NULL)
{
    perror(dirname);
    return -1;
}

// print the origin of the tree
if(level == 0)
{
    if(dirlen > 0 && dirname[dirlen-1] == '/')
    {
        puts(dirname);
    }
    else
    {
        printf("%s/\n", dirname);
    }
    level = 1;
}

while((e=readdir(d)))
{
    int len;

    // skip this and up
    if(strcmp(".", e->d_name) == 0 //
        strcmp("..", e->d_name) == 0)
    {
        continue;
    }
```

```
    // calc length
    len = strlen(e->d_name);

    // the directory part + 1 for the seperator('/') +
    // the file name part + 1 for the terminating null('\0')
    if((newpath = realloc(newpath, dirlen+1+len+1)) == NULL)
    {
      fprintf(stderr, "out of memory");
      exit(1);
    }

    // create new string
    sprintf(newpath, "%s/%s", dirname, e->d_name);

    fprintf(stderr, "path: %s\n", newpath);

    // stat like normal but if we can't find it then it
    // is a dangling link so we have to lstat() it
    if(stat(newpath, &st) != 0)
    {
      if(lstat(newpath, &st) != 0)
      {
        perror(newpath);
        continue;
      }
    }

if(S_ISDIR(st.st_mode))
{
  int i;

 for(i=0; i<level; i++) { printf("  "); }
fprintf(stdout, "%s/\n", newpath+dirlen+1);
 if(recursfs(newpath, level+1) != 0)
  {
    continue;
  }
}
else
{
  int i;
```

```c
    for(i=0; i<level; i++) { printf("  "); }
     fprintf(stdout, "%s\n", e->d_name);
       }
    }
  }
  closedir(d);

  if(newpath) { free(newpath); }

     return 0;
  }

  int main(int argc, char **argv)
  {
     char *root_dir;
     int exitcode = 0;

  if(argc>1)
  {
     int i;

  for(i=1; i<argc; i++)
  {
     if(recursfs(argv[i], 0) != 0)
       {
          exitcode = 1;
       }
  }
  }
  else
     {
        root_dir = ".";
     }

  return(exitcode);
  }
```

link()

The UNIX system file structure allows more than one named reference to a given file, a feature called "aliasing". Making an alias to a file means that the file has more than one name, but all names of the file refer to the same data. Since all names refer to the same data, changing the contents of one file changes the contents of all aliases to that file. Aliasing a file in the UNIX system amounts to the system creating a new directory entry that contains the alias file name and then copying the i-number of a existing file to the i-number position of this new directory entry. This action is accomplished by the link() system call. The link() system call links an existing file to a new file.

The prototype for `link()` is :

```
int link(original_name, alias_name)
char *original_name, *alias_name;
```

where both original_name and alias_name are character strings that name the existing and new files respectively, `link()` will fail and no link will be created if any of the following conditions holds :

a path name component is not a directory.
a path name component does not exist.
a path name component is off-limits.
original_name does not exist.
alias_name does exist.
original_name is a directory and you are not the superuser.
a link is attempted across file systems.
the destination directory for alias_name is not writable.
the destination directory is on a mounted read-only file system.

Example 5

```
#include <stdio.h>
int main()
{
   if ((link("foo.old", "foo.new")) == -1)
     {
     perror(" ");
     exit (1); /* return a non-zero exit code on error */
     }
   exit(0);
}
```

`unlink()`

The opposite of the link() system call is the unlink() system call. unlink() removes a file by zeroing the i-number part of the file's directory entry, reducing the link count field in the file's inode by 1, and releasing the data blocks and the inode if the link count field becomes zero. unlink() is the only system call for removing a file in the UNIX system.

The prototype for unlink() is :

```
int unlink(file_name)
char*file_name;
```

where `file_name` names the file to be unlinked. unlink() fails if any of the following conditions holds :

> a path name component is not a directory.
> a path name component does not exist.
> a path name component is off-limits.
> file_name does not exist.
> file_name is a directory and you are not the superuser.
> the directory for the file named by file_name is not writable.
> the directory is contained in a file system mounted read-only.

It is important to understand that a file's contents and its inode are not discarded until all processes close the unlinked file.

Example 6

```c
#include <stdio.h>

int main()
{
   if ((unlink("foo.bar")) == -1)
     {
     perror(" ");
     exit (1); /* return a non-zero exit code on error */
     }
   exit (0);
}
```

Example 7

This program emulates 'du' command of Unix and prints file names and their sizes in blocks.

```c
#include <stdio.h>
#include <stdlib.h>
#include <unistd.h>
#include <dirent.h>
#include <sys/types.h>
#include <sys/stat.h>

void du(const char *path)
{
    struct dirent *dir;
   DIR *D;
   struct stat X;
   char *name = 0;
```

```c
    D = opendir(path);
    while((dir = readdir(D)))
    {
      char *tmp = dir->d_name;
      if((strcmp(tmp,".")==0) || strcmp(tmp,"..")==0)
          continue;
      name = (char*)malloc(strlen(path)+dir->d_reclen+2);
      sprintf(name,"%s/%s",path,tmp);
      stat(name, &X);
      if(S_ISDIR(X.st_mode))
          {
          du(name);
                printf("%ld\t%s\n",X.st_blocks,name);
          }
          free(name);
       }
        closedir(D);
    }

int main(int argc, char **argv)
{
   if (argc == 1)
          du(".");
   else du(argv[1]);
   return 0;
}
```

Example 8

Program which takes disk partition name along the command line and then print how many blocks are occupied, free, and block size and percentage of freeness etc.,.

```c
    #include<stdio.h>
    #include<sys/vfs.h>

    int main(int argc, char **argv)
    {
        struct statfs fs;
        if (argc == 1) argv[1] = "/dev/hda";
        if (statfs(argv[1], &fs) < 0)
        {
          perror("Statfs");
          return -1;
        }
```

```
    printf("Total blocks occupied :%d\n",fs.f_blocks -
    fs.f_bfree);
    printf("Number free blocks :%d\n",fs.f_bfree);
    printf("Block size :%d\n",fs.f_bsize);
    printf("Percentage of freeness :%d %\n",100*fs.f_bfree/
    fs.f_blocks);
    return 0;
}
```

Example 9

Displays name of those files whose sizes are more than an environment variable 'L'
size if it is defined. Otherwise display the files whose sizes are more than 10k in
given directory

```
#include <stdio.h>
#include <sys/types.h>
#include <dirent.h>
#include <sys/stat.h>
#include <unistd.h>

int main(int argc, char **argv)
{
  struct stat X;
  DIR *D;
  struct dirent *dir;
  char *t=NULL;
  size_t size;
  if (argc == 1)
  {
    printf("Usage: %s [DIR]\n",argv[0]);
    return -1;
  }
  if ((D = opendir(argv[1])) == NULL)
  {
    perror("Opendir");
    return -1;
  }
  if (t = (char*)getenv("L"))
        size = atoi(t);
  else size = 10000;
  t = NULL;
  while((dir = readdir(D)))
```

```
    {
      t = (char*)realloc(t, dir->d_reclen+strlen(argv[1])+2);
      sprintf(t,"%s/%s",argv[1],dir->d_name);
      if(stat(t, &X) < 0)
      {
        printf("%s  ",dir->d_name); fflush(stdout);
        perror("Stat");
        continue;
      }
      if (X.st_size > size)
      printf("%s ",dir->d_name);
    }
    closedir(D);
    return 0;
    }
```

Example 10

This program takes a directory name along the command line and then displays names of the files which are having more than 1 link, i.e for which hard link files in the same directory.

```
#include <stdio.h>
#include <unistd.h>
#include <dirent.h>
#include <string.h>
#include <stdlib.h>
#include <sys/types.h>
#include <sys/stat.h>

int main(int argc, char **argv)
{
    struct stat X;
  struct dirent *dir;
  DIR *D;
    int no_of_files = 0, i, j;
    long *size, *Ino,1;
  char *name = NULL, **file;
  if (argc == 1)
  {
    printf("Usage: %s [DIR]\n", argv[0]);
    return -1;
  }
  if ((D = opendir(argv[1])) == NULL)
```

```c
{
        perror("Opendir");
        return -1;
}
while((dir = readdir(D)))
{
        name = (char*)realloc(name, strlen(argv[1])+dir-
        >d_reclen+2);
        sprintf(name,"%s/%s",argv[1],dir->d_name);
        stat(name, &X);
        if(S_ISREG(X.st_mode))
        no_of_files++;
}
    size = (long*)malloc(no_of_files*sizeof(long));
    Ino  = (long*)malloc(no_of_files*sizeof(long));
    file = (char **)malloc(no_of_files*sizeof(char*));

    rewinddir(D);
    i = 0; name = NULL;
    while((dir = readdir(D)))
    {
      name  =  (char*)realloc(name,  strlen(argv[1])+dir-
         >d_reclen+2);
      sprintf(name,"%s/%s",argv[1],dir->d_name);
      stat(name, &X);
      if(S_ISREG(X.st_mode))
      {
        size[i] = X.st_size;
        Ino[i] =  dir->d_ino;
        file[i] = dir->d_name;
        i++;
      }
    }
    for (i = 0; i < no_of_files-1; i++)
    for (j = 0; j < no_of_files-i-1; j++)
    if (Ino[j] > Ino[j+1])
    {
      long t;
      t = Ino[j]; Ino[j] = Ino[j+1]; Ino[j+1] = t;
      t = size[j]; size[j] = size[j+1]; size[j+1] = t;
      name = file[j]; file[j] = file[j+1]; file[j+1] = name;
    }
```

```
        l = 0;
        for (i = 0; i < no_of_files; i++)
        {
          if(Ino[i] != l)
          {   l = Ino[i];  printf("%ld  ",l);  }
          printf("%s  ",file[i]);
          if(Ino[i] != Ino[i+1])
          printf("%ld\n",size[i]);
        }
      return 0;
}
```

Example 11

Program which takes a filename along the command line and also the directory name and then print whether the file is existing in any of   the sub directories of the given directory or not.

```
#include <stdio.h>
#include <string.h>
#include <dirent.h>
#include <stdlib.h>
#include <sys/stat.h>
#include <sys/types.h>

int find(const char *path, const char *file)
{
  DIR *D;
  struct dirent *dir;
  char *name = 0;
  struct stat X;
  static short flag = 0;
  if ((D = opendir(path)) == NULL)
  {
    perror("Opendir");
    exit(-1);
  }
  while((dir = readdir(D)))
  {
    char *str = dir->d_name;
    if ((strcmp(str,".")==0) || (strcmp(str,"..")==0))
    continue;
    name = (char*)realloc(name, strlen(path)+dir->d_reclen+2);
    sprintf(name,"%s/%s",path,str);
```

```c
      stat(name, &X);
      if (strcmp(str,file) == 0)
      {
        printf("%s\n", name);
        flag++;
      }
      if(S_ISDIR(X.st_mode))
        find(name,file);
    }
    closedir(D);
    free(name);
    return flag;
}

int main(int argc, char **argv)
{
    int chk;
    if(argc != 3)
    {
      printf("Usage: %s [DIR] [FILE]\n\n",argv[0]);
      return -1;
    }
    chk = find(argv[1], argv[2]);
    (chk > 0) ? printf("%d File(s) Exist\n",chk) :
        printf("File doesn't exist\n");
    return 0;
}
```

Example 12

Program to display names of different links to same inode

```c
      #include <stdio.h>
      #include <dirent.h>
      #include <sys/types.h>
      #include <sys/stat.h>
      #include <string.h>
      #include <stdlib.h>

      unsigned long *inode;
      char **filename;

      void list(char *a)
      {
        struct dirent *file;
        DIR *D;
```

```c
int count = 0, i, j;
if((D = opendir(a)) == 0)
{
   perror("Opendir");
   return ;
}
while((file = readdir(D)))
   count++;
inode = (unsigned long*)malloc(count*sizeof(unsigned long));
filename = (char**)malloc(count*sizeof(char*));
printf("The number of regular files are: %d\n",count);
count = 0;
printf("Loop...");
rewinddir(D);
while((file = readdir(D)))
{
   struct stat st;
   stat(file->d_name, &st);
   if(S_ISREG(st.st_mode))
   {
      inode[count] = st.st_ino;
      filename[count] = file->d_name;
      count++;
   }
}
for (i = 0; i < count - 1; i++)
   for (j = 0; j < count-i-1; j++)
 if(inode[j] < inode[j+1])
  {
      char *t; unsigned long n;
      n = inode[j]; inode[j] = inode[j+1]; inode[j+1] = n;
      t = filename[j]; filename[j] = filename[j+1];
      filename[j+1] = t;
  }
for(j = 0; j < count; j++)
{
   if(j == 0 || inode[j-1] != inode[j])
   printf("\n%ld", inode[j]);
   printf("%s", filename[j]);
}
printf("\n");
}
```

```c
int main(int n, char **a)
{
   if(n==1)
   {
      printf("Usage: %s DIR\n",a[0]);
      return -1;
   }
   list(a[1]);
   return 0;
}
```

Example 13

Program reads a program name along the command line and prints from which directory
it get executed.

```c
#include <stdio.h>
#include <dirent.h>
#include <unistd.h>
#include <string.h>

int find_dir(const char *file, const char *path)
{
   DIR *D;
   struct dirent *dir;
   if ((D = opendir(path)) == NULL)
   {
      perror("Opendir");
      return 0;
   }
   while((dir = readdir(D)))
   {
      if (strcmp(dir->d_name,file) == 0)
      return 1;
   }
   return 0;
}

int main(int argc, char **argv)
{
   char *p, *q;
   int k;
   if(argc == 1)
   {
      printf("Usage: %s  [FILE]\n",argv[0]);
      return -1;
   }
```

```
    p = getenv("PATH");
    while(1)
    {
      q = index(p, ':');
      p = strtok(p, ":");
      if ((k = find_dir(argv[1], p))) break;
      if (q == 0) break;
      p = q+1;
    }
    (k) ? printf("\n%s\n",p) : printf("File not found\n");
    return 0;
}
```

Example 14

The program takes a directory name along the command line and prints whether it is consistent or not interms of no of links

```
#include <stdio.h>
#include <unistd.h>
#include <sys/types.h>
#include <sys/stat.h>
#include <dirent.h>
#include <stdlib.h>
#include <string.h>

typedef struct node
{
   long Ino;
   short nlink;
   short lnk_count;
   struct node *next;
}node;

void print(node *head)
{
   while(head)
   {
      printf("%ld   ",head->Ino);
      head = head->next;
   }
}
```

```c
node *Head = NULL;

void inode_list(const char *path)
{
  struct stat X;
  DIR *D;
  struct dirent *dir;
  char *name=0,*str;
  node *nod,*tnod;
  if((D = opendir(path)) == NULL)
  {
    perror("Opendir");
    return ;
  }
  while((dir = readdir(D)))
  {
    str = dir->d_name;
    if((strcmp(str,".")==0) || (strcmp(str,"..")==0))
        continue;
    name = (char*)realloc(name,strlen(path)+dir->d_reclen+2);
    sprintf(name,"%s/%s",path,str);
    stat(name, &X);

    if (!Head)
    {
      nod = (node*)malloc(sizeof(node));
      nod->next = NULL;
      nod->lnk_count = 1;
      nod->nlink = X.st_nlink;
      nod->Ino = X.st_ino;
      Head = nod;
    }
    else
    {
      node *tmp;
      tnod = Head;
      while (tnod && (tnod->Ino != X.st_ino))
      {
          tmp = tnod;
          tnod = tnod->next;
      }
```

```c
          if (tnod && (tnod->Ino == X.st_ino))
              tnod->lnk_count++;
          else
          {
            nod = (node*)malloc(sizeof(node));
            nod->lnk_count = 1;
            nod->Ino = X.st_ino;
            nod->nlink = X.st_nlink;
            nod->next = 0;
            tmp->next = nod;
          }
        }
        if(S_ISDIR(X.st_mode))  inode_list(name);
      }
    return ;
}

void destroy(node *head)
{
    node *t;
    while(head)
    {
      t = head;
      head = head->next;
      free(t);
    }
}

int main(int argc, char **argv)
{
    node *tnode;
    if (argc == 1)
    argv[1] = ".";
    inode_list(argv[1]);
    tnode = Head;
    while(tnode)
    {
      if (tnode->lnk_count != tnode->nlink)
      break;
      tnode = tnode->next;
    }
```

```
    if(tnode)
    {
       printf("\nInconsistent\n");
       printf("Ino :%ld\nnlink :%d\ncount :%d\n",
          tnode->Ino,tnode->lnk_count,tnode->nlink);
    }
    else
       printf("\nConsistent\n");
    destroy(Head);
    return 0;
}
```

Please note that this program checks for a given directory only or current working directory only. While experimenting, create afresh a directory, and files, only hard links to them in that directory and then run the above program on freshly created directory. You should get file system as consistent. Then create a hard link for a file of this directory such that this hard link file is another directory and then run the above program by giving this directory name. You should now get file system as inconsistent as you are traversing in the given directory only whreas the one of the hard link file is in the another directory!! This is after all to simulate!!

Similarly, you can simulate on entire partition also.

Conclusions

In this chapter we have described how files in a directory can be traversed element by element using readdir() and opendir() system calls. How to traverse directory recursively is explained with live examples. Also, a live example is given to demonstrate how file system is checked for inconsistency.

Questions

1. Write a program which takes a filename along the command name and checks whether any of its hard link files are there in the current working directory or not. If exists print their name.

2. Write a program which takes a number, say p (0-100) and prints names of the n largest files whose total size is atleast p% of the total file sizes of current working directory.

3. Write a program which prints the files of current working directory in accordance with their creation times.

4. Write a program from emulate du command of unix.

5. Write a program which takes two directory names along the command line and then displays for each file of the first directory its hard links (if exists) in second directory.

13 Standard Library Functions

The `<stdio.h>` library handles the standard input and output functions for C programmers. It is by far the largest library. Functions of this library uses file related Unix system calls.

Now before we talk about files we need to agree on the words that we are going to use. A file or device is considered to be a stream of data. This stream of data that is associated with a file or hardware device and is accessed by your program by opening the file or device. Once the stream is opened then you can read and/or write into it.

Three streams are opened automatically when you execute a program. Standard input (`stdin`), standard output (`stdout`), and standard error (`stderr`). These can all be redirected by your shell when you run the program but normally `stdin` is your keyboard and `stdout` and `stderr` both go to your monitor. This discussion is already made in previous chapters.

After we are done with our streams we need to tell the operating system to clean up buffers and finish saving data to the devices. We do this by closing the stream. If we don't close our stream then it is possible to lose data. `stdin, stdout` and `stderr` are all closed automatically the same way they are opened automatically.

One of the most important things to remember when dealing with devices and files is that you are dealing with the real world. Don't assume that the function is going to work. Even something like printf can fail. Disks fill up or occasionally fail, users input the wrong data, processors get too busy, other programs have your files locked. Every function that deals with the real world returns an error condition if the function failed. Always check every return value and take the appropriate action when there is an error condition. Exceptions are not errors unless they are handled badly. Exceptions are opportunities for extra computation .

The first example is to basically show how to open a file for reading. It just dumps contents of a file called "test" in the current directory to the standard out. All exceptions are reported to standard error and then program is halted with an error. It should produce an error if a file called "test" doesn't exist.

Example 1

```
#include <stdio.h>  /*  this is a compiler directive that
                        tells the  the compiler that
                        you are going to be using  functions
                        that are in the standard
                        input/output library
                     */
main ()
{
FILE *stream; /* need a pointer to FILE for the stream */
int buffer_character; /*needan int toholda single character */

/*openthe file calledtest for reading inthe current directory*/
  stream = fopen ("test", "r");

/*ifthe file wasn't opened correctly than the stream will be
  equal to NULL. It is now customary to represent NULL by
  casting the value of 0 to the correct type yourself
  rather than having the compiler guess at the type
  of NULL to use. */

if (stream == (FILE *)0) {

fprintf(stderr, "Error opening file (printed to
               standard error)\n");
exit (1);
}    /* end if */

/* read and write the file one character at a time until you
   reach end-of-file on either our file or output. If the EOF
   is on file_descriptor then drop out of the while loop. if
   the end-of-file is on report write errors to standard out
   and exit the program with an error condition
*/
```

```c
    while ((buffer_character=getc(stream))!=EOF) {

    /* write the character to standard out and check for errors */
        if((putc(buffer_character, stdout)) == EOF) {

        fprintf(stderr,"Error writing to standard out.
                            (printed to standard error)\n");
    fclose(stream);
    exit(1);
    }     /* end if */
    }     /* end while */

    /* close the file after you are done with it, if file doesn't
        close then report and exit */

    if ((fclose(stream)) == EOF) {

    fprintf(stderr,"Error closing stream. (printed to
                                    standard error)\n");
    exit(1);
    }     /* end if */
    /* report success back to environment */
    return 0;
    }     /* end main*/
```

The above simple program is an example of opening a file, reading the file, and then closing the file while also using `stdout`, and `stderr`.

What follows is a quick summary of the file operations in the <stdio.h> library. These are the operations that work directly with streams.

Opening Streams

Before a stream can be used we must associate the stream with some device or file. This is called opening the stream. Our program is asking for permission from the operating system to read or write to a device. If we have the correct permissions, the file exists or we can create the file and no-one else has the file locked then the operating system allows us to open the file and gives us back an object that is the stream. Using this object we can read and write to the stream and when we are done you can close the stream.

Looking at the first line below we see that the fopen function takes two pointers to strings, one is a path to a file and the other is the open mode of the program. The function will return a pointer to FILE type which is a complex object that is defined in the <stdio.h> library. So in order to accept the return type we must have declared a variable of type pointer to FILE, like the stream variable in the example above. In the example you can see where we call the function fopen with the static filename of "test" and a mode of "r" and then accept the return value into the stream object.

A stream can be opened by any of these three functions:

```
FILE    *fopen   (char  *path,    char    *mode)
FILE    *fdopen  (int   fildes,   char    *mode)
FILE    *freopen (char *path, char *mode, FILE *stream)
```

char *path is a pointer to a string with the filename in it.

char *mode is the mode of opening the file (table follows.) int fildes is a file descriptor (explained in previous chapters) which has already been opened and whose mode matches.

fopen is used to open the given filename with the respective mode. This is the function that is used the most to open files.

fdopen is used to assign a stream to a currently opened file descriptor. The file descriptor mode and the fdopen mode must match.

freopen is normally used redirect `stdin`, `stdout` and `stderr` to file. The stream that is given will be closed and a new stream opened to the given path with the given mode.

The following are the modes of file opening.

```
"r"  Open an existing file for reading.
"r+" Open an existing file for both reading and writing
"w"  Open a file for writing. If the file already exists its
     content will be wiped out. Otherwise afresh file is
     created for writing.
"w+" Open a file for writing and reading. If the file already
     exists its content will be wiped out. Otherwise afresh
     file is created for writing.
"a"  Open a file for appending. If the file already exists
     its content will be wiped out. Otherwise afresh
     file is created for writing.
"a+" Open a file for appending and reading. If the file
     already exists its content will be wiped out. Otherwise
     afresh file is created for writing.
```

Stream Flushing

Sometimes we want your program to ensure that what we have written to a file has actually gone to the disk and is not waiting in the buffer. Or we might want to throw out a lot of user input and get fresh input, for a game. The following two functions are useful for emptying the streams buffers, though one just throws the data away while the other stores it safely on to the stream.

```
int fflush(FILE *stream)

int fpurge(FILE *stream)
```

FILE *stream is an already existing stream.

These functions return a 0 on success. On a failure they return an EOF.

fflush is used to write out the buffers of the stream to a device or file.

fpurge is used to clear the buffers of unwritten or unread data that is in a buffer waiting. We think of this as a destructive purge because it clears the read and write buffers by dumping the contents.

Closing Streams

When we are done with a stream we must clean up after our program. When we close a stream the command ensures that the buffers are successfully written and that the stream is truly closed. If we just exit a program without closing our files then more than likely the last few bytes that we wrote will be there. But we won't know unless we check. Also there is a limit to how many streams a single process can have open at one time. So if we keep on opening streams without closing the old streams we will use up system resources. Only one command is used to close any stream.

```
int fclose(FILE *stream)
```

FILE *stream is an already existing stream.

Returns a 0 on success, or an EOF otherwise.

fclose flushes the given streams buffers and then disassociates the stream from the pointer to FILE.

Renaming and Removing Files

These two commands work just like `rm` and `mv`, but without the options. They are not recursive.

```
int remove(char *path)
int rename(char *oldpath, const char *newpath)
```

char *path, oldpath and newpath are all pointers to existing files.

Returns a 0 on success and a non-zero otherwise.

remove works just like `rm` to remove the file in the string pointed to by path.

rename works just like move to rename a file from oldpath to newpath, changing directories if need be.

Temporary Files

You can create your own temp files by using the following functions:

FILE *tmpfile(void)

This command returns a pointer to a FILE of stream which is a temp file that magically goes away when your program is done running. You never even know the files name. If the function fails it returns a NULL pointer of type (FILE *)0.

char *tmpnam(char *string)

This function returns a filename in the tmp directory that is unique, or a NULL if there is an error. Each additional call overrides the previous name so you must move the name somewhere else if you need to know the name after you open the file.

Stream Buffering

Normally a stream is block buffered, unless it is connected to a terminal like stdin or stdout. In block buffered mode the stream reads ahead a set amount and then gives you what the input that we ask for. Sometimes we want this to be bigger or smaller to improve performance in some program. The following four functions can be used to set the buffering type and the size of the buffers. The defaults are normally pretty good so we shouldn't have to worry too much about these.

```
int setbuf( FILE *stream, char *buf);
int setbuffer( FILE *stream, char *buf, size_t size);
int setlinebuf( FILE *stream);
int setvbuf(FILE *stream, char *buf, int mode , size_t size);
```

Where mode is one of the following :

_IONBF unbuffered, output sent as soon as received.

_IOLBF line buffered, output sent as soon as a newline is received.

_IOFBF fully buffered, output isn't sent until size characters are received.

setbuf is an alias for setvbuf(stream, buf, buf ? _IOFBF : _IONBF, BUFSIZ);
setbuffer is an alias for setvbuf(stream, buf, buf ? _IOFBF : _IONBF, size);
setlinebuf is an alias for setvbuf(stream, (char *)NULL, _IOLBF, 0);
setvbuf sets a buffer for the given stream of size_t size and of buffer mode.

Stream Positioning

Once you open a stream we are located at a certain postition depending on what mode we opened the stream in, as we read or write your position increases with each character. We can see where we are at in the stream and jump to any position in the stream. If we are writing a database program we don't want to have to read and ignore a million characters to get to the record that we want, we want to be able to jump right to the record and start reading.

Note that terminals cannot have their stream repositioned, only block devices (like hard drives) will allow this.

Also note that if we open a file for writing and use fseek to go out 10,000 bytes, write one character and then close the file that we will not have a file of 10,001 bytes. The file will be much smaller. This is called a sparse file. If we move a sparse file using the mv command it will not change size because a mv is only a change to the directory structure, not the file. If we cp or tar a sparse file then it will expand out to its true size.

```
int fseek( FILE *stream, long offset, int whence);
long ftell( FILE *stream);
void rewind( FILE *stream);
int fgetpos( FILE *stream, fpos_t *pos);
int fsetpos( FILE *stream, fpos_t *pos);
```

FILE *stream is a pointer to an already existing stream.

long offset is added to the position indicated by the whence.

int whence is SEEK_SET (0), SEEK_CUR(2), or SEEK_END(1) depending on where you want the offset to be applied to: the beginning, the current position or the end. fpos_t *pos is a complex file position indicator. On some systems you must use this to get and set stream positions.

If these functions are successful fgetpos, fseek, fsetpos return 0, and ftell returns the current offset. Otherwise, EOF is returned. There is no return value from rewind.

fseek sets the file position in the stream to the value of offset plus the position indicated by the whence, either the beginning, the current or the end of file to get the new position in the stream. This is useful for reading along, adding something to the end of the stream and then going back to reading the stream where you left off.

ftell returns the current position of the stream.

rewind sets the current position to the beginning of the stream. Notice that no error code is returned. This function is assumed to always succeed.

fgetpos is used like ftell to return the position of the stream. The position is returned in the pos variable which is of type fpos_t.

fsetpos is used like fseek in that it will set the current postion of the stream to the value in pos. On some systems you have to use **fgetpos** and **fsetpos** in order to reliably position your stream.

Error Codes

When any of the above functions return an error you can see what the error was and even get a text error message to display for the user. There are a group of functions that deal with error values.

If anyone is interested the functions are : **clearerr**, **feof**, **ferror**, and **fileno**.

```
int fgetc(FILE *ip);
int fputc(char V, FILE *ip);
char *fgets(char *s, int n, FILE *ip);
fputs(char *s, FILE *ip);
```

Example 2

This program takes a file name along the command line and prints its size.

```
#include <stdio.h>

void main(int argc, char*argv[])
{
FILE *ip;

if(argc!=2) {printf("One argument is needed\n"); exit(-1); }

ip=fopen(argv[1], "r");

if(ip==0) { printf("Error in opening file"); exit(-1); }

fseek(ip,0,SEEK_END);

printf("File Size=%ld\n", ftell(ip));
}
```

Example 3

The same program can be realised using system calls as follows.

```
/* lseek.c */
#include <stdio.h>
#include <fcntl.h>
int main()
{
int fd;
long position;
fd = open("datafile.dat", O_RDONLY);
if ( fd != -1)
{
position = lseek(fd, 0L, 2); /* seek 0 bytes from end-of-file */
if (position != -1) printf("The length of datafile.dat is %ld
                           bytes.\n", position);
```

```
else
perror("lseek error");
}
else
printf("can't open datafile.dat\n");
close(fd);
}
```

Example 4

This program takes source file name as the first command line argument and duplicate file name as the second command line argument and then copies the content of the source file to destination file.

```
#include <stdio.h>

void main(int argc, char*argv[])
{
FILE *ip, *op;

if(argc!=3) {printf("Two arguments are needed\n");exit(-1); }
ip=fopen(argv[1], "r");

if(ip==0) { printf("Error in opening file"); exit(-1); }

op=fopen(argv[2],"w");

while(!feof(ip))
fputc(fgetc(ip),op);

fclose(ip);
fclose(op);
}
```

Example 5

Write a program which opens a file "xyz" in current working directory and writes "Hello" in it. If environment variable "TMP" is defined then the file "xyz" has to be created in the directory pointed by the value of this variable.

```
#include <stdio.h>

void main(int argc, char*argv[])
{
FILE *ip;
char s[40], *p;
```

```
if((p=getenv("TMP"))!=NULL)
   sprintf(s,"%s/%s", p, "xyz");
else
   sprintf(s,"xyz");

ip=fopen(s, "w");

if(ip==0) { printf("Error in opening file"); exit(-1); }

fprintf(ip,"Hello\n");

fclose(ip);
}
```

If the above program is compiled and the resultant executable file name is "xx" then the following commands at the shell prompt can be used to test the program.

```
xx
cat xyz
TMP=/tmp
export TMP
xx
cat/tmp/xyz
```

Example 6

Write a program to emulate UNIX's cat command; however with different interface. If an environment variable UP is defined and its value is YES then the file content has to be converted to uppercase and then written into the destination file. If an environment variable LOW is defined and its value is YES then the file content has to be converted to lowercase and then written into the destination file. If both the environment variables are defined then uppercase characters has to be converted to lowercase and vice-versa. If both the environment variables are not defined or not having value YES then the program has to simply behave similar to normal UNIX cat command and copy the source file content as it is to destination.

```
#include <stdio.h>
#include <string.h>
#include <stdlib.h>
void main(int argc, char*argv[])
{
FILE *ip, *op;

int up=0,low=0;
char  V;
```

```c
if(argc!=3){printf("Two arguments are needed\n"); exit(-1); }
ip=fopen(argv[1], "r");

if(ip==0) { printf("Error in opening file"); exit(-1); }

op=fopen(argv[2],"w");

if(strcmp(getenv("UP"),"YES")==0) up=1;

if(strcmp(getenv("LOW"),"YES")==0)low=2;

while(!feof(ip))
{
V=fgetc(ip);
switch(up+low)
{
case 0:  fputc(V,op); break;
case 1:  fputc(toupper(V),op); break;
case 2:  fputc(tolower(V),op); break;
case 3:   if(isupper(V))
            fputc(tolower(V),op);
      else
            fputc(toupper(V),op);
      break;
}
}

fclose(ip);
fclose(op);

}
```

If the above program is compiled and the resultant executable file name is "yy" then the following commands at the shell prompt can be used to test program.

```
yy rao raj      #copies the content of file rao to raj. Assum-
                ing UP, LOW are undefined.

UP=YES
export UP
yy rao raj1     #copies the content of file rao to raj1 and
                coverts all the characters to uppercase
```

```
UP=
LOW=YES
export LOW
yy rao raj2    #copies the content of file rao to raj2 and
               coverts all the characters to lowercase
UP=YES
export UP
yy rao raj3    # copies the content of file rao to raj3
               and coverts all the lower case characters to
               uppercase and upper case to lower case.
               Assuming all the above commands are executed
               sequentially.
```

Example 7

Write a program which takes source file name as a first command line argument and duplicate file names as subsequent command line arguments and copies the content of the source file to destination files.

```c
#include <stdio.h>

void main(int argc, char*argv[])
{
FILE *ip, *op;
int i;

if(argc<3) {printf("Atleast minimum two arguments are
                    needed\n"); exit(-1); }

ip=fopen(argv[1], "r");

if(ip==0) { printf("Error in opening file"); exit(-1); }

for(i=2;i<argc;i++)
{
op=fopen(argv[i],"w");

while(!feof(ip))
fputc(fgetc(ip),op);

fclose(op);
rewind(ip);
}

fclose(ip);

}
```

Example 8

This program demonstrates the use of temporary files. It creates a temporary file and writes a string into it and then reads the same and prints it on the screen.

```c
#include <stdio.h>
#include <stdlib.h>
#define MAXLINE 100

int main()
{
   char name [L_tmpnam],line[MAXLINE];
   FILE *op;
   printf("%s\n",tmpnam(NULL));
   tmpnam(name);
   printf("%s\n",name);
   printf("%s",p_tmpdir);
   if((op=tmpfile())==NULL)
            perror("tmpfile");
   fputs("Oneline!",op);
   rewind(op);
   fgets(line,sizeof(line),op);
   fputs(line,stdout);
   sleep(10);
   abort();
}
```

Conclusions

In this chapter C standard library function are explore in detail. Examples are given from demonstrate binary I/O and formatted I/O. Also, file stream pointers and file descriptors are related with live examples. How temporary files can be used and their necessity in practical programs is high lighted at the end.

Questions

1. Write a program from emulate cp command of unix. Compare the time requirements of the same with that of the question 5 chapter 11.

2. In DOS, **copy sourcefilename destionafilename /v** copies the content of source file to dsetination file and then further verifies. Can you implement the same?.

3. Write a program which takes a source file name along the command line and duplicate file names also along the command line and copies the content of soruces file from the destantion files.

4. Read about "ed" command (a line editor) in unix (probably old unix books you have from refer) and then write program from emulate the same.

14 Process

Processes

In the chronological development of operating systems, concept of multi tasking is most important and gave path way to all modern operating systems. Concepts of multi tasking, concurrency etc got more popularity after their realizations in Unix operating system.

At various levels, the concept of multi processing is employed in Unix design. For example, the Shell, the command line interpreter is a process which accepts user's commands and creates a new process and in that process the command is executed (see Shell Programming chapter). Similarly, the **init** process is an ever running process in Unix OS which takes the responsibility of all boot time administration such as mounting devices, loading device drivers, initializing interfaces etc.

It is very common practice in concurrent programming to create multiple processes and let each process to execute a program. For example, in **client server computing** the server (daemon) process will be looking at its well known port for connect requests from client and when such a request arrives it creates (spawns) a new process and via that process it will extend the service to the client while the parent process (daemon process) immediately returns to listening mode. Similarly, we can have one process to capture incoming packets and store in shared memory while another process takes the responsibility of processing these packets for finding possible intruders or organizations security violations.

Also, in scientific computing we can have multiple processing running parallely to reduce the execution time requirements of the program.

A program under excution is a process which can be identified through its PCB, (process control block) a structure in which process state information such as state registers (PC, SP, Flags) values, page table address, etc., are saved. Every process will have its own (virtual) address space (*see* Figure 14.1).

The memory for any process is divided into

- text - relocatable program code (fixed size)
- data - fixed data such as static variables, strings (fixed size)
- stack - user stack (grows downwards)
- bss - unintialised data for the heap (grows upwards)

In a virtual memory system (which all modern Unix's are) this may look like

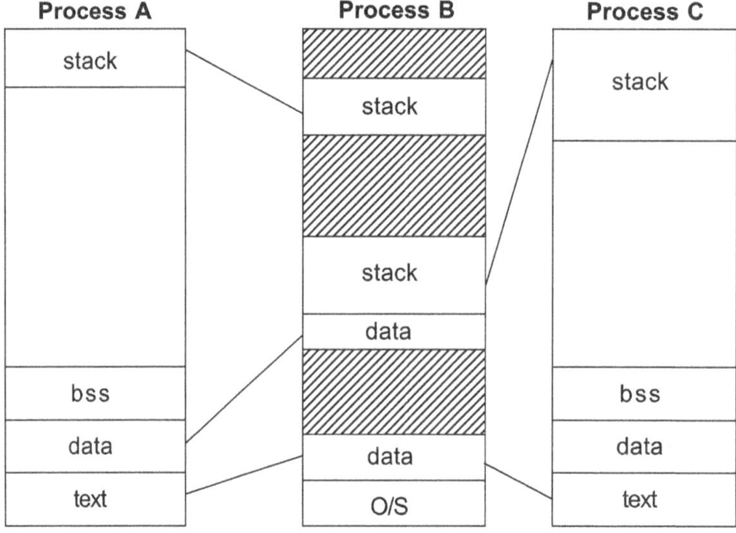

Figure 14.1

To create a new process from a program (or process), we may use the `fork()` system call. The prototype for the fork() system call is :

```
pid_t fork()
```

Function `fork()` causes the UNIX system to create a new process which can be called as the "child process", with a new process ID. The contents of the child process are identical to the contents of the parent process. Entire address space of the parent process is duplicated for child process. All the statements after `fork()` are executed in both the process; child and parent. Thus, child behaviour is same as the parent process.

The new process inherits several characteristics of the old process. Among the characteristics inherited are :

- process credentials (real/effective/saved UIDs and GIDs)
- environment
- stack
- memory
- open file descriptors (note that the underlying file positions are shared between the parent and child)
- close-on-exec flags
- signal handling settings
- nice value
- scheduler class
- process group ID
- session ID
- current working directory
- root directory
- file mode creation mask (umask)
- resource limits
- controlling terminal

Unique to the child :

- process ID
- different parent process ID
- Own copy of file descriptors and directory streams.
- process, text, data and other memory locks are NOT inherited.
- process times, in the tms struct
- resource utilizations are set to 0
- pending signals initialized to the empty set
- timers created by timer_create not inherited
- asynchronous input or output operations are not inherited

We can not tell which process runs soon after the `fork()`, child or parent? This is difficult to understand at first because you only call `fork()` once, yet it returns twice - once per process. To differentiate which process is which, `fork()` returns zero in the child process and non-zero (the child's process ID) in the parent process.

Example 1

The following program explains about the fork system call.

```c
#include <sys/types.h>
#include <unistd.h>
#include<stdio.h>

void main(){
pid_t pid;

switch (pid = fork()){
case -1:

   /* Here if pid is -1, the fork failed */
   /* Some possible reasons are that you're */
   /* out of process slots or virtual memory */

   perror("The fork failed!");
   break;

case 0:
   /* if pid is zero then it is the child */
      printf("From Child\n");
      _exit(0);
default:
/* pid greater than zero is parent getting the child's pid */

printf("From Parent: Child's pid is %d\n",pid);
}
```

What's the difference between `fork()` and `vfork()`?

Some systems have a system call `vfork()`, which was originally designed as a lower-overhead version of `fork()`. Since `fork()` involved copying the entire address space of the process, and was therefore quite expensive. The `vfork()` function was introduced in some BSD versions.

However, since `vfork()` was introduced, the implementation of `fork()` has improved drastically, most notably with the introduction of 'copy-on-write', where the copying of the process address space is transparently faked by allowing both processes to refer to the same physical memory until either of them modify it. This largely removes the justification for `vfork()`; indeed, a large proportion of systems now lack the original functionality of vfork() completely. For compatibility, though, there may still be a `vfork()` call present, that simply calls `fork()` without attempting to emulate all of the `vfork()` semantics.

As a result, it is very unwise to actually make use of any of the differences between `fork()` and `vfork()`. Indeed, it is probably unwise to use `vfork()` at all, unless you know exactly *why* you want to. The basic difference between the two is that when a new process is created with `vfork()`, the parent process is temporarily suspended, and the child process might borrow the parent's address space. This strange state of affairs continues until the child process either exits, or calls `execve()`, at which point the parent process continues.

This means that the child process of a `vfork()` must be careful to avoid unexpectedly modifying variables of the parent process. In particular, the child process must **not** return from the function containing the `vfork()` call, and it must **not** call exit() (if it needs to exit, it should use `_exit()`; actually, this is also true for the child of a normal `fork()`).

Example 2

The following program explains about the process tree. Here, `fork()` is called 3 times thus 2^3 processes will be created in total. Thus, in total we may see 8 times Hello message to be printed on the screen.

```
#include <sdtio.h>

void main()
{
fork();
fork();
fork();
printf("Hello\n");
}
```

Example 3

The following program creates a process chain.

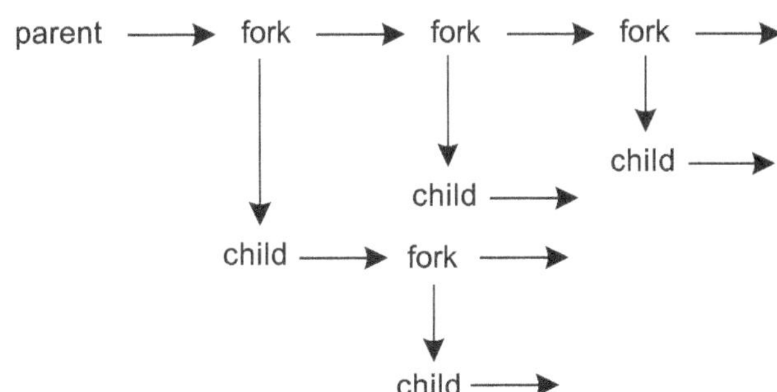

```
#include <stdio.h>

void main()
{
if(fork() ==0)
     if(fork()==0)
fork();
printf("Hello\n");
}
```

The above program creates in total four processes such that *every* parent has one child exactly.

Eample 4

The following example creates a chain of processes i.e. *every* parent has only one child.

Also check the process ID's of the processes created by running the following program.

```
#include <unistd.h>

int main()
{
if (fork() == 0)
{
   printf("Pid: %d\tpid: %d\n",getpid(),getppid());
     if(fork()==0)
     {
        printf("Pid: %d\tpid: %d\n",getpid(),getppid());
          if (fork()==0)
          printf("Pid: %d\tpid: %d\n",getpid(),getppid());
     }
}
return 0;
}
```

Example 5

The following example takes a integer along the command line and creates a process chian with that many processes in the chain.

```c
#include <stdio.h>
#include <stdlib.h>
#include <sys/types.h>
#include <unistd.h>

void main(int argc, char **argv)
{

int i;
pid_t childpid;
int n;

if(argc!=2){
   fprintf(stderr, "Usage: %s processes \n", argv[0]);
   exit(1);
}
n=atoi(argv[1]);

childpid=0;
for(i=1; i<n; ++i)
   if(childpid=fork())
      break;
   if(childpid==-1){
      perror("the fork failed\n");
      exit(1);
}

fprintf(stderr"i:%dprocessID:%ldparent ID:%ld child ID:%ld\n",
i, (long)getpid(), (long)getppid(), (long)childpid);
exit(0);

}
```

Example 6

The following example indicates that the variable x value will be printed as same from both the processes. This is because both the processes will have their own address spaces and when they modify this variable, really modification takes place on the variable "x" in their address space. Thus, the other processes can not see the modifications done by the other processes.

```c
#include <unistd.h>

int main()
{
    int x=10;
    if(fork() == 0)
    {
        sleep(10);
        x = x+10;
        printf("From child %d\n",x);
    }
    else
        printf("From parent %d\n",x);
    return 0;
}
```

`wait()` **System Call**

You can control the execution of child processes by calling `wait()` in the parent. `wait()` forces the parent to suspend execution until the child is finished. `wait()` returns the process ID of a child process that finished. If the child finishes before the parent gets around to calling `wait()`, then when `wait()` is called by the parent, it will return immediately with error message. (It is possible to have more than one child process by simply calling `fork()` more than once.). The prototype for the `wait()` system call is :

```c
int wait(status)
int *status;
```

where status is a pointer to an integer where the UNIX system stores the value returned by the child process. `wait()` returns the process ID of the process that ended. `wait()` fails if any of the following conditions hold:

The process has no children to wait for.

Status points to an invalid address.

The format of the information returned by wait() is as follows :

If the child process ended by calling the `exit()` system call, the second lowest byte of status is set to the argument given to `exit()` and the lowest byte of status is set to zeroes. If the process ended because of a signal, the second lowest byte of status is set to zeroes and the lowest byte of status contains the signal number that ended the process. If the seventh bit of the lowest byte of status is set (i.e. status &0200 == 0200) then the UNIX system produced a core dump of the process.

Example 7

The following program demonstrates use of exit() returning a status to `wait()`.

```c
int main()
{
   unsigned int status;

   if ( fork () == 0 )  {          /*  == 0 means in child  */
      scanf ("%d", &status);
      exit (status);
   }
   else  {                         /* != 0 means in parent */
      wait (&status);
      printf("child exit status = %d\n", status >>8);
   }
}
```

    Note : Since `wait()` returns the exit status multiplied by 256 (contained in the upper 8 bits), the status value is shifted right 8 bits (divided by 256) to obtain the correct value.

Example 8

In this example 'wait' system call is called in parent such that child runs first. In the child process, a SIGINT (signal number 2. See chapter on signal handling) is sent to the child process itself. Thus child terminates and the signal number is saved in first byte of status variable which is printed from the parent process.

```c
#include <unistd.h>
//#include <sys/types.h>
#include <sys/wait.h>

int main()
{
   int pid, id;
   if (fork()==0)
   {
      printf("From child %d\n",getpid());
      raise(2); /* sends SIGINT to this process. It is as good
                   as typing ^c */
   }
   pid = wait(&id);
   printf("From parent\n");
   printf("Signal No=%d\n", id&255);
   return 0;
}
```

Example 9

In this example 'wait' system call is called in parent such that child runs first. In the child process a SIGALRM is sent to the child process itself. Thus child terminates and the signal number is saved in first byte of status variable which is printed from the parent process.

```c
#include <unistd.h>
//#include <sys/types.h>
#include <sys/wait.h>

int main()
{
   int pid, id;
   if(fork()==0)
   {
     printf("From child %d\n",getpid());
     alarm(20);  /* sends SIGALRM to this process */
     while(1); /* busy wait */
   }
   pid = wait(&id);
   printf("From parent\n");
   printf("Signal No=%d\n", id&255);
   return 0;
}
```

Note : replace alarm() with abort() system call and run the program and find signal number of SIGABRT.

Example 10

Run this program in one terminal and note down the PID of the child (say 13216) which apprears on the screen. Go to another terminal then kill the child process by using command like **kill –2 13216**. Here 2 is the signal number 2 (SIGINT) and we are sending this to child process whose PID is 13216. Switch back to previous terminal and observe the output.

```c
#include <unistd.h>

int main()
{
   int x;
   if(fork()==0)
   {
     printf("%d\n",getpid());
     while(1);
   }
```

```
      else
      {
        wait(&x);
        printf("%d   %d\n",x&255, (x>>8)&255);
      }
      return 0;
}
```

What is a Zombie ?

When a program forks and the child finishes before the parent, the kernel still keeps some of its information about the child in case the parent might need it - for example, the parent may need to check the child's exit status. To be able to get this information, the parent calls wait(); when this happens, the kernel can discard the information. In the interval between the child terminating and the parent calling wait(), the child is said to be a 'zombie'. (If you do 'ps', the child will have a 'Z' in its status field to indicate this.) Even though it's not running, it's still taking up an entry in the process table. (It consumes no other resources, but some utilities may show bogus figures for e.g. CPU usage; this is because some parts of the process table entry have been overlaid by accounting info to save space.) This is not good, as the process table has a fixed number of entries and it is possible for the system to run out of them. Even if the system doesn't run out, there is a limit on the number of processes each user can run, which is usually smaller than the system's limit. This is one of the reasons why you should always check if fork() failed, by the way! If the parent terminates without calling wait(), the child is 'adopted' by init, which handles the work necessary to cleanup after the child. (This is a special system program mentioned earlier with process ID 1 - it's actually the first program to run after the system boots up).

How do I prevent them from occuring ?

You need to ensure that your parent process calls `wait()` (or `waitpid()`, `wait3()`, etc.) for every child process that terminates; or, on some systems, you can instruct the system that you are uninterested in child exit states.

Another approach is to `fork()` *twice*, and have the immediate child process exit straight away. This causes the grandchild process to be orphaned, so the init process is responsible for cleaning it up.

Environment Variables

How can I read the whole environment?

We have discussed about the environment variables in the previous chapters. The following discussion explains how we can know the environment variables from a C program. A global variable, **environ**, holds a pointer to an array of pointers to environment strings, each string in the form "NAME=value". A NULL pointer is used to mark the end of the array. Here's a program to print the current environment (like printenv or env) :

Example 11

```
#include <stdio.h>

extern char **environ;

int main()
{
  char **ep = environ;
  char *p;
  while((p = *ep++))
    printf("%s\n", p);
  return 0;
}
```

In general, the environ variable is also passed as the third, optional, parameter to `main()`; that is, the above could have been written:

Example 12

```
#include <stdio.h>

int main(int argc, char **argv, char **envp)
{
  char *p;
  while ((p = *envp++))
    printf("%s\n", p);
  return 0;
}
```

However, while pretty universally supported, this method isn't actually defined by the POSIX standards. (It's also less useful, in general.)

How can I get/set an environment variable from a program?

Getting the value of an environment variable is done by using getenv().

```
#include <stdlib.h>

char *getenv(const char *name);
```

Setting the value of an environment variable is done by using putenv().

```
#include <stdlib.h>

int putenv(char *string);
```

The string passed to putenv must *not* be freed or made invalid, since a pointer to it is kept by `putenv()`. This means that it must either be a static buffer or allocated off the heap. The string can be freed if the environment variable is redefined or deleted via another call to `putenv()`.

Remember that environment variables are inherited; each process has a separate copy of the environment. As a result, you can't change the value of an environment variable in another process, such as the shell. Suppose you wanted to get the value for the TERM environment variable. You would use this code :

```
char *envvar;

envvar=getenv("TERM");

printf("The value for the environment variable TERM is ");
if(envvar)
{
   printf("%s\n",envvar);
}
else
{
printf("not set.\n");
}
```

Now suppose you wanted to create a new environment variable called MYVAR, with a value of MYVAL. This is how you'd do it.

```
static char envbuf[256];

sprintf(envbuf,"MYVAR=%s","MYVAL");

if(putenv(envbuf))
{
printf("Sorry, putenv() couldn't find the memory for
%s\n",envbuf);
/* Might exit() or something here if you can't live without
it */
}
```

Example 13

Whenever a process calls sleep it goes to waiting state next process will be picked by the schedular.

```
#include <unistd.h>
#include <stdlib.h>

int main()
{
   char *p;
   putenv("XZ=Hello");
   if(fork()==0)
```

```
{
  putenv("YZ=How are you");
  if(p = getenv("XZ")) printf("%s\n",p);
  if(p = getenv("YZ")) printf("%s\n",p);
}
else
{
  sleep(5);
  if(p = getenv("XZ")) printf("%s\n",p);
  if(p = getenv("YZ")) printf("%s\n",p);
}
return 0;
}
```

Here, child process runs first always as sleep() is called in the parent first. Thus, even if parent starts first, it goes to sleeping state. Child gives output as :

```
Hello

How are You.
```

Then parent gives output as :

```
Hello
```

In the parent process, we can see the environment variable "YZ". As parent can not inherit properties from child process. That is whatever environment variables defined in child process or modified in child process are visible only its children process but in its parent.

Example 14

The following example is to show that the child process will inherit all the environment information from parent process. When you run this program same environment variables are printed two times.

```
#include <unistd.h>
#include <stdio.h>
#include <fcntl.h>

extern char **environ;

int main(int n, char **a)
```

```
{
  int i;
  fork();
  for(i = 0; environ[i]; i++)
    printf("%s\n",environ[i]);
  return 0;
}
```

Example 15

To show that the child process inherit opened files from parent. Here, a file is opened first and then `fork()` is executed. With the help of write system call "Hello" message is written into file. As this statement is executed both in child and parent process we will find "Hello" two times in the given file. Also, we can see that the same file descriptor value is printed from both the processes.

```
#include <unistd.h>
#include <stdio.h>
#include <fcntl.h>

extern char **environ;

int main(int n, char **a)
{
  int  fd;
  fd = open("xyz",O_WRONLY|O_CREAT);
  fork();
  printf("File descriptor = %d\n",fd);
  write(fd,"Hello",5);
  return 0;
}
```

Exec Family Functions

The UNIX system calls that transform a executable binary file into a process are the "exec" family of system calls. That is, from a program by calling either of these functions we can load a executable (machine language) file of a program into the address space of the current process.

The prototypes for these calls are :

```
int execl(file_name, arg0 [, arg1, ..., argn], NULL)
char *file_name, *arg0, *arg1, ..., *argn;

int execv(file_name, argv)
char *file_name, *argv[];
```

```
int execle(file_name, arg0 [, arg1, ..., argn], NULL, envp)
char *file_name, *arg0, *arg1, ..., *argn, *envp[];

int execve(file_name, argv, envp)
char *file_name, *argv[], *envp[];

int execlp(file_name, arg0 [, arg1, ..., argn], NULL)
char *file_name, *arg0, *arg1, ..., *argn;

int execvp(file_name, argv)
char *file_name, *argv[];
```

where file_name names the executable binary file to be transformed into a process, arg0 through argn and argv define the arguments to be passed to the process, and envp defines the environment, also to be passed to the process. By convention, `arg0` and `argv[0]` name the last path name component of the executable binary file named by file_name. For `execl()`, `execv()`, `execle()`, and `execve()`, file_name must be the fully qualified path name of the executable binary file. However for `execlp()` and `execvp()`, the PATH variable is used to find the executable binary file. When the environment is not explicitly given as an argument to an exec system call, the environment of the current process is used. Furthermore, the last array element of both argv and envp must be null to signify the end of the array.

Unlike the other system calls and subroutines, a successful exec system call does not return. Instead, control is given to the executable binary file named as the first argument. When that file is made into a process, that process replaces the process that executed the exec system call - a new process is not created. If an exec call should fail, it will return a −1.

When transforming an executable binary file into a process, the UNIX system preserves some characteristics of the replaced process. Among the items saved by the exec system call are :

The "nice" value for scheduling.

The process ID and the parent process ID.

The time left until an alarm clock signal.

The current working directory and the root directory.

The file creation mask as established with umask().

All open files.

The last of these is the most interesting because the shell uses this feature to handle input/output redirection.

Letters added to the end of exec indicate the type of arguments :

l   argn is specified as a list of arguments.

v   argv is specified as a vector (array of character pointers).

e   environment is specified as an array of character pointers.

p   user's PATH is searched for command, and command can be a shell program

Following is a brief description of the six routines that make up the collective family of exec routines :

`execl`   Takes the path name of an executable program (binary file) as its first argument. The rest of the arguments are a list of command line arguments to the new program (`argv[]`). The list is terminated with a null pointer :

```
execl("/bin/cat", "cat", "f1", "f2", (char *) 0);
execl("a.out", "a.out", (char *) 0);
```

Note that, by convention, the argument listed after the program is the name of the command being executed (`argv[0]`).

`execle`   Same as `execl()`, except that the end of the argument list is followed by a pointer to a null-terminated list of character pointers that is passed as the environment of the new program (i.e., the place that `getenv()` searches for exported shell variables) :

```
static char *env[] = {
"TERM=vt100",
"PATH=/bin:/usr/bin",
(char *) 0 };

execle("/bin/cat", "cat", "f1", "f2", (char *) 0, env);
```

`execv`   Takes the path name of an executable program (binary file) as its first argument. The second argument is a pointer to a list of character pointers (like `argv[]`) that is passed as command line arguments to the new program :

```
static char *args[] = {
"cat",
"f1",
"f2",
(char *) 0 };

execv("/bin/cat", args);
```

      `execve` Same as `execv()`, except that a third argument is given as a pointer to a list of character pointers (like `argv[]`) that is passed as the environment of the new program :

```
static char *env[] = {
"TERM=vt100",
"PATH=/bin:/usr/bin",
(char *) 0 };

static char *args[] = {
"cat",
"f1",
"f2",
(char *) 0 };

execve("/bin/cat", args, env);
```

      `execlp` Same as `execl()`, except that the program name doesn't have to be a full path name, and it can be a shell program instead of an executable module :

```
execlp("ls", "ls", "-l", "/usr", (char *) 0);
```
      `execlp()` searches the PATH environment variable to find the specified program.

      `execvp`   Same as `execv()`, except that the program name doesn't have to be a full path name, and it can be a shell program instead of an executable module :

```
static char *args[] = {
"cat",
"f1",
"f2",
(char *) 0 };

execvp("cat", args);
```

Example 16

To demonstrate use of `execl()` function.

```
#include <unistd.h>
#include <stdio.h>

void main()
{
printf("Before execl function\n");
execl("/bin/ls", "ls", "-a", "-l",0);
printf("After execl call\n");
exit(10);
}
```

In the above program, the last printf statement will never get executed because when `execl()` call is called machine language file of "ls" command is loaded to the address space of the current process. That is, text area, data areas of the current processes are loaded with that of "ls" command. Moreover, you may find that the exit status of this program is not 10 (use echo $? after running this program). Rather it is zero which is the exit status of "ls" command. Thus, we conclude that when we load a program into a processes address space, that processes exit status is same as the exit status of the program loaded.

Example 17

To demonstrate use of `execv()` function.

```
#include<unistd.h>
#include<stdio.h>

void main()
{
char *a[4];
a[0]="ls";
a[1]="-a";
a[2]="-l";
a[3]=0;
execv("/bin/ls", a);
}
```

In this example, all the arguments are stored in a character pointer array with last element as zero (null) and this pointer array is sent as argument to the function.

Example 18

To demonstrate use of `execvp()` function.

```
#include <unistd.h>
#include <stdio.h>

void main()
{
char *a[4];
a[0]="ls";
a[1]="-a";
a[2]="-l";
a[3]=0;
execvp("ls", a);
}
```

In this example, all the arguments are stored in a character pointer array with last element as zero (null) and this pointer array is sent as argument to the function. The executable file of the "ls" command is located with the help of PATH environment variable.

Example 19

To demonstrate use of `execlp()` function.

```
#include <unistd.h>
#include <stdio.h>

void main()
{
printf("Before execl function\n");
execlp("ls", "ls", 0);
}
```

Here, machine language file of "ls" command is located with the help PATH environment variable and then loaded into the current processes address space.

Example 20

Demo to demonstrate use of function `excle()`.

```
#include <unistd.h>

extern char **environ;

int main()
{
char *x[3];
int i;
x[0] = "xyz=/tmp";
x[1] = "pqr=/bin";
x[2] = 0;
if(fork()==0)
{
   for(i = 0; environ[i]; i++)
    printf("%s\n",environ[i]);
   execle("./aa","aa",0,x);
}
wait(&i);
return 0;
}

/* file 'aa.c'
*
* extern char **environ;
* int main()
* {
*    int i;
*   for(i = 0; environ[i]; i++)
*     printf("%s\n",environ[i]);
* }
 */
```

First compile file aa.c to get an executable file with name "**aa**" then run the above program. We can find that the environment variables which are available in the child process before `execle()` are available to the process "aa" also (actually "aa" prints environment variables information).

Example 21

Program to demonstrate use of function `excve()`.

```
#include <unistd.h>

extern char **environ;

int main()
{
  char x[3],y[2];
  int i;
  x[0] = "xyz=/tmp";
  x[1] = "pqr=/bin";
  x[2] = 0;

  y[0]="aa";
  y[1]=0;
  if(fork()==0)
  {
     for(i = 0; environ[i]; i++)
     printf("%s\n",environ[i]);
     execve("./aa",y,x);
  }
  wait(&i);
  return 0;
}
```

Example 22

This program is a simple command interpreter that uses `execlp()` to execute commands typed in by the user. Please note that the commands which user has to enter should not have any arguments.

```
#include <stdio.h>

int main()
{
  int process;
  char line[81];

  for (;;)
```

```
            {
                fprintf(stderr, "cmd: ");
                if (gets (line) == (char *) NULL)  /* blank line input */
                    exit (0);

        /* create a new process */

        process = fork ();

        if (process > 0)    /* parent */
        wait ((int *) 0);  /* null pointer - return value not saved */
        else if (process == 0)        /* child */
            {                         /* execute program */
            execlp (line, line, (char *) NULL);
                            /* some problem if exec returns */
            fprintf (stderr, "Can't execute %s\n", line);
            exit (1);
            }
            else if (process == -1)  /* can't create a new process */
                {
                    fprintf (stderr, "Can't fork!\n");
                    exit (2);
                }
            }
        }
```

Example 23

The following program demonstrates a practical use of fork () and exec () to create a
new directory. Only the superuser has the permission to use the mknod () system call to
create a new directory - an ordinary user cannot use mknod () to create a directory. So,
we use fork/exec to call upon the UNIX system's mkdir command that anyone can use to
create a directory.

```
        #include <stdio.h>

        int main()
        {
           int fd;

           if ( fork() != 0)
             wait ((int *) 0);
           else
```

```
    {
    execl ("/bin/mkdir", "mkdir", "newdir", (char *) NULL);
    fprintf (stderr, "exec failed!\n");
    exit (1);
    }

    /*  now use newdir  */
    if ((fd = open("newdir/foo.bar", O_RDWR | O_CREAT, 0644))
    == -1)
      {
      fprintf (stderr, "open failed!\n");
      exit (2);
      }
    write (fd, "Hello, world\n", 14);
    close (fd);
    exit (0);
    }
```

User Indentification

```
getlogin()
```

The function getlogin() is defined by

```
char *getlogin(void)
```

It returns a string holding the login name, or NULL on failure. You should not modify the returned string.

Example 24

```
#include <stdio.h>

int main(int argc, char **argv)
{
  char *login;

  if ((login = getlogin()) != NULL) {
  printf("Login name %s\n", login);
  } else {
    fprintf(stderr, "Can't find login name\n");
    exit(1);
  }
  exit(0);
}
```

passwd

Information about users is stored in the file /etc/passwd. The function getpwnam()
returns such information given a user's name as a string.

```
#include <pwd.h>

struct passwd *getpwnam(char *name)
```

The returned structure is

```
struct passwd
{
  char *pw_name;                        /* Username.  */
  char *pw_passwd;                      /* Password.  */
  uid_t pw_uid;                         /* User ID.  */
  gid_t pw_gid;                         /* Group ID.  */
  char *pw_dir;                         /* Home directory.  */
  char *pw_shell;                       /* Shell program.  */
};
```

Example 25

```
#include <stdio.h>
#include <pwd.h>

int main(int argc, char *argv[])
{
  struct passwd *pass;
  char *name = "jan";

  if ((pass = getpwnam(name)) != NULL) {
  printf("Home dir of %s is %s \n", name,
    pass->pw_dir);
  } else {
  fprintf(stderr, "Can't find password info for %s\n",
        name);
  exit(1);
  }
  exit(0);
}
```

Example 26

This Program dumps out all defined users and their user information from `/etc/passwd` file.

```c
#include <pwd.h>
#include <sys/types.h>
#include <error.h>
#include <stdio.h>

int main()
{
  struct passwd *psw;
  if((psw = getpwnam("guest")) == NULL)
  {
    perror("Getpwnam");
    return -1;
  }
  printf("Name: %s\nPasswd: %s\n",psw->pw_name,
                                  psw->pw_passwd);\
  printf("Uid: %d\nGid: %d\nReal name: %s\nHome: %s\
      \nDefault shell: %s\n",psw->pw_uid,psw->pw_gid,\
      psw->pw_gecos,psw->pw_dir,psw->pw_shell);
  setpwent();
  printf("Name Passwd uid gid RealName HomeDir
          currentShell\n");
  while((psw = getpwent()))
  {
    printf("%-10s%-6s  ",psw->pw_name,psw->pw_passwd);
    printf("%4d%4d  %-12s %-8s   %s\n",psw->pw_uid,
                                  psw->pw_gid,\
    psw->pw_gecos,psw->pw_dir,psw->pw_shell);
  }
  endpwent();
  return 0;
}
```

uname

System information is given by the call

```c
#include <sys/utsname.h>

int uname(struct *utsname name)
```

Given the address of an existing structure, the fields are filled in. A value of -1 is returned on error. The structure is

```
#define _SYS_NMLN 257

struct utsname {
   char sysname[_SYS_NMLN];
   char nodename[_SYS_NMLN];
   char release[_SYS_NMLN];
   char version[_SYS_NMLN];
   char machine[_SYS_NMLN-65];
}
```

Example 27

```
#include <stdio.h>
#include <sys/utsname.h>

int main(int argc, char *argv[])
{
   struct utsname name;

   if (uname(&name) != -1) {
      printf("System name: %s\n",
               name.sysname);
   } else {
      fprintf(stderr, "Can't find system name\n");
      exit(1);
   }
   exit(0);
}
```

Conclusions

Unix process creation is explained in relation to multiprocessing. The fork() system call from create child process is dealt in detail in a lucid and with simple concept oriented example. Process chains, process trees and their creations are explained with examples. The wait(), waitpid() system calls and their use for process synchronization is dealt in detail. Child process behavior in relation to its parent and zombie process's etc are also emphasized in detail.

Also, use of exec() family of functions is critically analyzed and live examples are included.

Questions

1. Write a program from check the value of a volatile variable both in child and parent process. What is your comment?

2. Observe what is going from happened if you execute the following program. Probably run "ps –Al" on another terminal.

```
#include<stdio.h>

void main()
{
   sleep(5);
   main();
}
```

3. Write a program to emulate DOS commands COPY, DEL, DELETE, ERASE, DIR (with out any options), REN, RENAME, MOVE, TYPE, MORE. That the program has from give a prompt, say DOS and that prompt user can type any of the DOS commands.

15   Process Timers

Clocks and timers have been part of UNIX systems for sometime. Standard UNIX (POSIX.1) has three clocks. One tells the time and is directly accessible to the user. The other two have other purposes which don't often concern the application programmer. There are two types of timers: one-shot timers and repeating. The one-shot timer only expires once and is used to signal a special event that needs to occur only once. Repeating timers go off at regular intervals and are used to schedule periodic events.

There is, basically, only one clock which application programs use in standard UNIX. The UNIX operating system keeps track of the current date and time by storing the number of seconds that have elasped since midnight January 1, 1970 UTC (Coordinated Universal Time, also known as Greenwich Mean Time (GMT)) which is called as epoch. This date is considered the informal "birthday" of the UNIX operating system. The time is stored in a signed long integer. (For the curious, assuming a 32 bit signed long integer, UNIX time will break at 03:14:08 January 19, 2038 UTC.)

The time function can be used to know how much in seconds is elapsed since Jan 1, 1970 UTC. The prototype for the time call is :

```
#include< time.h>

time_t time(time_t *tloc);
```

In all versions of UNIX, the `time()` system call may be used to obtain the time of day. This call is peculiar in that if given the address of a long integer as an argument, it places the time in that integer and returns it. If, however, a null pointer is passed, the time of day is just returned.

The `time_t` is convenient for calculating differences between times, but difficult to print dates. Several routines are available to convert the long integer returned by `time()` into an ASCII date string. With the UNIX operating system, an ASCII date string is a string as shown below :

```
Day Mon dd hh:mm:ss yyyy
```

Example : Sat Mar 24 11:03:36 1990

The `ctime()` library function can be used to do the above conversion. Its prototype is :

```
#include<time.h>

char *ctime(const time_t *clock)
```

Example

This example print the current date and time in a format similar to the output of the date command.

Example 1

```
#include <stdio.h>
#include <time.h>        /* may need to be #include <sys/time.h>
                            instead on some systems*/

int main()
{
   long now, time();
   char *ctime();

   time (&now);
   printf("It is now %s\n", ctime (&now));

   exit (0);
}
```

Often you need access to specific information about the current date and time. The `localtime()` and `gmtime()` functions will provide it. They do this by converting the long integer returned by `time()` into a data structure called `tm`, which is defined in the `time.h` header file. In fact, this is what the header file looks like :

```
struct tm {
   int   tm_sec;    /* seconds after the minute - [0,59] */
   int   tm_min;    /* minutes after the hour - [0,59] */
   int   tm_hour;   /* hours since midnight - [0,23] */
   int   tm_mday;   /* day of the month - [1,31] */
```

```
int    tm_mon;      /* months since January - [0,11] */
int    tm_year;     /* years since 1900 */
int    tm_wday;     /* days since Sunday - [0,6] */
int    tm_yday;     /* days since January 1 - [0,365] */
int    tm_isdst;    /* daylight savings time flag */
};
```

As you can see, there is quite a bit of information you can access. The `tm_isdst` member is non-zero if Daylight Savings Time is in effect. The `localtime()` function returns the time in the local time zone, whereas the `gmtime()` function returns the time in the UTC (or GMT) time zone. Both `localtime()` and `gmtime()` take as their argument a pointer to a long integer that represents the date and time as the number of seconds since January 1, 1970 (such a returned by `time()`). The return pointers to a tm structure, where the converted data is placed. The following example prints the local date in the familiar mm/dd/yy format:

Example 2

This example prints date in mm/dd/yy format

```
#include <stdio.h>
#include <time.h>       /* may need to be #include <sys/time.h>
                           instead */

int main()
{
   long now, time();
   struct tm *today, *localtime();

   time (&now);
   today = localtime (&now);

   printf("Today  is:    %d/%d/%d\n", today->tm_mon + 1,
   today->tm_mday, today->tm_year);
   exit (0);
}
```

The time function measures **real time** or wall-clock time. In a multiprogramming environment, we may be more interested in the amount of time an individual process uses. This is called **virtual time**. The system call times returns information about the execution times of a process and its children.

```
#include <sys/times.h>
clock_t times(struct tms *buffer);
```

The `clock_t` type holds a number of clock ticks. The structure `tms` contains at least the following members

```
clock_t   tms_utime;   /*user CPU time*/
clock_t   tms_stime;   /*system CPU time*/
clock_t   tms_cutime; /*user CPU time of terminated children*/
clock_t   tms_sutime; /*system CPU time of terminated children*/
```

The function returns the amount of elapsed time in clock ticks since an arbitrary point in the past. The following code segment caculates the fraction of time that a process is running on a processor while performing a computation.

Example 3

```
#include <sys/times.h>
#include <limits.h>
#include <stdio.h>

void main()
{
   clock_t real_start;
   clock_t real_end;
   clock_t ticks_used;
   struct tms process_start;
   struct tms process_end;

if ((real_start = times(&process_start)) == -1)
   perror("Could not get starting times");
else {
   /* perform calculation to be timed */
if ((real_end = times(&process_end)) == -1)
   perror("Could not get ending times");
else {
   ticks_used = process_end.tms_utime + process_end.tms_cstime-
   process_start.tms_utime - process_start.tms_cstime;
   printf("Fraction of time running = %f\n",
   (double)(ticks_used)/(real_end - real_start));
      }
   }
}
```

One Shot Timers

The most well known example of a one-shot timer is the sleep call.

```
#include <unistd.h>

unsigned sleep(unsigned seconds);
```

When a process executes sleep, it blocks for the number of seconds specified. The sleep function can be used as a sort of crude interval timer. For example, let's examine the following code segment

```
while (1) {
sleep(nsec);
/*do something*/
}
```

This code attempts to execute the "do something" code segment every nsec seconds. The problem, however, is that nsec is in "seconds". In many situations, this sort of timing is much too coarse for actual control applications. In addition to this, the actual period for the while loop will be nsec plus some "drift" associated with the amount of time required to "do something". In a multitasking environment where signals can asynchronously interrupt processes, it is impossible to determine precisely how long it takes to "do something". To get around this difficulty, the standard UNIX interval timers were created.

Standard UNIX Interval Timers

The standard UNIX interval timers were defined in the Berkeley and SR4(1170) versions of UNIX. A conforming Spec 1170 implementation must provide each process with the following three interval timers.

- `ITIMER_REAL` : decrements in real time and generates a SIGALRM signal when it expires.
- `ITIMER_VIRTUAL` : decrements in virtual time (time used by the process) and generates a SIGVTALRM signal when it expires
- `ITIMER_PROF` : decrements in virtual time and system time for the process and generates a SIGPROF signal when it expires.

Interval timers use a struct `itimerval` structure to contain the following members:

```
struct timeval it_value;   /*time until next expiration*/
struct timeval it_interval; /*value to reload into timer*/
```

The system call `setitimer` is provided for starting and stopping interval timers.

```
#include<sys/time.h>

int setitimer(int which, const struct itimerval *value,
                    struct itimerval *ovalue);
```

The `setitimer` function returns 0 on success. It returns –1 and sets errno on failure. The which parameter specifies the timer. The caller specifies the time interval for setting the timer in *value. The system call fills the members of the structure point to by ovalue with the current timer values. This pointer may be NULL if we don't need to see the information.

Use getitimer to determine the amount of time remaining on a Spec 1170 timer

```
#include <sys/time.h>

int getitimer(int which,struct itimerval *value);
```

The system call sets *value to the time remaining on timer which and returns 0 on success. It returns –1 and sets errno on failure.

Example 4

The following program causes the process to print out an asterisk for each two seconds of CPU time used. The ITIMER_PROF timer generates a SIGPROF signal after every two seconds of CPU time used by the process. The process catches the SIGPROF signal and handles it with myhandler.

```
#include <stdio.h>
#include <stdlib.h>
#include <signal.h>
#include <sys/time.h>

char astbuf[] = "*";
static void myhandler(int s)
{
   write(STDERR_FILENO, astbuf, sizeof(char));
}

/* set up the myhandler handler for signal SIGPROF */
void init_timer_interrupt(void)
{
   struct sigaction newact;
   newact.sa_handler = myhandler;
   newact.sa_flags = SA_RESTART;
   sigemptyset(&newact.sa_mask);
   sigaction(SIGPROF, &newact, NULL);
}

/* set the ITIMER_PROF interval timer for 2-second intervals */
void setup_interval_timer(void)
{
   struct itimerval value;
   value.it_interval.tv_sec = 2;
   value.it_interval.tv_usec = 0;
   value.it_value = value.it_interval;
   setitimer(ITIMER_PROF, &value, NULL);
}
```

```
void main(int argc, char *argv[])
{
  init_timer_interrupt();
  setup_interval_timer();
  /* execute rest of main program here */
  exit(0);
}
```

POSIX Interval Timers

The 1170 specification timers do not provide sufficient flexiblity to deal with real time tasks. To be useful in a realtime programming environment, we need the following

- support of additional clocks beyond `ITIMER_REAL`, `ITIMER_VIRTUAL`, and `ITIMER_PROF`.
- allowance for greater time resolution (i.e. nanosecond resolution)
- ability to determine timer overruns.
- ability to use something other than `SIGALRM` to indicate timer expiration.

As a result, POSIX.1b defines a new set of timer functions that meet the additional requirements stated above. In POSIX.1, each process has only three timers. In POSIX.1b, there are a small number of clocks such as `CLOCK_REALTIME` and a process can create many independent timers based on these hardware clocks.

Conclusions

In this chapter, Unix timers are explored. How timers can be used to find out the CPU time requirements of a program for benchmarking is emphasized. Also, interval timers are explained.

Questions

1. Assume from see assignment the students have from type a program name, say assignments. Whenver executes this program, his user name, time has from be stored in a log file which no one can disturb (Find out is there any need for setuid for this program).

2. Find out how much time is required for the program which is written for the 5 question of chapter 11 by you.

3. Write a program which when executed gives either "Good Morning", "Good Evening", "Good Night" and "Good After Noon" depending on the time.

16 Signals

What Are Signals ?

We are familiar with interrupts which are sent to the operating system by the hardware. Signals are also very similar in their behavior with the difference that they are sent to the process by the operating system, or by other processes or explicitly by the user by pressing some special key sequences such as `^c`, `^d`, `^\` etc.,. Note that signals have nothing to do with software interrupts, which are still sent by the hardware (the CPU itself, in this case).

Signals, to be short, are various notifications sent to a process in order to notify it of various "important" events. By their nature, they interrupt whatever the process is doing at this minute, and force it to handle them immediately. Each signal has an integer number that represents it (1, 2 and so on), as well as a symbolic name that is usually defined in the file /usr/include/signal.h or one of the files included by it directly or indirectly (HUP, INT and so on. Use the command 'kill -l' to see a list of signals supported by your system).

Each signal may have an associated signal handler, which is a function that gets called when the process receives that signal. The function is called in "asynchronous mode", meaning that no where in your program you have code that calls this function directly. Instead, when the signal is sent to the process, the operating system stops the execution of the process, and "forces" it to call the signal handler function. When that signal handler function returns, the process continues execution from wherever it happened to be before the signal was received, as if this interruption never occurred.

What Are Signals Used For ?

Signals are usually used by the operating system to notify processes that some event occurred, without these processes needing to poll for the event. Signals should then be *handled*, rather then *used* to create an event notification mechanism for a specific application. When we say that "Signals are being handled", we mean that our program is ready to handle such signals that the operating system might be sending it (such as signals notifying that the user asked to terminate it, or that a network connection we tried writing into, was closed, etc). Failing to properly handle various signals, would likely cause our application to terminate, when it receives such signals.

Sending Signals To Processes

Sending Signals using the Keyboard

The most common way of sending signals to processes is using the keyboard. There are certain key presses that are interpreted by the system as requests to send signals to the process with which we are interacting:

`Ctrl-C`

Pressing this key causes the system to send an INT signal (SIGINT) to the running process. By default, this signal causes the process to immediately terminate.

`Ctrl-Z`

Pressing this key causes the system to send a TSTP signal (SIGTSTP) to the running process. By default, this signal causes the process to suspend execution.

`Ctrl-\`

Pressing this key causes the system to send a ABRT signal (SIGABRT) to the running process. By default, this signal causes the process to immediately terminate. Note that this redundancy (i.e. Ctrl-\ doing the same as Ctrl-C) gives us some better flexibility.

Sending Signals from the Command Line

Another way of sending signals to processes is done using various commands, usually internal to the shell:

`kill`

The kill command accepts two parameters: a signal name (or number), and a process ID. Usually the syntax for using it goes something like:

```
kill -<signal> <PID>
```

For example, in order to send the INT signal to process with PID 5342, type :

```
kill -INT 5342
```

This has the same affect as pressing `Ctrl-C` in the shell that runs that process. If no signal name or number is specified, the default is to send a TERM signal to the process, which normally causes its termination, and hence the name of the kill command.

Kill system call

By using the kill system call from within a C program we can send a signal to a process. This call takes a process ID and a signal number as parameters

```
#include<sys/types.h>
#include<signal.h>

int kill(pid_t pid, int sig);
```

If the process id is positive, `kill` sends the specified signal to the process with that pid. If pid is negative, then `kill` sends the signal to the process group with group ID equal to `|pid|`. If `pid=0`, then `kill` sends the message to all processes of the caller's process group.

Raise System Call

A process can send a signal to itself with the `raise` function. This function has only one argument, the signal parameter

```
#include < signal.h>

int raise(int sig);
```

Alarm System Call

The `alarm` function causes a `SIGALRM` to be sent to the calling process after a specified number of real time seconds have passed.

```
#include < unistd.h>

unsigned int alarm(unsigned int seconds);
```

Requests to alarm are not stacked, so that if a program calls `alarm` before the previous one expires, the alarm is reset to the new value. The default action for `SIGALRM` is to terminate the process.

Abort System Call

This sends SIGABRT to the process which calls this function.

fg

On most shells, using the '`fg`' command will resume execution of the process (that was suspended with Ctrl-Z), by sending it a CONT signal.

Sending Signals Using System Calls

A third way of sending signals to processes is by using the kill system call. This is the normal way of sending a signal from one process to another. This system call is also used by the 'kill' command or by the 'fg' command. Here is an example code that causes a process to suspend its own execution by sending itself the STOP signal :

```
#include <unistd.h> /*standard unix functions, likegetpid()*/
#include <sys/types.h> /*various type definitions, like pid_t*/
#include <signal.h>   /* signal name macros, and the
                             kill()prototype */

/* first, find my own process ID */
pid_t my_pid = getpid();

/* now that I got my PID, send myself the STOP signal. */
kill(my_pid, SIGSTOP);
```

An example of a situation when this code might prove useful, is inside a signal handler that catches the TSTP signal (Ctrl-Z, remember?) in order to do various tasks before actually suspending the process. We will see an example of this later on.

Catching Signals - Signal Handlers

Catchable and Non-Catchable Signals

Most signals may be caught by the process, but there are a few signals that the process cannot catch, and cause the process to terminate. For example, the KILL signal is such a signal. This is why you usually see a process being shut-down using this signal if it gets "wild". One process that uses this signal is a system shutdown process. It first sends a TERM signal to all processes, waits a while, and after allowing them a "grace period" to shut down cleanly, it kills whichever are left using the KILL signal.

STOP is also a signal that a process cannot catch, and forces the process's suspension immediately. This is useful when debugging programs whose behavior depends on timing. Suppose that process A needs to send some data to process B, and you want to check some system parameters after the message is sent, but before it is received and processed by process B. One way to do that would be to send a STOP signal to process B, thus causing its suspension, and then running process A and waiting until it sends its oh-so important message to process B. Now you can check whatever you want to, and later on you can use the CONT signal to continue process B's execution, which will then receive and process the message sent from process A.

Now, many other signals are catchable, and this includes the famous SEGV and BUS signals. You probably have seen numerous occasions when a program has exited with a message such as '*Segmentation Violation - Core Dumped*', or '*Bus Error - core dumped*'. In the first occasion, a SEGV signal was sent to your program due to accessing an illegal memory address. In the second case, a BUS signal was sent to your program, due to accessing a memory address with invalid alignment. In both cases, it is possible to catch these signals in order to do some cleanup - kill child processes, perhaps remove temporary files, etc. Although in both cases, the memory used by your process is most likely corrupt, it's probable that only a small part of it was corrupt, so cleanup is still usually possible.

Exampe 1

```
#include<stdio.h>
void main()
{
int X;

scanf("%d", X);

}
```

This program compiles and while running you will get memory segment violation. This can be attributed to scanf function which reads an integer from key board and tries to store at the location pointed by the value of X; which is a garbage value. As the memory pointed by this X value is not guaranteed to be allocated to this process, our program makes memory violation thus SIGSEGV signal is sent to this process and thus we get the above error message and program gets terminated.

The type of signals which a unix system supports vary a little from system to system. (Most commonly available signals are listed in Table 16.1).

Table 16.1 Common Signals

Signal	Description
SIGABRT	Process abort signal.
SIGALRM	Alarm clock.
SIGFPE	Erroneous arithmetic operation.
SIGHUP	Hangup.
SIGILL	Illegal instruction.
SIGINT	Terminal interrupt signal.
SIGKILL	Kill (cannot be caught or ignored).
SIGPIPE	Write on a pipe with no one to read it.
SIGQUIT	Terminal quit signal.
SIGSEGV	Invalid memory reference.
SIGTERM	Termination signal.
SIGUSR1	User-defined signal 1.

Table 16.1 Contd...

Signal	Description
SIGUSR2	User-defined signal 2.
SIGCHLD	Child process terminated or stopped.
SIGCONT	Continue executing, if stopped.
SIGSTOP	Stop executing (cannot be caught or ignored).
SIGTSTP	Terminal stop signal.
SIGTTIN	Background process attempting read.
SIGTTOU	Background process attempting write.
SIGBUS	Bus error.
SIGPOLL	Pollable event.
SIGPROF	Profiling timer expired.
SIGSYS	Bad system call.
SIGTRAP	Trace/breakpoint trap.
SIGURG	High bandwidth data is available at a socket.
SIGVTALRM	Virtual timer expired.
SIGXCPU	CPU time limit exceeded.
SIGXFSZ	File size limit exceeded.

Default Signal Handlers

Whenever a signal arrives to a process it executes the function associated with that signal which we may call as its handler. Every signal will have their default signal handlers i.e if you install no signal handlers of your own (remember what a signal handler is? yes, that function handling a signal?), the runtime environment sets up a set of default signal handlers for your program. For example, the default signal handler for the TERM signal calls the exit() system call. The default handler for the ABRT is to dump the process's memory image into a file named 'core' in the process's current directory, and then exit. Note that the 'core' file might actually have some suffix (such as 'core.567') on some systems.

Installing Signal Handlers

If we want a process to execute a specified function when a signal arrives then we have to install that function as a signal handler for that signal. Once it is done, whenever that signal arrives to this process this function will be executed automatically. We don't require to call this function explicitly. This is known as signal handling (like exit handlers or exception handlers in object oriented languages). There are several ways to install signal handlers.

The signal() System Call: An Unreliable Way Of Signal Handling

The signal() system call is used to set a signal handler for a single signal type. signal() accepts a signal number and a pointer to a signal handler function, and sets that handler to accept the given signal. As an example, here is a code snippest that causes the program to print the string "Don't do that" when a user presses Ctrl-C.

The prototype of the signal function is given as :

```c
int signal(int signo, void (*f)(int) );

#include <stdio.h> /*standard I/O functions */
#include <unistd.h> /*standard unix functions, like getpid()*/
#include <sys/types.h> /* various type definitions, like pid_t*
#include <signal.h>     /*signal name macros, and the signal()
                         prototype */

/* first, here is the signal handler */
void catch_int(int sig_num)
{
  /* re-set the signal handler again to catch_int,
    for next time */
  signal(SIGINT, catch_int);
  /* and print the message */
  printf("Don't do that");
  fflush(stdout);
}

/* and somewhere later in the code.... */

/* set the INT (Ctrl-C) signal handler to 'catch_int' */
signal(SIGINT, catch_int);

/* now, lets get into an infinite loop of doing nothing. */
for ( ;; )
pause();
```

Example 2

The complete source code for this program is as follows :

```c
#include <stdio.h> /* standard I/O functions */

#include <unistd.h> /* standard unix functions, like getpid()*/
#include <signal.h> /* signal name macros, and the signal()
                       prototype */
```

```c
/* first, here is the signal handler */
void catch_int(int sig_num)
{

/* re-set the signal handler again to catch_int,
   for next time */
signal(SIGINT, catch_int);
printf("Don't do that\n");
fflush(stdout);
}

int main(int argc, char* argv[])
{
   /* set the INT (Ctrl-C) signal handler to 'catch_int' */
   signal(SIGINT, catch_int);

   /* now, lets get into an infinite loop of doing nothing. */
   for ( ;; )
      pause();
}
```

Notes :

- the pause() system call causes the process to halt execution, until a signal is received. It is surely better than a 'busy wait' infinite loop.
- the name of a function in C/C++ is actually a pointer to the function, so when you're asked to supply a pointer to a function, you may simply specify its name instead.
- On some systems (such as Linux), when a signal handler is called, the system automatically resets the signal handler for that signal to the default handler. Thus, we re-assign the signal handler immediately when entering the handler function. Otherwise, the next time this signal is received, the process will exit (default behavior for INT signals). Even on systems that do not behave in this way, it still won't hurt, so adding this line always is a good idea.

Pre-defined Signal Handlers

For our convenience, there are two pre-defined signal handler functions that we can use, instead of writing our own: SIG_IGN and SIG_DFL.

```
SIG_IGN
```

Causes the process to ignore the specified signal. For example, in order to ignore Ctrl-C completely (useful for programs that must NOT be interrupted in the middle, or in critical sections), write this :

```c
signal (SIGINT, SIG_IGN);
```

SIG_DFL

Causes the system to set the default signal handler for the given signal (i.e. the same handler the system would have assigned for the signal when the process started running):

```
signal(SIGTSTP, SIG_DFL);
```

Exampe 3

This exaple is used to demonstrate signal SIGSEGV. As explained earlier, when we try to access memory which is not allocated SIGSEGV is raised. In this program, a handler is written and is registered as signal handler for this signal using signal() system call. This will be executed.

```
void sig_mem(int signo)
{
printf("You are accessing memory which is not
        allocated to you\n");
}

#include <stdio.h>
#include <signal.h>
#include <unistd.h>

void main()
{
int X;

signal(SIGSEGV,sig_mem);

scanf("%d", X);

}
```

Example 4

```
#include <signal.h>
#include <unistd.h>
#include <stdio.h>

void xyz(int n)
{
  printf("Hello: %d\n",getpid());
  signal(2,SIG_DFL);
}
```

```
int main()
{
  signal(2,xyz);
      fork();
  while(1); /*busy wait */
  return 0;
}
```

This example is to explain about signal handlers and `fork()` system calls. The child process inherits all the system handlers also. Thus, while running this program if we press ^c we get "Hello" message two times: once from parent and next from child. Also, when we press next time ^c the process will be terminated as we are making the handler as SIG_DFL in signal system call.

Example 5

```
#include <signal.h>
#include <unistd.h>

void xyz(int n)
{
  printf("Hello: %d\n",getpid());
  signal(2,xyz);
}
void pqr(int n)
{
  printf("From pqr: %d\n",getpid());
}
int main()
{
  signal(2,xyz);   // 2 for <ctrl>+c
  if(fork()==0)
{
  signal(2,pqr);
  kill(0,2);
}
  while(1);
  return 0;
}
```

In this program, a signal handler is defined for SIGINT before fork. However, in the child process, `pqr()` is made as the signal handler. By calling the `kill()` with first argument as 0, we are sending SIGINT to all processes whose process groupid is same as child. Thus, child and parent also receives the signal. However, when child receives the signal, it executes `pqr()` function, whereas parent executes `xyz()`.

Example 6

Program shows a simple signal handler that catches either of the two user defined signals and prints the signal number.

```c
#include <stdio.h>
#include <unistd.h>
#include <signal.h>

static void sig_usr(int signo)
{
   if (signo == SIGUSR1)
     printf("Recieved SIGUSR1\n");
   else if (signo == SIGUSR2)
     printf("received SIGUSR\n");
   else
   {
     printf("Received signal %d\n",signo);
     exit();
   }
}

int main()
{
   if (signal(SIGUSR1, sig_usr) == SIG_ERR)
   {
     perror("SIGUSR1");
     return -1;
   }
   if (signal(SIGUSR2, sig_usr) == SIG_ERR)
   {
     perror("SIGUSR2");
     return -1;
   }
   for(;;)
   pause();
return 0;
}
```

Run the above program in background and the following command at the shell prompt to send userdefined signals to this process.

```
kill -USR1 PID (of the above program)
kill -USR2 PID (of the above program)
```

Example 7

The following program runs for approximately ten seconds of wall-clock time. Here, with the help of SIGALRM and signal call we are making a process to sleep for ten seconds.

```c
#include <unistd.h>

void main()
{
   alarm(10);
   while(1);
}
```

Example 8

```c
#include <unistd.h>
#include <stdio.h>
#include <signal.h>
#include <stdlib.h>
#include <sys/wait.h>

volatile int child_res;
pid_t p;

void handle_child(int sig)
{
   printf("got sig: %d\n", sig);
   p = wait(&child_res);
}

int main(int argc, char **argv)
{
   int res;
   int r;
   int child_randmod = 10;
   int parent_randmod = 10;

   p = -1;

   if(argc > 1)
{
   parent_randmod = child_randmod = atoi(argv[1]);
}
```

```c
if(argc > 2)
{
  child_randmod = atoi(argv[2]);
}

signal(SIGCHLD, handle_child);

srand(getpid());
res = fork();

switch(res)
{
  case -1:
    perror("fork");
    exit(1);
    break;

  case 0:
    printf("I'm the kid, my name is: %d, my parent is: %d\n",
        (int)getpid(),
        (int)getppid());
    r = rand()% child_randmod;
    printf("sleeping for: %d\n", r);
    sleep(r);
    exit(r);
    break;

  default:
    printf("I'm the parent, my name is: %d, I have a
            kid: %d\n",
        (int)getpid(),
        res);
    break;
}

rand();
r = rand()% parent_randmod;
printf("sleeping for: %d\n", r);
sleep(r);

if(p != -1)
```

```c
{
  printf("got res: %d(%d) from %d\n", child_res,
          WEXITSTATUS(child_res), (int)p);
}
else
{
  printf("child did not return :-(\n");
}

return 0;
}
```

Example 9

```c
#include <signal.h>
#include <stdio.h>
#include <unistd.h>
static volatile int last_sig = 0;

void generic_sig_handler(int sig)
{
  last_sig = sig;
}

int main( int argc, char **argv )
{
  signal(SIGINT, generic_sig_handler);
  signal(SIGHUP, generic_sig_handler);

for(;;)
{
  if(last_sig != 0)
  {
    printf("received signal %d\n", last_sig);
    last_sig = 0;
  }

  fprintf(stderr, ".");
  sleep(1);
}

return 0;
}
```

The above program prints 2 whenever we press `^c` (SIGINT). Similarly, it may print the signal number of the signal SIGHUP whenever it receives the SIGHUP.

SIGHUP is a signal that means, by convention, "the terminal line got hung up". It has nothing to do with parent processes, and is usually generated by the tty driver (and delivered to the foreground process group).

However, as part of the session management system, there are exactly two cases where SIGHUP is sent on the death of a process:

- When the process that dies is the session leader of a session that is attached to a terminal device, SIGHUP is sent to all processes in the foreground process group of that terminal device.

- When the death of a process causes a process group to become orphaned, and one or more processes in the orphaned group are *stopped*, then SIGHUP and SIGCONT are sent to all members of the orphaned group. (An orphaned process group is one where no process in the group has a parent which is part of the same session, but not the same process group.)

Avoiding Signal Races - Masking Signals

One of the nasty problems that might occur when handling a signal, is the occurrence of a second signal while the signal handler function executes. Such a signal might be of a different type than the one being handled, or even of the same type. Thus, we should take some precautions inside the signal handler function, to avoid races.

Luckily, the system also contains some features that will allow us to block signals from being processed. These can be used in two 'contexts' - a global context which affects all signal handlers, or a per-signal type context - that only affects the signal handler for a specific signal type.

Reliable Signal Handling

Handling signals using `signal()` system call is said to be unreliable way of handling as there is chance of loosing the signals especially during some critical junctures. For example, as mentioned earlier in some Unix systems, signal handler will be reset to default once after executing the signal handler. However, in order to make a function a default signal handler, we will call `signal()` function in the handler itself to re-register the signal handler. The problem with this solution is that if another time same signal arrives when its signal handler is running there is a possibility of taking default handler or the registered ones. This is the unreliability. With the help of reliable way handling signals, we can take care of this situation.

Signal sets

Signal sets are data types (structures) to represent multiple signals. The following functions are used to manipulate them.

```
int sigemptyset(sigset_t *set);
```

This function initializes the signal set pointed by set variable such that it contains no signals in it.

```
int sigfillset(segset_t *set);
```

This function fills the signal set pointed by set variable such that it contains all signals in it.

```
int sigaddset(segset_t *set,int signo);
```

This function adds a signal (with signal number `signo`) to the signal set pointed by set variable.

```
int sigdelset(segset_t *set,int signo);
```

This function removes a signal (with signal number `signo`) from the signal set pointed by set variable.

```
int issigmember(segset_t *set,int signo);
```

This function checks a signal (with signal number `signo`) is in the signal set pointed by set variable or not.

```
int sigpending(sigset_t *set);
```

This function returns the set of signals that are blocked from delivery and currently pending to the signal set pointed by set variable.

```
int sigsuspend(sigset_t *set);
```

This function sets the signal mask of the process to the signal set pointed by set variable. Also, the process is suspended until a signal is caught or until a signal occurs that terminates the process.

Masking signals with sigprocmask()

The (modern) "POSIX" function used to mask signals in the global context, is the sigprocmask() system call. It allows us to specify a set of signals to block, and returns the list of signals that were previously blocked. This is useful when we'll want to restore the previous masking state once we're done with our critical section.

Note : *Each process on a unix system has its own signals mask, which is used by the operating system to specify which signals should be delivered to the process, and which should be blocked. The sigprocmask system call is used to take a signals mask we created in user space, and update the one in stored in the kernel, using this user-space mask. The mask stored in the kernel is the one later considered by the operating system, when deciding whether to deliver a signal to the process, or block it.*

sigprocmask(int how, const sigset_t *set , sigset_t *oldset);

```
int how
```

defines if we want to add signals to the current process's mask (SIG_BLOCK), remove them from the current mask (SIG_UNBLOCK), or completely replace the current mask with the new mask (SIG_SETMASK).

```
const sigset_t *set
```

The set of signals to be blocked, or to be added to the current mask, or removed from the current mask (depending on the 'how' parameter).

```
sigset_t *oldset
```

If this parameter is not NULL, then it'll contain the previous mask. We can later use this set to restore the situation back to how it was before we called sigprocmask().

Note : Older systems do not support the *sigprocmask()* system call. Instead, one should use the *sigmask()* and *sigsetmask()* system calls. If you have such an operating system handy, please read the manual pages for these system calls. They are simpler to use than sigprocmask, so it shouldn't be too hard understanding them once you've read this section.

int sigaction(int signo, const struct sigaction *act, struct sigaction *oact);

The sigaction function allows us to examine or modify the action associated with a particular signal. That is, it supercedes `signal()` system call decribed in unreliable signal handling.

signo It is the signal number for which handler is defining or examining or modifying.

act If it is null we are modifying the action for the signal.

oact If it is non-null the system returns the previous action for the signal to this variable.

```
struct sigaction{
   void (*sa_handler)();   /*pointer to function or SIG_DFL
                           or SIG_IGN*/
```

```
sigset_t sa_mask/          /* additional signal to be
                              blocked during
                              execution of hander*/
int sa_flags;              /*special flags and options*/
}
```

See the following code fragments to know the use of the above functions.

```
/* define a new mask set */
sigset_t mask_set;

/* first clear the set (i.e. make it contain no signal numbers) */

sigemptyset(&mask_set);

/* lets add the TSTP and INT signals to our mask set */
sigaddset(&mask_set, SIGTSTP);
sigaddset(&mask_set, SIGINT);

/* and just for fun, lets remove the TSTP signal from the set. */
sigdelset(&mask_set, SIGTSTP);

/* finally, lets check if the INT signal is defined in our set */
if (sigismember(&mask_set, SIGINT)
   printf("signal INT is in our set\n");
else
   printf("signal INT is not in our set - how strange...\n");

/* finally, lets make the set contain ALL signals
   available on our system */
   sigfillset(&mask_set)
```

Now that we know all these little secrets, lets see a short code example that counts the number of Ctrl-C signals a user has hit, and on the 5th time (note - this number was "Stolen" from some quite famous Unix program) asks the user if they really want to exit. Further more, if the user hits Ctrl-Z, the number of Ctrl-C presses is printed on the screen.

```
/* first, define the Ctrl-C counter, initialize it with zero. */

int ctrl_c_count = 0;
#define CTRL_C_THRESHOLD 5

/* the Ctrl-C signal handler */
void catch_int(int sig_num)
```

```c
{
  sigset_t mask_set;  /* used to set a signal masking set. */
  sigset_t old_set;   /* used to store the old mask set.   */

  /* re-set the signal handler again to catch_int, for next time */
  signal(SIGINT, catch_int);

  /* mask any further signals while we're inside the handler. */
  sigfillset(&mask_set);
  sigprocmask(SIG_SETMASK, &mask_set, &old_set);

  /* increase count, and check if threshold was reached */
  ctrl_c_count++;
  if (ctrl_c_count >= CTRL_C_THRESHOLD) {
  char answer[30];

  /* prompt the user to tell us if to really exit or not */
  printf("\nRealy Exit? [y/N]: ");
  fflush(stdout);
  gets(answer);
  if (answer[0] == 'y' || answer[0] == 'Y') {
     printf("\nExiting...\n");
     fflush(stdout);
      exit(0);
}
else {
        printf("\nContinuing\n");
        fflush(stdout);
        /* reset Ctrl-C counter */
        ctrl_c_count = 0;
     }
  }
/* no need to restore the old signal mask-this
   is done automatically,*/
/* by the operating system, when a signal handler
   returns. */
  }

/* the Ctrl-Z signal handler */
void catch_suspend(int sig_num)
{
  sigset_t mask_set;  /* used to set a signal masking set. */
  sigset_t old_set;   /* used to store the old mask set. */
```

```
    /* re-set the signal handler again to catch_suspend,
       for next time */
    signal(SIGTSTP, catch_suspend);

    /* mask any further signals while we're inside the handler. */
    sigfillset(&mask_set);
    sigprocmask(SIG_SETMASK, &mask_set, &old_set);

    /* print the current Ctrl-C counter */
       printf("\n\nSo far, '%d' Ctrl-C presses were counted\n\n",
                         ctrl_c_count);
    fflush(stdout);

    /* no need to restore the old signal mask-this
       is done automatically, */{{/COMMENT_FONT}}*/
    /* by the operating system, when a signal handler
       returns. */{{/COMMENT_FONT}}*/
}

    /* and somewhere inside the main function... */

    /* set the Ctrl-C and Ctrl-Z signal handlers */
    signal(SIGINT, catch_int);
    signal(SIGTSTP, catch_suspend);
    .
    /* and then the rest of the program */
    .
```

Example 10

The complete source code for this program is given below.

You should note that using `sigprocmask()` the way we did now does not resolve all possible race conditions. For example, it is possible that after we entered the signal handler, but before we managed to call the `sigprocmask()` system call, we receive another signal, which WILL be called. Thus, if the user is VERY quick (or the system is very slow), it is possible to get into races. In our current functions, this will probably not disturb the flow, but there might be cases where this kind of race could cause problems.

The way to guarantee no races at all, is to let the system set the signal masking for us before it calls the signal handler. This can be done if we use the sigaction() system call to define both the signal handler function AND the signal mask to be used when the handler is executed.

One final note - signal handling for processes is done quite differently than it is done for threads. With threads, the situation is more complicated (e.g. signals masked by one thread could still be sent to another thread). How signals are handled for threads, is out of the scope of this tutorial.

```c
#include <stdio.h>     /*standard I/O functions */
#include <unistd.h>  /* standard unix functions, like getpid()*/
#include <signal.h> /*  signal name macros, and the
                           signal() prototype */

/* first, define the Ctrl-C counter, initialize it with zero.*/
int ctrl_c_count = 0;
#defineCTRL_C_THRESHOLD 15

/* the Ctrl-C signal handler */
void catch_int(int sig_num)
{
   sigset_t mask_set; /* used to set a signal masking set. */
   sigset_t old_set;  /* used to store the old mask set. */


/* re-set the signal handler again to catch_int, for next time */
signal(SIGINT, catch_int);

/* mask any further signals while we're inside the handler. */
sigfillset(&mask_set);
sigprocmask(SIG_SETMASK, &mask_set, &old_set);

/* increase count, and check if threshold was reached */
ctrl_c_count++;
if (ctrl_c_count >= CTRL_C_THRESHOLD) {
char answer[30];

/* prompt the user to tell us if to really exit or not */
printf("\nRealy Exit? [y/N]: ");
fflush(stdout);
fgets(answer, sizeof(answer), stdin);
if (answer[0] == 'y' || answer[0] == 'Y') {
    printf("\nExiting...\n");
    fflush(stdout);
    exit(0);
}
```

```c
else {
        printf("\nContinuing\n");
        fflush(stdout);

        /* reset Ctrl-C counter */
        ctrl_c_count = 0;
    }
}
/* no need to restore the old signal mask - this is
   done automatically, */
/* by the operating system, when a signal handler
   returns. */
}


/* the Ctrl-Z signal handler */
void catch_suspend(int sig_num)
{
   sigset_t mask_set; /* used to set a signal masking set. */
   sigset_t old_set;   /* used to store the old mask set.   */

   /* re-set the signal handler again to catch_suspend,
      for next time */
   signal(SIGTSTP, catch_suspend);

   /* mask any further signals while we're inside the
      handler. */
   sigfillset(&mask_set);
   sigprocmask(SIG_SETMASK, &mask_set, &old_set);

   /* print the current Ctrl-C counter */
   printf("\n\nSo far, '%d' Ctrl-C presses were
          counted\n\n", ctrl_c_count);
   fflush(stdout);

   /* no need to restore the old signal mask - this
      is done automatically, */
   /* by the operating system, when a signal handler
      returns. */
}


int main(int argc, char* argv[])
```

```
{
  /* set the Ctrl-C and Ctrl-Z signal handlers */
  signal(SIGINT, catch_int);
  signal(SIGTSTP, catch_suspend);

  /* enter an infinite loop of waiting for signals */
  for ( ;; )
    pause();

  return 0;
}
```

Catching and Ignoring Signals in Reliable Signal Handling

The following code segment illustrates how to use sigaction to install a handler for SIGINT.

```
#include <signal.h>
#include <stdio.h>
struct sigaction newact;

newact.sa_handler = mysighand;  /*set the new handler*/
sigemptyset(&newact.sa_mask);   /*no other signals blocked*/
newact.sa_flags=0;              /*no special options*/
if(sigaction(SIGINT, &newact, NULL) ==-1)
  perror("could not install SIGINT signal handler");
```

Waiting for Signals

One reason for using signals is to avoid **busy waiting**. Busy waiting means that CPU cycles are continuously used to wait for an event (i.e. a big while loop). A more efficient method is to suspend the process until the waited for event occurs. UNIX provides two functions that allow a process to suspend itself until a signal occurs; pause and sigsuspend.

pause suspends the calling process until a signal that is not being ignored is delivered to the process. If a signal is caught by the process, the pause returns after the signal handler returns. The pause function always returns –1.

```
#include <unistd.h>
int pause(void);
```

The following code segment causes a process to wait for a particular signal with pause by having the signal handler set the signal_received variable to 1. Initially, this variable is zero. This example uses a loop because the pause returns when any signal is delivered to the process. If the signal was not the right one, then signal_received is still 0 and the loop calls pause again.

```
#include <unistd.h>
int signal_received=0;

while(signal_received==0) pause();
```

Note that if a signal is delivered between the testing of `signal_received` and `pause`, then `pause` will not catch that signal and return from it.

The following example is a negative example showing an incorrect approach to solving the preceding problem found in our example above.

```
#include <unistd.h>
#include <signal.h>
int signal_received=0;

sig_set_t sigset;
int signum;

sigemptyset(&sigset);
sigaddset(&sigset,signum);
sigprocmask(SIG_BLOCK,&sigset, NULL);
while(signal_received==0) pause();
```

The preceding program executes the `pause` while the signal is blocked. As a result the program never receives the signal and `pause` never returns. The only way to fix this is to have the program unblock the signal before executing pause. However, we might still receive a signal between the unblocking and pause command, so that our problem persists.

Basically, there is no way around this problem using `pause`. The actions of unblocking the signal and pausing must be done **atomically**, i.e. in one logically indivisible unit. This requires a new system function `sigsuspend`.

```
#include <signal.h>
int sigsuspend(const sigset_t *sigmask);
```

The `sigsuspend` functions set the signal mask to the one pointed to by `sigmask` and suspends until a signal is delivered to the process. The sigmask can be used to unblock the signal the program is looking for. When `sigsuspend` returns, the signal mask is reset to the value it had before the `sigsuspend`. The following code segment suspends a process until the signal given by the value of `signum` occurs. It then restores the original signal mask.

```
#include <signal.h>
int signal_received=0;

sigset_t sigset;
sigset_t sigoldmask;
int signum;
```

```
sigprocmask(SIG_SETMASK, NULL, &sigoldmask);
sigprocmask(SIG_SETMASK, NULL, &sigset);
sigaddset(&sigset, signum);
sigprocmask(SIG_BLOCK, &sigset, NULL);

sigdelset(&sigset, signum);

while(signal_received==0) sigsuspend(&sigset);
sigprocmask(SIG_SETMASK, &sigoldmask, NULL);
```

Implementing Timers Using Signals

One of the weak aspects of Unix-like operating systems is their lack of proper support for timers. Timers are important to allow one to check timeouts (e.g. wait for user input up to 30 seconds, or exit), check some conditions on a regular basis (e.g. check every 30 seconds that a server we're talking to is still active, or close the connection and notify the user about the problem), and so on. There are various ways to get around the problem for programs that use an "event loop" based on the select() system call (or its new replacement, the poll() system call), but not all programs work that way, and this method is too complex for short and simple programs.

Yet, the operating system gives us a simple way of setting up timers that don't require too much hassles, by using special alarm signals. They are generally limited to one timer active at a time, but that will suffice in simple cases.

The alarm() System Call

The alarm() system call is used to ask the system to send our process a special signal, named ALRM, after a given number of seconds. Since Unix-like systems don't operate as real-time systems, your process might receive this signal after a longer time than requested. Combining this system call with a proper signal handler enables us to do some simple tricks. Lets see an example of a program that waits for user input, but exits if none was given after a certain timeout.

```
#include <unistd.h>   /* standard unix functions, like alarm()*/
#include <signal.h> /* signal name macros, and the
                          signal() prototype */

char user[40];   /* buffer to read user name from the user */

/* define an alarm signal handler. */
void catch_alarm(int sig_num)
{
    printf("Operation timed out. Exiting...\n\n");
    exit(0);
}
```

```
/* and inside the main program... */

/* set a signal handler for ALRM signals */
signal(SIGALRM, catch_alarm);

/* prompt the user for input */
printf("Username: ");
fflush(stdout);
/* start a 30 seconds alarm */
alarm(30);
/* wait for user input */
gets(user);
/* remove the timer, now that we've got the user's input */
alarm(0);
.

.
/* do something with the received user name */
.

.
```

Example 11

The complete source code for this program is as follows.

As you can see, we start the timer right before waiting for user input. If we started it earlier, we'll be giving the user less time than promised to perform the operation. We also stop the timer right after getting the user's input, before doing any tests or processing of the input, to avoid a random timer from setting off due to slow processing of the input. Many bugs that occur using the alarm() system call occur due to forgetting to set off the timer at various places when the code gets complicated. If you need to make some tests during the input phase, put the whole piece of code in a function, so it'll be easier to make sure that the timer is always set off after calling the function. Here is an example of how NOT to do this:

```
#include <stdio.h>  /* standard I/O functions */
#include <unistd.h> /* standard unix functions, like alarm()*/
#include <signal.h>  /* signal name macros, and the
                               signal() prototype */

char user[40];   /* buffer to read user name from the user */

/* define an alarm signal handler. */
void catch_alarm(int sig_num)
```

```c
{
  printf("Operation timed out. Exiting...\n\n");
  exit(0);
}

int main(int argc, char* argv[])
{
/* set a signal handler for ALRM signals */
signal(SIGALRM, catch_alarm);

/* prompt the user for input */
printf("Username: ");
fflush(stdout);
/* start a 30 seconds alarm */
alarm(30);
/* wait for user input */
gets(user);
/* remove the timer, now that we've got the user's input */
alarm(0);

printf("User name: '%s'\n", user);

return 0;
}

int read_user_name(char user[])
{
  int ok_len;
  int result = 0; /* assume failure */

/* set an alarm to timeout the input operation */
alarm(3); /* Mistake 1 */
printf("Enter user name: "); /* Mistake 2 */
fflush(stdout);
if (gets(user) == NULL) {
  printf("End of input received.\n");
  return 0;    /* Mistake 3 */
}
/* count the size of prefix of 'user' made only of characters */
/* in the given set. if all characters in 'user' are in the   */
/* set, then ok_len will be equal to the length of 'user'. */
ok_len = strspn(user, "abcdefghijklmnopqrstuvwxyz0123456789");
if (ok_len == strlen(user)) {
```

```
/* check if the user exists in our database */
result = find_user_in_database(user); /* Mistake 4 */
}
alarm(0);

return result;
}
```

Lets count the mistakes and bad programming practices in the above function :

1. *Too short timeout :* 3 seconds might be enough for superman to type his user name, but a normal user obviously needs more time. Such a timeout should actually be tunable, because not all people type at the same pace, or should be long enough for even the slowest of users.

2. *Printing while timer is ticking :* This printing should have been done before starting up the timer. Printing may be a time consuming operation, and thus will leave less time than expected for the user to type in the expected input.

3. *Exiting function without turning off timer :* This kind of mistake is hard to catch. It will cause the program to randomly exit somewhere LATER during the execution. If we'll trace it with a debugger, we'll see that the signal was received while we were already executing a completely different part of the program, leaving us scratching our head and looking up to the sky, hoping somehow inspiration will fall from there to guide us to the location of the problem.

4. *Making long checks before turning off timer :* As if it's not enough that we gave the poor user a short time to check for the input, we're also inserting some database checking operation while the timer is still ticking. Even if we also want to timeout the database operation, we should probably set up a different timer (and a different ALRM signal handler), so as not to confuse a slow user with a slow database server. It will also allow the user to know why we are timing out. Without this information, a person trying to figure out why the program suddenly exits, will have hard time finding where the fault lies.

"Do" and "Don't" inside A Signal Handler

- *Make it short* – the signal handler should be a short function that returns quickly. Instead of doing complex operations inside the signal handler, it is better that the function will raise a flag (e.g. a global variable, although these are evil by themselves) and have the main program check that flag occasionally.

- *Proper Signal Masking* – don't be too lazy to define proper signal masking for a signal handler, preferably using the sigaction() system call. It takes a little more effort than just using the signal() system call, but it'll help you sleep better at night, knowing that you haven't left an extra place for race conditions to occur. Remember if some bug has a probability of 1/10,000 to occur, it WILL occur when many people use that program many times, as tends to be the case with good programs (you write only good programs, no?).

- *Careful with "fault" signals* – If you catch signals that indicate a program bug (SIGBUS, SIGSEGV, SIGFPE), don't try to be too smart and let the program continue, unless you know exactly what you are doing (which is a very rare case) - just do the minimal required cleanup, and exit, preferably with a core dump (using the abort() function). Such signals usually indicate a bug in the program, that if ignored will most likely cause it to crush sooner or later, making you think the problem is somewhere else in the code.

- *Careful with timers* – when you use timers, remember that you can only use one timer at a time, unless you also (ab)use the VTALRM signal. If you need to have more than one timer active at a time, don't use signals, or devise a set of functions that will allow you to have several virtual timers using a delta list of some sort. If you've no idea what I'm talking about, you probably don't need several simultaneous timers in the first place.

- *Signals are NOT an event driven framework* – it is easy to get carried away and try turning the signals system into an event-driven driver for a program, but signal handling functions were not meant for that. If you need such a thing, use some framework that is more suitable for the application (e.g. use an event loop of a windowing program, use a select-based loop inside a network server, etc.).

Example 12

This example is used to explain about critical section problems in classical OS's. Here, before entering to the critical section a set of signals are blocked. Run the program and give it SIGINTs (CNTRL-C) and notice that the critical section is undaunted. After leaving the critical section all the signals which are blocked are restored.

```
#include <unistd.h>
#include <stdio.h>
#include <signal.h>
#include <errno.h>

char* sMessage = "I got a signal!\n";

int criticalSection( void )
{
    char buf[BUFSIZ];
    printf("starting critical section\n");
```

```c
   printf("input text: ");
   fgets(buf, BUFSIZ, stdin);
   printf("your text: %s\n", buf);
   printf("critical section done\n");
   return 0;
}

void sigHandler( int sig )
{
// write is okay, printf is not
write(1, sMessage, 16);
}

int main( int argc, char **argv )
{
   sigset_t newSignals;
   sigset_t oldSignals;
   struct sigaction newAction;

   printf("starting\n");

   printf("my pid is: %d\n", (int)getpid() );

   // install handler for INT
   sigemptyset(&(newAction.sa_mask));
   newAction.sa_handler = sigHandler;
   newAction.sa_flags = 0;
   sigaction(SIGINT, &newAction, NULL);

   // create our set, never block FPE, ILL, or SEGV
   sigfillset(&newSignals);
   sigdelset(&newSignals, SIGFPE);
   sigdelset(&newSignals, SIGILL);
   sigdelset(&newSignals, SIGSEGV);

   sleep( 20 );

   // block signals
   sigprocmask(SIG_BLOCK, &newSignals, &oldSignals);

   criticalSection();
   // restore the mask to it's previous state
   sigprocmask(SIG_SETMASK, &oldSignals, NULL);
```

```
    // unblock signals
    sigprocmask(SIG_UNBLOCK, &newSignals, NULL);

    sleep( 20 );

    printf("done\n");

    return 0;
}
```

Example 13

This example is used to demonstrate how we can catch SIGCHLD signal.

```
#include <sys/types.h>  /* include this before any
                               other sys headers */
#include <sys/wait.h>   /* header for waitpid()
                               and various macros */
#include <signal.h>     /* header for signal functions */
#include <stdio.h>      /* header for fprintf() */
#include <unistd.h>     /* header for fork() */

void sig_chld(int);   /* prototype for our SIGCHLD handler */

int main()
{
  struct sigaction act;
  pid_t pid;

  /* Assign sig_chld as our SIGCHLD handler */
  act.sa_handler = sig_chld;

  /* We don't want to block any other signals in this example */
  sigemptyset(&act.sa_mask);
  /*
  * We're only interested in children that have
     terminated, not ones
  * which have been stopped (eg user pressing control-Z
     at terminal)
  */
  act.sa_flags = SA_NOCLDSTOP;
```

```c
    /*
     * Make these values effective. If we were writing a real
     * application, we would probably save the old
        value instead of
     * passing NULL.
    */
    if (sigaction(SIGCHLD, &act, NULL) < 0)
    {
      fprintf(stderr, "sigaction failed\n");
      return 1;
    }

    /* Fork */
      switch (pid = fork())
      {
        case -1:
        fprintf(stderr, "fork failed\n");
        return 1;

        case 0:      /* child — finish straight away */
        _exit(7);    /* exit status = 7 */

        default:        /* parent */
        sleep(10);   /* give child time to finish */
      }

    return 0;
    }

/*
* The signal handler function — only gets called when a SIGCHLD
* is received, ie when a child terminates
*/
void sig_chld(int signo)
{
int status, child_val;

/* Wait for any child without blocking */
if (waitpid(-1, &status, WNOHANG) < 0)
{
/*
* calling standard I/O functions like fprintf() in a
* signal handler is not recommended, but probably OK
* in toy programs like this one.
*/
```

```
    fprintf(stderr, "waitpid failed\n");
    return;
    }


    /*
    * We now have the info in 'status' and can
       manipulate it using
    * the macros in wait.h.
    */
    if (WIFEXITED(status))   /* did child exit normally? */
    {
    child_val = WEXITSTATUS(status); /* get child's
                                        exit status */
    printf("child's exited normally with status %d\n", child_val);
    }
}
```

How can I kill all descendents of a process?

There isn't a fully general approach to doing this. While you can determine the relationships between processes by parsing `ps` output, this is unreliable in that it represents only a snapshot of the system.

However, if you're launching a subprocess that might spawn further subprocesses of its own, and you want to be able to kill the entire spawned job at one go, the solution is to put the subprocess into a new process group, and kill that process group if you need to.

The preferred function for creating process groups is `setpgid()`. Use this if possible rather than `setpgrp()` because the latter differs between systems (on some systems `setpgrp();` is equivalent to `setpgid(0,0);`, on others, `setpgrp()` and `setpgid()` are identical).

Putting a subprocess into its own process group has a number of effects. In particular, unless you explicitly place the new process group in the foreground, it will be treated as a background job with these consequences:

- it will be stopped with `SIGTTIN` if it attempts to read from the terminal
- if `tostop` is set in the terminal modes, it will be stopped with SIGTTOU if it attempts to write to the terminal (attempting to change the terminal modes should also cause this, independently of the current setting of `tostop`)
- The subprocess will not receive keyboard signals from the terminal (e.g. `SIGINT` or `SIGQUIT`)

In many applications input and output will be redirected anyway, so the most significant effect will be the lack of keyboard signals. The parent application should arrange to catch at least `SIGINT` and `SIGQUIT` (and preferably `SIGTERM` as well) and clean up any background jobs as necessary.

Given a pid, how can I tell whether it's a running program ?

```
Use kill() with 0 for the signal number.
```

There are four possible results from this call :

- `kill()` returns 0 – this implies that a process exists with the given PID, and the system would allow you to send signals to it. It is system-dependent whether the process could be a zombie.

- `kill()` returns -1, `errno == ESRCH` – either no process exists with the given PID, or security enhancements are causing the system to deny its existence. (On some systems, the process could be a zombie.)

- `kill()` returns -1, `errno == EPERM` – the system would not allow you to kill the specified process. This means that either the process exists (again, it could be a zombie) or draconian security enhancements are present (e.g. your process is not allowed to send signals to anybody).

- `kill()` returns -1, with some other value of `errno` you are in trouble!

The most-used technique is to assume that success or failure with `EPERM` implies that the process exists, and any other error implies that it doesn't.

An alternative exists, if you are writing specifically for a system (or all those systems) that provide a '`/proc`' filesystem : checking for the existence of '`/proc/PID`' may work.

Conclusions

This chapter deals with handling signals both in reliable and unreliable manner. First, signals and their source of arrivals are high lighted with live examples related SIGSEGV, SIGABRT, SIGALRM. Also, we have discussed about how child processes will inherit signals from their parent. Signalmask, signalprocmask(), sigpending() functions are described in detail with easy examples.

Questions

1. Write a program which shows how a child process pauses, waiting for a signal (SIGINT) from the parent which when received responds by sending the paused parent a signal(SIGINT). Both in parent and child prcoess's register separate signal handlers which may display from in which process signal handler is running.

2. Write a program which when started calls signal() system call from ignore ^c, ^d and ^\ and then loads the shell (bash) through execl() function. Check whether new shell really ignores them or not.

3. Repeat the above program while remapping the ^c, ^d and ^\ from some other keys.

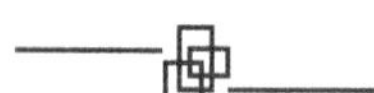

17   Unix Memory Management

Unix operating system uses virtual memory management. To allow a program to access more memory than might be physically installed in the machine, most modern operating systems including all Unix variants employs this concept. Virtual memory works by the operating system (in tight cooperation with the CPU) by mapping virtual addresses used by a process, into physical addresses. When a process allocates a new block of memory, the operating system assigns this block to some section (called 'page') of physical memory, using a virtual memory translation table. Each access to a memory location by the process is translated to access to the matching physical memory page. In order to avoid slowing down the program, this translation is done directly by the CPU.

Memory Protection

The operating system uses a translation table to map virtual memory to physical memory. Taking this a further step, the system can use a different translation table for each process, thereby giving each process its own address space. This means that the same virtual memory address used by two different processes, will be mapped into two different physical memory addresses. This means that one process cannot access the contents of the memory used by the other process, and thus one process corrupting its memory won't interfere with the contents of the memory of any other process in the system. This feature is known as "memory protection", and is used now by most operating systems (including all Unix variants).

Run-time Management Of Virtual Memory

Some of the virtual memory sections might be mapped to no physical memory page. When a process tries to access a memory cell in such a section, the CPU identifies a page fault, and invokes an operating system routine that needs to handle this fault. Most operating systems use this feature to store part of the virtual memory sections on disk, rather than in RAM, thereby allowing the program to use an address space larger than the physical RAM of the machine. When a page fault occurs, the operating system loads the contents of the faulted virtual memory section from the disk, copies it into a free physical memory page, and updates the virtual memory translation table so the CPU will know to map the virtual memory section to the new physical RAM page.

During the search for a free page, it might be that no free page is found. In such case, the operating system takes the contents of a busy physical memory page, copies it to the hard disk, and uses this memory page to load the data of the desired virtual memory section. The virtual memory section that was previously mapped to this physical memory page, is now marked as paged out.

As you can see from this, the algorithm used to decide which memory page should be taken when there are no free pages, has to be efficient. With a bad algorithm, a process that accesses two virtual memory sections alternately, might cause the system to keep paging these sections in and out. Since access to the disk is much slower than access to RAM, this will slow down the system tremendously. A common algorithm used to find candidates for paging out is called LRU - Least Recently Used. In this algorithm, the memory page that was used least recently, is the page that will have its contents paged out. This algorithm works well due to the locality principle - if a process accessed a given memory page, it is likely to access this same page or one near it on the next instruction.

Signals : SIGSEGV & SIGBUS

We saw that some virtual memory sections aren't mapped to physical memory. While some of them were simply paged out, others were never allocated by the process. When a process runs, its virtual memory table is small. As it allocates more memory pages, the table grows. However, if the process tries to access a virtual memory address of a section it hasn't allocated yet, the operating system has no where to bring this page from. The designers of the Unix system decided that this situation indicates a program bug, and thus instead of making an automatic allocation of a memory page in such a case, they chose to send a signal to the process. This signal is a SEGV signal (or SIGSEGV), and its default signal handler prints out a "Segmentation violation - core dumped" message, and dumps the memory image of the process into a file named 'core' in the process's current directory (see example in chapter on signals).

Another way to cause a 'segmentation violation' is trying to access an illegal location of virtual memory. Because many invalid pointer problems occur with very low pointer values, the operating system does not allow a process to allocate a memory page for the virtual memory section beginning with the virtual address '0'. This is what causes programs to receive a SEGV signal when trying to de-reference a NULL pointer (NULL on most machine architectures is defined as '0').

Example 1

```
#include<stdio.h>
int main()
{
   char *s;
   s=(char *)0;
   printf("%c\n",  *s);
   return 0;
}
```

The above program gives run time error "segment violation" as memory location 0 is not accessible. When you say " *s", the hardware sees that you want to read memory location zero. It checks with the operating system, which says "I haven't allocated the page containing location zero for you". Thus, this results in a segmentation violation.

Example 2

```
#include<stdio.h>
int main()
{
int x;

scanf("%d", x);
}
```

The above program compiles but gives run time error "segment violation". In this program, we are calling scanf function with x as argument whose value is undefined and we are asking scanf to read an integer from keyboard and store the same in the memory pointed by the value of this variable x. If that memory is not allocated to our program we get this error. By chance if that value refers to an allocated memory then we will not be getting any such error.

What about a BUS (or SIGBUS) signal? this signal is sent to a program that tries to access a non-aligned pointer. For instance, on many machine architectures, access to 'long' (4 byte) numbers must be done using a memory address that divides by 4. Trying to access such an entity using an address that does not abide by this rule will cause the CPU to emit a trap. The operating system's kernel catches this trap, and then sends a BUS signal to the program. The default signal handler for this signal emits a "Bus error - core dumped" message, and dumps the memory contents to a 'core' file, much like the handler for the SEGV signal does.

Load On Demand

As we have seen, the efficiency of virtual memory is based on the locality principle. The same principle can be used when loading programs into memory. There is no point in loading all the executable file during application startup. Large parts of the code are likely not to be ever executed during the process's lifetime. Furthermore, loading all of the code at once will mean it will take more time until the process can start running.

Thus, what Unix systems do, is just allocate the page table entries, and mark the pages as "load on demand". When the process tries to access a virtual memory cell in a page that wasn't loaded yet, a page fault will occur, causing the operating system to load the contents of this specific page into memory. The code part of shared libraries is treated in a similar manner.

This feature, together with some properties of file management could explain the following phenomena: if you have a process executing program file 'foo', and you then compile a new version of 'foo' and copy it on top of the original 'foo' file - the process is likely to crash very quickly. The reason for this is that the process is likely to access a virtual memory cell of a page whose contents were not loaded yet. This will cause the system to load the page from the new binary file - which is most likely different from the original binary file. Thus, the program will be executing a random machine instruction, instead of the machine instruction it was supposed to perform, most likely resulting a process crash.

Example 3

```
#include<stdio.h>
void main()
{
while(1);
}
```

Let this file name be "a.c", the following sequence of commands are executed at the command prompt.

```
gcc  -o  a  a.c
./a&
gcc -o a a.c
```

In the first command, we have compiled a.c and created an executable file "a". The second command starts this program in background. In the third command we are trying to recompile the same program 'a.c'. This may give raise to an error message "**text file busy**" on some Unix systems. The reason is as explained above.

In order to avoid the above scenario, there are several options. One is killing all processes currently executing the program's binary, before updating it. A better method is to rename the old binary file to a new name (e.g. foo.old) and then copy the new binary to 'foo'. This will work, because the name of a file is relevant only when a process tries to open it. After the file was opened, the process accesses it via its disk location (I-node number) - which is different for the old and the new files. Actually, you may even erase the old binary file without renaming it - the file will be removed from the directory, but not from the disk. It will be removed from disk only when all processes keeping it open (e.g. processes executing this binary program file) will close it (or exit). Note that this is NOT true if the binary file is accessed via NFS, only if it is accessed on a local file system. NFS file accesses always use the file name, whether for open operations or for read operations.

Read-Only Memory

Some of the virtual memory space used by a process does not ever need to change during the process's life. This fact can be used to optimize handling of such memory pages by the paging code of the operating system. For example, executable memory pages are read-only pages, and are marked so by the system. Trying to write into them would fail, and generate a CPU trap which will be caught by the operating system, that will send a SEGV signal to the process.

When the system needs to page out read-only code pages of this sort, it doesn't even have to page them out to disk - it already has a copy of them inside the binary executable (or the shared library) they were taken from. Thus, paging these pages out just requires marking them as free.

The process can mark other memory pages as read-only too (see the man page for the mmap() system call, for example). This could be useful to make sure no part of the code tries to modify the contents of that memory - useful for trapping down some bugs.

Shared Memory

Another feature supported by Unix systems is shared memory. Using this feature, virtual memory sections of different processes are marked as shared, and thus point to the same physical memory pages. When one process changes the contents of this memory, the other processes immediately see the new contents. Of course this means that access to this shared memory should be synchronized among the processes sharing it, using some locking mechanism.

Writable memory pages can be shared by processes using various system APIs, such as the System-V shared memory API (see the man page of shmget() and shmat() for details) or using the mmap() system call. Note that a page may be shared between more than 2 processes, and some of these processes might only require read-only access to these shared memory pages.

Read-only shared memory is easier to manage. One place where sharing read-only memory pages comes in very handy is sharing of executable code coming from program binary files and from shared libraries. The system automatically takes care of that-if a process tries to execute a program that is already loaded to memory due to being executed by another process, the memory pages holding the binary code will be mapped to the virtual address space of the new process, and thus overall memory usage of the system would not increase (other than the memory needed to hold the translation table for the new process - this table is not shared between processes). Note that dynamic data won't be shared by processes in this manner, since it is stored to writable memory pages. This is, ofcourse, the expected behavior - you wouldn't want one process changing a variable's contents, affecting another process running the same program, would you?.

Memory Managers

Memory managers are software libraries that perform memory allocation and de-allocation on behalf of the program. Every programming language comes with a runtime environment that includes at least one memory manager. Since the programming languages we deal with tend to be general purpose, the memory manager is also general purpose - it does not assume anything about the pattern of allocations, sizes of memory chunks allocated and the likes. Therefore, it is possible to find an allocation pattern that will cause a given memory allocation to perform poorly. Thus, having an idea regarding how a memory manager works could allow us to write programs that make more efficient use of memory, in terms of speed and of overall memory usage.

Memory Alignment

One property of all memory managers is that they return memory chunks which are aligned best for the architecture of the machine on which they are run. Alignment means that the memory chunks returned to the user begin on an address that divides by the size of a word for the CPU they are running on. This size is often of 4 bytes (for 32 bit architectures) or 8 bytes (for 64 bit architectures). Further, the size of returned chunks is also kept to a multiple of the word size. This ensures that the returned memory blocks can be used to store the largest data type the machine supports (e.g. a long integer).

The price of this mechanism is that often memory is wasted. For example, suppose that I have a machine with a word size of 4 bytes. Further, suppose that I want to store a string whose length is 5 bytes (including the terminating null character, if we're referring to a C language string). The memory manager will give me a memory chunk whose size is 8 bytes (2 words). I use 5 bytes, and 3 are wasted. Thus, general-purpose memory managers cause a lot of memory waste for programs that allocate many small memory chunks. We will discuss methods of overcoming this problem when we discuss specialized memory managers. We will also see how this affects issues with pointers and memory smearing (memory contents corrupting).

Because of the same reason, on most of the systems the following program prints complete string even if its size is declared as 4 bytes.

Example 4

```
#include <stdio.h>
void main()
{
char x[4]="Ramya";
printf("%s\n",x);
}
```

We have claimed that the memory manager begins with one chunk on its list of free memory chunks. This chunk has to be taken from some place - this is the role of the operating system's virtual memory manager. As you remember, the memory the process accesses is actually virtual memory. Also, most virtual memory sections are not mapped anywhere. This is done for efficiency - when a process's virtual address space is of a size of several giga-bytes, it will be wasteful to allocate a map to handle this amount of virtual memory, especially since most processes use a much smaller amount of memory.

The way the operating system handles this situation is by not allocating any memory for the process, unless it asks for it. Of course, the program's binary and shared library sizes can be known in advance, but memory used to store data is of an arbitrary size. When the process requires more memory to store data pages, it uses the `brk()` system call (or `sbrk()`) to ask the system to enlarge its allocated address space. The system then adds entries to the translation map for this process, and the pages themselves will be then mapped into physical memory when they are accessed.

As the program runs, and memory is allocated from the heap using **malloc()**, the heap grows. To figure out the boundary of the heap, we must use **brk()** or **sbrk()**. Both are system calls, and you can read their man pages.

```
caddr_t sbrk(int incr);
```

A caddr_t is a "c address pointer". It is the same as a (**char ***) or a (**void ***).

This specifies for the operating system to give **incr** more bytes to the heap. It returns a pointer to the end of the heap before **sbrk()** was called. Thus, the new end of the heap after an **sbrk()** call is at address

```
sbrk(incr) + incr;
```

If you call sbrk(0), then it returns the current end of the heap.

Now, **malloc()** (and the related programs **realloc()** and **calloc()**) all call **sbrk()** to get the memory to allocate in the heap. They are the only routines that call **sbrk()**. Thus, the only way that you can get memory in the heap is through **malloc()** or **sbrk()**. However, you should use **malloc()**, as it is more efficient.

Actually, the system call interface is hardly ever used by programmers. The memory manager of the runtime environment of our programming language is the one that uses this interface. Thus, whenever it runs out of free memory chunks on its list, it'll call the brk() system call to allocate more memory pages, and add the new block to its chunks list. The amount of memory it will ask the system to allocate can vary. Asking for too small sizes will cause many calls to brk(), which is time consuming. Allocating a too large block will take time for the system to update the virtual translation map for the process.

> ***Note 1 :*** there is usually no system call that can be used to return unused memory back to the operating system. when you free memory, the memory manager cannot return this memory back to the operating system. If this freed memory is never used again, it will eventually be paged out to disk-but won't be freed until the process exits. Thus, the amount of virtual memory used by a process always increases - never decreases.

> ***Note 2 :*** the above rule has an exception-shared memory, and mapped memory. Shared memory is counted as part of the memory space used by the process. Thus, when the process attached to a shared memory chunk, its 'accounted' virtual address space size is increased by the amount of space in the shared memory page. When the process releases a shared memory chunk, the process's 'accounted' virtual address space size is decreased. The same goes for memory mapped using the mmap() system call.

Memory Manager's Interaction With Program's Code

As we have seen, the memory manager keeps its own data structures in the address space of the process for which it works. This means that if the process overwrites memory out of bounds (e.g. referencing a location right before an array it has allocated using the manager) - the data structures of the memory manager itself may be corrupted. This would explain cases where a program we write crashes, and the stack shows it was in a middle of a call to the memory manager's functions.

Note that these kinds of bugs are not always easy to track - the memory corruption might have occurred in a completely different part of the code, and just looking at the functions on the stack and the code they execute often won't help locating the cause of the problem.

The cause of such a problem could be that our program had overwritten a location that had stored the size of a chunk, and thus when it was freed, the memory manager overtook a larger chunk than had originally been allocated. The manager later allocated parts of this chunk for other purposes, and thus we get the same chunk of memory used by different parts of our code for different purposes. Or a bug in our code might cause the list of free memory chunks to be corrupted, causing one of its pointers to contain an invalid value (e.g. pointing outside the process's address space).

C Runtime Memory Management

The C programming language and its runtime environment serve as the basic language used on Unix systems. The runtime environment defines not only how memory is allocated and freed, but also how the process's different pieces of information are layered out in memory. Also, being a language that works on a low level, it allows the programmer a lot of control on how memory is used. This means a lot of power - together with responsibility.

Program Memory Segments

A C program is layered out in memory in several separate segments - code segment, stack segment and data segment. These segments are layered out inside the virtual address space of the process.

The code segment holds the executable code of the program (both coming from the program's binary itself, and any shared libraries it loads). All memory pages of the code segment are marked as read-only, and are shared with any other process using the same program file and/or shared library files.

> ***Note :*** not all pages are shared in this way, due to 'relocation' issues. There are cases when a part of the program needs to know the address of another part, but the exact address will only be known at run-time. This address might be different for different processes (since they load a different set of shared libraries, for example), and thus cannot be written in a shared page. The dynamic loader (which is responsible for handling such situations, among other things) uses "indirect jumps" - it stores non-shared pages that contain these varied addresses in them, and the program's code is compiled in a way that it will read the addresses from these non-shared pages. If this was not done, complete pages of executable code will need to be copied, just to change one or two locations holding such addresses.

The stack segment is used to hold the contents of the stack of the process. The stack size is defined at process startup, and cannot be increased while the process runs. For a multi-threaded process, several stacks will exist in the stack segment.

The data segment occupies the space from the stack segment, to the last address allocated by the process using the `brk()` system call. This segment can grow as the process runs and needs more virtual memory.

Example 5

```
#include <stdio.h>

extern end;
extern etext;

int I;
```

```
main(int argc, char **argv)
{

    int i;
    int *ii;

    printf("&etext = 0x%lx\n", &etext);
    printf("&end  = 0x%lx\n", &end);

    printf("\n");
    ii = (int *) malloc(sizeof(int));

    printf("main  = 0x%lx\n", main);
    printf("&I    = 0x%lx\n", &I);
    printf("&i    = 0x%lx\n", &i);
    printf("&argc = 0x%lx\n", &argc);
    printf("&ii   = 0x%lx\n", &ii);
    printf("ii    = 0x%lx\n", ii);

}
```

```
&etext and &end.
```

These are two external variables that are defined as follows :

```
extern etext;
extern end;
```

Note that they are typeless. You never use just "**etext**" and "**end**". Instead, you use their addresses - these variables point to the end of the text and globals (data) segments respectively.

When we run the above program it prints out the addresses of **etext** and **end**. Then it also prints out 6 values :

- **main** is a pointer to the first instruction of the **main()** procedure. This is simply a location in the code segment, which should be familiar to you from the assembler lectures.
- I is a global variable. Thus **&I** should be an address in the globals segment.
- i is a local variable. Thus **&i** should be an address in the stack.
- argc is an argument to **main()**. Thus, **&argc** should be an address in the stack.
- ii is another local variable. Thus, **&ii** should be an address in the stack. However, ii is a pointer to memory that has been **malloc**'d. Thus, **ii** should be an address in the heap.

When we run **testaddr1**, we get something like the following :

```
&etext = 0x80484d7
&end   = 0x8049674

main   = 0x804835c
&I     = 0x8049670
&i     = 0xbfffe5c4
&argc  = 0xbfffe5d0
&ii    = 0xbfffe5c0
ii     = 0x80496c8
```

So, what this says is that the code segment is upto 0x80484d7. The globals segment goes upto 0x8049674.

Run the following program to check which range of addresses are meaningful (i.e which don't give any segment violation error) and which are not meaningful. This is done by taking a HEX address from the user and trying to read and write into it. If the location is not accessible then we may get SIGSEGV error and some times if the location is read only type (such as code area) then during writing we will get error. Run this program and play it by giving different addresses.

Example 6

```
#include <stdio.h>

extern end;
extern etext;

main()
{
   char *s;
   char c;

   printf("&etext = 0x%lx\n", &etext);
   printf("&end   = 0x%lx\n", &end);

   printf("\n");

   printf("Enter memory location in hex (start with 0x): ");
   fflush(stdout);

   scanf("0x%x", &s);

   printf("Reading 0x%x:  ", s);
   fflush(stdout);
```

```
        c = *s;
        printf("%d\n", c);
        printf("Writing %d back to  0x%x:  ", c, s);
        fflush(stdout);
        *s = c;
        printf("ok\n");
    }
```

When we give address is 0x862121 we will get the following result and segment violation.

```
        &etext = 0x804855b
        &end   = 0x804973c
```

Enter memory location in hex (start with 0x) : Reading 0x862121 :

When the first **malloc()** is called, a call to **sbrk()** is made to get a new chunk of memory. To support this run the following program and see the values of &end and sbrk(0) values.

Example 7

```
        #include <stdio.h>

        extern end;
        extern etext;

        main()
        {
          char *s;
          char c;

          printf("&etext = 0x%lx\n", &etext);
          printf("&end   = 0x%lx\n", &end);
          printf("sbrk(0)= 0x%lx\n", sbrk(0));
          printf("&c     = 0x%lx\n", &c);

          printf("\n");

          printf("Enter memory location in hex (start with 0x): ");
          fflush(stdout);

          scanf("0x%x", &s);

          printf("Reading 0x%x:  ", s);
          fflush(stdout);
          c = *s;
```

```
    printf("%d\n", c);
    printf("Writing %d back to  0x%x:   ", c, s);
    fflush(stdout);
    *s = c;
    printf("ok\n");
}
```

Results of the above program supports the above statement. That is before, malloc() call sbrk(0) value is same as &end.

```
&etext = 0x80485c3
&end   = 0x80497e0
sbrk(0)= 0x80497e0
&c     = 0xbfffdcc3
```

Enter memory location in hex (start with 0x) : Reading 0x812121 :

Now, run the following program in which malloc() is called before printing values and we can find that the &end and sbrk(0) values as different.

Example 8

```
#include <stdio.h>

extern end;
extern etext;

main()
{
    char *s;
    char c;
    char *buf;

    buf = (char *) malloc(1000);

    printf("&etext = 0x%lx\n", &etext);
    printf("&end   = 0x%lx\n", &end);
    printf("sbrk(0)= 0x%lx\n", sbrk(0));
    printf("&c     = 0x%lx\n", &c);

    printf("\n");

    printf("Enter memory location in hex (start with 0x): ");
    fflush(stdout);

    scanf("0x%x", &s);
```

```
    printf("Reading 0x%x:  ", s);
    fflush(stdout);
    c = *s;
    printf("%d\n", c);
    printf("Writing %d back to  0x%x:  ", c, s);
    fflush(stdout);
    *s = c;
    printf("ok\n");
}
```

Results of the above program

```
&etext = 0x8048607
&end   = 0x8049824
sbrk(0)= 0x804b000
&c     = 0xbfffe7c3
```

Enter memory location in hex (start with 0x): Reading 0x8612121:

The function malloc keeps a big buffer of memory in the heap and carves it up and doles it out whenever the user calls **malloc()**. If there is not enough room in the buffer for what the user desires, then sbrk() is called to get heap storage for a big enough buffer.

Malloc really maintain a linked list of free memory. When **malloc()** is called, it looks on its list for a piece of memory that is big enough. If it finds one, then it removes that memory from the linked list and returns it to the user. When **free()** is called, the memory is put back on the linked list. Now, to be efficient, if there is a chunk of memory on the free list that much bigger than what is requested, then it breaks up that chunk into two chunks - one which is the size of the request (padded to a multiple of 8), and the remainder. The remainder is put on the free list and the one the size of the request is returned to the user. This is the standard way that you view **malloc** - it manages a free list of memory. **Malloc()** takes memory from the free list and gives it to the user, and **free()** gives memory back to the free list.

When the first **malloc()** is called, we call **sbrk()** to get a new chunk of memory for the free list. This memory is split up so that some is returned to the user, and the rest goes back onto the free list. Similarly, nodes of the free lists are also coalesced. The link may maintain the address of previous and next lists in addition to the size of the chunk which we may call as book keeping.

Example 9

```
    #include <stdio.h>
    #include <sys/types.h>

    main()
```

```
{
  int *i1, *i2, *i3;

  printf("sbrk(0) before malloc(4): 0x%x\n", sbrk(0));
  i1 = (int *) malloc(4);
  printf("sbrk(0) after `i1 = (int *) malloc(4)':
                               0x%x\n", sbrk(0));
  i2 = (int *) malloc(4);
  printf("sbrk(0) after `i2 = (int *) malloc(4)':
                               0x%x\n", sbrk(0));
  printf("i1 = 0x%x, i2 = 0x%x, sbrk(0)-i2 = %d\n", i1, i2,
     (char *) sbrk(0)- (char *) i2);
  i3 = (int *) malloc(8164);
  printf("sbrk(0) after `i3 = (int *) malloc(8164)':
                               0x%x\n", sbrk(0));
  printf("i3 = 0x%x\n", i3);

}

Results of the above program  are as follows.
sbrk(0) before malloc(4): 0x804978c
sbrk(0) after `i1 = (int *) malloc(4)': 0x804b000
sbrk(0) after `i2 = (int *) malloc(4)': 0x804b000
i1 = 0x80497e0, i2 = 0x80497f0, sbrk(0)-i2 = 6160
sbrk(0) after `i3 = (int *) malloc(8164)': 0x804c000
i3 = 0x8049800
```

This corroborates of our statements such as :

1. malloc() calls sbrk() first time and gets a chunk of free memory. Also, after both malloc() calls also sbrk(0) value did not change. Which supports the above discussion of free list.

2. Also, check the addresses of i1 and i2 which are differed by 16 bytes. Though we have asked for 4 bytes, malloc() allocated 16 bytes. That is remaining memory book keeping information and empty bytes as explained earlier.

3. When we try to allocate memory of 8192 bytes again sbrk(0) values is changed. Which indicates that sbrk() is called again to accommodate the required memory request.

To support the second statement given above, run the following program and check the results.

Example 10

```
#include <stdio.h>
int main()
```

```
{
int *s; char *p; int i;
s=(int *)malloc(sizeof(int));
scanf("%d", s);
printf("%d\n",*s);
p=(char *)s;
for(i=0;i<8;i++)
printf("%c\n",  *(p+i));
return 0;
}
```

Here, first memory (4 bytes) is allocated for an integer and its address is assigned to "s" and the same address is assigned to a character pointer "p" through typecasting. Then, by running a for loop eight elements (characters) are printed. Though actually, we should be in a position to access only 4 bytes, we are able to access some of the next bytes also. This supports that malloc() allocates memory more than what we have asked for. Ofcourse, the next location may contain book keeping information of the chunk. Refer for dope vectors in principles of programming language books.

The Stack And Local Variables

The stack is used by the process to store the chain of functions which are currently in the middle of execution. Each function call causes the process to add an execution frame to the top of the stack. This execution frame would contain the contents of CPU registers as they were before the function call was made, the return address (i.e. where in the code this function was invoked, so we can return there when the function returns), the parameters passed to the function and all local variables of the function. Thus, when we have fucntion 'main' calling function 'a' which calls function 'b', we will have 3 frames on the stack.

The 'allocation' of a stack frame does not require performing real memory allocation - as the space for the stack was reserved during process startup. Instead, this is done by merely marking a part of the stack as containing the frame, and copying data to that frame. Note that local variables are "allocated" by simply advancing the stack pointer beyond their location on the stack, so allocating local variables takes a fixed amount of time, no matter their size. When a function returns - its stack frame is freed by simply modifying the stack pointer to point below its frame.

The local variables are not initialized-they just contain the values that were accidentally placed in the memory locations these variables occupy. You may consider a situation in which a function was called, its variables used and given some values. Later the function returned, and its frame was released. Then, another function was called. the stack frame of this new function is located in the same place in memory as the frame of the former function, so the new function's local variables will get the values that were left there by the local variables of the former function. This can explain why the values of un-intialised local variables are often neither 0, nor look like total garbage.

Since all local variables are stored in consecutive memory on the stack, if we take a pointer to such a variable, and later on write right above or right below this pointer, we'll be modifying the contents of another local variable, or even that of the function's return address, if we're "lucky". For example, consider the following code:

```
int foo()
{
   int numbers[2];
   int j;

   j = 2;
   printf("j - %d\n", j);
   numbers[2] = 3;
   printf("j - %d\n", j);
}
```

During execution of this function, we first assign 2 to 'j', and thus the first print command will show "j - 2". Then, we try to assign a value to 'numbers[2]'. However, the 'numbers' array only has 2 cells - 0 and 1. Writing into subscript '2' of this array will cause us to write just beyond the array (which is fully located on the stack). The variable 'j' just happens to be stored in that location in memory, and thus, the value '3' will be actually assigned to 'j'. Our second print command will thus show "j - 3". Note that this assumes that the variables are stored in memory in the same order as they were declared inside the function's code. With some compilers, this might not be the case, and the out-of-range assignment might overwrite a different variable, or a part of the stack that does not hold variables, leading to other unexpected results.

> ***Note :*** local variables (as well as function parameters) might be stored in registers, rather than on the stack. This could be either because we used the 'register' keyword when declaring these variables, or because the compiler's optimization chose to place a variable in a register. Ofcourse, such variables cannot be over-written by stack overflows.

Now, lets break the stack. This can be done by writing a program that allocates too much stack memory. One such program is given below performs infinite recursion, and at each recursive step it allocates 10000 bytes of stack memory in the variable iptr. When you run this, you'll see that you get a segmentation violation when the recursive call is made. Often when you have infinite recursion and overflow the stack, you get "illegal instruction" instead of Segmenation fault.

Example 11

```
#include <stdio.h>

extern end;
extern etext;
```

```
main()
{
  char c;
  char iptr[100000];

  printf("&c      = 0x%lx, iptr = 0x%x  ...  ", &c, iptr);
  fflush(stdout);
  c = iptr[0];
  printf("ok\n");
  main();
}
```

The second way to break the stack is to simply allocate too much local memory. E.g. look at the following program. It tries to allocate 10M of memory in the stack.

Example 12

```
#include <stdio.h>

extern end;
extern etext;

a()
{
  char c;
  char iptr[10000000];

  printf("&c      = 0x%lx, iptr = 0x%x  ...  ", &c, iptr);
  fflush(stdout);
  c = iptr[0];
  printf("ok\n");
}

main()
{
  printf("Calling a\n");
  a();
}
```

Also, recursive function calls may lead to stack overflow. Normally, tail recursion is employed to alleviate this problem.

See the following program to show stack information.

Example 12

```c
#include <stdio.h>

a(int j, int *k)
{
  char **s;
  char *s2;
  int i;

  s = (char **) &s;

  printf("a: &i = 0x%x, &j = 0x%x, &k = 0x%x\n", &i, &j, &k);

  for (i = 0; i < 10; i++) {
  s++;
  s2 = (char *) s;
  printf("0x%x : %15d 0x%-8x\n", s, *s, *s);
  }
}

b(int j)
{
  int i;

  j++;
  i = j+15;

  printf("b: &i = 0x%x, &j = 0x%x\n", &i, &j);

  a(49, &j);
}

main()
{
  int i;

  i = 333;

  b(i);
}
```

If we run the above program we may get the results which displays the details of
the stack frames.

```
b: &i = 0xbffff624, &j = 0xbffff630
a: &i = 0xbffff5fc, &j = 0xbffff610, &k = 0xbffff614
0xbffff608 :   -1073744344 0xbffff628
0xbffff60c :    134513603 0x80483c3
0xbffff610 :    49 0x31
0xbffff614 :   -1073744336 0xbffff630
0xbffff618 :   -1073744336 0xbffff630
0xbffff61c :    134513318  0x80482a6
0xbffff620 :    1108545272 0x42130ef8
0xbffff624 :     349 0x15d
0xbffff628 :   -1073744312 0xbffff648
0xbffff62c :    134513642 0x80483ea
```

This example also explains the status of the stack.

Example 13

```c
#include <stdio.h>
safechar(char c)
{
   if (c >= 'a' && c <= 'z') return(c);
   if (c >= 'A' && c <= 'Z') return(c);
   if (c >= '0' && c <= '9') return(c);
   if (c == ' ') return(c);
   if (c == '.') return(c);
   if (c == '-') return(c);
   if (c == ',') return(c);
   if (c == '(') return(c);
   if (c == ')') return(c);
   if (c == '[') return(c);
   if (c == ']') return(c);
   if (c == '{') return(c);
   if (c == '}') return(c);
return '@';
}
main(int argc, char **argv, char **envp)
{
   char **s;
   char *s2;
   int i, top;

if (argc < 2) {
fprintf(stderr, "usage: printstack nentries (& other junk
                if you want)\n");
exit(1);
}
```

```
top = atoi(argv[1]);

printf("&s = 0x%x\n", &s);
printf("&argc = 0x%x\n", &argc);
printf("&argv = 0x%x\n", &argv);
printf("&envp = 0x%x\n", &envp);
printf("\n");

s = (char **) &s;
for (i = 0; i < top; i++) {
s++;
s2 = (char *) s;
printf("0x%x : %15d 0x%-8x %2c %2c %2c %2c\n",
        s, *s, *s, safechar(s2[0]),
   safechar(s2[1]), safechar(s2[2]), safechar(s2[3]));
   }
}
```

Results of the above program is as follows.

```
&s = 0xbfffe044
&argc = 0xbfffe050
&argv = 0xbfffe054
&envp = 0xbfffe058

0xbfffe048 :  -1073749912 0xbfffe068  h  @  @  @
0xbfffe04c :   1107383668 0x42015574  t  U  @  B
```

```
Free()
```

When we want to free a memory chunk previously allocated by `malloc()`, we use the free function. This function accepts a char pointer to a previously allocated memory chunk, and frees it - that is, adds it to the list of free memory chunks, that may be re-allocated. Several notes about free():

- The size of the chunk was stored by `malloc()` previously in its memory map, and that is how `free()` knows how many bytes to free.

- The freed memory is not being cleared or erased in any manner. This is why accessing memory that was just freed often does not cause a crash - any data in it is still the same as before calling `free()`.

- The free() function cannot nullify pointers to the given memory chunk that might still exist in our program. After we call free(), it is up to us (the programmers) not to try and dereference pointers that still point to that memory chunk. Such pointers are known as 'dangling pointers' - they point to memory that was already freed, and thus they should NOT be dereferenced again, unless they are assigned the address of a different (not-freed) memory chunk.

As you can see, `free()` only marks the memory chunk as free - there is no enforcement of this freeing operation. Accessing memory chunks that were previously freed is the cause of many memory errors for novices and experienced programmers. A good practice is that always nullify a pointer that was just freed, as in :

```
char* p = malloc(10);
strcpy(p, "hello");
printf("%s\n", p);
free(p);
p = NULL;
```

One might ask-what if accidentally free a memory chunk twice? this kind of bug could occur, for example, if we free a data point but don't nullify it, and during cleanup later, we see its not NULL, and try to free it again.

To understand what this kind of error might cause, we should remember how the memory manager normally works. Often, it stores the size of the allocated chunk right before the chunk itself in memory. If we freed the memory, this memory chunk might have been allocated again by another `malloc()` request, and thus this double-free will actually free the wrong memory chunk - causing us to have a dangling pointer somewhere else in our application. Such bugs tend to show themselves much later than the place in the code where they occured. Sometimes we don't see them at all, but they still lurk around, waiting for an opportunity to rear their ugly heads.

Another problem that might occur, is that this double-free will be done after the freed chunk was merged together with neighbouring free chunks to form a larger free chunk, and then the larger chunk was re-allocated. In such a case, when we try to `free()` our chunk for the 2nd time, we'll actually free only part of the memory chunk that the application is currently using. This will cause even more unexpected problems.

Example 14

The following example sets the end of the data segment to a pointer variable. Whenever, we try to store some thing in that location segment violation occurs which makes the signal handler to run which in turn calls sbrk(256) to increase the data segment size.

```
#include <unistd.h>
#include <signal.h>

void catcher(int signo)
{
    char *cp2;
    printf("%d Occured", signo);
    cp2 = sbrk(256);
    printf("Current brk value = %d\n", (int)cp2);
```

```
        sleep(5);
        signal(SIGSEGV, catcher);
    }

    int main()
    {
        char *old, *cp;
        void catcher();
        old = sbrk(0);
        cp = old;
        signal(SIGSEGV, catcher);
        for(;;)
        *cp++ = 1;
    }
```

Realloc()

The functin prototype is given as :

```
Void * realloc( void *oldaddress, int size)
```

This function takes two arguments, one pointer to already allocated memory and size of the new memory required. It not only allocates the memory (new memory) but also copies the content of the old memory. If the required size of the new memory is smaller than the existing one it will not allocates new memory.

Example 15

```
        #include <stdio.h>
        int main()
        {
            char  *p, *q;

            p=(char *) malloc(10);
            scanf("%s", p);

            printf("%s\n", p);
            q=realloc(p,20);

            printf("%s\n", q);

        }
```

calloc()

This function also works similar to malloc() with the exception that it initializes allocated memory also.

Conclusions

This chapter discusses about unix memory management in practical manner. Program strcture and paging concepts are emphasized in detail. Programs are included from explain about dynamic memory allocation, deallocation, stack management etc. Also, some programs are included from explain about system calls brk() and sbrk(). C runtime memory management is described in an elaborate manner.

Questions

1. What is a dangling pointer ?

2. What is dangling memory ?

3. Write testing programs to know where memory is allocated for a static array, static array which is initialized, global array, global array which is initialized, automatic array in main, automatic array which is initialized, and an array in a function and an array in a function which is initialized 9Hint run size command on the executable programs you have developed).

4. How do you create a 2-D array flexibly in pointer from pointer representation.

5. How do you free a 2-D dynamic array represented in pointer from pointer fashion.

6. Do you face any dangling memory problem with the above program ? When ?

18 File Locking

When a file can be accessed by more than one process, a synchronization problem occurs: what happens if two processes try to write in the same file location? Or again, what happens if a process reads from a file location while another process is writing into it? In traditional Unix systems, concurrent accesses to the same file location produce unpredictable results.

However, the systems provide a mechanism that allows the processes to lock a file region so that concurrent accesses may be easily avoided. However, this may limit parallism in some applications. Thus, File locking provides a very simple yet incredibly useful mechanism for coordinating file accesses.

There are two types of locking mechanisms :

- Mandatory Locking
- Advisory Locking

Traditional System V variants provide the `lockf()` system call, which is just an interface to `fcntl()`. More importantly, System V Release 3 introduced mandatory locking : the kernel checks that every invocation of the `open()`, `read()`, and `write()` system calls does not violate a mandatory lock on the file being accessed. Therefore, mandatory locks are enforced even between non-cooperative processes. A file is marked as a candidate for mandatory locking by setting its set-group bit (SGID) and clearing the group-execute permission bit. Since the set-group bit makes no sense when the group-execute bit is off, the kernel interprets that combination as a hint to use mandatory locks instead of advisory ones.

Oddly enough, a process may still unlink (delete) a file even if some other process owns a mandatory lock on it! This perplexing situation is possible because, when a process deletes a file hard link, it does not modify its contents but only the contents of its parent directory.

In an advisory lock system, processes can still read and write from a file while it's locked. Useless ? Not quite, since there is a way for a process to check for the existence of a lock before a read or write. See, it's a kind of cooperative locking system. This is easily sufficient for almost all cases where file locking is necessary. This kind of lock does not keep out another process that is ignorant of locking. The lock is considered *"advisory"* because it doesn't work unless other processes cooperate in checking the existence of a lock before accessing the file. Therefore, locks are known as advisory locks.

Traditional BSD variants implement advisory locking through the `flock()` system call. This call does not allow a process to lock a file region, just the whole file.

There are two types of (advisory!) locks: read locks and write locks (also referred to as shared locks and exclusive locks, respectively.) The way read locks work is that they don't interfere with other read locks. For instance, multiple processes can have a file locked for reading at the same. However, when a process has an write lock on a file, no other process can activate either a read or write lock until it is relinquished. One easy way to think of this is that there can be multiple readers simultaneously, but there can only be one writer at a time.

As mentioned earlier, there are many ways to lock files in Unix systems. System V likes lockf(), which is not effective. Some other better systems support `flock()` which offers better control over the lock, but still lacks in certain ways. For portability and for completeness, we will be talking about how to lock files using `fcntl()`. We encourage you, though, to use one of the higher-level flock()-style functions if it suits your needs, but we want to portably demonstrate the full range of power you have at your fingertips.

Setting a Lock

The `fcntl()` function does just about everything on the planet, but we'll just use it for file locking. Setting the lock consists of filling out a struct flock (declared in fcntl.h) that describes the type of lock needed, open()ing the file with the matching mode, and calling `fcntl()` with the proper arguments.

```
struct flock fl;
int fd;

fl.l_type   = F_WRLCK;  /* F_RDLCK, F_WRLCK, F_UNLCK    */
fl.l_whence = SEEK_SET; /* SEEK_SET, SEEK_CUR, SEEK_END */
fl.l_start  = 0;        /* Offset from l_whence         */
fl.l_len    = 0;        /* length, 0 = to EOF           */
fl.l_pid    = getpid(); /* our PID                      */

fd = open("filename", O_WRONLY);

fcntl(fd, F_SETLKW, &fl);  /* F_GETLK, F_SETLK, F_SETLKW */
```

What just happened ? Let's start with the struct flock since the fields in it are used to describe the locking action taking place. Here are some field definitions :

l_type

This is where you signify the type of lock you want to set. It's either F_RDLCK, F_WRLCK, or F_UNLCK if you want to set a read lock, write lock, or clear the lock, respectively.

l_whence

This field determines where the l_start field starts from (it's like an offset for the offset). It can be either SEEK_SET, SEEK_CUR, or SEEK_END, for beginning of file, current file position, or end of file.

l_start

This is the starting offset in bytes of the lock, relative to l_whence.

l_len

This is the length of the lock region in bytes (which starts from l_start which is relative to l_whence.

l_pid

The process ID of the process dealing with the lock. Use getpid() to get this.

In our example, we told it make a lock of type F_WRLCK (a write lock), starting relative to SEEK_SET (the beginning of the file), offset 0, length 0 (a zero value means "lock to end-of-file), with the PID set to getpid().

The next step is to open() the file, since flock() needs a file descriptor of the file that's being locked. Note that when you open the file, you need to open it in the same mode as you have specified in the lock, as shown in Table 18.1. If you open the file in the wrong mode for a given lock type, open() will return EBADF.

l_type	mode
F_RDLCK	O_RDONLY or O_RDWR
F_WRLCK	O_WRONLY or O_RDWR

Table 18.1 Lock types and corresponding open() modes.

Finally, the call to fcntl() actually sets, clears, or gets the lock. See, the second argument (the cmd) to fcntl() tells it what to do with the data passed to it in the struct flock. The following list summarizes what each fcntl() cmd does.

F_SETLKW

This argument tells fcntl() to attempt to obtain the lock requested in the struct flock structure. If the lock cannot be obtained (since someone else has it locked already), fcntl() will wait (block) until the lock has cleared, then will set it itself. This is a very useful command. I use it all the time.

F_SETLK

This function is almost identical to F_SETLKW. The only difference is that this one will not wait if it cannot obtain a lock. It will return immediately with -1. This function can be used to clear a lock by setting the l_type field in the struct flock to F_UNLCK.

F_GETLK

If you want to only check to see if there is a lock, but don't want to set one, you can use this command. It looks through all the file locks until it finds one that conflicts with the lock you specified in the struct flock. It then copies the conflicting lock's information into the struct and returns it to you. If it can't find a conflicting lock, fcntl() returns the struct as you passed it, except it sets the l_type field to F_UNLCK.

In our above example, we call fcntl() with F_SETLKW as the argument, so it blocks until it can set the lock, then sets it and continues.

Clearing a Lock

After all the locking stuff up there, it's time for something easy : unlocking! Actually, this is a piece of cake in comparison. We will just reuse that first example and add the code to unlock it at the end:

```
struct flock fl;
int fd;

fl.l_type   = F_WRLCK;  /* F_RDLCK, F_WRLCK, F_UNLCK   */
fl.l_whence = SEEK_SET; /* SEEK_SET, SEEK_CUR, SEEK_END */
fl.l_start  = 0;        /* Offset from l_whence         */
fl.l_len    = 0;        /* length, 0 = to EOF           */
fl.l_pid    = getpid(); /* our PID                      */

fd = open("filename", O_WRONLY); /* get the file descriptor */
fcntl(fd, F_SETLKW, &fl);/* set the lock, waiting if necessary */
.

.

.

fl.l_type   = F_UNLCK;  /* tell it to unlock the region */
fcntl(fd, F_SETLK, &fl); /* set the region to unlocked */
```

Now, we left the old locking code in there for high contrast, but you can tell that we just changed the l_type field to F_UNLCK (leaving the others completely unchanged!) and called fcntl() with F_SETLK as the command. Easy!

When a process acquires locks to two regions of a file which are adjacent then the locked regions are merged. This is known as lock promotion. Similarly, if a process acquires lock for a region and subsequenctly it removes lock for a some portion of the region which may lead to two regions with locks. This is known as lock splitting.

Example 1

Here, we will include a demo program, lockdemo.c, that waits for the user to hit return, then locks its own source, waits for another return, then unlocks it. By running this program in two (or more) windows, you can see how programs interact while waiting for locks.

Basically, usage is this: if you run lockdemo with no command line arguments, it tries to grab a write lock (F_WRLCK) on its source (lockdemo.c). If you start it with any command line arguments at all, it tries to get a read lock (F_RDLCK) on it.

```c
#include <stdio.h>
#include <stdlib.h>
#include <errno.h>
#include <fcntl.h>
#include <unistd.h>

int main(int argc, char *argv[])
{
  struct flock fl = { F_WRLCK, SEEK_SET, 0, 0, 0 };
  int fd;

  fl.l_pid = getpid();

  if (argc > 1)
  fl.l_type = F_RDLCK;

  if ((fd = open("lockdemo.c", O_RDWR)) == -1) {
    perror("open");
    exit(1);
  }

  printf("Press <RETURN> to try to get lock: ");
  getchar();
  printf("Trying to get lock...");

  if (fcntl(fd, F_SETLKW, &fl) == -1) {
    perror("fcntl");
    exit(1);
  }

  printf("got lock\n");
  printf("Press <RETURN> to release lock: ");
  getchar();

  fl.l_type = F_UNLCK;  /* set to unlock same region */
```

```
    if (fcntl(fd, F_SETLK, &fl) == -1) {
       perror("fcntl");
       exit(1);
    }

    printf("Unlocked.\n");

    close(fd);
}
```

Compile the above program. Notice that when one lockdemo has a read lock, other instances of the program can get their own read locks with no problem. It's only when a write lock is obtained that other processes can't get a lock of any kind.

If we run the above program in one window we may get the following messages on the screen.

```
Press <RETURN> to try to get lock
Trying to get lock..
got lock
Press <RETURN> to release lock
```

Now, in another window, if we run it again we get the following messages

```
Press <RETURN> to try to get lock
Trying to get lock..
```

That is the second instance is blocked while attempting to lock the file. Go back to the first window and press Enter:
unlocking

The program running in the second window immediately acquires the lock.

Another thing to notice is that you can't get a write lock if there are any read locks on the same region of the file. The process waiting to get the write lock will wait until all the read locks are cleared. One upshot of this is that you can keep piling on read locks (because a read lock doesn't stop other processes from getting read locks) and any processes waiting for a write lock will sit there and starve. There isn't a rule anywhere that keeps you from adding more read locks if there is a process waiting for a write lock. You must be careful.

The fcntl version has a major advantage: It works with files on NFS file systems (as long as the NFS server is reasonably recent and correctly configured). So, if you have access to two machines that both mount the same file system via NFS, you can repeat the previous example using two different machines. Run lock-file on one machine, specifying a file on NFS file system, and then run it again on another machine, specifying the same file. NFS wakes up the second program when the lock is released by the first program.

Practically, though, you will probably mostly be using write locks to guarantee exclusive access to a file for a short amount of time while it's being updated; which is the most common use of locks.

Locks rule. Sometimes, though, you might need more control over your processes in a producer-consumer situation. For this reason, if no other, you should *see* **semaphores** if your system supports such a beast. They provide a more extensive and at least equally function equivalent to file locks.

Example 2

In this example, if some one is accessing "/tmp/INFO" file no other can access it. That is, if once we start this program is started we can not have another instance of the same program. Like this we can make sure that always only one instance of this program will be running on the system. Experiment by typing this programs machine language file name multiple times at command line. This program can not be terminated by sending any signals.

```c
#include <stdio.h>
#include <signal.h>
#define LOCK "/tmp/INFO"
void unlock(int n)
{
signal(SIGINT,SIG_IGN);
signal(SIGQUIT,SIG_IGN);
signal(SIGHUP,SIG_IGN);
signal(SIGTERM,SIG_IGN);
unlink(LOCK);
exit(0);
}

int main()
{
signal(SIGINT,unlock);
signal(SIGQUIT,unlock);
signal(SIGHUP,unlock);
signal(SIGTERM,unlock);
if(access(LOCK,0)==0) {
printf("Someone is using this program. Try later\n");
exit(2);
}
fopen(LOCK,"w");
sleep(100);
/* some procesing can be done */
}
```

Example 3

```c
#include <stdio.h>
#include <signal.h>
#include <sys/types.h>
#include <fcntl.h>
#include <unistd.h>

int main(int XX, char *a[])
{
  struct flock fvar;
  int fd;

  if((fd=open("LOCK",O_RDWR))==-1) {perror("open");
                                    exit(-1); }

  fvar.l_type=F_RDLCK;
  fvar.l_whence=SEEK_SET;
  fvar.l_start=0;
  fvar.l_len=10;
  fvar.l_pid=getpid();
  fcntl(fd,F_SETLK, &fvar);

  fvar.l_type=F_RDLCK;
  fvar.l_start=50;
  fvar.l_len=25;
  fcntl(fd,F_SETLK,&fvar);

  fvar.l_type=F_RDLCK;
  fvar.l_start=10;
  fvar.l_len=40;
  fcntl(fd,F_SETLK,&fvar);

  fvar.l_type=F_WRLCK;
  fvar.l_start=80;
  fvar.l_len=40;
  fcntl(fd,F_SETLK,&fvar);

  sleep(atoi(a[1]));
  fvar.l_type=F_WRLCK;
  fvar.l_whence=SEEK_SET;
  fvar.l_start=0;
  fvar.l_len=0;
  while(fcntl(fd,F_SETLK,&fvar)==-1)
  {
    while(fcntl(fd,F_GETLK,&fvar)!=-1&& fvar.l_type!=F_UNLCK)
    {
    printf("From Process = %d Locked by %d From %d Length
      %d\n",getpid(),  fvar.l_pid, fvar.l_start, fvar.l_len);
```

```
          if(!fvar.l_len)break;
          fvar.l_start +=fvar.l_len;

          fvar.l_len=0;
      }
  }
  return 0;
  }
```

Let a.out is the executable file of the above program.

Execute the following command

```
./a.out 30 &
```

(the first instance of the above program starts in background and acquires 3 read locks and a write lock and then sleeps for 30 sec).

Now execute the following command

```
./a.out 0
```

We will get the following results

```
From Process =1405 Locked by 1404 From 0 Length 75
From Process =1405 Locked by 1404 From 80 Length 40
```

The above indicates that all the 3 read locks are considered as single read lock, i.e lock growing or merging. Similarly, we can find the write lock from 80'th byte to 40 bytes.

Conclusions

This chapter explains about file locking mechanisms available in Unix and their practical use. Both advisory and mandatory locking methods are explored. A live example is included to explain how multiple process will employ locks while accessing shared files.

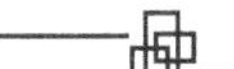

19 Pipes

Introduction

There is no form of IPC that is simpler than pipes (also known as nameless pipes), which are implemented on every flavor of Unix. The `pipe()` and `fork()` make up the functionality behind the " | " in shell commands such as "`ls | more`" which are discussed in previous chapters. Pipes are marginally useful for cool things, but are a good way to learn about basic methods of IPC.

The syntax of the `pipe()` system call is as follows (requires a 1-D array with two elements as argument)

```
int pipe(int fd[])
```

Basically, a call to the `pipe()` function returns a pair of file descriptors (Fig. 19.1). One of these descriptors is connected to the write end of the pipe, and the other is connected to the read end. Anything can be written to the pipe from one end, and can be read from the other end in the order it came in. On many systems, pipes will fill up after you write about 10K to them without reading anything out.

Figure 19.1 How a pipe is organized

Example 1

The following program creates, writes to, and reads from a pipe.

```c
#include <stdio.h>
#include <stdlib.h>
#include <errno.h>
#include <unistd.h>
int main()
{   int pfds[2];
    char buf[30];

    if (pipe(pfds) == -1) {perror("pipe");
    exit(1);}
    printf("writing to file descriptor #%d\n", pfds[1]);
    write(pfds[1], "test", 5);
    printf("reading from file descriptor #%d\n", pfds[0]);
    read(pfds[0], buf, 5);
    printf("read \"%s\"\n", buf);
}
```

From the above example, it's pretty hard to see how these would even be useful. Now, let's put a `fork()` in the mix and see what happens. First, we'll have the parent make a pipe. Secondly, we'll `fork()`. The child will receive a copy of all the parent's file descriptors, and this includes a copy of the pipe's file descriptors. Thus, the child will be able to send stuff to the write-end of the pipe, and the parent will get it off the read-end.

Before fork() system call in the following program may create pipe.

After fork() both parent and child process will have both the descriptors of the pipe as shown below.

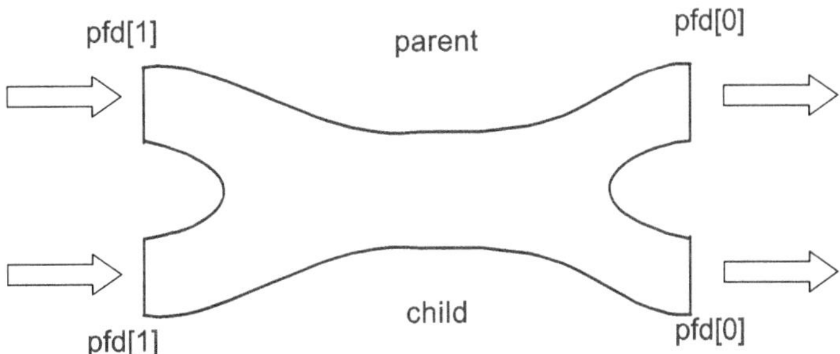

By closing reading descriptor in one process and in another writing end we can have a communication media can be created such that following :

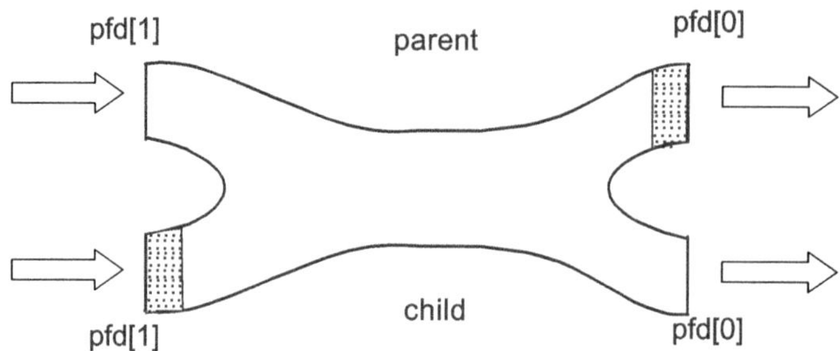

Example 2

```c
#include <stdio.h>
#include <stdlib.h>
#include <sys/types.h>
#include <unistd.h>

int main()
{
   int pfd[2];
   char buf[30];

   if ( pipe(pfd)==-1)
{
   perror("pipe failed");
   exit(1);
}
   if (!fork()) {
   printf(" CHILD: writing to the pipe\n");
     write(pfd[1], "test", 5);
    printf(" CHILD: exiting\n");
     exit(0);
  } else
    {
    printf("PARENT: reading from pipe\n");
    read(pfd[0], buf, 5);
    printf("PARENT: read \"%s\"\n", buf);
     wait(NULL);
    }
   }
```

Anyway, this example is just like the previous one, except now we fork() of a new process and have it write to the pipe, while the parent reads from it. The resultant output will be something similar to the following:

```
PARENT: reading from pipe
CHILD: writing to the pipe
CHILD: exiting
PARENT: read "test"
```

In this case, the parent tried to read from the pipe before the child writes to it. When this happens, the parent is said to *block*, or sleep, until data arrives to be read. It seems that the parent tried to read, went to sleep, the child wrote and exited, and the parent woke up and read the data.

Thus, one of the mechanisms that allow related-processes to communicate is the pipe, or the anonymous pipe. A pipe is a one-way mechanism that allows two related processes (i.e. one is an ancestor of the other) to send a byte stream from one of them to the other one. Naturally, to use such a channel properly, one needs to form some kind of protocol in which data is sent over the pipe

For example, in the following program in child process, system() function call executes "ls -l" command after closing file descriptor 1 and calling dup() system call. Here, file descriptor "1" becomes duplicate for writing file descriptor (pfd[1]) of the pipe. Thus, standard output of "ls -l" command is now redirected to pipe and is read by the parent process and prints the same on the standard output.

Example 3

```c
#include <stdio.h>
#include <stdlib.h>
#include <sys/types.h>
#include <unistd.h>

int main()
{
   int pfd[2];
   char buf[80];

   if( pipe(pfd)==-1){
   perror("pipe failed");      exit(1);
}
   if (!fork()) {
                   close(1);
                   dup(pfd[1]);
                   system("ls -l");
               }
                   else
```

```
                {printf ("PARENT : reading from pipe\n");
        while (read(pfd[0], buf, 80))
        printf ("%s\n", buf);
        }
    }
```

In Unix Shell, we use piping commands (such as "ls | wc -l") and are discussed in previous chapters. The following is an example of using pipe() in such a situations. This requires usage of a couple more functions such as : exec() and dup(). We will connect the standard output of the ls to the standard input of wc. See, stdout of ls flows into the pipe, and the stdin of wc flows in from the pipe.

Example 4

```
#include <stdio.h>
#include <stdlib.h>
#include <unistd.h>

int main()
{
  int pfd[2];

  if(pipe(pfd) ==-1) {
                        perror ("pipe failed");    exit(1);
                    }
  if (!fork()) {
      close(1);        /* close normal stdout */
      dup(pfd[1]);   /* make stdout same as pfds[1] */
      close(pfd[0]); /* we don't need this */
      execlp("ls", "ls", NULL);
  }
  else {
      close(0);        /* close normal stdin */
      dup(pfd[0]);   /* make stdin same as pfds[0] */
      close(pfd[1]); /* we don't need this */
      execlp("wc", "wc", "-l", NULL);
      }
  }
```

Here, close(1) frees up file descriptor 1 (standard output). dup(pfd[1]) makes a copy of the write-end of the pipe in the first available file descriptor, which is "1", since we just closed that. In this way, anything that ls writes to standard output (file descriptor 1) will instead go to pfd[1] (the write end of the pipe). The wc section of code works the same way, except in reverse.

The above example can be even implemented using `dup2()` system call also as follows.

Example 5

```c
#include <stdio.h>
#include <stdlib.h>
#include <unistd.h>

int main(void)
{  int pfd[2];
   int pid;

if (pipe(pfd) == -1)    {
                                   perror("pipe failed"); exit(1);
                          }
if ((pid = fork()) < 0) {
                                   perror("fork failed");
                                   exit(2);
                          }
if (pid == 0)
{
   close(pfd[1]);
   dup2(pfd[0], 0);
   close(pfd[0]);
   execlp("wc", "wc",
      (char *) 0);
   perror("wc failed");
   exit(3);
}
else {
close(pfd[0]);
dup2(pfd[1], 1);
close(pfd[1]);
execlp("ls", "ls",
   (char *) 0);
perror("ls failed");
exit(4);
}
exit(0);
}
```

Here, the parent process will replace "ls" command be calling exec, and the child will exec the command "wc". The write end of the pipe may be descriptor 3 and the read end may be descriptor 4 "ls" normally writes to 1 and "wc" normally reads from 0.

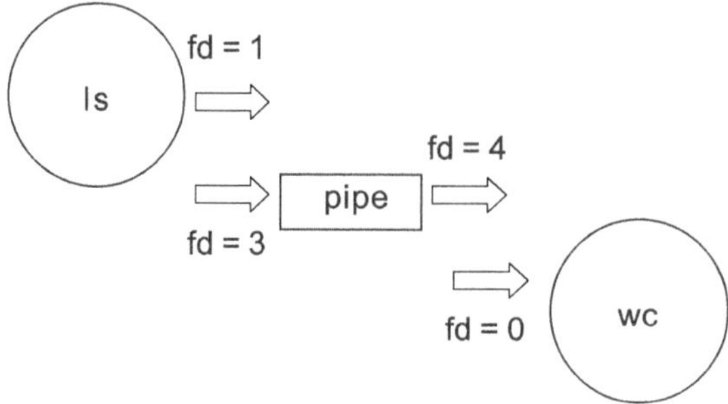

The "dup2" function call takes an existing file descriptor, and another one that it "would like to be". Here, fd=3 would also like to be 1, and fd=4 would like to be 0. So we dup2 fd=3 as 1, and dup2 fd=4 as 0. Then the old fd=3 and fd=4 can be closed as they are no longer needed.

After dup2

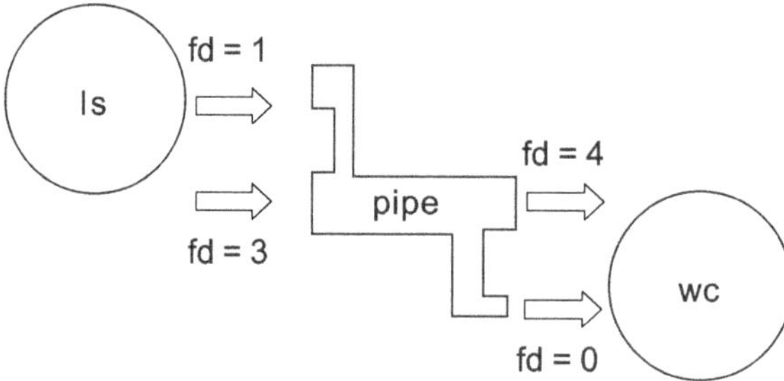

After close

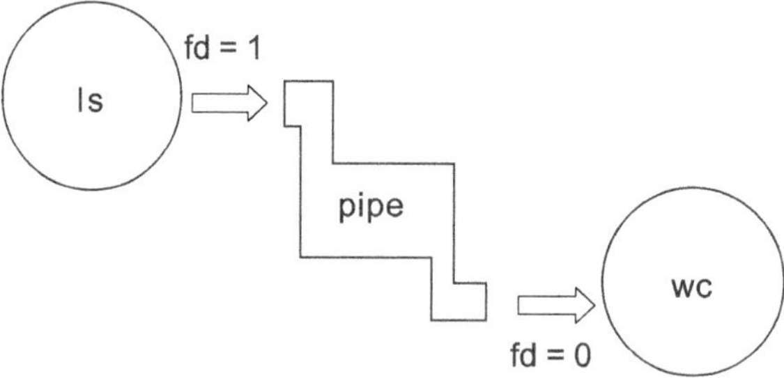

In a more complex system, one-way communications is too limiting. Thus, we'd want to be able to communication in both directions - from parent to child, and from child to parent. Here, what we need to do is open two pipes - one to be used in each direction. However, using two pipes might cause us to get into a situation known as 'deadlock':

Deadlock

A situation in which a group of two or more processes are all waiting for a set of resources that are currently taken by other processes in the same group, or waiting for events that are supposed to be sent from other processes in the group.

Such a situation might occur when two processes communicate via two pipes. Here are two scenarios that could led to such a deadlock :

1. Both pipes are empty, and both processes are trying to read from their input pipes. Each one is blocked on the read (cause the pipe is empty), and thus they'll remain stuck like this forever.

2. This one is more complicated. Each pipe has a buffer of limited size associated with it. When a process writes to a pipe, the data is placed on the buffer of that pipe, until it is read by the reading process. If the buffer is full, the write() system call gets blocked until the buffer has some free space. The only way to free space on the buffer, is by reading data from the pipe.

Thus, if both processes write data, each to its 'writing' pipe, until the buffers are filled up, both processes will get blocked on the write() system call. Since no other process is reading from any of the pipes, our two processes have just entered a deadlock.

Lets see an example of a (hopefully) deadlock-free program in which child process writes a message "test" in to the first pipe; where as the parent process reads the same and translates to upper-case letters and sends the same data back to the child process via the other pipe. The child reads the same and writes on to standard output.

Example 6

```c
#include <stdio.h>
#include <stdlib.h>
#include <unistd.h>

int main()
{
  int pfds[2], p1fds[2];
  char buf[10];
  int I;

  pipe(pfds);
  pipe(p1fds);

  if (fork()==0) {

    close(pfds[0]);  /* reading descriptor is closed
                        for first pipe*/
    close(p1fds[1]); /* writing descriptor is closed
                        for second pipe*/
```

```
write(pfds[1], "test", 5);   /* writes into first pipe */
read(p1fds[0],buf,5);    /* reads from second pipe */
write(1,buf,5);  /*writes on to standard output */
}
  else
{
  close(pfds[1]); /* writing descriptor is closed
                      for first pipe*/
  close(p1fds[0]); /* reading descriptor is closed
                      for second pipe*/
  read(pfds[0], buf, 5);  /* reads from  first pipe*/

  for (I=0;I<4;I++)
       buf[I]=toupper(buf[I]);

write(p1fds[1],buf,5);  /* writes into second pipe */
}
}
```

Let us see another example of a (hopefully) deadlock-free program in which one process reads input from the user, writes it to the other process via a pipe. the second process translates each upper-case letter to a lower-case letter and sends the data back to the first process. Finally, the first process writes the data to standard output.

Two processes communicating both ways by using two pipes. One process reads input from the user and handles it. The other process makes some translation of the input (translates upper-case letters to lower-case), and hands it back to the first process for printing.

Example 7

```
#include <stdio.h>
#include <unistd.h>
#include <ctype.h>

/* function executed by the user-interacting process. */

void user_handler(int input_pipe[], int output_pipe[])
{
   int c; /* user input-must be 'int', to recognize EOF (= -1).*/
   char ch;  /* the same - as a char. */
   int rc;   /* return values of functions. */

/* first, close unnecessary file descriptors */
```

```c
close(input_pipe[1]); /* we don't need to write to this pipe.*/
close(output_pipe[0]); /* we don't need to read from
                         this pipe. */

/* loop: read input from user, send via one pipe
         to the translator, */
/* read via other pipe what the translator returned,
   and write to   */
/* stdout. exit on EOF from user.*/

while ((c = getchar()) > 0) {

/* note - when we 'read' and 'write', we must deal
         with a char, */
/* rather then an int, because an int is longer than a char,*/
/* and writing only one byte from it, will lead to unexpected */
/* results, depending on how an int is stored on the system.*/

ch = (char)c;

/* write to translator */

rc = write(output_pipe[1], &ch, 1);

if (rc == -1) {/* write failed - notify the user and exit. */
   perror("user_handler: write");
   close(input_pipe[0]);
   close(output_pipe[1]);
    exit(1);
  }
/* read back from translator */

rc = read(input_pipe[0], &ch, 1);
c = (int)ch;
if (rc <= 0) { /* read failed - notify user and exit. */
   perror("user_handler: read");
   close(input_pipe[0]);
   close(output_pipe[1]);
    exit(1);
 }
/* print translated character to stdout. */
putchar(c);
}
```

```c
/* close pipes and exit. */
close(input_pipe[0]);
close(output_pipe[1]);
exit(0);
}

/* now comes the function executed by the translator process.*/
void translator(int input_pipe[], int output_pipe[])
{
int c; /* user input-must be 'int', to recognize EOF (= -1). */
char ch;   /* the same - as a char. */
int rc;    /* return values of functions. */

/* first, close unnecessary file descriptors */

close(input_pipe[1]); /* we don't need to write to this pipe. */
close(output_pipe[0]); /* we don't need to read from this pipe.*/

/* enter a loop of reading from the user_handler's pipe,
   translating */
/* the character, and writing back to the user handler. */

while (read(input_pipe[0], &ch, 1) > 0) {
  c = ch;

  /* translate any upper-case letter to lower-case. */

  if (isascii(c) && isupper(c))    c = tolower(c);

  ch = c;

  /* write translated character back to user_handler. */

  rc = write(output_pipe[1], &ch, 1);
  if (rc == -1) { /* write failed - notify user and exit. */
    perror("translator: write");
    close(input_pipe[0]);
    close(output_pipe[1]);
    exit(1);
  }
}
```

```c
/* close pipes and exit. */
close(input_pipe[0]);
close(output_pipe[1]);
exit(0);
}


/* and finally, the main function: spawn off two processes,*/
/* and let each of them execute its function.             */

int main(int argc, char* argv[])
{
   /* 2 arrays to contain file descriptors, for two pipes. */
   int user_to_translator[2];
   int translator_to_user[2];
   int pid; /* pid of child process, or 0, as returned via fork.*/
   int rc;  /* stores return values of various routines. */

   /* first, create one pipe. */
   rc = pipe(user_to_translator);
   if (rc == -1) {
   perror("main: pipe user_to_translator");
   exit(1);
}

/* then, create another pipe. */

rc = pipe(translator_to_user);
if (rc == -1) {
   perror("main: pipe translator_to_user");
   exit(1);
}

/* now fork off a child process, and set their handling routines.*/

pid = fork();

switch (pid) {
   case -1:  /* fork failed. */
      perror("main: fork");
      exit(1);
   case 0:   /* inside child process.  */
      translator(user_to_translator, translator_to_user); /*
                line 'A' */
```

```
      /* NOT REACHED */
      default:  /* inside parent process. */
      user_handler(translator_to_user, user_to_translator); /*
                        line 'B' */
        /* NOT REACHED */
      }


  return 0; /* NOT REACHED */
  }
```

Please note that SIGPIPE is reported when we try to write into a pipe whose read end is closed.

A piping command may consist of three or more process (ps|sed 1d|wc -l). In this case there are many choices available such as :

3.   The parent can fork twice to give two children.

4.   The parent can fork once and the child can fork once, giving a parent, child and grandchild.

5.   The parent can create two pipes before any forking. After a fork there will then be a total of 8 ends open (2 processes * two ends * 2 pipes). Most of these will have to be closed to ensure that there ends up only one read and only one write end.

6.   As many ends as possible of a pipe may be closed before a fork. This minimizes the number of closes that have to be done after forking

FIFO Pipes (Named Pipes)

One limitation of anonymous pipes is that only processes 'related' to the process that created the pipe (i.e. siblings of that process) may communicate using them. If we want two un-related processes to communicate via pipes, we need to use named pipes.

A FIFO ("First In, First Out") is sometimes known as a *named pipe*. That is, it's like a pipe, except that it has a name! In this case, the name is that of a file that multiple processes can open() and read and write to.

This latter aspect of FIFOs is designed to let them get around one of the shortcomings of normal pipes: we can't grab one end of a normal pipe that was created by an unrelated process. See, if we run two individual copies of a program, they can both call pipe () all they want and still not be able to speak to one another. (This is because we must pipe (), then fork () to get a child process that can communicate to the parent via the pipe.) With FIFOs, though, each unrelated process can simply open () the pipe and transfer data through it.

Since the FIFO is actually a file on disk, we have to to call `mknod() system call` with the proper arguments to create the same. Here is a `mknod()` call that creates a FIFO:

```
mknod("myfifo", S_IFIFO | 0644 , 0);
```

In the above example, the FIFO file will be called "myfifo". The second argument is the creation mode, which is used to tell mknod() to make a FIFO (the S_IFIFO part of the OR) and sets access permissions to that file (octal 644, or rw-r—r—) which can also be set by ORing together macros from sys/stat.h. This permission is just like the one you'd set using the chmod command. Finally, a device number is passed. This is ignored when creating a FIFO, so we can put anything we want in there.

A FIFO can also be created from the command line using the Unix mknod command.

Example

```
mknod pipefilename p
```

We can do the same with mkfifo command on some versions of Unix.

Example

```
mkfifo pipefilename
```

Opening a named pipe is done just like opening any other file in the system, using the open() system call, or using the `fopen()` standard C function. If the call succeeds, we get a file descriptor (in the case of `open()`, or a 'FILE' pointer (in the case of `fopen()`), which we may use either for reading or for writing, depending on the parameters passed to `open()` or to `fopen()`.

Reading from a named pipe is very similar to reading from a file, and the same goes for writing to a named pipe. Yet there are several differences:

7. *Either Read Or Write* - a named pipe cannot be opened for both reading and writing. The process opening it must choose one mode, and stick to it until it closes the pipe.

8. *Read/Write Are Blocking* - when a process reads from a named pipe that has no data in it, the reading process is blocked. It does not receive an end of file (EOF) value, like when reading from a file. When a process tries to write to a named pipe that has no reader (e.g. the reader process has just closed the named pipe), the writing process gets blocked, until a second process re-opens the named pipe.

Thus, when writing a program that uses a named pipe, we must take these limitations into account. We could also turn the file descriptor via which we access the named pipe to a non-blocking mode.

To give you an idea of how all of these can work together, here is a brief example showing how a sender might set up a connection to FIFO file and send a message. Please make sure that before you run this program you have to create file "/tmp/myFIFO" with the either mknod or mkfifo commands at the command prompt.

Example 8

```c
#include <sys/types.h>
#include <sys/stat.h>
#include <unistd.h>
#include <fcntl.h>
#include <stdio.h>
#include <stdlib.h>
#include <errno.h>

#define MAX_LINE 80

int main(int argc, char** argv) {
char line[MAX_LINE];
int pipe;

// open a named pipe
pipe = open("/tmp/myFIFO", O_WRONLY);

// get a line to send
printf("Enter line: ");
fgets(line, MAX_LINE, stdin);

// actually write out the data and close the pipe
write(pipe, line, strlen(line));

// close the pipe
close(pipe);
return 0;
}
```

As an example to an obscure usage of named pipes, we will borrow some idea from a program that allows one to count how many times they have been "fingered" an account. As described in the previous chapters, finger daemon, that accepts requests from users running the "finger" program, with a possible user name, and tells them when this user last logged on, as well as some other information. Amongst other thing, the finger daemon also checks if the user has a file named '.plan' (that is dot followed by "plan") in users home directory. If there is such a file, the finger daemon opens it, and prints its contents to the client.

This feature of the finger daemon may be used to create a program that tells the client how many times it was fingered. For that to work, we first create a named pipe, where the '.plan' file resides :

```
mknod /home/rao/.plan p
```

When you run the program, it gets into an endless loop of opening the named pipe in writing mode, write a message to the named pipe, close it, and sleep for a second. Look at the program's source code for more information. A sample of its output looks like this:

When you have done playing the program, stop the program, and don't forget to remove the named pipe from the file system.

Example 9

An example of using a named pipe, in order to make the finger daemon tell whoever fingers our account, how many times we were fingered recently. Uses a named pipe instead of a regular '.plan' file.

```c
#include <stdio.h>
#include <unistd.h>
#define PLAN_FILE "/home/rao/.plan"
     /* full path to my '.plan' file */

void main()
{
   FILE* plan;     int count = 0;

/* run an infinite loop of opening the named pipe, writing */
/* our message into it, and closing it.                    */

while (1) {
/* open the '.plan' file. This blocks until someone, */
/* (such as the finger daemon) opens the file for reading. */
plan = fopen(PLAN_FILE, "w");
if (!plan) {
   perror("fopen");    exit(1);
           }
   count++;
   fprintf(plan, "Ihave been fingered %d times today\n", count);

/* close  the  named pipe. This will cause the reader to get an EOF */
   fclose (plan);
```

```
/* suspend execution, give the reader process enough time to
read the message, get the EOF sign, and close the pipe.
otherwise, we might get to re-open the pipe before the reader
closes it, and thus write several messages to the same reader.
*/
   sleep(1);
   }
}
```

FIFO's are used

1. to create complex unix commands without creating temporary files
2. to pass data between client-server applications

Producers and Consumers Example

Once the FIFO has been created, a process can start up and open it for reading or writing using the standard open() system call. Here, we present two programs which will send data through a FIFO (speak.c), and the other is called tick.c, which sucks data out of the FIFO.

Example 10

```
#include <stdio.h>
#include <stdlib.h>
#include <errno.h>
#include <string.h>
#include <fcntl.h>
#include <sys/types.h>
#include <sys/stat.h>
#include <unistd.h>

#define FIFO_NAME "XYZ"

main()
{
   char s[300];
   int num, fd;

   mknod(FIFO_NAME, S_IFIFO | 0666, 0);

   printf("waiting for readers...\n");
   fd = open(FIFO_NAME, O_WRONLY);
   printf("got a reader—type some stuff\n");
```

```
while (gets(s), !feof(stdin)) {
  if ((num = write(fd, s, strlen(s))) == -1)
      perror("write");
  else
      printf("speak: wrote %d bytes\n", num);
  }
}
```

What speak does is creates the FIFO, then try to open() it. Now, what will happen is that the open() call will block until some other process (tick.c given below) opens the other end of the pipe for reading.

Example 11

```
#include <stdio.h>
#include <stdlib.h>
#include <errno.h>
#include <string.h>
#include <fcntl.h>
#include <sys/types.h>
#include <sys/stat.h>
#include <unistd.h>

#define FIFO_NAME "XYZ"

main()
{
  char s[300];
  int num, fd;

  mknod(FIFO_NAME, S_IFIFO | 0666, 0);

  printf("waiting for writers...\n");
  fd = open(FIFO_NAME, O_RDONLY);
  printf("got a writer:\n");

  do {
    if ((num = read(fd, s, 300)) == -1)
      perror("read");
    else {
      s[num] = '\0';
      printf("tick: read %d bytes: \"%s\"\n", num, s);
    }
  } while (num > 0);
}
```

Like `speak.c`, `tick` will block on the `open()` if there is no one writing to the FIFO. As soon as someone opens the FIFO for writing, `tick` will spring to life. Try it! Start `speak` and it will block until you start tick in another window. (Conversely, if you start tick, it will block until you start `speak` in another window.) Type away in the `speak` window and `tick` will suck it all up. Now, break out of speak. Notice what happens : the `read()` in tick returns 0, signifying EOF. In this way, the reader can tell when all writers have closed their connection to the FIFO.

What happens when you break out of tick while speak is running. You get "Broken Pipe"! What does this mean? Well, what has happened is that when all readers for a FIFO close and the writer is still open, the writer will receiver the signal SIGPIPE the next time it tries to write(). The default signal handler for this signal prints "Broken Pipe" and exits. Of course, you can handle this more gracefully by catching SIGPIPE through the `signal()` call.

O_NDELAY! I'm UNSTOPPABLE!

Earlier, it is mentioned that you could get around the blocking `open()` call if there was no corresponding reader or writer. The way to do this is to call `open()` with the O_NDELAY flag set in the mode argument:

```
fd = open(FIFO_NAME, O_RDONLY | O_NDELAY);
```

This will cause `open()` to return -1 if there are no processes that have the file open for reading.

Likewise, you can open the reader process using the O_NDELAY flag, but this has a different effect: all attempts to `read()` from the pipe will simply return 0 bytes read if there is no data in the pipe. (That is, the `read()` will no longer block until there is some data in the pipe.) Note that you can no longer tell if `read()` is returning 0 because there is no data in the pipe, or because the writer has exited. This is the price of power, but my suggestion is to try to stick with blocking whenever possible.

Multiple Writers - How do I multiplex all these ?

```
"What?" you ask "There can be multiple writers to the same pipe?"
```

Let us say, you have a pipe with one reader and one writer connected to it. There's no problem for the reader, since there is only one place its data could be coming from (namely, the one writer.) Suddenly another writer leaps snarling from the shadows! Without provocation, it begins spewing random data into the pipe! How is the poor reader going to sort the data from the two writers?

Well, there are lots of ways, and they all depend on what kind of data you are passing back and forth. One of the simplest ways would occur if all the writers were sending the same amount of data every time (lets say, 1024 bytes). Then the reader could read 1024 bytes at a time and be assured that it's getting a single packet (as opposed to, say 512 bytes from one writer and 512 from the other.) Still, though, there is no way to tell which writer sent which packet.

One of the best solutions to this is for each writer to use (or prepend to) the first couple bytes of the packet for some kind of unique identifier. The reader can pick up this identifier and determine which writer sent the packet. This "id" can be thought of as a petite packet header.

Allowing for a packet header gives us a lot more flexibility with what we can send through a pipe. For instance, you could also add a length field that tells the reader how many bytes of data accompany the header. A sample data structure to hold one of these packets might be :

```
typedef struct {
short id;
short length;
char data[1024]
} PACKET;
```

By transmitting a packet with structure similar to the above, you could have an arbitrary number of writers sending packets of varying lengths. The reader will be able to sort it all out since it gets the "id" of the source writer and the length of the packet.

Finally, what happens if you have multiple readers? Well, strange things happen. Sometimes one of the readers get everything. Sometimes it alternates between readers. Why do you want to have multiple readers, anyway?

popen() and pclose() functions

The standard I/O library has provided popen(), pclose() functions for creating pipes and closing them. These two things can handle all the necessary things needed to communicate two processes such as creating pipe, fork'ing, calling exec family of functions, closing unused ends of the pipe in the both processes and returns either reading or writing file stream pointer to parent process. The syntax of the functions are as follows.

```
FILE * popen( char* cmdstring, char *type);
int pclose(FILE *)
```

Here, when popen() function called the following actions takes place :

(a) pipe() system call is called

(b) fork() system call is called and new (child) process is created.

(c) execve() system call is called to start the shell. Also, it returns either reading or writing file stream pointer to the parent process with the help of which parent process can either read the output of the child process from pipe or write into the pipe such that child process can read the same when it runs.

(d) The shell interprets the **cmdstring**

(e) Shell starts the command. If not, shell return an error from popen() function.

Example 12

```
#include <stdio.h>
#include <string.h>
#include <stdlib.h>
#include <unistd.h>

int main()
{
  char buf[256]; FILE *p;

  if( !(p=popen("ps -al", "r")))  {
                                    perror("popen");
                                    exit (-1);
                                    }
  while ((fgets(buf, sizeof(buf),p)!=0)
  fputs(buf, stdout);

  if(pclose(p))
  {
  perror("pclose");
  exit(-1);
  }
  return 0;
  }
```

If we run the above program we may see that the following processes are running on the terminal.

(a) current program

(b) shell

(c) ps -al

The following program explains how to write into pipe such that the child process can use it. Here, by calling popen() function mail program is made as a child process and writing stream pointer will be returned to parent process. In the parent process, a message written into pipe using this file stream pointer which in turn delivered to the user as a email message.

Example 13

```
#include <pwd.h>
#include <sys/types.h>
#include <stdio.h>
#include <string.h>
#include <stdlib.h>
#include <unistd.h>
```

```c
int main()
{
   char cmd[256];
   FILE *p;
   struct passwd *pw=0;

   if(!(pw=getpwuid(geteuid()))) {
                                   perror("getpwuid");
                                   exit(-1);
                                   }

   sprintf(cmd, "mail -s 'A Message From ' %s", pw->pw_name);

   if( !(p=popen(cmd, "w"))) {
                               perror("popen");
                               exit (-1);
                               }

   fprintf(p,"This is a Test Message\n");

   if(pclose(p))
   {
   perror("pclose");
   exit(-1);
   }
   return 0;
}
```

Conclusions

The basic IPC communication mechanism, pipes are explained with live examples. Both nameless and named pipes and their relative applicability for IPC is outlined. How two related processes can communicate in full duplex manner is high lighted. The classical producer consumer problem of Operating system is implemented using pipes. Standard C library functions popen() and pclose() are also used for IPC.

Questions

1. When do you require nameless pipes.

2. When do you required from use named pipes.

3. What will be difficulties if we want from use pipes for client server applications ?

4. Can you see pipes are alternatives for packet communication ?

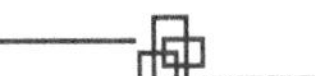

20   IPC - Message Queues

Inter Process Communication

Many variants of Unix these days support a set of inter-process communications methods, which includes message queues (used for sending and receiving messages), shared memory (used to allow several processes share data in memory) and semaphores (used to co-ordinate access by several processes, to other resources). Each of these resource types is handled by the system, and unlike anonymous pipes, may out-live the process that created it. These resources also have some security support by the system, that allows one to specify which processes may access a given message queue, for example.

The fact that these resources are global to the system has two contradicting implications. On one hand, it means that if a process exits, the data it sent through a message queue, or placed in shared memory is still there, and can be collected by other processes. On the other hand, this also means that the programmer has to take care of freeing these resources, or they occupy system resources until the next reboot, or until being removed by hand.

Permission Issues

Before delving into the usage of the different IPC mechanisms, we will describe the security model used to limit access to these resources.

Private Vs. Public

Each resource in IPC may be either private or public. Private means that it may be accessed only by the process that created it, or by child processes of this process. Public means that it may be potentially accessed by any process in the system, except when access permission modes state otherwise.

Access Permission Modes - The 'ipc_perm' Structure

IPC resources may be protected using access mode permissions, much like files and directories are protected by the Unix system. Each such resource has an owning user and an owning group. Permission modes define if and how processes belonging to different users in the system may access this resource. Permissions may be set separately for the owning user, for users from the owning group, and everyone else. Permissions may be set for reading the resource (e.g. reading messages from a message queue), or writing to the resource (e.g. sending a message on a queue, changing the value of a semaphore). A structure of type 'ipc_perm', which is defined as follows is used.

```
struct ipc_perm
{
key_t  key; /* key identifying the resource  */
ushort uid; /* owner effective user ID and effective group ID*/
ushort gid;
ushort cuid;   /* creator effective user ID and
                  effective group ID */
ushort cgid;
ushort mode;  /* access modes  */
ushort seq;   /* sequence number */
};
```

These fields have the following meanings :

- key - the identifier of the resource this structure refers to.
- uid - effective user ID owning the resource.
- gid - effective group ID owning the resource.
- cuid - effective user ID that created the resource.
- cgid - effective group ID that created the resource.
- mode - access permission modes for the given resource. This is a bit field, with the lowest 9 bits denoting access flags, and are a bit-wise 'or' of the following (octal) values:
- 0400 - owning user may read from this resource.
- 0200 - owning user may write to this resource.
- 0040 - owning group may read from this resource.
- 0020 - owning group may write to this resource.
- 0004 - every other user may read from this resource.
- 0002 - every other user may write to this resource.
- seq - used to keep system-internal info about the resource. for further info, check your kernel's sources (you are working on a system with free access to its source code, right?).

Part of the IPC API allows us to modify the access permissions for the resources. We will encounter them when discussing the different IPC methods.

System Utilities to Administer IPC Resources

Since IPC resources live outside the scope of a single process, there is a need to manage them somehow - delete resources that were left by irresponsible processes (or process crashes); check the number of existing resources of each type (especially to find if the system-global limit was reached), etc. Two utilities (commands) were created for handling these jobs: '**ipcs**' - to check usage of IPC resources, and '**ipcrm**' - to remove such resources.

Running '**ipcs**' will show us statistics separately for each of the three resource types (shared memory segments, semaphore arrays and message queues). For each resource type, the command will show us some statistics for each resource that exists in the system. It will show its identifier, owner, size of resources it occupies in the system, and permission flags. We may give '**ipcs**' a flag to ask it to show only resources of one type ('**-m**' for shared Memory segments, **-q** for message Queues and '**-s**' for Semaphore arrays). We may also use '**ipcs**' with the '**-l**' flag to see the system enforced limits on these resources, or the '**-u**' flag to show us usage summary. Refer to the manual page of '**ipcs**' for more information.

The '**ipcrm**' command accepts a resource type ('**shm**', '**msg**' or '**sem**') and a resource ID, and removes the given resource from the system. We need to have the proper permissions in order to delete a resource.

Using Message Queues

One of the problems with pipes is that it is up to you, as a programmer, to establish the protocol. Now, usually this protocol is based on sending separate messages. With a stream taken from a pipe, it means you have to somehow parse the bytes, and separate them to packets to get meaningful information. Another problem is that data sent via pipes always arrives in a FIFO order. This means that before you can read any part of the stream, you have to consume all the bytes sent before the piece you're looking for, and thus you need to construct your own queuing mechanism on which you place the data you just skipped, to be read later. If that's what you're interested at, this is a good time to get acquainted with message queues.

What Are Message Queues ?

A message queue is a queue onto which messages can be placed. A message is composed of a message type (which is a number), and message data. A message queue can be either private, or public. If it is private, it can be accessed only by its creating process or child processes of that creator. If it's public, it can be accessed by any process that knows the queue's key. Several processes may write messages onto a message queue, or read messages from the queue. Messages may be read by type, and thus not have to be read in a FIFO order as is the case with pipes.

Creating A Message Queue - `msgget()`

In order to use a message queue, it has to be created first. The msgget() system call is used to do just that. This system call accepts two parameters - a queue key, and flags. The key may be one of:

- IPC_PRIVATE - used to create a private message queue.
- a positive integer - used to create (or access) a publicly-accessible message queue.

The second parameter contains flags that control how the system call is to be processed. It may contain flags like IPC_CREAT or IPC_EXCL, which behave similar to O_CREAT and O_EXCL in the open() system call, and will be explained later, and it also contains access permission bits. The lowest 9 bits of the flags are used to define access permission for the queue, much like similar 9 bits are used to control access to files. The bits are separated into 3 groups - user, group and others. In each set, the first bit refers to read permission, the second bit to write permission, and the third bit is ignored (no execute permission is relevant to message queues).

Lets see an example of a code that creates a private message queue :

Example 1

```
#include <stdio.h>     /* standard I/O routines. */
#include <sys/types.h> /* standard system data types. */
#include <sys/ipc.h>  /* common system V IPC structures. */
#include <sys/msg.h>  /* message-queue specific functions. */

void main()
{
  int queue_id;
/* create a private message queue, with access only
  to the owner. */

queue_id = msgget(IPC_PRIVATE, 0600); /* <-this is
                                   an octal number. */
if (queue_id == -1) {
  perror("msgget");
  exit(1);
}

printf("Message Queue ID=%d\n", queue_id);

}
```

A Few notes about this Code

1. The system call returns an integer identifying the created queue. Later on we can use this key in order to access the queue for reading and writing messages.

2. The queue created belongs to the user whose process created the queue. Thus, since the permission bits are '0600', only processes run on behalf of this user will have access to the queue.

Example 2

The following program creates a public message queue by specifying some key value.

```
#include <stdio.h>      /* standard I/O routines.          */
#include <sys/types.h> /* standard system data types.     */
#include <sys/ipc.h>  /* common system V IPC structures.  */
#include <sys/msg.h> /* message-queue specific functions. */

void main()
{
int queue_id;

queue_id = msgget((key_t) 10, IPC_CREAT | 0644);
if (queue_id == -1) {
  perror("msgget");
  exit(1);
}

printf("Message Queue ID=%d\n", queue_id);
}
```

Into the queue created, this process can read and write where as other processes can only read. Also, if we run the above program more than once with same key then new queue will not be created rather it returns the IPC ID of the existing queue associated with that key to the calling program.

When we execute the unix command "`ipcs -q`" we may get the following output which indicates that message queue is created in the kernel space.

Message Queues

key	msqid	owner	perms	used-bytes	messages
0x0000000a	0	root	644	0	0

Example 3

The following program creates a public message queue by specifying some key value if it is not already existing otherwise it prints a error message.

```c
#include <stdio.h>      /* standard I/O routines.    */
#include <sys/types.h> /* standard system data types. */
#include <sys/ipc.h>  /* common system V IPC structures. */
#include <sys/msg.h>  /*message-queue specific functions. */

void main()
{
int queue_id;

queue_id = msgget((key_t) 10, IPC_CREAT | IPC_EXCL);
if (queue_id <0) {
printf("msgget() failed\n");
exit(1);
}
else
printf("Message Queue ID=%d\n", queue_id);
}
```

Example 4

Run the following program and find out how many queue's can be created on your machine. The result may vary from machine to machine Also identify the queue IPC ID's returned by the system.

```c
#include <stdio.h>      /* standard I/O routines. */
#include <sys/types.h> /* standard system data types. */
#include <sys/ipc.h>  /* common system V IPC structures.   */
#include <sys/msg.h>  /*message-queue specific functions. */

void main()
{
   int queue_id,i;

   for(i=0; i<1024; i++)
   {
      queue_id = msgget((key_t) i,  IPC_PRIVATE| 0644);

      printf("%d\t %d\n", i, queue_id);
```

```
        if (queue_id == -1) {
        perror("msgget");
        exit(1);
    }


}


}
```

The last value of variable I indicates the limit on number of message queues that can be created by a process.

The Message Structure - `struct msgbuf`

Before we go to writing messages to the queue or reading messages from it, we need to see how a message looks. The system defines a structure named 'msgbuf' for this purpose. Here is how it is defined :

```
struct msgbuf {
long mtype; /*messagetype, apositivenumber(cannotbezero).*/
char mtext[1]; /*message body array. usually larger
                  than one byte. */
};
```

The message type part is rather obvious. But how do we deal with a message text that is only 1 byte long? Well, we actually may place a much larger text inside a message. For this, we allocate more memory for a msgbuf structure than `size of(struct msgbuf)`. Lets see how we create an "hello world" message:

```
/* first, define the message string */
   char* msg_text = "hello world";
/* allocate a message with enough space for length of
   string and */
/* one extra byte for the terminating null character. */
   struct msgbuf* msg =
      (struct msgbuf*)malloc(sizeof(struct msgbuf) +
      strlen(msg_text));
/* set the message type. for example - set it to '1'. */
      msg->mtype = 1;
/* finally, place the "hello world" string inside
              the message. */
strcpy(msg->mtext, msg_text);
```

Few Notes

1. When allocating a space for a string, one always needs to allocate one extra byte for the null character terminating the string. In our case, we allocated strlen(msg_text) more than the size of "struct msgbuf", and didn't need to allocate an extra place for the null character, cause that's already contained in the msgbuf structure (the 1 byte of mtext there).

2. We don't need to place only text messages in a message. We may also place binary data. In that case, we could allocate space as large as the msgbuf struct plus the size of our binary data, minus one byte. Ofcourse then to copy the data to the message, we'll use a function such as memset(), and not strcpy().

Writing Messages Onto A Queue - `msgsnd()`

Once we created the message queue, and a message structure, we can place it on the message queue, using the `msgsnd()` system call. This system call copies our message structure and places that as the last message on the queue. It takes the following parameters:

1. `int msqid` - id of message queue, as returned from the msgget() call.

2. `struct msgbuf* msg` - a pointer to a properly initializes message structure, such as the one we prepared in the previous section.

3. `int msgsz` - the size of the data part (mtext) of the message, in bytes.

4. `int msgflg` - flags specifying how to send the message. may be a logical "or" of the following:

   - `IPC_NOWAIT` - if the message cannot be sent immediately, without blocking the process, return '-1', and set `errno` to `EAGAIN`. to set no flags, use the value '0'.

So in order to send our message on the queue, we'll use `msgsnd()` like this:

```
int rc = msgsnd(queue_id, msg, strlen(msg_text)+1, 0);
if (rc == -1) {
  perror("msgsnd");
  exit(1);
}
```

Note that we used a message size one larger than the length of the string, since we're also sending the null character. Function msgsnd() assumes the data in the message to be an arbitrary sequence of bytes, so it cannot know we've got the null character there too, unless we state that explicitly.

Reading A Message From The Queue - `msgrcv()`

We may use the system call `msgrcv()` in order to read a message from a message queue. This system call accepts the following list of parameters :

1. `int msqid` - id of the queue, as returned from `msgget()`.

2. `struct msgbuf* msg` - a pointer to a pre-allocated msgbuf structure. It should generally be large enough to contain a message with some arbitrary data (*see more below*).

3. `int msgsz` - size of largest message text we wish to receive. Must NOT be larger than the amount of space we allocated for the message text in 'msg'.

4. `int msgtyp` - Type of message we wish to read, may be one of :

   - 0 - The first message on the queue will be returned.

   - a positive integer - the first message on the queue whose type (mtype) equals this integer (unless a certain flag is set in msgflg, *see below*).

   - a negative integer - the first message on the queue whose type is less than or equal to the absolute value of this integer.

6. `int msgflg` - a logical 'or' combination of any of the following flags :

   - `IPC_NOWAIT` - if there is no message on the queue matching what we want to read, return '-1', and set errno to ENOMSG.

   - `MSG_EXCEPT` - if the message type parameter is a positive integer, then return the first message whose type is NOT equal to the given integer.

   - `MSG_NOERROR` - If a message with a text part larger than 'msgsz' matches what we want to read, then truncate the text when copying the message to our msgbuf structure. If this flag is not set and the message text is too large, the system call returns '-1', and errno is set to E2BIG.

Lets then try to read our message from the message queue :

```c
/* prepare a message structure large enough to
   read our "hello world". */
struct msgbuf* recv_msg =
    (struct msgbuf*)malloc(sizeof(struct msgbuf)+strlen
    ("hello world"));
/* use msgrcv() to read the message. We agree to get
   any type, and thus */
/* use '0' in the message type parameter, and use no
   flags (0). */
int rc = msgrcv(queue_id, recv_msg, strlen
        ("hello world")+1, 0, 0);
if (rc == -1) {
perror("msgrcv");
exit(1);
}
```

Few Notes

1. If the message on the queue was larger than the size of "hello world" (plus one), we would get an error, and thus exit.

2. If there was no message on the queue, the `msgrcv()` call would have blocked our process until one of the following happens:
   - a suitable message was placed on the queue.
   - the queue was removed (and then `errno` would be set to `EIDRM`).
   - our process received a signal (and then `errno` would be set to `EINTR`.

Removing Message Queue, getting message queue status : `msgctl()`

With the help of `msgctl()` function we can remove a queue, get status of the queue, etc.,. The syntax of the `msgctl()` function is :

```
msgctl(int msqid, int flags, struct msqid_ds *buf)
```

1. msqid is the IPC ID as returned by the msgget() function.
2. The flags argument is used to specify the action to be performed.
   (a) IPC_RMID to remove the message queue.
   (b) IPC_STAT to get the queue status information
   (c) IPC_SET to change the properties of the queue such as queue size etc.,.
3. When you want to remove (IPC_RMID) the queue this argument can be NULL, where as with two options we have to send valid address. In the case of IPC_STAT, the queue information is stored at this address. Where as with IPC_SET, we have fill the required fields in a struct msqid_ds type of variable to required values and then its address can be passed as third argument.

```
struct msqid_ds
{
  struct ipc_perm msg_perm;
  struct msg *msg_first;
  struct msg *msg_last;
  ushort msg_cbytes;
  ushort msq_qnum;
  ushort msg_qbytes;
  ushort msg_lspid;    /*  pid of the process which
                           received the message last */
  ushort msg_lrpid;    /*  pid of the process which
                           sent the message last */
  time_t msg_stime;    /*  when the last message is
                           sent in to queue */
  time_t msg_rtime;    /*  when the last message is read  */
  time_t msg_ctime;    /*  queue cretaion time */
};
```

Example 5

The following program takes message queue's IPC ID number from the command line and removes the same from the system resource list.

```c
#include <stdio.h>  /* standard I/O routines. */
#include <sys/types.h> /* standard system data types. */
#include <sys/ipc.h>  /* common system V IPC structures. */
#include <sys/msg.h> /* message-queue specific functions. */
#include<stdlib.h>

void main(int N, char **a)
{
   int q_id_to_be_removed=atoi(a[1]);

   if(msgctl(q_id_to_be_removed, IPC_RMID,0)<0)
   {
     perror("msgctl");
     exit(1);
   }

   printf("Successfully removed\n");

}
```

Before running this program, make sure that queue is created and its IPC ID is given as command line argument to the above program. Of course, the message queue can be removed by executing **ipcrm -q** command.

Example 6

Now that you've seen all the different parts, you're invited to look at the following program, for the complete program. Here, a single process creates a message queue and sends itself a "hello world" message via this queue.

```c
#include <stdio.h>
#include <sys/types.h>
#include <sys/ipc.h>
#include <sys/msg.h>

int main(int argc, char* argv[])
{
   /* create a private message queue, with access
      only to the owner. */
```

```c
      int queue_id = msgget(IPC_PRIVATE, 0600);
                      struct msgbuf* msg;
   struct msgbuf* recv_msg;
   int rc;

   if (queue_id == -1) {
     perror("main: msgget");
     exit(1);
   }
printf("message queue created, queue id '%d'.\n", queue_id);
msg = (struct msgbuf*)malloc(sizeof(struct
        msgbuf)+strlen("hello world"));
msg->mtype = 1;
strcpy(msg->mtext, "hello world");
rc = msgsnd(queue_id, msg, strlen(msg->mtext)+1, 0);
if (rc == -1) {
   perror("main: msgsnd");
   exit(1);
}
free(msg);
printf("message placed on the queue successfully.\n");
recv_msg = (struct msgbuf*)malloc(sizeof(struct
            msgbuf)+strlen("hello world"));
rc = msgrcv(queue_id, recv_msg, strlen("helloworld")+1,0,0);
if (rc == -1) {
   perror("main: msgrcv");
   exit(1);
}

printf("msgrcv: received message: mtype '%d'; mtext '%s'\n",
      recv_msg->mtype, recv_msg->mtext);

return 0;
}
```

Example 7

By executing the following program we can print the status information about the queue.
We have to give queue IPC ID as the command line argument.

```c
#include <stdio.h>    /* standard I/O routines. */
#include <sys/types.h> /* standard system data types. */
#include <sys/ipc.h>  /* common system V IPC structures. */
#include <sys/msg.h>  /* message-queue specific functions. */
#include<stdlib.h>
```

```c
void main(int N, char **a)
{
struct msqid_ds X;
int qid=atoi(a[1]);

if(msgctl(qid, IPC_STAT, &X)<0)
{
  perror("msgctl");
  exit(-1);
}

printf("Pid of the Process which sent the last message to
queue=%d\n", X.msg_lspid);
printf("Pid of the Process which read the last message from
the queue=%d\n", X.msg_lrpid);
printf("Message Queue size=%d\n", X.msg_nbytes);

}
```

Example 8 : Message Queues - A Complete

As an example of using non-private message queues, we will show a program, named "queue_sender", that creates a message queue, and then starts sending messages with different priorities onto the queue. A second program, named "queue_reader", may be run that reads the messages from the queue, and does something with them (in our example - just prints their contents to standard output). The "queue_reader" is given a number on its command line, which is the priority of messages that it should read. By running several copies of this program simultaneously, we can achieve a basic level of concurrency. Such a mechanism may be used by a system in which several clients may be sending requests of different types, that need to be handled differently.

```c
#ifndef QUEUE_DEFS_H
# define QUEUE_DEFS_H

/*
* queue_defs.h-common macros and definitions for the
     public message
*  queue example. */

#define QUEUE_ID 137   /* ID of queue to generate. */
#define MAX_MSG_SIZE 200  /* size(in bytes) of largest
                              message we'll send.*/
#define NUM_MESSAGES 100 /* number of messages the
                             sender program will send.*/
```

```c
#endif /* QUEUE_DEFS_H */


/*
    * queue_reader.c - a program that reads messages
    * with a given identifier off of a message queue. */


#include <stdio.h>     /* standard I/O functions. */
#include <stdlib.h>  /* malloc(), free() etc. */
#include <unistd.h>  /* sleep(), etc. */
#include <sys/types.h> /* various type definitions. */
#include <sys/ipc.h>  /* general Sys V IPC structures */
#include <sys/msg.h>  /* message queue functions and structs.*/
#include "queue_defs.h"  /* definitions shared by both programs*/


void main(int argc, char* argv[])
{
   int queue_id;  /* ID of the created queue.   */
   struct msgbuf* msg;  /* structure used for received messages.*/
   int rc;      /* error code returned by system calls.  */
   int msg_type;   /* type of messages we want to receive.  */

   /* read message type from command line */
   if (argc != 2) {
     fprintf(stderr, "Usage: %s <message type>\n", argv[0]);
     fprintf(stderr, "<message type> must be between 1 and 3.\n");
     exit(1);
   }
   msg_type = atoi(argv[1]);
   if (msg_type < 1 || msg_type > 3) {
     fprintf(stderr, "Usage: %s <message type>\n", argv[0]);
     fprintf(stderr, "<message type> must be between 1 and 3.\n");
     exit(1);
   }


   /* access the public message queue that the
      sender program created. */
   queue_id = msgget(QUEUE_ID, 0);
   if (queue_id == -1) {
     perror("main: msgget");
   exit(1);
   }
```

```c
    printf("message queue opened, queue id '%d'.\n", queue_id);
    msg = (struct msgbuf*)malloc(sizeof(struct
            msgbuf)+MAX_MSG_SIZE);

    /* form a loop of receiving messages and printing them out.*/
    while (1) {
    rc = msgrcv(queue_id, msg, MAX_MSG_SIZE+1, msg_type, 0);
    if (rc == -1) {
      perror("main: msgrcv");
      exit(1);
    }
    printf("Reader '%d' read message: '%s'\n",
            msg_type, msg->mtext);
    /* slow down a little... */
    sleep(1);
    }
/* NOT REACHED */
}


/*
   * queue_sender.c-a program that reads messages with
   * one of 3 identifiers to a message queue. */

#include <stdio.h>     /* standard I/O functions. */
#include <stdlib.h>    /* malloc(), free() etc.  */
#include <sys/types.h> /* various type definitions.  */
#include <sys/ipc.h> /* general SysV IPC structures  */
#include <sys/msg.h> /* message queue functions and structs.*/

#include "queue_defs.h"    /* definitions shared by
                                both programs */

int main(int argc, char* argv[])
{
   int queue_id; /* ID of the created queue.    */
   struct msgbuf* msg;  /* structure used for sent messages.*/
   /*struct msgbuf* recv_msg;*/
   int i;                     /* loop counter                 */
   int rc; /* error code retuend by system calls. */
```

```
/* create a public message queue, with access
   only to the owning user. */
queue_id = msgget(QUEUE_ID, IPC_CREAT | IPC_EXCL | 0600);
if (queue_id == -1) {
  perror("main: msgget");
  exit(1);
}
printf("message queue created, queue id '%d'.\n", queue_id);
msg = (struct msgbuf*)malloc(sizeof(struct
        msgbuf)+MAX_MSG_SIZE);


/* form a loop of creating messages and sending them. */
for (i=1; i <= NUM_MESSAGES; i++) {
msg->mtype = (i % 3) + 1; /* create message type
                             between '1' and '3' */
sprintf(msg->mtext, "hello world - %d", i);
rc = msgsnd(queue_id, msg, strlen(msg->mtext)+1, 0);
if (rc == -1) {
  perror("main: msgsnd");
  exit(1);
  }
}
/* free allocated memory. */
free(msg);

printf("generated %d messages, exiting.\n", NUM_MESSAGES);

return 0;
}
```

Once a message is received (read) by a process it will be removed from the queue. Also, note that message queues along with message will persist even after the process which created them has expired (completed). Unlike pipes, un-related processes can exchange information through message queues.

Conclusions

The message queues, another IPC mechanism is dealt in this chapter with live examples. The need for message queues are explained initially. Message queue creation, message packets communication and reception is explained.

Questions

1. Write a server and client programs to simulate Distributed Time Server (*see* distributed operating systems concepts in OS books).

2. Write a program which creates a message queue and writes message into queue which contains number of users working on the machine along with observed time in hours and minutes. This rs repeated for *every* 10 minutes. Write another program which reads this information from the queue and calculates on average in each hour how many users are working.

3. What is difference between pipes and message queues.

4. If the speed difference between producer processes and consumer process is more, which one do you prefer, pipes or queues ?

5. Does the information sent by a process from queue is available in the even after the process which created it is dead ?

6. Answer the above question assuming that the process which created and sent the messages is dead and system is also rebooted.

21 Shared Memory

Shared Memory : An Introduction

Pipes, message queues are created in order to let processes communicate. The problem is that all these methods are sequential in nature. What can we do in order to allow processes to share data in a random-access manner? Shared memory comes to the rescue. As you might know, on a Unix system, each process has its own virtual address space, and the system makes sure no process would access the memory area of another process. This means that if one process corrupts its memory's contents, this does not directly affect any other process in the system. With shared memory, we declare a given section in the memory as one that will be used simultaneously by several processes. Thus the data found in this memory section (or memory segment) will be seen by several processes. Ofcourse, these processes might try to alter this memory area at the same time, and thus some method should be used to synchronize their access to this memory area ("apply mutual exclusion using a semaphore" which will be explained in later chapters).

Background - Virtual Memory Management Under Unix

In order to understand the concept of shared memory, we should first check how virtual memory is managed on the system. When the process is started, it is being allocated a memory segment to hold the runtime stack, a memory segment to hold the program's code which is also known as text area (the code segment), and a memory for data (the data segment). Each such segment might be composed of many memory pages. When ever the process needs to allocate more memory, new pages are being allocated for it, to enlarge its data segment. When a process is being forked (discussed in previous chapters) off from another process, the memory page table of the parent process is being copied to the child process, but not the pages themselves. If the child process will try to update any of these pages, then this page specifically will be copied, and then only the copy of the child process will be modified. This behavior is very efficient for processes that call `fork()` and immediately use the `exec()` system call to replace the program it runs.

With shared memory, we declare a given section in the memory as one that will be used simultaneously by several processes. Thus the data found in this memory section (or memory segment) will be seen by several processes. What all we need in order to support shared memory, is to some memory pages to be declared as shared, and to allow a way to identify them. This way, one process will create a shared memory segment, other processes will attach to them (by placing their physical address in the process's memory pages table). That is we can let multiple processes attach a segment of physical memory to their virtual address spaces. From now all these processes will access the same physical memory when accessing these pages, thus sharing this memory area.

Allocating A Shared Memory Segment

A shared memory segment first needs to be allocated (created), using the `shmget()` system call. This call gets a key for the segment (like the keys used in `msgget()` and `semget()`), the desired segment size, and flags to denote access permissions and whether to create this page if it does not exist yet. `shmget()` returns an identifier that can be later used to access the memory segment. It is prototyped by :

```
int shmget(key_t key, size_t size, int shmflg);
```

- The `key` argument is a access value associated with the IPC ID.
- The `size` argument is the size in bytes of the requested shared memory.
- The `shmflg` argument specifies the initial access permissions and creation control flags.

Here is how to use this call.

```
/* this variable is used to hold the returned segment
   identifier. */
int shm_id;

/* allocate a shared memory segment with size of 2048 bytes, */
/* accessible only to the current user.
   */
shm_id = shmget(100, 2048, IPC_CREAT | IPC_EXCL | 0600);

if (shm_id == -1) {
  perror("shmget: ");
  exit(1);
}
```

One of the problems with SysV IPC methods is the need to choose a unique identifier for our processes. How can we make sure that the identifier of a semaphore.message queue/shared memory in our project won't collide with the identifier of other program installed on the system? To help with that, the ftok() system call was introduced. This system call accepts two parameters, a path to a file and a character, and generates a more-or-less unique identifier. It does that by finding the "i-node" number of the file (more or less the number of the disk sector containing this file's information), combines it with the second parameter, and thus generates an identifier, that can be later fed to semget, shmget() or msgget(). Here is how to use ftok() :

```
/* identifier returned by ftok() */
key_t set_key;

/* generate a "unique" key for our set, using the */
/* directory "/usr/local/lib/ourprojectdir".      */
set_key = ftok("/usr/local/lib/ourprojectdir", 'a');
if (set_key == -1) {
  perror("ftok: ");
  exit(1);
}
```

If we remove the file and then re-create it, the system is very likely to allocate a new disk sector for this file, and thus activating the same ftok call with this file will generate a different key. Thus, the file used should be a steady file, and not one that is likely to be moved to a different disk or erased and re-created.

When the call succeeds, it returns the shared memory segment ID. This call is also used to get the ID of an existing shared segment (from a process requesting sharing of some existing memory portion). That is, if several processes try to allocate a segment using the same ID, they will all get same identifier for the same page, unless they defined IPC_EXCL in the flags to shmget(). In that case, the call will succeed only if the page did not exist before.

Example 1

The following example demonstrates the creation of shared memory.

```
#include <sys/shm.h>
#include <sys/ipc.h>
#include <stdio.h>
#include <fcntl.h>

int main()
{
  char *p;
  int smid,i,st,fd;
```

```
smid=shmget(10,getpagesize(),IPC_CREAT|0644);

/* here we are asking shared memory  of one page,
    i.e 4096 bytes */

}
```

When we execute "ipcs -m" command before running the above program we may get results on the screen as follows:

Message Queues

key   msqid owner   permsused-bytes   messages

After executing the above program if we run "ipcs -m" command we will get results on the screen as follows:

Shared Memory Segments

key	shmid	owner	perms	bytes	nattch	status
0x0000000a	32768	root	644	4096	0	

Controlling a Shared Memory Segment

The `system call shmctl()` is used to alter the permissions and other characteristics of a shared memory segment. It's prototype is as follows :

```
int shmctl(int shmid, int cmd, struct shmid_ds *buf);
```

The process must have an effective `shmid` of owner, creator or superuser to perform this command. The cmd argument is one of following control commands :

SHM_LOCK

Lock the specified shared memory segment in memory. The process must have the effective ID of superuser to perform this command.

SHM_UNLOCK

Unlock the shared memory segment. The process must have the effective ID of superuser to perform this command.

IPC_STAT

Return the status information contained in the control structure and place it in the buffer pointed to by buf. The process must have read permission on the segment to perform this command.

```
IPC_SET
```

Set the effective user and group identification and access permissions. The process must have an effective ID of owner, creator or superuser to perform this command.

```
IPC_RMID
```

Remove the shared memory segment.

Attaching And Detaching A Shared Memory Segment

After we allocated a memory page, we need to add it to the memory page table of the process. This is done using the `shmat()` (shared-memory attach) system call. Assuming 'shm_id' contains an identifier returned by a call to `shmget()`, here is how to do this:

```
/* these variables are used to specify where the
   page is attached. */

char* shm_addr;
char* shm_addr_ro;

/* attach the given shared memory segment,
    at some free position */
/* that will be allocated by the system. */

shm_addr = shmat(shm_id, NULL, 0);
if (!shm_addr) { /* operation failed. */
  perror("shmat: ");
  exit(1);
}

/* attach the same shared memory segment again, this time in  */
/* read-only mode. Any write operation to this page using this*/
/* address will cause a segmentation violation (SIGSEGV) signal.*/

shm_addr_ro = shmat(shm_id, NULL, SHM_RDONLY);
if (!shm_addr_ro) { /* operation failed. */
  perror("shmat: ");
  exit(1);
}
```

As you can see, a page may be attached in read-only mode, or in read-write mode. The same page may be attached several times by the same process, and then all the given addresses will refer to the same data. In the example above, we can use 'shm_addr' to access the segment both for reading and for writing, while 'shm_addr_ro' can be used for read-only access to this page. Attaching a segment in read-only mode makes sense if our process is not supposed to alter this memory page, and is recommended in such cases. The reason is that if a bug in our process causes it to corrupt its memory image, it might corrupt the contents of the shared segment, thus causing all other processes using this segment to possibly crush. By using a read-only attachment, we protect the rest of the processes from a bug in our process.

Destroying A Shared Memory Segment

After we finished using a shared memory segment, we should destroy it. It is safe to destroy it even if it is still in use (i. e. attached by some process). In such a case, the segment will be destroyed only after all processes detach it. Here is how to destroy a segment :

```
/*    this structure is used by the shmctl() system call. */
      struct shmid_ds shm_desc;

/*    destroy the shared memory segment. */
      if (shmctl(shm_id, IPC_RMID, &shm_desc) == -1) {
      perror("main: shmctl: ");
}
```

Note that any process may destroy the shared memory segment, not only the one that created it, as long as it has write permission to this segment.

Example 2

```
#include <stdio.h>
#include <stdlib.h>
#include <sys/stat.h>
#include <sys/ipc.h>
#include <sys/shm.h>
#include <sys/types.h>
#include <sys/mman.h>
#include <fcntl.h>

void main()
{
   int shmid,i;
   void *p;
   shmid=shmget(14,getpagesize(),IPC_CREAT|0644);
   p=shmat(shmid,0,SHM_RND);
   i=fork();
```

```
    sleep(3);
    if(i==0)shmdt(p);
    sleep(15);
    shmctl(shmid,IPC_RMID,0);
}
```

After executing the above program if we execute "ipcs -m" command with small delay in between we may get the following results on the screen.

Shared Memory Segments

key	shmid	owner	perms	bytes	nattch	status
0x0000000a	32768	root	644	4096	0	
0x0000000e	262145	root	644	4096	2	

Shared Memory Segments

key	shmid	owner	perms	bytes	nattch	status
0x0000000a	32768	root	644	4096	0	
0x0000000e	262145	root	644	4096	1	

In the above program a shared memory is created and attached and then fork() system call is made. As the shared memory is also inherited by the child process, we may find that in total 2 processes are attached to the shared memory; which can be supported by the results of "ipcs -m". After some time, child process is getting detached from the shared memory thus number of processes attached to the shared memory becomes 1. This can be also seen from the "ipcs -m" command output.

Placing Data In Shared Memory

Placing data in a shared memory segment is done by using the pointer returned by the shmat() system call. Any kind of data may be placed in a shared segment, except for pointers. The reason for this is simple: pointers contain virtual addresses. Since the same segment might be attached in a different virtual address in each process, a pointer referring to one memory area in one process might refer to a different memory area in another process. We can try to work around this problem by attaching the shared segment in the same virtual address in all processes (by supplying an address as the second parameter to shmat(), and adding the SHM_RND flag to its third parameter), but this might fail if the given virtual address is already in use by the process.

Here is an example of placing data in a shared memory segment, and later on reading this data. We assume that 'shm_addr' is a character pointer, containing an address returned by a call to shmat().

```c
/* define a structure to be used in the given shared memory segment. */

struct country {
   char name[30];
   char capital_city[30];
   char currency[30];
   int population;
};

/* define a countries array variable. */
int* countries_num;
struct country* countries;

/* create a countries index on the shared memory segment. */
countries_num = (int*) shm_addr;
*countries_num = 0;
countries = (struct country*) ((void*)shm_addr+sizeof(int));

strcpy(countries[0].name, "U.S.A");
strcpy(countries[0].capital_city, "Washington");
strcpy(countries[0].currency, "U.S. Dollar");
countries[0].population = 250000000;
(*countries_num)++;

strcpy(countries[1].name, "Israel");
strcpy(countries[1].capital_city, "Jerusalem");
strcpy(countries[1].currency, "New Israeli Shekel");
countries[1].population = 6000000;
(*countries_num)++;

strcpy(countries[2].name, "France");
strcpy(countries[2].capital_city, "Paris");
strcpy(countries[2].currency, "Frank");
countries[2].population = 60000000;
(*countries_num)++;

/* now, print out the countries data. */
for (i=0; i < (*countries_num); i++) {
   printf("Country %d:\n", i+1);
   printf("  name: %s:\n", countries[i].name);
   printf("  capital city: %s:\n", countries[i].capital_city);
   printf("  currency: %s:\n", countries[i].currency);
   printf("  population: %d:\n", countries[i].population);
}
```

Few Notes about this Code

1. No usage of `malloc()`. Since the memory page was already allocated when we called `shmget()`, there is no need to use malloc() when placing data in that segment. Instead, we do all memory management ourselves, by simple pointer arithmetic operations. We also need to make sure the shared segment was allocated enough memory to accommodate future growth of our data - there are no means for enlarging the size of the segment once allocated (unlike when using normal memory management - we can always move data to a new memory location using the `realloc()` function).

2. Memory alignment. In the example above, we assumed that the page's address is aligned properly for an integer to be placed in it. If it was not, any attempt to try to alter the contents of 'countries_num' would trigger a bus error (SIGBUS) signal. further, we assumed the alignment of our structure is the same as that needed for an integer (when we placed the structures array right after the integer variable).

3. Completeness of the data model. By placing all the data relating to our data model in the shared memory segment, we make sure all processes attaching to this segment can use the full data kept in it. A naive mistake would be to place the countries counter in a local variable, while placing the countries array in the shared memory segment. If we did that, other processes trying to access this segment would have no means of knowing how many countries are in there.

Example 3

The following program creates a shared memory segment and stores first nine 'A's and then calls fork() system call. The shared memory segment is available in both the parent and child processes. While parent process waits the child process replaces all 'A's in the shared memory with lower case 'a's. When the parent process starts it simply reads these 'a's and prints on the screen. Thus, we can find that automatically shared memory segments are inherited by child process. This program also prints some system level details such as minimum size of shared memory etc. See the content of the file created by this program.

```c
#include <sys/shm.h>
#include <sys/ipc.h>
#include <stdio.h>
#include <fcntl.h>
int main()
{
    char *p;
    int smid,i,st,fd;
```

```c
smid=shmget(10,getpagesize(),IPC_CREAT|0644);
p=shmat(smid,0,SHM_RND);

printf("%d-Max no. of shared regions\n",SHMMNI);
printf("%d-Min size of shared memory\n",SHMMIN);
printf("%d-Max size of shared memory\n",SHMMAX);

for(i=0;i<10;i++)  p[i]='A';
p[i]='\0';

fd=open("abc",O_WRONLY|O_CREAT|O_TRUNC);

if(fork()==0)
{
    i=0;
    while(p[i]!='\0')
    {
        write(fd,p+i,1);
        write(1,p+i,1);
        p[i]='a';
        i++;
    }
}
else
{
    wait(&st);

    i=0;
    while(p[i]!='\0')
    {
        write(fd,p+i,1);
        write(1,p+i,1);
        i++;
    }
}

}
```

Example 4

Run the following program and accesses the same shared memory segment created in
the previous program and prints the content there in it. This example is to indicate that
the shared memory created will be available even after the process which created it is

exited. Actually, this behavior is very much needed in some time critical applications. That is, a process (such as packet sniffer) can collects the data (incoming packets) and store them in shared memory while other process can process the same packets at a later stage such that this sniffer process can miss only very minimal number of incoming packets. If we plan to develop a sniffer which itself gathers incoming packets and processes. Then there is a danger of missing some incoming packets especially if packet arrival rate is very high.

```c
#include <sys/shm.h>
#include <sys/ipc.h>
#include <stdio.h>
#include <fcntl.h>

int main()
{
    char *p;
    int smid,i,st,fd;
    smid=shmget(10,getpagesize(),IPC_CREAT|0644);
    p=shmat(smid,0,SHM_RND);
    i=0;
    while(p[i]!='\0')
    {

        write(1,p+i,1);
        i++;
    }

}
```

Example 5 : Two processes communicating via shared memory.

We develop two programs here that illustrate the passing of a simple piece of memory (a string) between the processes if running simultaneously:

```
shm_server.c
```

simply creates the string and shared memory portion.

```
shm_client.c
```

attaches itself to the created shared memory portion and uses the string (prints).

The code listings of the 2 programs now follow :

```c
shm_server.c
#include <sys/types.h>
#include <sys/ipc.h>
```

```c
#include <sys/shm.h>
#include <stdio.h>

#define SHMSZ     27

main()
{
    char c;
    int shmid;
    key_t key;
    char *shm, *s;

    /*
     * We'll name our shared memory segment
     * "5678".
     */
    key = 5678;

    /*
     * Create the segment.
     */

    if ((shmid = shmget(key, SHMSZ, IPC_CREAT | 0666)) < 0) {
        perror("shmget");
        exit(1);
    }

    /*
     * Now we attach the segment to our data space.
     */
    if ((shm = shmat(shmid, NULL, 0)) == (char *) -1) {
        perror("shmat");
        exit(1);
    }

    /*
    Now put some things into the memory for the other process to read.
    */
    s = shm;

    for (c = 'a'; c <= 'z'; c++)
    *s++ = c;
    *s = NULL;
```

```c
/*
   Finally,  we wait until the other process changes
               the first character of our memory to `*',
               indicating that it has read what we put there.
*/
 while (*shm != `*')
   sleep(1);

exit(0);
}


shm_client.c
/*
 * shm-client - client program to demonstrate shared memory.
 */

#include <sys/types.h>
#include <sys/ipc.h>
#include <sys/shm.h>
#include <stdio.h>

#define SHMSZ     27

main()
{
   int shmid;
   key_t key;
   char *shm, *s;

/*
 * We need to get the segment named
 * "5678", created by the server.
 */
key = 5678;

/*
 * Locate the segment.
 */
if ((shmid = shmget(key, SHMSZ, 0666)) < 0) {
    perror("shmget");
    exit(1);
}
```

```c
/*
 * Now we attach the segment to our data space.
 */
if ((shm = shmat(shmid, NULL, 0)) == (char *) -1) {
  perror("shmat");
  exit(1);
}

/*
 * Now read what the server put in the memory.
 */
for (s = shm; *s != NULL; s++)
  putchar(*s);
  putchar('\n');

/*
  Finally, change the first character of the segment to '*',
          indicating we have read the segment.
 */

* shm = '*';

exit(0);
}
```

Example 6 (*Please read this after reading semaphores*)

As a naive example of using shared memory, we collected the source code from the above sections into a file named shared-mem.c. It shows how a single process uses shared memory. Naturally, when two processes (or more) use a single shared memory segment, there may be race conditions, if one process tries to update this segment, while another is reading from it. To avoid this, we need to use some locking mechanism - SysV semaphores (used as mutexes) come to mind here. An example of two processes that access the same shared memory segment using a semaphore to synchronize their access, is found in the file shared-mem-with-semaphore.c in the chapter on semaphores.

```c
/*
 * shared-mem.c - demonstrates basic usage of shared memory.
 */

#include <stdio.h>  /* standard I/O routines.  */
#include <sys/types.h>  /* various type definitions.  */
#include <sys/ipc.h>   /* general SysV IPC structures  */
#include <sys/shm.h>  /* shared memory functions and structs*/
```

```c
/* define a structure to be used in the given
   shared memory segment. */
struct country {
  char name[30];
  char capital_city[30];
  char currency[30];
  int population;
};

int main(int argc, char* argv[])
{
  int shm_id;    /* ID of the shared memory segment.   */
  char* shm_addr;  /* address of shared memory segment.  */
  int* countries_num;  /* number of countries in shared mem.*/
  struct country* countries; /*countries array in shared mem.*/
  struct shmid_ds shm_desc;
  int i;    /* counter for loop operation.       */

  /* allocate a shared memory segment with size of 2048 bytes.*/
  shm_id = shmget(100, 2048, IPC_CREAT | IPC_EXCL | 0600);
  if (shm_id == -1) {
    perror("main: shmget: ");
    exit(1);
  }

  /* attach the shared memory segment to our process's
     address space. */
  shm_addr = shmat(shm_id, NULL, 0);
  if (!shm_addr) { /* operation failed. */
    perror("main: shmat: ");
    exit(1);
  }

  /* create a countries index on the shared memory segment. */
  countries_num = (int*) shm_addr;
  *countries_num = 0;
  countries = (struct country*) ((void*)shm_addr+sizeof(int));

  strcpy(countries[0].capital_city, "U.S.A");
  strcpy(countries[0].capital_city, "Washington");
  strcpy(countries[0].currency, "U.S. Dollar");
  countries[0].population = 250000000;
  (*countries_num)++;
```

```c
strcpy(countries[1].capital_city, "Israel");
strcpy(countries[1].capital_city, "Jerusalem");
strcpy(countries[1].currency, "New Israeli Shekel");
countries[1].population = 6000000;
(*countries_num)++;

strcpy(countries[2].capital_city, "France");
strcpy(countries[2].capital_city, "Paris");
strcpy(countries[2].currency, "Frank");
countries[2].population = 60000000;
(*countries_num)++;

/* now, print out the countries data. */
for (i=0; i < (*countries_num); i++) {
printf("Countery %d:\n", i+1);
printf("name: %s:\n", countries[i].name);
printf("capital city: %s:\n", countries[i].capital_city);
printf("currency: %s:\n", countries[i].currency);
printf("population: %d:\n", countries[i].population);
}

/* detach the shared memory segment from our process's
   address space. */
if (shmdt(shm_addr) == -1) {
   perror("main: shmdt: ");
}

/* de-allocate the shared memory segment. */
if (shmctl(shm_id, IPC_RMID, &shm_desc) == -1) {
   perror("main: shmctl: ");
}

return 0;
}
```

Example 7

This program does one of two things: if you run it with no command line parameters, it prints the contents of the shared memory segment. If you give it one command line parameter, it stores that parameter in the shared memory segment.

```c
#include <stdio.h>
#include <stdlib.h>
#include <string.h>
#include <sys/types.h>
```

```c
#include <sys/ipc.h>
#include <sys/shm.h>

#define SHM_SIZE 1024  /* make it a 1K shared memory segment */

int main(int argc, char *argv[])
{
    key_t key;
    int shmid;
    char *data;
    int mode;

    if (argc > 2) {
        fprintf(stderr, "usage: shmdemo [data_to_write]\n");
        exit(1);
    }

    /* make the key: */

    if ((key = ftok("shmdemo.c", 'R')) == -1) {
        perror("ftok");
        exit(1);
    }

    /* connect to (and possibly create) the segment: */

    if ((shmid = shmget(key, SHM_SIZE, 0644 | IPC_CREAT)) == -1) {
        perror("shmget");
        exit(1);
    }

    /* attach to the segment to get a pointer to it: */

    data = shmat(shmid, (void *)0, 0);
        if (data == (char *)(-1)) {
        perror("shmat");
        exit(1);
    }

    /* read or modify the segment, based on the command line: */

    if (argc == 2) {
        printf("writing to segment: \"%s\"\n", argv[1]);
        strncpy(data, argv[1], SHM_SIZE);
```

```c
    } else
printf("segment contains: \"%s\"\n", data);

    /* detach from the segment: */

if (shmdt(data) == -1) {
    perror("shmdt");
    exit(1);
    }

    return 0;
}
```

Run the above program first time with some message along the command line which will be stored in the shared memory. When we run the same with out any argument the information available in the shared memory is printed.

Conclusions

The chapter starts with introduction from shared and memory and its necessity. How shared memory is created and attached to a processes address space to explained with examples. With some examples, how multiple processes can use shared memory for IPC is explained. The Unix command, ipcs and ipcrm are also used in the chapter.

Questions

1. Write a program which creates a shared memory and gets the same attached. Repeatedly execute the same program by writing a shell program and find out after attaching how many processes we will get error.
2. Simultaneously check ipcs command result from another terminal.
3. Also, find out the shared memory created by a process is avialable from other processes even after the process which is created is dead.
4. What happens from shared memory when system reboots ?
5. Is there any mechanism from save all the shared resources during booting time and restore during the next booting ? Does such need arises ?

22 Semaphores

Process Synchronization With Semaphores

All the inter-process communication methods described in the previous chapters are used to exchange information between processes. However, sometimes we need to synchronize operations amongst more than two processes, or to synchronize access to data resources that might be accessed by several processes in parallel. Semaphores are a means supplied with IPC that allow us to synchronize such operations.

What Is A Semaphore? What Is A Semaphore Set?

A semaphore is a resource that contains an integer value, and allows processes to synchronize by testing and setting this value in a single atomic operation. This means that the process that tests the value of a semaphore and sets it to a different value (based on the test), is guaranteed no other process will interfere with the operation in the middle. Two types of operations can be carried on a semaphore: wait and signal. A set operation first checks if the semaphore's value equals some number. If it does, it decreases its value and returns. If it does not, the operation blocks the calling process until the semaphore's value reaches the desired value. A signal operation increments the value of the semaphore, possibly awakening one or more processes that are waiting on the semaphore. How this mechanism can be put to practical use will be explained soon. A semaphore set is a structure that stores a group of semaphores together, and possibly allows the process to commit a transaction on part or all of the semaphores in the set together. In here, a transaction means that we are guaranteed that either all operations are done successfully, or none is done at all. Note that a semaphore set is not a general parallel programming concept, it's just an extra mechanism supplied by IPC.

Usually, some form of synchronization is needed while dealing with resources. The Unix semaphores gives freedom to group resources into one set and the caller can obtain all resources needed in one system call without worrying about deadlock. If any of the resource requests are not available, the caller simply waits until all the resources are available.

Creating A Semaphore Set - `semget()`

Creation of a semaphore set is done using the `semget()` system call. Similar to the creation of message queues, we supply some ID for the set, and some flags (used to define access permission mode and a few options). We also supply the number of semaphores we want to have in the given set. This number is limited to SEMMSL, as defined in file /usr/include/sys/sem.h. Also, it is necessary that the semaphore values should be initialized soon after their creation for maximum portability as default values for semaphores changes from implementation to implementation.

The semget() functions prototype is :

```
int semget(key_t key, in nsems, int flag);
```

`key` is same as other IPC mechanisms such as messages, shared memory etc.

nsems is the number of semaphores required in the set.

flag is as same as other IPC mechanisms such as message queues, etc.

Lets see an example :

Example 1

```
#include <stdio.h>
#include <unistd.h>
#include <sys/types.h>
#include <sys/ipc.h>
#include <sys/sem.h>
#include <sys/wait.h>
int main()
{

/* ID of the semaphore set.     */
int sem1;
int sem2;

/* create a private semaphore set with one semaphore in it, */
/* with access only to the owner. */

sem1 = semget(IPC_PRIVATE, 1, IPC_CREAT | 0600);
```

```
if (sem1 == -1) {
    perror("main: semget");
    exit(1);
}

/* create a semaphore set with ID 250, three semaphores */
/* in the set, with access only to the owner.           */

sem2 = semget(250, 3, IPC_CREAT | 0600);
if (sem2 == -1) {
    perror("main: semget");
    exit(1);
}

}
```

Note that in the second case, if a semaphore set with ID 250 already existed, we would get access to the existing set, rather than a new set to be created. This works just like it worked with message queues.

Before executing the above program if we execute the command "ipcs -s" we may get the following results on the screen.

Semaphore Arrays

key	semid	owner	perms	nsems
0x00000000	65536	apache	600	1
0x00000000	98305	apache	600	1
0x00000000	131074	apache	600	1

The above results indicates that apache server is currently using some semaphores.

After running the above program if we execute the command "ipcs -s" we may get the following results on the screen which indicates the creation of semaphores in the kernel space.

Semaphore Arrays

key	semid	owner	perms	nsems
0x00000000	65536	apache	600	1
0x00000000	98305	apache	600	1
0x00000000	131074	apache	600	1
0x0000000a	163843	root	644	1

The above output indicates that a semaphore set is created by the root user and IPC ID is 163843; this number is usually used in other semaphore manipulation functions such as semctl(), semop(), etc.

Setting And Getting Semaphore Values With `semctl()`

After the semaphore set is created, we need to initialize the value of the semaphores in the set. We do that using the `semctl()` system call. Note that this system call has other uses, but they are not relevant to our needs right now. It is prototyped as follows :

```
int semctl(int semid, int semnum, int cmd, union semun arg);
```

It must be called with a valid semaphore ID, `semid`. The `semnum` value selects a semaphore within an array by its index. The cmd argument is one of the following control flags:

GETVAL

Return the value of a single semaphore.

SETVAL

Set the value of a single semaphore. In this case, arg is taken as arg.val, an int.

GETPID

Return the `PID` of the process that performed the last operation on the semaphore or array.

GETNCNT

Return the number of processes waiting for the value of a semaphore to increase.

GETZCNT

Return the number of processes waiting for the value of a particular semaphore to reach zero.

GETALL

Return the values for all semaphores in a set. In this case, `arg` is taken as `arg.array`, a pointer to an array of unsigned shorts (see below).

SETALL

Set values for all semaphores in a set. In this case, `arg` is taken as `arg.array`, a pointer to an array of unsigned shorts.

IPC_STAT

Return the status information from the control structure for the semaphore set and place it in the data structure pointed to by `arg.buf`, a pointer to a buffer of type `semid_ds`.

```
IPC_SET
```

Set the *effective* user and group identification and permissions. In this case, `arg` is taken as `arg.buf`.

```
IPC_RMID
```

Remove the specified semaphore set.

Any process with read permission can test whether a semaphore has a zero value. To increment or decrement a semaphore requires write permission. When an operation fails, none of the semaphores is altered.

A process must have an effective user identification of owner, creator, or superuser to perform an `IPC_SET` or `IPC_RMID` command. Read and write permission is required as for the other control commands. The following code illustrates `semctl ()`.

The fourth argument `union semun arg` is optional, depending upon the operation requested. If required it is of type `union semun`, which must be *explicitly* declared by the application program as :

```
union semun {
int val;
struct semid_ds *buf;
ushort *array;
} arg;
```

Lets assume we want to set the values of the three semaphores in our second set to values 3, 6 and 0, respectively. The ID of the first semaphore in the set is '0', the ID of the second semaphore is '1', and so on.

```
/* use this to store return values of system calls.   */
int rc;

/* initialize the first semaphore in our set to '3'.  */
rc = semctl(sem_set_id_2, 0, SETVAL, 3);
if (rc == -1) {
  perror("main: semctl");
  exit(1);
}

/* initialize the second semaphore in our set to '6'. */
rc = semctl(sem_set_id_2, 1, SETVAL, 6);
if (rc == -1) {
  perror("main: semctl");
  exit(1);
}
```

```
/* initialize the third semaphore in our set to '0'.  */
rc = semctl(sem_set_id_2, 2, SETVAL, 0);
if (rc == -1) {
  perror("main: semctl");
  exit(1);
}
```

There is one comment to be made about the way we used semctl() here. According to the manual, the last parameter for this system call should be a union of type union semun. However, since the SETVAL (set value) operation only uses the int val part of the union, we simply passed an integer to the function. The proper way to use this system call was to define a variable of this union type, and set its value appropriately, like this :

```
/* use this variable to pass the value to the semctl() call */
union semun sem_val;

/* initialize the first semaphore in our set to '3'. */
sem_val.val = 0;
rc = semctl(sem_set_id_2, 2, SETVAL, sem_val);
if (rc == -1) {
  perror("main: semctl");
  exit(1);
}
```

We used the first form just for simplicity. From now on, we will only use the second form.

Using Semaphores For Mutual Exclusion With semop()

With the help of semop() function we can perform an array of operations on a semaphore set. This function's prototype is as follows:

```
int semop(int semid, struct sembuf semoparray[], size_t nops);
```

The structure variable sembuf definition is as follows :

```
Struct sembuf
{
ushort sem_num; /* semaphore number in the set. 0...nsems-1 */
short sem_op; /* operation on the semaphore. See the table 22.1 */
short sem_flg;   /* IPC_NOWAIT or SEM_UNDO */
};
```

semid is the IPC ID returned by the semget() function.

Semoparray is a pointer to an array of semaphore operations
nops is number of operations. That is on how many semaphores we wanted to do operations at a time.

sem_op	What happens
Positive	The value of sem_op is added to the semaphore's value. This is how a program uses a semaphore to mark a resource as allocated.
Negative	If the absolute value of sem_op is greater than the value of the semaphore, the calling process will block until the value of the semaphore reaches that of the absolute value of sem_op. Finally, the absolute value of sem_op will be subtracted from the semaphore's value. This is how a process releases a resource guarded by the semaphore.
Zero	This process will wait until the semaphore in question reaches 0.

Table 22.1 sem_op values and their effects.

Sometimes we have a resource that we want to allow only one process at a time to manipulate. Simultaneous requests by different processes are performed in an arbitrary order. When an array of operations is given by a semop() call, no updates are done until all operations on the array can finish successfully.

If a process with exclusive use of a semaphore terminates abnormally and fails to undo the operation or free the semaphore, the semaphore stays locked in memory in the state the process left it. To prevent this, the SEM_UNDO control flag makes semop() allocate an undo structure for each semaphore operation, which contains the operation that returns the semaphore to its previous state. If the process dies, the system applies the operations in the undo structures. This prevents an aborted process from leaving a semaphore set in an inconsistent state. If processes share access to a resource controlled by a semaphore, operations on the semaphore should not be made with SEM_UNDO in effect. If the process that currently has control of the resource terminates abnormally, the resource is presumed to be inconsistent. Another process must be able to recognize this to restore the resource to a consistent state. When performing a semaphore operation with SEM_UNDO in effect, you must also have it in effect for the call that will perform the reversing operation. When the process runs normally, the reversing operation updates the undo structure with a complementary value. This ensures that, unless the process is aborted, the values applied to the undo structure are cancel to zero. When the undo structure reaches zero, it is removed.

Note : Using SEM_UNDO inconsistently can lead to excessive resource consumption because allocated undo structures might not be freed until the system is rebooted.

For example, we have a file that we only want written into only by one process at a time, to avoid corrupting its contents. Of-course, we could use various file locking mechanisms to protect the file, but we will demonstrate the usage of semaphores for this purpose as an example. Later on we will see the real usage of semaphores, to protect access to shared memory segments. Anyway, here is a code snippest. It assumes the semaphore in our set whose id is "sem_set_id" was initialized to 1 initially:

```
/* this function updates the contents of the file with the given path name. */
        void update_file(char* file_path, int number)
        {
        /* structure for semaphore operations.   */
        struct sembuf sem_op;
        FILE* file;

        /* wait on the semaphore, unless it's value is non-negative.*/
        sem_op.sem_num = 0;
        sem_op.sem_op = -1;    /* <- Comment 1 */
        sem_op.sem_flg = 0;
        semop(sem_set_id, &sem_op, 1);

        /* Comment 2 */
        /* we "locked" the semaphore, and are assured exclusive
           access to file.   */
        /* manipulate the file in some way. for example,
           write a number into it. */

        file = fopen(file_path, "w");
        if (file) {
           fprintf(file, "%d\n", number);
           fclose(file);
        }

        /* finally, signal the semaphore-increase its value by one. */
        sem_op.sem_num = 0;
        sem_op.sem_op = 1;    /* <- Comment 3 */
        sem_op.sem_flg = 0;
        semop(sem_set_id, &sem_op, 1);
        }
```

This code needs some explanations, especially regarding the semantics of the `semop()` calls.

1. Comment 1 - before we access the file, we use semop() to wait on the semaphore. Supplying '-1' in sem_op.sem_op means: If the value of the semaphore is greater than or equal to '1', decrease this value by one, and return to the caller. Otherwise (the value is 1 or less), block the calling process, until the value of the semaphore becomes '1', at which point we return to the caller.

2. Comment 2 - The semantics of semop() assure us that when we return from this function, the value of the semaphore is 0. Why? it couldn't be less, or else semop() won't return. It couldn't be more due to the way we later on signal the semaphore. And why it cannot be more than '0'? read on to find out...

3. Comment 3 - after we are done manipulating the file, we increase the value of the semaphore by 1, possibly waking up a process waiting on the semaphore. If several processes are waiting on the semaphore, the first that got blocked on it is wakened and continues its execution.

Now, lets assume that any process that tries to access the file, does it only via a call to our "update_file" function. As you can see, when it goes through the function, it always decrements the value of the semaphore by 1, and then increases it by 1. Thus, the semaphore's value can never go above its initial value, which is '1'. Now lets check two scenarios :

1. No other process is executing the "update_file" concurrently. In this case, when we enter the function, the semaphore's value is '1'. after the first semop() call, the value of the semaphore is decremented to '0', and thus our process is not blocked. We continue to execute the file update, and with the second semop() call, we raise the value of the semaphore back to '1'.

2. Another process is in the middle of the "update_file" function. If it already managed to pass the first call to semop(), the value of the semaphore is '0', and when we call semop(), our process is blocked. When the other process signals the semaphore with the second semop() call, it increases the value of the semaphore back to '0', and it wakes up the process blocked on the semaphore, which is our process. We now get into executing the file handling code, and finally we raise the semaphore's value back to '1' with our second call to semop().

Example 2

We have the source code for a program demonstrating the mutex concept, in the file named sem-mutex.c. The program launches several processes (5, as defined by the NUM_PROCS macro), each of which is executing the "update_file" function several times in a row, and then exits. Try running the program, and scan its output. Each process prints out its PID as it updates the file, so you can see what happens when. Try to play with the DELAY macro (specifying how long a process waits between two calls to "update_file") and see how it effects the order of the operations. Check what happens if you replace the delay loop in the "do_child_loop" function, with a call to sleep().

```
/*
 * sem-mutex.c -demonstrates the usage of a semaphore as a mutex that
 *  that synchronizes accesses of multiple processes
 *  to a file.
 */
```

```c
#include <stdio.h>  /* standard I/O routines.   */
#include <stdlib.h>  /* rand() and srand() functions */
#include <unistd.h>   /* fork(), etc.      */
#include <time.h>   /* nanosleep(), etc. */
#include <sys/types.h>   /* various type definitions.   */
#include <sys/ipc.h>   /* general SysV IPC structures */
#include <sys/sem.h>  /* semaphore functions and structs. */
#include <sys/wait.h>  /* wait(), etc.   */


#define NUM_PROCS  5   /* number of processes to launch. */
#define SEM_ID 250   /* ID for the semaphore. */
#define FILE_NAME "sem_mutex" /* name of file to manipulate */
#define DELAY 400000 /* delay between file updates by one process.*/


/* this function updates the contents of the file
   with the given path name. */
void update_file(int sem_set_id, char* file_path, int number)
{
/* structure for semaphore operations.   */
struct sembuf sem_op;
FILE* file;


/*wait on thesemaphore,unless it's value is non-negative. */
sem_op.sem_num = 0;
sem_op.sem_op = -1;   /* <- Comment 1 */
sem_op.sem_flg = 0;
semop(sem_set_id, &sem_op, 1);


/* Comment 2 */
/* we "locked" the semaphore, and are assured exclusive
   accessto file. */
/* manipulate the file in some way. for example,
   write a number into it. */
file = fopen(file_path, "w");
if (file) {
  fprintf(file, "%d\n", number);
  printf("%d\n", number);
  fclose(file);
}


/* finally, signal the semaphore-increase its value by one. */
sem_op.sem_num = 0;
sem_op.sem_op = 1;   /* <- Comment 3 */
```

```c
sem_op.sem_flg = 0;
semop(sem_set_id, &sem_op, 1);
}

/* this function calls "file_update" several times in a row,  */
/* and waiting a little time between each two calls, in order */
/* to allow other processes time to operate.                 */
void do_child_loop(int sem_set_id, char* file_name)
{
pid_t pid = getpid();
int i, j;

for (i=0; i<3; i++) {
update_file(sem_set_id, file_name, pid);
for (j=0; j<400000; j++)
;
}
}

/* finally, the main() function. */
void main()
{
int sem_set_id;     /* ID of the semaphore set. */
union semun sem_val; /* semaphore value, for semctl(). */
int child_pid;       /* PID of our child process.      */
int i;    /* counter for loop operation.   */
int rc;   /* return value of system calls.  */

/* create a semaphore set with ID 250, with one semaphore  */
/* in it, with access only to the owner.                   */
sem_set_id = semget(SEM_ID, 1, IPC_CREAT | 0600);
if (sem_set_id == -1) {
  perror("main: semget");
  exit(1);
}

/* intialize the first (and single) semaphore in our set to '1'.*/
sem_val.val = 1;
rc = semctl(sem_set_id, 0, SETVAL, sem_val);
if (rc == -1) {
  perror("main: semctl");
  exit(1);
}
```

```c
/* create a set of child processes that will compete
   on the semaphore */
for (i=0; i<NUM_PROCS; i++) {
child_pid = fork();
switch(child_pid) {
  case -1:
    perror("fork");
    exit(1);
  case 0:  /* we're at child process. */
    do_child_loop(sem_set_id, FILE_NAME);
    exit(0);
    default: /* we're at parent process. */
      break;
  }
}

/* wait for all children to finish running */
for (i=0; i<NUM_PROCS; i++) {
int child_status;

wait(&child_status);
}

printf("main: we're done\n");
fflush(stdout);
}
```

File Locking using System V Semaphores

There are occasions when multiple processes want to share some resource. It is essential that some for of mutual exclusion be provided so that only one process at a time accesses the resource. Consider the following scenario. Consider a line printer daemon. The process that places a job on the print queue has to assign a unique sequence number to each print job. We cannot use the process ID as the sequence number as it is possible for a print job to exist long enough for a given pid to be reused. The technique used by the UNIX printer spoolers is to have a file for each printer that contains the next sequence number to be used. The file is just a single line containing the sequence number in ASCII. Each process that needs to assign a sequence number goes through three steps.

1. it reads the sequence number file
2. it uses the number
3. it increments the number and writes it back.

The problem is that in the time it takes a single process to execute these three steps, another process can perform the same three steps. What is needed is for a process to be able to set a lock so that no other process can access the file until the first process has finished with the file. In other words we need to synchronize the access of the processes to the sequence number file. To lock and unlock the resource we may call `semop`.

Example 3

The following code segment shows the implementation of our semaphore synchronization,

```
/*
*Locking routines using semaphores
*/

#include <sys/types.h>
#include <sys/ipc.h>
#include <sys/sem.h>

#define SEMKEY 123456L   /* key value for semget() */
#define PERMS  0666

static struct sembuf    op_lock[2]={
0 , 0, 0    /*wait for sem#0 to become 0*/
0 , 1, 0    /*increment sem#0 to 1 */
};

static struct sembuf op_unlock[1]={
0, -1 , IPC_NOWAIT  /*decrement sem#0 by 1 */
};

int semid = -1     /* semaphore id */

void my_lock(int fd){
if (semid < 0) {
   if( (semid = semget(SEMKEY, 1, IPC_CREAT | PERMS)) < 0)
     err_sys("semget error");
}
if (semop(semid, &op_lock[0],2)<0)
   err_sys("semop lock error");
}

void my_unlock(int fd){
if(semop(semid, &op_unlock[0], 1) < 0)
   err_sys("semop unlock error");
}
```

```
void main(int argc, char **argv){
int fd,i,n,pid,seqno;
char buff[MAXBUFF+1];

pid=getpid();
if( (fd=open(SEQFILE,2)) < 0)
  perror("can't open %s",SEQFILE);

for(i=0;i<20;i++){
  my_lock(fd);
  lseek(fd,0L,0);
  if( (n=read(fd,buff,MAXBUFF))<=0)
    perror("read error");

  buff[n]='\0';
  if( (n=sscanf(buff, "%d\n", &seqno))!=1)
    perror("sscanf error");

  printf("pid=%d, seqno=%d\n",pid,seqno);

  seqno++;

  sprintf(buff, "%03d\n",seqno);
  n=strlen(buff);
  lseek(fd,0L,0);

  if(write(fd,buff,n)!=n)
    perror("write error");
  my_unlock(fd);
  }

}
```

Using Semaphores For Producer-Consumer Operations With `semop()`

Using a semaphore as a mutex is not utilizing the full power of the semaphore. As we saw,
a semaphore contains a counter, that may be used for more complex operations. Those
operations often use a programming model called "producer-consumer". In this model,
we have one or more processes that produce something, and one or more processes that
consume that something. For example, one set of processes accept printing requests from
clients and place them in a spool directory, and another set of processes take the files from
the spool directory and actually print them using the printer. To control such a printing
system, we need the producers to maintain a count of the number of files waiting in the
spool directory and incrementing it for every new file placed there. The consumers check

this counter, and whenever it gets above zero, one of them grabs a file from the spool, and sends it to the printer. If there are no files in the spool (i.e. the counter value is zero), all consumer processes get blocked. The behavior of this counter sounds very familiar.... it is the exact same behavior of a counting semaphore.

Lets see how we can use a semaphore as a counter. We still use the same two operations on the semaphore, namely "signal" and "wait".

```
/* this variable will contain the semaphore set. */
int sem_set_id;

/* semaphore value, for semctl().  */
union semun sem_val;

/* structure for semaphore operations.   */
struct sembuf sem_op;

/* first we create a semaphore set with a single semaphore, */
/* whose counter is initialized to '0'.  */
sem_set_id = semget(IPC_PRIVATE, 1, 0600);
if (sem_set_id == -1) {
  perror("semget");
  exit(1);
}
sem_val.val = 0;
semctl(sem_set_id, 0, SETVAL, sem_val);

/* we now do some producing function, and then signal the   */
/* semaphore, increasing its counter by one.  */
.

.
sem_op.sem_num = 0;
sem_op.sem_op = 1;
sem_op.sem_flg = 0;
semop(sem_set_id, &sem_op, 1);
.

.

.
/* meanwhile, in a different process, we try to consume the */
/* resource protected (and counter) by the semaphore.  */
/* we block on the semaphore, unless it's value is non-negative. */
```

```
sem_op.sem_num = 0;
sem_op.sem_op = -1;
sem_op.sem_flg = 0;
semop(sem_set_id, &sem_op, 1);


/* when we get here, it means that the semaphore's value is '0' */
/* or more, so there's something to consume. */
    .

    .
```

Note that our "wait" and "signal" operations here are just like we did with when using the semaphore as a mutex. The only difference is in who is doing the "wait" and the "signal". With a mutex, the same process did both the "wait" and the "signal" (in that order). In the producer-consumer example, one process is doing the "signal" operation, while the other is doing the "wait" operation.

Example 4

Find the following programs to explain the usage of semop(), semctl() functions.

```
Source code for x.c

#include <stdio.h>
#include <stdlib.h>
#include <errno.h>
#include <sys/types.h>
#include <sys/ipc.h>
#include <sys/sem.h>

int main(int N, char **a)
{
key_t key=20;
int semid,val;

val=atoi(a[1]);

if ((semid = semget(key, 1, IPC_CREAT|0644)) == -1) {
  perror("semget");
  exit(1);
}

semctl(semid,0,SETVAL,val);
return 0;
}
```

Source code for y.c

```c
#include <stdio.h>
#include <stdlib.h>
#include <errno.h>
#include <sys/types.h>
#include <sys/ipc.h>
#include <sys/sem.h>

int main(int N, char **a)
{
key_t key=20;
int semid,retval;
struct sembuf sop={0,0,0};

if ((semid = semget(key, 1, IPC_CREAT|0644)) == -1) {
   perror("semget");
   exit(1);
}
printf("Before Semop\n");
retval=semop(semid, &sop, 1);
printf("%d\n", retval);
return 0;
}
```

If the above program "x" is executed with zero as command line argument and then followed by "y" is executed then "y" prints 0.

If "x" is executed with 1 as command line argument or any other number as command line argument and "y" is executed then "y" gets blocked.

By running 'x" again the "y" program gets terminated.

Example 5

We fork() a child process so that we have two processes running : Each process communicates via a semaphore. The respective process can only do its work (not much here) When it notices that the semaphore track is free when it returns to 0. Each process must modify the semaphore accordingly

```c
#include <stdio.h>
#include <sys/types.h>
#include <sys/ipc.h>
#include <sys/sem.h>

union semun {
   int val;
   struct semid_ds *buf;
   ushort *array;
};
```

```c
main()
{ int i,j;
  int pid;
  int semid; /* semid of semaphore set */
  key_t key = 1234; /* key to pass to semget() */

  int semflg = IPC_CREAT | 0666; /* semflg to pass to semget() */
  int nsems = 1; /* nsems to pass to semget() */
  int nsops; /* number of operations to do */
  struct sembuf *sops = (struct sembuf *) malloc(2*sizeof
                            (struct sembuf));

/* ptr to operations to perform */

/* set up semaphore */

(void) fprintf(stderr, "\nsemget:Settingupseamaphore:
      semget(%#lx, %\ %#o)\n",key, nsems, semflg);

if ((semid = semget(key, nsems, semflg)) == -1) {
  perror("semget: semget failed");
  exit(1);
}
else
(void) fprintf(stderr, "semget: semget succeeded:
                            semid =%d\n", semid);

/* get child process */

if ((pid = fork()) < 0) {
  perror("fork");
  exit(1);
}

if (pid == 0)
{ /* child */
i = 0;

while (i  < 3) {/* allow for 3 semaphore sets */

nsops = 2;

/* wait for semaphore to reach zero */
```

```
sops[0].sem_num = 0; /* We only use one track */
sops[0].sem_op = 0;
/* wait for semaphore flag to become zero */
sops[0].sem_flg = SEM_UNDO; /*take off semaphore asynchronous*/

sops[1].sem_num = 0;
sops[1].sem_op = 1; /* increment semaphore-take
                          control of track */
sops[1].sem_flg = SEM_UNDO | IPC_NOWAIT; /* take off
                                          semaphore */

/* Recap the call to be made. */

(void) fprintf(stderr,"\nsemop:Child  Calling semop
                      (%d, &sops, %d) with:", semid, nsops);
for (j = 0; j < nsops; j++)
{
(void) fprintf(stderr, "\n\tsops[%d].sem_num = %d, ", j,
                      sops[j].sem_num);
(void) fprintf(stderr, "sem_op = %d, ", sops[j].sem_op);
(void) fprintf(stderr, "sem_flg = %#o\n", sops[j].sem_flg);
}

/* Make the semop() call and report the results. */
if ((j = semop(semid, sops, nsops)) == -1) {
  perror("semop: semop failed");
}
else
{
(void) fprintf(stderr, "\tsemop: semop returned %d\n", j);

(void) fprintf(stderr, "\n\nChild Process Taking Control
                          of Track: %d/3 times\n", i+1);
sleep(5); /* DO Nothing for 5 seconds */

nsops = 1;

/* wait for semaphore to reach zero */
sops[0].sem_num = 0;
sops[0].sem_op = -1; /* Give UP COntrol of track */
sops[0].sem_flg = SEM_UNDO | IPC_NOWAIT; /* take off
                          semaphore, asynchronous  */
```

```c
    if ((j = semop(semid, sops, nsops)) == -1) {
      perror("semop: semop failed");
    }
    else
    (void) fprintf(stderr, "Child Process Giving up Control
                            of Track: %d/3 times\n", i+1);
    sleep(5); /* halt process to allow parent to catch
                semaphor change first */
    }
    ++i;
    }


    }
    else /* parent */
    {  /* pid hold id of child */

    i = 0;

while (i  < 3) { /* allow for 3 semaphore sets */

nsops = 2;

/* wait for semaphore to reach zero */
sops[0].sem_num = 0;
sops[0].sem_op = 0; /* wait for semaphore flag to become zero */
sops[0].sem_flg = SEM_UNDO; /* take off semaphore
                               asynchronous  */

sops[1].sem_num = 0;
sops[1].sem_op = 1; /* increment semaphore—take
                       control of track */
sops[1].sem_flg = SEM_UNDO | IPC_NOWAIT; /* take off
                                            semaphore */


(void) fprintf(stderr,"\nsemop:Parent Calling semop(%d, &sops,
                       %d) with:", semid, nsops);
for (j = 0; j < nsops; j++)
{
(void) fprintf(stderr, "\n\tsops[%d].sem_num = %d, ", j,
                       sops[j].sem_num);
(void) fprintf(stderr, "sem_op = %d, ", sops[j].sem_op);
(void) fprintf(stderr, "sem_flg = %#o\n", sops[j].sem_flg);
}
```

```
    /* Make the semop() call and report the results. */
    if ((j = semop(semid, sops, nsops)) == -1) {
      perror("semop: semop failed");
    }
    else
    {
    (void) fprintf(stderr, "semop: semop returned %d\n", j);

    (void) fprintf(stderr, "Parent Process Taking Control of
                            Track: %d/3 times\n", i+1);
    sleep(5); /* Do nothing for 5 seconds */

    nsops = 1;

    /* wait for semaphore to reach zero */
    sops[0].sem_num = 0;
  sops[0].sem_op = -1; /* Give UP COntrol of track */
    sops[0].sem_flg = SEM_UNDO | IPC_NOWAIT; /* take off sema-
phore, asynchronous  */

    if ((j = semop(semid, sops, nsops)) == -1) {
      perror("semop: semop failed");
      }
      else
    (void) fprintf(stderr, "Parent Process Giving up Control
                            of Track: %d/3 times\n", i+1);
    sleep(5); /* halt process to allow child to catch
              semaphor change first */
    }
    ++i;

    }

    }
    }
```

The key elements of this program are as follows :

* After a semaphore is created with as simple key 1234, two prcesses are forked.
* Each process (parent and child) essentially performs the same operations:
* Each process accesses the same semaphore track (sops[].sem_num = 0).
* Each process waits for the track to become free and then attempts to take control of track
* This is achieved by setting appropriate sops[].sem_op values in the array.

* Once the process has control it sleeps for 5 seconds (in reality some processing would take place in place of this simple illustration)
* The process then gives up control of the track sops[1].sem_op = –1
* An additional sleep operation is then performed to ensure that the other process has time to access the semaphore before a subsequent (same process) semaphore read.

Note : There is no synchronization here in this simple example and we have no control over how the OS will schedule the processes.

Example 6

The full source code for a simple program that implements a producer-consumer system with two processes, is as follows :

```
/*
 * sem-producer-consumer.c -demonstrates a basic
   producer-consumer
 *  implementation.
 */

#include <stdio.h>  /* standard I/O routines.  */
#include <stdlib.h> /* rand() and srand() functions  */
#include <unistd.h>   /* fork(), etc.    */
#include <time.h>   /* nanosleep(), etc. */
#include <sys/types.h>   /* various type definitions. */
#include <sys/ipc.h> /* general SysV IPC structures  */
#include <sys/sem.h> /* semaphore functions and structs. */

#define NUM_LOOPS  20 /* number of loops to perform. */

int main(int argc, char* argv[])
{
int sem_set_id;        /* ID of the semaphore set.        */
union semun sem_val; /* semaphore value, for semctl(). */
int child_pid;       /* PID of our child process.       */
int i;           /* counter for loop operation.    */
struct sembuf sem_op;    /* structure for semaphore ops.   */
int rc;           /* return value of system calls.  */
struct timespec delay;    /* used for wasting time.        */

/* create a private semaphore set with one semaphore in it, */
/* with access only to the owner.   */
sem_set_id = semget(IPC_PRIVATE, 1, 0600);
if (sem_set_id == -1) {
```

```c
    perror("main: semget");
    exit(1);
}
printf("semaphore set created, semaphore set id '%d'.\n",
        sem_set_id);

/* intialize the first (and single) semaphore in our set
   to '0'. */
sem_val.val = 0;
rc = semctl(sem_set_id, 0, SETVAL, sem_val);

/* fork-off a child process, and start a  producer/consumer job.*/
child_pid = fork();
switch (child_pid) {
  case -1:  /* fork() failed */
    perror("fork");
    exit(1);
  case 0:   /* child process here */
   for (i=0; i<NUM_LOOPS; i++) {
   /* block on the semaphore, unless it's value is
      non-negative. */
   sem_op.sem_num = 0;
   sem_op.sem_op = -1;
   sem_op.sem_flg = 0;
   semop(sem_set_id, &sem_op, 1);
   printf("consumer: '%d'\n", i);
   fflush(stdout);
     }
   break;
default:  /* parent process here */
    for (i=0; i<NUM_LOOPS; i++) {
   printf("producer: '%d'\n", i);
   fflush(stdout);
   /* increase the value of the semaphore by 1. */
   sem_op.sem_num = 0;
   sem_op.sem_op = 1;
   sem_op.sem_flg = 0;
   semop(sem_set_id, &sem_op, 1);
   /* pause execution for a little bit, to allow the */
   /* child process to run and handle some requests. */
   /* this is done about 25% of the time.            */
   if (rand() > 3*(RAND_MAX/4)) {
```

```
      delay.tv_sec = 0;
      delay.tv_nsec = 10;
      nanosleep(&delay, NULL);
        }
      }
    break;
  }

  return 0;
}
```

Example 8

In the following program (copy), we define two shared memory segments, and a semaphore set with two semaphores. A child process is created with the help of fork() system call. This program can be started by typing "`copy<inputfile >outputfile`" at the command prompt. The parent process reads from the standard input (inputfile) and stores the same in first shared memory segment while the child process copies the content of second shared memory segment to standard output (outputfile). Similarly, while parent process is writing into second shared memory segment the child process reads from the first shared memory segment. Thus parent and child processes communicate via two shared memory segments at a time.

```
#define SIZ  5*1024
#define SHMKEY1 (key_t) 0x10
#define SHMKEY2 (key_t) 0x15
#define SEMKEY  (key_t) 0x20

struct databuf{ int nread;  char buf[SIZ];};
static int semid,shmid1,shmid2;
struct sembuf P1,V1,P2,V2;

void main()
{
struct databuf *buf1,*buf2;   int semid, pid;
int pid;

semid=semget(SEMKEY, 2, IPC_CREAT|0600);
semctl(semid,0,SETVAL,0);
semctl(semid,1,SETVAL,0);

shmid1=shmget(SHMKEY1,sizeof(struct databuf), IPC_CREAT|600);
shmid2=shmget(SHMKEY2,sizeof(struct databuf), IPC_CREAT|600);

buf1=(struct databuf*)shmat(shmid1,0,0);
buf2=(struct databuf*)shmat(shmid2,0,0);
```

```c
if((pid=fork())==0)  {
   writer(semid,buf1,buf2);
   remove();
   exit(0);
                             }
else  {
   reader(semid,buf1,buf2);
   exit(1);
   }
}
voidreader(int semid,struct databuf *buf1, struct databuf *buf2)
{
P2.sem_num=1; P2.sem_op=-1; P2.sem_flg=0;
 V1.sem_num=0; V1.sem_op=1; V1.sem_flg=0;

 while(1)
 { buf1->nread=read(0,buf1->buf,SIZ);
 semop(semid,&V1,1);  semop(semid,&P2,1);
 if(buf1->nread <=0) return;

 buf2->nread=read(0,buf2->buf,SIZ);
 semop(semid,&V1,1);   semop(semid,&P2,1);
 if(buf2->nread<=0) return;
 }
 }

 remove(){
 shmctl(shmid1,IPC_RMD,0); shmctl(shmid2,IPC_RMD,0);
 semctl(semid,IPC_RMD,0);    }

 void writer(int semid,struct databuf *buf1,
            struct databuf *buf2)
 {   P1.sem_num=0; P1.sem_op=-1; P1.sem_flg=0;
 V2.sem_num=1; V2.sem_op=1; V2.sem_flg=0;

 while(1)  {
 semop(semid,&P1,0); semop(semid,&V2,0);
 if(buf1->nread <=0) return;

 write(1,buf1->buf,buf1->nread);
 semop(semid,&P1,1);  semop(semid,&V2,1);
 if(buf2->nread<=0) return;
 write(1,buf2->buf,buf2->nread);
 }
 }
```

Example 9

This is another example to explain about use of shared memory while sharing shared memory segment

```
/*
 * shared-mem-with-semaphore.c  -using a semaphore
                                  to synchronize access
 * to a shared memory segment.
 */


#include <stdio.h>  /* standard I/O routines.  */
#include <sys/types.h> /* various type definitions.  */
#include <sys/ipc.h> /* general SysV IPC structures  */
#include <sys/shm.h> /* semaphore functions and structs.  */
#include <sys/sem.h>  /* shared memory functions and structs.*/
#include <unistd.h>   /* fork(), etc.    */
#include <wait.h>   /* wait(), etc.        */
#include <time.h>   /* nanosleep(), etc. */
#include <stdlib.h>   /* rand(), etc.    */

#define SEM_ID    250 /* ID for the semaphore. */

/* define a structure to be used in the given
   shared memory segment. */
struct country {
  char name[30];
  char capital_city[30];
  char currency[30];
  int population;
};

/*
 * function: random_delay. delay the executing process
                           for a random number
 * of nano-seconds.
 * input:    none.
 * output:   none.
 */
void
random_delay()
{
  static int initialized = 0;
  int random_num;
  struct timespec delay;  /* used for wasting time. */
```

```c
    if (!initialized) {
      srand(time(NULL));
      initialized = 1;
  }


  random_num = rand() % 10;
  delay.tv_sec = 0;
  delay.tv_nsec = 10*random_num;
  nanosleep(&delay, NULL);
}


/*
* function: sem_lock. locks the semaphore,
                        for exclusive access to a resource.
* input:    semaphore set ID.
* output:   none.
*/
void
sem_lock(int sem_set_id)
{
/* structure for semaphore operations.   */
struct sembuf sem_op;

/* wait on the semaphore, unless it's value
   is non-negative. */
  sem_op.sem_num = 0;
  sem_op.sem_op = -1;
  sem_op.sem_flg = 0;
  semop(sem_set_id, &sem_op, 1);
}


/*
* function: sem_unlock. un-locks the semaphore.
* input:    semaphore set ID.
* output:   none.
*/
void
sem_unlock(int sem_set_id)
{
/* structure for semaphore operations. */
struct sembuf sem_op;
```

```c
/* signal the semaphore - increase its value by one. */
sem_op.sem_num = 0;
sem_op.sem_op = 1;    /* <- Comment 3 */
sem_op.sem_flg = 0;
semop(sem_set_id, &sem_op, 1);
}


/*
 * function: add_country. adds a new country to
                            the counties array in the
 *  shard memory segment. Handles locking using a semaphore.
 * input:semaphore id, pointer to countries counter, pointer to
 *  counties array, data to fill into country.
 * output:none.
 */
void
add_country(int sem_set_id, int* countries_num,
            struct country*  countries,
    char* country_name, char* capital_city, char* currency,
    int population)
{
   sem_lock(sem_set_id);
   strcpy(countries[*countries_num].name, country_name);
   strcpy(countries[*countries_num].capital_city,
                                    capital_city);
   strcpy(countries[*countries_num].currency, currency);
   countries[*countries_num].population = population;
   (*countries_num)++;
   sem_unlock(sem_set_id);
}


/*
 * function: do_child. runs the child process's code,
            for populating
 *  the shared memory segment with data.
 *  input: semaphore id, pointer to countries counter, pointer to
 *  counties array.
 * output: none.
 */
void
do_child(int sem_set_id, int* countries_num,
          struct country* counties)
```

```c
{
add_country(sem_set_id, countries_num, counties,
   "U.S.A", "Washington", "U.S. Dollar", 250000000);
random_delay();
add_country(sem_set_id, countries_num, counties,
   "Israel", "Jerusalem", "New Israeli Shekel", 6000000);
random_delay();
add_country(sem_set_id, countries_num, counties,
   "France", "Paris", "Frank", 60000000);
random_delay();
add_country(sem_set_id, countries_num, counties,
   "Great Britain", "London", "Pound", 55000000);
}


/*
 * function: do_parent. runs the parent process's code,
                        for reading and
 *  printing the contents of the 'countries' array in the shared
 *  memory segment.
 * input: semaphore id, pointer to countries counter, pointer to
 *  counties array.
 * output: printout of countries array contents.
 */
void
do_parent (int sem_set_id, int* countries_num,
           struct country* countries)
{
int i, num_loops;

for (num_loops=0; num_loops < 5; num_loops++) {
/* now, print out the countries data. */
sem_lock(sem_set_id);
printf("———————————————————————\n");
printf("Number Of Countries: %d\n", *countries_num);
for (i=0; i < (*countries_num); i++) {
  printf("Country %d:\n", i+1);
  printf("  name: %s:\n", countries[i].name);
  printf("  capital city: %s:\n", countries[i].capital_city);
  printf("  currency: %s:\n", countries[i].currency);
  printf("  population: %d:\n", countries[i].population);
}
sem_unlock(sem_set_id);
  random_delay();
}
}
```

```c
int main(int argc, char* argv[])
{
int sem_set_id;  /* ID of the semaphore set.    */
union semun sem_val; /* semaphore value, for semctl(). */
int shm_id;    /* ID of the shared memory segment.   */
char* shm_addr;     /* address of shared memory segment. */
int* countries_num;   /* number of countries in shared mem. */
struct country* countries; /* countries array in shared mem.*/
struct shmid_ds shm_desc;
int rc;   /* return value of system calls. */
pid_t pid;  /* PID of child process.      */

/* create a semaphore set with ID 250, with one semaphore  */
/* in it, with access only to the owner. */
sem_set_id = semget(SEM_ID, 1, IPC_CREAT | 0600);
if (sem_set_id == -1) {
  perror("main: semget");
  exit(1);
}


/* intialize the first (and single) semaphore
   in our set to '1'. */
sem_val.val = 1;
rc = semctl(sem_set_id, 0, SETVAL, sem_val);
if (rc == -1) {
  perror("main: semctl");
  exit(1);
}


/* allocate a shared memory segment with size of 2048 bytes. */
shm_id = shmget(100, 2048, IPC_CREAT | IPC_EXCL | 0600);
if (shm_id == -1) {
  perror("main: shmget: ");
  exit(1);
}


/* attach the shared memory segment to our process's
   address space. */
shm_addr = shmat(shm_id, NULL, 0);
if (!shm_addr) { /* operation failed. */
  perror("main: shmat: ");
  exit(1);
}
```

```c
/* create a countries index on the shared memory segment. */
countries_num = (int*) shm_addr;
*countries_num = 0;
countries = (struct country*) ((void*)shm_addr+sizeof(int));

/* fork-off a child process that'll populate the
   memory segment. */
pid = fork();
switch (pid) {
  case -1:
    perror("fork: ");
    exit(1);
    break;
case 0:
    do_child(sem_set_id, countries_num, countries);
    exit(0);
    break;
default:
    do_parent(sem_set_id, countries_num, countries);
    break;
}

/* wait for child process's termination. */
{
int child_status;

wait(&child_status);
}

/* detach the shared memory segment from our process's
   address space. */
if (shmdt(shm_addr) == -1) {
  perror("main: shmdt: ");
}

/* de-allocate the shared memory segment. */
if (shmctl(shm_id, IPC_RMID, &shm_desc) == -1) {
  perror("main: shmctl: ");
}

return 0;
}
```

Conclusions

This chapter describes when we require semaphores and how they can be created. Classical synchronization problems of operating systems such as producer consumer problem and signal and wait problems are explained with nice illustrative examples. The system calls semget(), semctl(), semop() etc are explained in detail.

Questions

1. Write a program to simulate sleep and wake up behaviours among two processes.
2. Does semaphore are available even after the process which created is dead?
3. Also comment what happens from semaphores created if system reboots.

23   Memory Mapped Files

Memory Mapping

Memory mapping is a file access technique that works very well under UNIX. Under Windows, it only makes sense in read-only applications, and even there, the "local copy" option (covered in a topic below) makes more sense. So it is for all practical purposes only of interest under UNIX. The concept is to map a disk file onto a processes memory address space, such that it can be accessed via memory operations rather than disk operations, that is the file is treated as an extension of virtual memory: Conceptually, the mapped file is simply another swap file mapped to a range of memory. The file doesn't have to fit entirely in memory, because the demand paging system (otherwise associated with virtual memory) takes care of swapping pages in and out of memory as needed.

It may appear that this is hardly different that ordinary disk caching, in which frequently accessed disk blocks are held in memory to minimize physical disk accesses. However, there is significant performance difference between accessing a cached disk record via a disk service call and accessing a memory record. Disk service calls require a context switch from user to supervisor mode, even if the data is in cache, whereas memory access calls do not. Such context switches are relatively expensive operations, being perhaps hundreds of times slower than ordinary instructions. So even though reading a disk record from cache and reading the equivalent data directory from memory may both appear to be "lightning fast", the difference can become significant when you have a lot of little disk accesses.

If memory mapping is so wonderful, you might ask why we don't just use it all the time. The answer would be that it can cause memory to be used inefficiently, which can have an adverse impact on the system performance. The recommendation would be to only use memory mapping with reasonably small files that are heavily accessed in specific programs. Good candidates would be any custom (non-ISAM) index files, or any small file whose records are accessed multiple times in a particular program. (ISAM files are not generally good candidates except perhaps in certain individual programs and when the files are not too large, because there is no convenient way to map the index without the data.)

Reading Large Files With File Mapping

Mapping a large file into memory (rather than performing a number of sequential read operations on that file) can significantly enhance I/O performance. Reading a file into a buffer can directly incur up to three I/O operations:

- paging out enough modified pages to allow for the allocation of the read buffer
- reading bytes from the file into the buffer
- later, paging out the buffer memory

Additionally, any pages paged out will likely need to be paged in again.

As mentioned earlier, mapping a file, on the other hand, causes the file to be treated as an extension of virtual memory: Conceptually, the mapped file is simply another swap file mapped to a range of memory. Thus, reading from the file can incur only two I/O operations directly: paging in the desired section of the file and paging out any modified pages needed to make room for the page in memory.

The pages of a file are maintained in a shareable state in memory. If the system runs low on memory, the pages are purged, but no I/O operation is incurred; if the data is referenced again, it is paged in again from the file.

Additionally, your code is often smaller with file mapping, because the file is accessed through a pointer, like all random-access memory, and **no file system calls need be used**.

However, the worst candidates examples are large files that are accessed sequentially or sporadically, with little repetitive access to the same records. For example, it would be a bad idea to memory map a customer master file probably in the customer maintenance program. Such a program is not likely to be disk-bound, and the amount of memory spent mapping the file would be better spent on other uses, like ordinary disk caching

Memory mapping can be used when you want to read and write to and from files so that the information is shared between processes. Think of it in this way: two processes both open the same file and both read and write from it, thus sharing the information. The problem is, sometimes it's a pain to do all those fseek()s and stuff to get around. However, with the help of memory mapping we can just map a section of the file into memory, and get a pointer to it and simply use pointer arithmetic to get (and set) data in the file. Ofcourse, If we have multiple processes manipulating the data in the same file concurrently, we could be in for troubles. We might have to lock the file or use semaphores to regulate access to the file while a process messes with it.

In some applications, any time when they start the same calculations or table initializations (data structures) has to be carried out before starting actual service. In order to improve the response time of such a programs we can use memory mapping. We can make this application program to do all necessary calculations when it is started first time and store the same in a file. Next time on wards when this program is started, simply it memory map's this file and uses the calculated tables and data structures in it. Thus, the response time becomes better.

Memory mapping must be activated within individual programs, and applies only to files opened after the memory mapping option is turned on, so in addition to identifying heavily accessed files, you would need to identify specific programs that were disk-bound in order to benefit from it.

It is safe and acceptable to allow a mixture of simultaneous memory-mapped and traditional I/O to any given file under UNIX.

Local Copies (Read-Only Access Under Windows)

Networked Windows environments are quite efficient at serving up entire files over the network from a fileserver (as in word processing applications), but they are relatively slow at serving up record-level operations. Here, the disk operation overhead is much higher than in the UNIX world because of the need for machine-to-machine communication. Loading a file from the server may require only a couple of units of machine-to-machine communication, but reading the file via thousands of individual record operations (which is typical of AMOS-style report programs) requires thousands of units of machine-to-machine communications. This overhead typically becomes the limiting factor in Windows installations of A-Shell.

Memory mapping doesn't really help here, since it doesn't eliminate the need for machine-to-machine communication, and in any case, it only works properly for read-only situations anyway. If we can limit ourselves to read-only access to a file in a particular program, then a better solution is to request that A-Shell give you a local copy of the file. In this case, when the file is opened, A-Shell copies the entire file (in one big transfer operation) from the server to the local workstation and then references the local copy until the file is closed (after which the local copy is deleted). This technique can significantly speed up report programs, or any other program that performs many read operations from a file, by eliminating that machine-to-machine communication overhead. As a side effect, it also reduces network traffic and the load on the fileserver, thus potentially speeding up other programs running across the network.

As mentioned earlier, before mapping a file to memory, you need to get a file descriptor for it by using the open() system call :

```
int fd;
fd = open("mapdemofile", O_RDWR);
```

In this example, we've opened the file for read/write access. You can open it in whatever mode you want, but it has to match the mode specified in the prot parameter to the mmap() call, below.

To memory map a file, you use the mmap() system call, which is defined as follows :

```
void *mmap(void *addr, size_t len, int prot, int flags,
int fildes, off_t off);
```

addr

This is the address we want the file mapped into. The best way to use this is to set it to (caddr_t)0 and let the OS choose it for you. If you tell it to use an address the OS doesn't like (for instance, if it's not a multiple of the virtual memory page size), it'll give you an error.

len

This parameter is the length of the data we want to map into memory. This can be any length you want. (Aside: if len not a multiple of the virtual memory page size, you will get a blocksize that is rounded up to that size. The extra bytes will be 0, and any changes you make to them will not modify the file.)

prot

The "protection" argument allows you to specify what kind of access this process has to the memory mapped region. This can be a bitwise-ORd mixture of the following values: PROT_READ, PROT_WRITE, and PROT_EXEC, for read, write, and execute permissions, respectively. The value specified here must be equivalent to the mode specified in the open() system call that is used to get the file descriptor.

flags

There are just miscellaneous flags that can be set for the system call. You'll want to set it to MAP_SHARED if you're planning to share your changes to the file with other processes, or MAP_PRIVATE otherwise. If you set it to the latter, your process will get a copy of the mapped region, so any changes you make to it will not be reflected in the original file-thus, other processes will not be able to see them. We won't talk about MAP_PRIVATE here at all, since it doesn't have much to do with IPC.

fildes

This is where you put that file descriptor you opened earlier.

```
off
```

This is the offset in the file that you want to start mapping from. A restriction: this **must** be a multiple of the virtual memory page size. This page size can be obtained with a call to `getpagesize()`.

The function `mmap()` returns -1 on error, and sets `errno`. Otherwise, it returns a pointer to the start of the mapped data.

We shall discuss a short demo that maps the second "page" of a file into memory. First we'll `open()` it to get the file descriptor, then we'll use `getpagesize()` to get the size of a virtual memory page and use this value for both the `len` and the `off`. In this way, we'll start mapping at the second page, and map for one page's length. (On my Linux box, the page size is 4K.)

```c
#include <unistd.h>
#include <sys/types.h>
#include <sys/mman.h>

int fd, pagesize;
char *data;

fd = fopen("foo", O_RDONLY);
pagesize = getpagesize();
data = mmap((caddr_t)0, pagesize, PROT_READ, MAP_SHARED,
        fd, pagesize);
```

Once this code stretch has run, you can access the first byte of the mapped section of file using data[0]. Notice there's a lot of type conversion going on here. For instance, mmap() returns caddr_t, but we treat it as a char*. Well, the fact is that caddr_t usually is defined to be a char*, so everything's fine.

Also notice that we've mapped the file PROT_READ so we have read-only access. Any attempt to write to the data (data[0] = 'B', for example) will cause a segmentation violation. Open the file O_RDWR with prot set to PROT_READ|PROT_WRITE if you want read-write access to the data.

Unmapping the File

There is, of course, a munmap() function to un-memory map a file:

```c
int munmap(caddr_t addr, size_t len);
```

This simply unmaps the region pointed to by *addr* (returned from mmap()) with length len (same as the len passed to mmap()). munmap() returns -1 on error and sets the errno variable.

Once you've unmapped a file, any attempts to access the data through the old pointer will result in a segmentation fault. You have been warned.

A simple Example

The following program maps its own source to memory and prints the byte that's found at whatever offset you specify on the command line.

The program restricts the offsets you can specify to the range 0 through the file length. The file length is obtained through a call to stat() which you might not have seen before. It returns a structure full of file info, one field of which is the size in bytes. Easy enough.

Example 1

Here is the source for mmapdemo.c :

```c
#include <stdio.h>
#include <stdlib.h>
#include <fcntl.h>
#include <unistd.h>
#include <sys/types.h>
#include <sys/mman.h>
#include <sys/stat.h>
#include <errno.h>

int main(int argc, char *argv[])
{
   int fd, offset;
   char *data;
   struct stat sbuf;

   if (argc != 2) {
      fprintf(stderr, "usage: mmapdemo offset\n");
      exit(1);
   }

   if ((fd = open("mmapdemo.c", O_RDONLY)) == -1) {
      perror("open");
      exit(1);
   }

   if (stat("mmapdemo.c", &sbuf) == -1) {
      perror("stat");
      exit(1);
   }
```

```
offset = atoi(argv[1]);
if (offset < 0 || offset > sbuf.st_size-1) {
fprintf(stderr, "mmapdemo: offset must be in the
                   range 0-%d\n", \
   sbuf.st_size-1);
  exit(1);
}

if ((data = mmap((caddr_t)0, sbuf.st_size, PROT_READ,
                  MAP_SHARED, \
fd, 0)) == (caddr_t)(-1)) {
  perror("mmap");
    exit(1);
 }

printf("byte at offset %d is '%c'\n", offset, data[offset]);

return 0;
}
```

Run it with some command line like :

```
$ mmapdemo 30
byte at offset 30 is 'e'
```

A memory mapped region is inherited by a child process across a fork (since its part of the parent's address space), but for the same reason is not inherited by the new program across an exec. A memory mapped region is automatically unmapped when the process terminates or by calling munmap directly.

Execute the above program by simply inserting a instruction **fork();**. We shall get the same byte information two times such as:

```
byte at offset 30 is 'e'
byte at offset 30 is 'e'
```

Example 2

In this example, We define a RECORD structure and then create NRECORDS versions each recording their number. These are appended to the file records.dat. Then, this file is memory mapped and a specified record is simply changed by accessing the same as an array.

```
#include <unistd.h>
#include <stdio.h>
#include <sys/mman.h>
#include <fcntl.h>
```

```c
typedef struct {
  int integer;
  char string[24];
} RECORD;

#define NRECORDS (100)

int main()
{
  RECORD record, *mapped;
  int i, f;
  FILE *fp;

  fp = fopen("records.dat","w+");
  for(i=0; i<NRECORDS; i++) {
    record.integer = i;
    sprintf(record.string,"RECORD-%d",i);
    fwrite(&record,sizeof(record),1,fp);
}
fclose(fp);

/*  We now change the integer value of record 43 to 143
    and write this to the 43rd record's string.  */

fp = fopen("records.dat","r+");
fseek(fp,43*sizeof(record),SEEK_SET);
fread(&record,sizeof(record),1,fp);

record.integer = 143;
sprintf(record.string,"RECORD-%d",record.integer);

fseek(fp,43*sizeof(record),SEEK_SET);
fwrite(&record,sizeof(record),1,fp);
fclose(fp);

/*  We now map the records into memory and access the
    43rd record in order to change the integer to 243
(and update the record string), again using memory mapping. */

f = open("records.dat",O_RDWR);

mapped = (RECORD *)mmap(0, NRECORDS*sizeof(record),
PROT_READ|PROT_WRITE, MAP_SHARED, f, 0);
```

```c
mapped[43].integer = 243;
sprintf(mapped[43].string,"RECORD-%d",mapped[43].integer);

msync((void *)mapped, NRECORDS*sizeof(record), MS_ASYNC);

/* this system call immediately writes the file
   information into disk */

munmap((void *)mapped, NRECORDS*sizeof(record));

close(f);

exit(0);
}
```

Example 3

The following functions can be used to memory map a file and related operations.

```c
void ProcessFile( char * inPathName )
{
size_t  dataLength;
void *  dataPtr;

if( MapFile( inPathName, &dataPtr, &dataLength ) == 0 )
{
//
// process the data and unmap the file
//

// ...

munmap( dataPtr, dataLength );
}
}


//
//  MapFile
//  Return the contents of the specified file as
//     a read-only pointer.
//
//  Enter:  inPathName is a "/"-delimited pathname
//
//  Exit: outDataPtra pointer to the mapped memory region
```

```c
//   outDataLength   size of the mapped memory region
//   return value    either an errno error condition
//   or zero for success
//
int MapFile( char * inPathName, void ** outDataPtr,
    size_t * outDataLength )
{
int  outError;
int  fileDescriptor;
struct stat statInfo;

// Return safe values on error.
outError       = 0;
*outDataPtr    = NULL;
*outDataLength = 0;

//
// Open the file.
//
fileDescriptor = open( inPathName, O_RDONLY, 0 );
if( fileDescriptor < 0 )
{
outError = errno;
}
else
{
//
// We now know the file exists. Retrieve the file size.
//
if( fstat( fileDescriptor, &statInfo ) != 0 )
{
outError = errno;
}
else
{
//
// Map the file into a read-only memory region.
//

* outDataPtr = mmap(NULL, statInfo.st_size, PROT_READ, 0,
    fileDescriptor,
    0);
```

```c
if( *outDataPtr == MAP_FAILED )
{
  outError = errno;
}
else
{
  //
  // On success, return the size of the mapped file.
  //
  *outDataLength = statInfo.st_size;
  }
}


//
// Now close the file.The kernel doesn't use
   our file descriptor.
//
close( fileDescriptor );
}


return outError;
}
```

Example 4

The following program is used to explain about the possible error which we get when we
try to access the memory mapped file.

```c
#include <stdio.h>
#include <unistd.h>
#include <sys/mman.h>
#include <sys/stat.h>
#include <fcntl.h>
#include <ctype.h>
#include <errno.h>
#include <stdlib.h>

static int alloc_size;
static char *memory;

void sighandle(int signo)
```

```
{
printf("Memory Accessed\n");
mprotect(memory, alloc_size, PROT_READ|PROT_WRITE);
}

int main()
{
int fd;
struct sigaction sa;

memset(&sa,0, sizeof(struct sigaction));

sa.sa_handler=sighandler;
sigaction(SIGSEGV,&sa, NULL);

alloc_size=getpagesize();

fd=open("/dev/zero", O_RDONLY);
memory=mmap(NULL,alloc_size, PROT_WRITE,MAP_PRIVATE, fd, 0);
close(fd);

memory[0]=0;
mprotect(memory, alloc_size, PROT_NONE);

memory[0]=0;
munmap(memory, alloc_size);
return (0);
}
```

Example 5

The following program has the following command line interface.

```
Programname <file> [perm] [shared/private] [size]
```

Whatever filename we will give along the command line is memory mapped and the same is accessed like a character array and each character will be displayed on the screen such that 80 characters are printed in one line. Whenever it encounters a non printable character it prints '*'.

```
#include <stdio.h>
#include <unistd.h>
#include <sys/mman.h>
#include <sys/stat.h>
#include <fcntl.h>
```

```c
#include <ctype.h>
#include <errno.h>
#include <stdlib.h>

#define BUFSIZE (1024-1)

static char *program_name;

void print_useage(void)
{
   fprintf(stdout, "usage: ");
   fprintf(stdout, "%s <file> [perm] [shared/private]
                    [size]\n", program_name);
}

void printdata(int len, const char *data)
{
   int i;

   for(i=0; i<len; i++)
   {
      if(isprint(data[i]))
      {
         putchar(data[i]);
      }
      else
      {
        putchar('*');
      }
      if(len % 79 == 79)
      {
        putchar('\n');
      }
   }
putchar('\n');
}

int main(int argc, char **argv)
{
struct stat statbuf;
int fd;
char *mmfilename;
char *mmdata;
```

```c
size_t len;
int mmmode = 0;
int mmflags = 0;
char buf[BUFSIZE+1];

buf[BUFSIZE] = '\0';
program_name = argv[0];

if(argc > 1)
{
mmfilename = argv[1];
}
else
{
print_useage();
exit(1);
}

if(argc > 2)
{
   if(strcmp("w", argv[2]) == 0 || strcmp("write",
                                          argv[2]) == 0)
   {
     mmmode |= PROT_WRITE;
   }
else if(strcmp("r", argv[2]) == 0 || strcmp("read",
                                            argv[2]) == 0)
   {
     mmmode |= PROT_READ;
   }
else if(strcmp("rw", argv[2]) == 0 || strcmp("read/write",
        argv[2]) == 0)
   {
     mmmode |= PROT_READ | PROT_WRITE;
   }
else
{
   fprintf(stderr, "unkown permissions `%s'\n", argv[4]);
   exit(1);
}
}
else
{
mmmode |= PROT_READ;
}
```

```c
if(argc > 3)
  {
    if(strcmp("shared", argv[3]) == 0)
    {
      mmflags |= MAP_SHARED;
    }
  else if(strcmp("private", argv[3]) == 0)
    {
      mmflags |= MAP_PRIVATE;
    }
  else
{
  fprintf(stderr, "unknown permissions `%s'\n", argv[4]);
  exit(1);
}
}
else
{
mmflags |= MAP_PRIVATE;
}

if((fd=open(mmfilename, O_RDWR | O_CREAT, 0666)) == -1)
{
  perror(mmfilename);
  exit(errno);
}

if(fstat(fd, &statbuf) != 0)
{
  perror("stat");
  exit(errno);
}

if(argc > 4)
{
  len = atoi(argv[4]);
}
else
{
  len = statbuf.st_size;
}

if((mmdata=mmap(NULL, len, mmmode, mmflags, fd, 0)) == NULL)
```

```c
{
  perror("mmap");
  exit(errno);
}

printf("mmap()'d %d bytes at addr 0x%08X\n", len,
(unsigned int)mmdata);

while(fgets(buf, BUFSIZE, stdin) != NULL)
{
printdata(len, mmdata);
}
```

munmap(mmdata, len);

return 0;
}

Example 6

This Program creates duplicate copy of a file by using the mmap function

```c
#include <unistd.h>
#include <sys/mman.h>
#include <sys/types.h>
#include <sys/stat.h>
#include <fcntl.h>

int main(int n, char **a)
{
  int fd1,fd2;
  size_t size, i=0;
  char *src, *dest;
  struct stat X;
  if(n != 3)
  {
    printf("Usage: %s SRC DEST\n",a[0]);
    return -1;
  }
if((fd1 = open(a[1],O_RDONLY)) < 0)
{
  perror("Open for read");
  return -1;
}
if((fd2 = open(a[2],O_RDWR|O_CREAT,S_IRWXU)) < 0)
{
  perror("Open for write");
  return -1;
}
```

```
fstat(fd1, &X);
size = X.st_size;
src = (char*)mmap(NULL,size,PROT_READ,
      MAP_FILE|MAP_SHARED,fd1,0);

lseek(fd2, size-1, SEEK_SET);
if (write(fd2, " ", 1) != 1)
{
   perror("write");
   return -1;
}

dest = (char*)mmap(NULL,size,PROT_WRITE,
      MAP_FILE|MAP_SHARED,fd2,0);
while(i < size)
{
   dest[i] = src[i];
   i++;
}
munmap(src, size);
munmap(dest, size);
return 0;
}
```

Conclusions

Memory mapping files and its advantages are described in the introduction. The system calls, mmap(), munmap() etc are explained in detail. Also, how memory mapped file can be used for IPC is demonstrated with live example.

Questions

1. Write program from emulate dd command through memory mapping concept.

2. Check the time requirements of the above program in relation from time requirement of the program 5 of chapter 11.

3. Write a program which when started first time reads order of a polynomial and opens a file and writes into it order, all the coefficients and all of its derivatives coefficients. (remember n'th order polynomial will have n derivatives). If the program is already executed more than once, then it reads polynomial order, coefficients, derivative coefficients from the file. Any time (including first time also) if we run the program and enter a value for x (point) then it displays polynomial value, all of its derivative values at x. Note your program has from memory map the polynomial details second time onwards.

24 Network Programming: A Brief Introduction

24.1 Introduction

Networks, connecting computers to networks and managing those networks are probably the most important, or at least the most hyped, areas of computing at the moment. The Internet is a global interconnected network of computers with which one can look at documents and images, view videos, listen to sound files from anywhere in the world. One can also use the Internet to publish so that others can look at our information in any of the number of standard file formats. One can also use the Internet to send messages through e-mail, as long as we know the e-mail address of the recipient. The Internet can also be used to transfer files between any two people or computers. The Internet also creates new communities of individuals, belonging to newsgroups where information is shared between people with similar interests, even though individuals could be geographically dispersed. Letters and files can be posted to newsgroups, where others can share them.

24.1.1   Some Popular Services on Intranet / Internet

The following is a list of the most common services that an Intranet might supply (by no means all of them). The list includes

- **file sharing**

    The common ability to share access to applications and data files. It's much simpler to install one copy of an application on a network server than it is to install 35 copies on each individual PC.

- **print sharing**

    The ability for many different machines to share a printer. It is especially economic if the printer is an expensive, good quality printer and

- **electronic mail**

    Sometimes called messaging. Electronic mail is fast becoming an essential tool for most businesses.

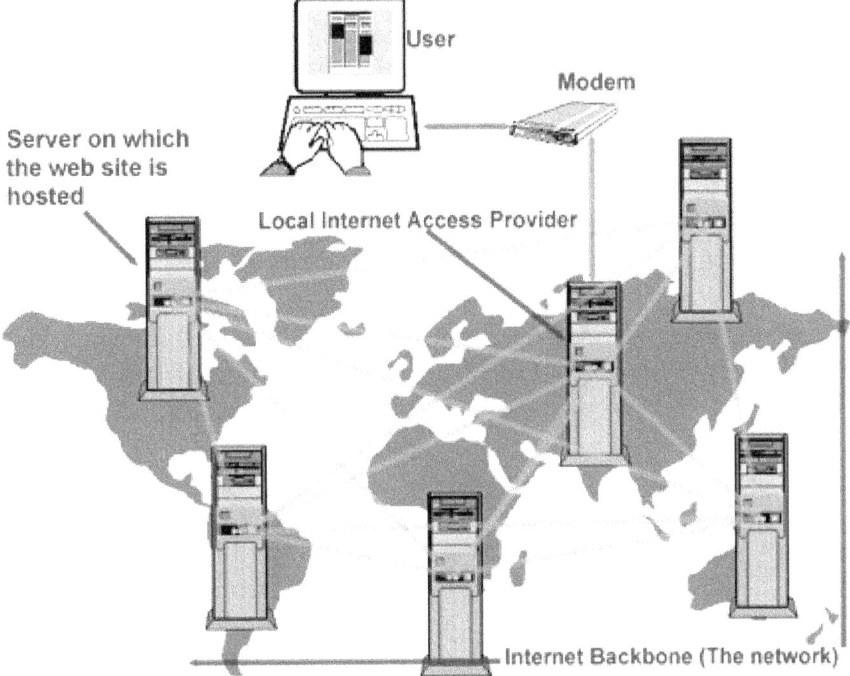

Fig. 24.1 Internet along with its components

The standard for communicating on the Internet is called "TCP/IP" (pronounced as TCPIP without the '/') which is short for Transmission Control Protocol/Internet Protocol. The key concept in TCP/IP is that every computer has to know where all other computers are on the network, and can send data by the quickest route. This is done by maintaining indexes of all IP addresses (IP address is a logical number assigned to a computer when it is in the Internet) in a domain at multiple servers strategically spread around the country, so that messages are quickly routed along the fastest path.

TCP/IP transfers information in small chunks called "packets". Each packet includes the following information: the computer the data came from, the computer to which it is headed, the data itself, and error-checking information (to ensure that the individual packet was accurately and completely sent and received). The elegance of TCP/IP is that a large file can be broken into multiple packets, each sent over different paths in the network. These packets then re-assembled at the other end into one file and saved on the destination computer.

To access the Internet, we need an Internet Service Provider (ISP). The ISP is connected to the Internet "backbone" which is the permanent cabling of the Internet. This backbone may consist of copper wire, fiber optic cable, microwave, and even satellite connections between any two points. To us it doesn't matter – the Internet's TCP/IP works this out for us. We can connect to the Internet in one of two basic ways, dialing into an ISPs computer, or with a direct connection to an ISP. The difference is mainly in the speed and cost.

Figure 24.1 gives a pictorial representation of how Internet works. We want to access a web site that is hosted on a server somewhere in the world (say USA) and we want to access the information from India. We connect (using a computer and modem - Dial up access) to our local Internet Access Provider (or internet service provider CISP), then we type in the address of our site. Our request is sent from the local ISP's server through the different computers in the network (Internet backbone) till it reaches the server where we have hosted our site. It is like a letter traveling. Through the various postal networks and reaching the addressee's place. Then the information stored on the web site that we are trying to access is sent back to our computer so that we can access it.

24.1.2 Three Unforgettable Addresses of TCP/IP Model

Popularly three addresses are used in computer networks which are explained in detail later. They are:

- Network card or Ethernet card address which is 48 bits long and is physical or hardwired.

- IP address which is 32 bits (as of now) and is logical. This is according to IPV4. In IPV6, IP address is 128 bits.

- Port address which is 16 bits and is logical.

A simple practical analogy for Internet Communication

Consider delivering an envelope through normal postal service. With the help of PIN number (is logical like IP address as it is not written on a city!!) a postal packet is delivered to a city. Further, with the help of door number it will be delivered to the apartment watchmen; which is further delivered to a specific flat owner, based on flat number (Probably door number and flat number can be considered as physical as they are written really!!). Then, with the help of person's name the packet is really delivered to the actual person (name is considered as logical like port as it is not written on the face of a person!!). Thus, in a nutshell we can assume port number as person's name, Flat number in an apartment building and door number of the apartment as network card address, and postal code as IP address.

In the same manner a packet (datagram) is delivered from source machine's router. In a nutshell, steps involved in a packets, delivery to an application (program) on a destination machine are as follows.

1. A packet is delivered to destination LAN with the help of network address (a portion of destination machine's IP address which is available in the packet itself) of it. That is, all the packets which are bound to a machine will have same IP address irrespective of their source. Also, all the packets which are bound to any machine of a LAN will be having their network part of their IP addresses as same.

2. Actually, LAN protocols are used to deliver a packet to machine in a LAN and LAN protocols requires Ethernet address to achieve this. When a packet arrives to destination router, using the **arp** protocol, destination machines network card address is found and is used for actual delivery of the packet to the machine using LAN protocols.

3. When a packet arrives to a machine, with the help of **port** number available in it, the same will be handed over to a program (running on that machine) which is looking for packets arrivals with that port number.

The **Internet protocol suite (TCP/IP suite)** is the set of <u>protocols</u> that implement the <u>protocol stack</u> on which the Internet runs. The Internet protocol suite can be described by analogy with the <u>OSI model</u>, which describes the layers of a <u>protocol stack</u>, not all of which correspond well with current Internet which is in practice. In a protocol stack, each layer solves a set of problems involving the transmission of data, and provides a well-defined service to the higher layers. Higher layers are logically closer to the user and deal with more abstract data, relying on lower layers to translate data into forms that can eventually be physically manipulated. The Internet model was produced as the solution to a practical engineering problem. The OSI model, on the other hand, was a more theoretical approach, and was also produced at an earlier stage in the evolution of <u>networks</u>. Therefore, the OSI model is easier to understand, but the TCP/IP model is the one in actual use. It is helpful to have an understanding of the OSI model before learning TCP/IP, as the same principles apply, but are easier to understand in the OSI model. The following diagram attempts to show where various TCP/IP and other protocols would reside in the original OSI model:

7	**Application**	e.g. HTTP, SMTP, SNMP, FTP, Telnet, NFS
6	**Presentation**	e.g. XDR, ASN.1, SMB, AFP
5	**Session**	e.g. ISO 8327 / CCITT X.225, RPC, NetBIOS, ASP
4	**Transport**	e.g. TCP, UDP, RTP, SPX, ATP
3	**Network**	e.g. IP, ICMP, IGMP, X.25, CLNP, ARP, OSPF, RIP, IPX, DDP
2	**Data Link**	e.g. Ethernet, Token ring, PPP, HDLC, Frame relay, ISDN, ATM
1	**Physical**	e.g. Electricity, Radio, Laser

Commonly, the top three layers of the OSI model (Application, Presentation and Session) are considered as a single Application Layer in the TCP/IP suite. Because the TCP/IP suite has no unified session layer on which higher layers are built, these functions are typically carried out (or ignored) by individual applications. A simplified TCP/IP interpretation of the stack is shown right.

Application
(HTTP, ftp, telnet, ...)

Transport
(TCP, UDP, ...)

Network
(IP, ...)

Link
(device driver, ...)

As we see in the diagram, computers running on the Internet communicate to each other using either the Transmission Control Protocol (TCP) or the User Datagram Protocol (UDP). When we write Java programs that communicate over the network, we are programming at the application layer. Typically, we don't need to concern ourself with the TCP and UDP layers. Instead, we can use the classes in the java.net package. These classes provide system-independent network communication. However, to decide which Java classes our programs should use, we do need to understand how TCP and UDP differ.

24.1.3   TCP

When two applications want to communicate with each other reliably, they establish a connection and send data back and forth over that connection. This is analogous to making a telephone call. If we want to speak to our friend in USA, a connection is established (thickline in Fig. 24.2) when we dial her phone number and she answers. We send data back and forth over the connection by speaking to one another over the phone lines. Like the phone company, TCP guarantees that data sent from one end of the connection actually gets to the other end and in the same order it was sent (see Fig 24.2). Otherwise, an error is reported. TCP provides a point-to-point channel for applications that require reliable communications.

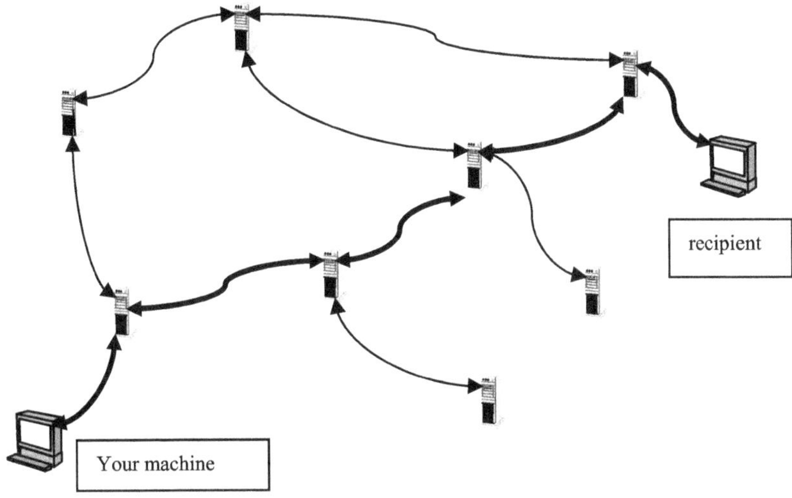

Fig. 24.2 TCP: connection oriented protocol

The Hypertext Transfer Protocol (HTTP), File Transfer Protocol (FTP), and Telnet are all examples of applications that require a reliable communication channel. The order in which the data is sent and received over the network is critical to the success of these applications. When HTTP is used to read from a URL, the data must be received in the order in which it was sent. Otherwise, we end up with a jumbled HTML file, a corrupt zip file, or some other invalid information.

24.1.4 UDP

The UDP protocol provides for communication that is not guaranteed between two applications on the network. UDP is not connection-based like TCP. Rather, it sends independent packets of data, called *datagrams*, from one application to another. Sending datagrams is much like sending a letter through the postal service: The order of delivery is not important and is not guaranteed, and each message is independent of any other. It is like a letter (postal) service. There is no active connection to the recipient machine. Your computer can package a piece of data into a packet, put a label on it that identifies the recipient and then send the packet to a machine on the network designated as a router. The router will then try to send the packet to another router (preferably the router nearest to the recipient machine that will then hopefully send the data directly to the recipient (see Fig 24.3). Note that when several packets are transmitted each may traverse in a different path across the network. There is no guarantee that a packet will actually end up at its destination nor that packets will arrive in the same order as they were transmitted. There is no automatic confirmation to the originator that a packet has arrived at its destination or that the packet has not been corrupted in the transmission process. This type of service is best used for single-shot communications.

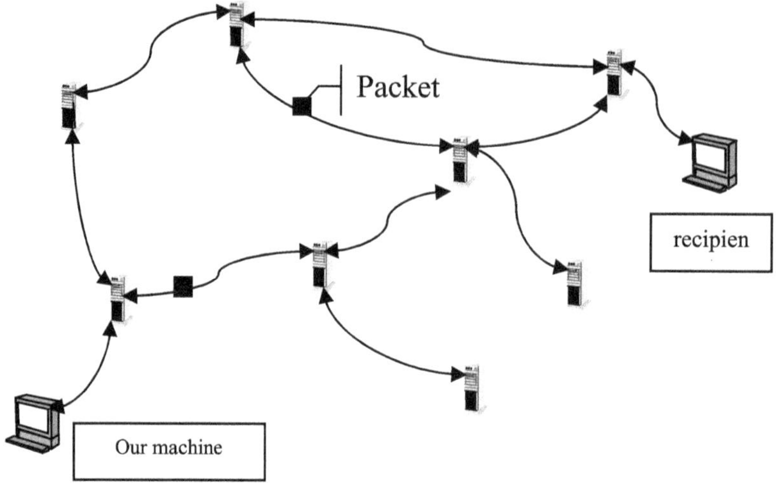

Fig. 24.3 UDP: Connection less service

For many applications, the guarantee of reliability is critical to the success of the transfer of information from one end of the connection to the other. However, other forms of communication don't require such strict standards. In fact, they may be slowed down by the extra overhead or the reliable connection may invalidate the service altogether. Consider, for example, a clock server that sends the current time to its client when requested to do so. If the client misses a packet, it doesn't really make sense recipient it because the time will be incorrect when the client receives it on the second try. If the client makes two requests and receives packets from the server out of order, it doesn't really matter because the client can figure out that the packets are out of order and make another request. The reliability of TCP is unnecessary in this instance because it causes performance degradation and may hinder the usefulness of the service. Another example of a service that doesn't need the guarantee of a reliable channel is the ping command. The purpose of the ping command is to test the communication between two programs over the network. In fact, ping needs to know about dropped or out-of-order packets to determine how good or bad the connection is. A reliable channel would invalidate this service altogether.

Note: Many firewalls and routers have been configured not to allow UDP packets. If we are having trouble in connecting to a service outside our firewall, or if clients are having trouble connecting to our service, ask our system administrator whether UDP is permitted or not.

24.1.5 Network Hardware

The first step in connecting a machine to a network is to find out what sort of network hardware you will be using. Currently the Linux kernel offers support for the networking hardware outlined in list below. For more detailed information about hardware support under Linux refer to the Hardware Compatibility HOWTO available from your nearest mirror of the Linux Documentation Project.

- arcnet
- ATM http://lrcwww.epfl.ch/linux-atm/
- AX25, amateur radio
- EQL
  EQL allows us to treat multiple point-to-point connections (SLIP, PPP) as a single logical TCP/IP connection.
- FDDI
- Frame relay
- ISDN
- PLIP
- PPP
- SLIP
- radio modem, STRIP, Starmode Radio IP
  http://mosquitonet.standford.edu/{mosquitonet.html | strip.html}
- token ring
- X.25
- WaveLan, wireless, card, and
- Ethernet

In most "normal" situations the networking hardware being used will be either

- Modem

  A modem is a serial device so your Linux kernel should support the appropriate serial port you have in your computer. The networking protocol used on a modem will be either SLIP or PPP which must also be supported by the kernel.

- Ethernet

Possibly the most common form of networking hardware at the moment. There are a number of different Ethernet cards. You will need to make sure that the kernel supports the particular Ethernet card you will be using. The Hardware Compatibility HOWTO includes this information.

24.1.6 Network Devices

Only way a program can gain access to a physical device is via a device file. Network hardware is still hardware so it follows that there should be device files for networking hardware. Under other versions of the UNIX operating system this is true. It is not the case under the Linux operating system.

Device files for networking hardware are created, as necessary, by the device drivers contained in the Linux kernel. These device files are not available for other programs to use. This means we can't execute the command

```
cat < /etc/passwd > /dev/eth0
```

The only way information can be sent via the network is by going through the kernel.

Remember, the main reason that the UNIX uses device files is to provide an abstraction which is independent of the actual hardware being used. A network device file must be configured properly before you can use it to send and receive information from the network. The process for configuring a network device requires a bit more background information than you have at the moment. The following provides that background and a later section in the chapter examines the process and the commands in more detail.

The installation process for most Linux variants will normally perform some network configuration for you. To find out what network devices are currently active on your system, have a look at the contents of the file /proc/net/dev

```
cat /proc/net/dev
```

```
Inter            Receive                          Transmit
face |packets errs drop fifo frame|packets errs drop fifo colls carrier
lo:        91   0    0    0    0       91   0    0    0     0    0
eth0:       0   0    0    0    0       60   0    0    0     0    60
```

On this machine there are two active network devices. lo: the loopback device and eth0: an Ethernet device file. If a computer has more than one Ethernet interface (network devices are usually called network interfaces) you would normally see entries for eth1 eth2 etc.,.

IP aliasing (talked about more later) is the ability for a single Ethernet card to have more than one Internet address. The following example shows the contents of the /proc/net/dev file for a machine using IP aliasing. *It is not normal for an Ethernet card to have multiple IP addresses, normally each Ethernet card/interface will have one IP address.*

```
cat /proc/net/dev
Inter-|   Receive                        |  Transmit
face  |packets errs drop fifo frame|packets errs drop fifo colls carrier
lo:285968         0   0    0      0    285968  0    0    0            0      0
eth0:61181891    59  59    0     89  77721923  0    0    0  11133617     57
eth0:0:48849      0   0    0      0       212  0    0    0            0      0
eth0:1: 10894     0   0    0      0       210  0    0    0            0      0
eth0:2: 481325    0   0    0      0       259  0    0    0            0      0
eth0:3: 29178     0   0    0      0       215  0    0    0            0      0
```

We can see that the device files for an aliased Ethernet device uses the format ethX:Y where X is the number for the Ethernet card and Y is the number of the aliased device. Since aliased devices use the same Ethernet card they must use the same network, after all you can't connect a single Ethernet card to two networks.

24.1.6 Kernel Support for Networking

Ensuring that the kernel includes support for your networking hardware is only the first step. In order to supply certain network services, it is necessary for them to be compiled into the kernel. The following is a list of some of the services that the Linux kernel can support

- **IP accounting**

  IP accounting must be compiled into the kernel and is configured with the ipfwadm command. IP accounting allows you to track the number of bytes and packets transmitted over the network connection. This is useful in situations where you must track the network usage of your users. For example, if you are a Internet Service Provider.

- **IP aliasing**

  Essentially, IP aliasing allows your computer to pretend as if it is more than one computer. In a normal configuration each network device is allocated a single IP address. However there are times when you wish to allocate multiple IP addresses to a computer with a single network interface. The most common example of this is web sites, for example, the websites http://cq-pan.cqu.edu.au/, http://webclass.cqu.edu.au/, and http://webfuse.cqu. edu.au/ are all hosted by one computer. This computer only has one Ethernet card and uses IP aliasing to create aliases for the Ethernet card. The Ethernet card's real IP address is 138.77.37.37 and its three alias addresses are 138.77.37.36, 138.77.37.59 and 138.77.37.108.

Normally the interface would only grab the network packets addressed to 138.77.37.37 but with network aliasing it will grab the packets for all three addresses.

You can see this in action by using the arp command. Have a look at the hardware addresses for the computers cq-pan, webclass and webfuse. What can you tell?

```
/sbin/arp
```

```
Address                 Hwtype      HWaddress        Flags Mask    Iface

centaurus.cqu.EDU.AU ether     AA:00:04:00:0B:1C  C        eth0

webfuse.cqu.EDU.AU    ether     00:60:97:3A:AA:85  C        eth0
cq-pan.cqu.EDU.AU     ether     00:60:97:3A:AA:85  C        eth0
science.cqu.EDU.AU    ether     00:00:F8:01:9E:DA  C        eth0
borric.cqu.EDU.AU     ether     00:20:AF:A4:39:39  C        eth0
webclass.cqu.EDU.AU   ether     00:60:97:3A:AA:85  C        eth0
138.77.37.46        incomplete)                       eth0
```

- **IP firewall**

  This option allows you to use a Linux computer to implement a firewall. A firewall works by allowing you to selectively ignore certain types of network connections. By doing this you can restrict what access there is to your computer (or the network behind it) and as a result help in increase of security.

  The firewall option is closely related to IP accounting, for example it is configured with the same command, ipfwadm.

- **IP encapsulation**

  IP encapsulation is where the IP packet from your machine is wrapped inside another IP packet. This is of particular use in mobile IP and IP multicast.

- **IPX**

  IPX protocol is used in Novel Netware systems. Including IPX support in the Linux kernel allows a Linux computer to communicate with Netware machines.

- **IPv6**

  IPv6, version 6 of the IP protocol, is the next generation of which is slowly being adopted. IPv6 includes support for the current IP protocol.

- **IP masquerade**

  IP masquerade allows multiple computers to use a single IP address. One situation where this can be useful is when you have a single dialup connection to the Internet via an Internet Service Provider (ISP). Normally, such a dialup connection can only be used by the machine which is connected. Even if the dialup machine is on a LAN with other machines connected they cannot access the Internet. However with IP masquerading it is possible to allow all the machines on that LAN access the Internet.

- **Network Address Translation**

  Support for network address translation for Linux is still at an alpha stage. Network address translation is the "next version" of IP masquerade.

- **IP proxy server**

  Mobile IP

  Since an IP address consists of both a network address and a host address it can normally only be used when a machine is connected to the network specified by the network address. Mobile IP allows a machine to be moved to other networks but still retain the same IP. IP encapsulation is used to send packets destined for the mobile machine to its new location.

- **IP multicast**

  IP multicast is used to send packets simultaneously to computers and separate IP networks. It is used for a variety of audio and video transmission.

24.1.7 Ethernet Basics

The following provides very brief background information on Ethernet which is a LAN protocol.

Ethernet addresses

Every Ethernet card has built into it a 48 bit address (called an Ethernet address or a Media Access Control (MAC) address or HW address). The high 24 bits of the address are used to assign a unique number to manufacturers of Ethernet addresses and the low 24 bits are assigned to individual Ethernet cards made by the manufacturer.

Some example Ethernet addresses. You will notice that Ethernet addresses are written using 6 tuple's of HEX numbers such as:

```
00:00:0C:03:79:2F
00:40:F6:60:4D:A4
```

Ethernet is a broadcast medium

Every packet, often called an Ethernet frame, of information sent on Ethernet contains a source and destination MAC address. The packet is placed on a Ethernet network and every machine, actually the Ethernet card, on the network looks at the packet. If the card recognizes the destination MAC as its own, it "grabs" the packet and passes it to the Network access layer.

It is possible to configure your Ethernet card so that it grabs all packets sent on the network. This is how it is possible to "listen in" on other people on a Ethernet network.

A single Ethernet network cannot cover much more than a couple of hundred meters. However, how far depends on the type of cabling used.

Converting hardware addresses to Internet addresses

The network access layer, the lowest level of the TCP/IP protocol stack is responsible for converting Internet addresses into hardware addresses. This is how TCP/IP can be used over a large number of different networking hardware.

Address Resolution Protocol

The mapping of Ethernet addresses into Internet addresses is performed by the Address Resolution Protocol (ARP). ARP maintains a table that contains the translation table between IP address and Ethernet address.

When the machine wants to send data to a computer on the local Ethernet network the ARP software is asked if it knows about the IP address of the machine (remember the software deals in IP addresses). If the ARP table contains the IP address the Ethernet address is returned.

If the IP address is not known a packet is broadcast to every host on the local network, the packet contains the required IP address. Every host on the network examines the packet. If the receiving host recognizes the IP address as its own, it will send a reply back that contains its Ethernet address. This response is then placed into the ARP table of the original machine (so it knows it next time).

The ARP table will only contain Ethernet addresses for machines on the local network. Delivery of information to machines not on the local network requires the intervention of routing software.

arp

On a UNIX machine, you can view, modify, remove the contents of the ARP table using the arp command. **arp -a** will display the entire table.

That is, we can see the arp cache, remove a host's entry from the arp cache, etc. In a networked system, when a packet arrives at router machine (often a UNIX machine) then the IP address to Ethernet address mapping is needed. This is achieved by arp protocol. These mappings are stored in arp cache such that next time another packet arrives with the same IP address then its Ethernet or physical address is calculated by carrying out a lookup operation on this arp cache. With arp command we can modify, view, delete the entries of this cache.

Some other options of arp command are shown in Table 24.1

Table 24.1 Options with arp command.

arp –a	Displays all entries are displayed
arp -a hostname	Displays entry of the given host
arp -d hostname	Removes the entry of the specified host
arp -s hostname HW_addr	Creates manually ARP entry for the host with the given hardware address (HW address has to be given in hexadecimal separated by colons)

To see how new entries are added to the cache we propose to ping command. Ping is often used to test a network connection and to see if a particular machine is alive. In this case we are pinging src.doc.ic.ac.uk.

```
ping src.doc.ic.ac.uk
PING src.doc.ic.ac.uk (138.77.37.102): 56 data bytes
64 bytes from 138.77.37.102: icmp_seq=0 ttl=64 time=19.0 ms

--- pug.cqu.edu.au ping statistics ---
1 packets transmitted, 1 packets received, 0% packet loss
round-trip min/avg/max = 19.0/19.0/19.0 ms
```

Now checkup the arp cache by running arp –a command. We will not find any new entry. Now, you can try by pinging a machine in our LAN and see the arp cache content. We find an entry for this local machine.

24.1.8 SLIP, PPP

SLIP and PPP, used to connect machines via serial lines (and modems) that are not broadcast media. They are simple "point-to-point" connections between two computers. This means that when information is placed on a SLIP/PPP connection, only the two computers at either end of that connection can see the information. SLIP/PPP are usually used when a computer is connected to a network via a modem or a serial connection.

24.2 More TCP/IP Basics

Before going any further, it is necessary to introduce some of the basic concepts related to TCP/IP networks. An understanding of these concepts is essential for the next steps in connecting a Linux machine to a network.

- **Hostnames**

  Every machine (also known as a host) on the Internet has a name known as hostname.

- **IP addresses**

  Each network interface on the network also has a unique IP address. This section discusses IP addresses, the components of an IP address, subnets, network classes and other related issues.

- **Name resolution**

  Human beings use hostnames while the IP protocols use IP addresses. There must be a way, name resolution, to convert hostnames into IP addresses. This section looks at how this is achieved.

- **Routing**

  When network packets travel from your computer to a Web site in the United States there are normally a multitude of different paths that packet can take. The decisions about which path it takes are performed by a routing algorithm. This section briefly discusses how routing occurs.

- **network ports**

  Network ports are the logical (that means that ports are an imaginary construct which exists only in software) connections through which the information flows into and out of a machine. A single machine can have thousands of programs all sending and receiving information via the network at the same time. The delivery of this information to the right programs is achieved through ports.

- **network servers**

  Network servers are the programs that sit listening at pre-defined ports waiting for connections from other hosts. These servers wait for a request, perform some action and send a response back to the program that requested the action. In general network servers operate as daemons.

- **network clients**

  Users access network services using client programs. Example network clients include Netscape, Eudora and the ftp command on a UNIX machine.

  - **network protocols**

  Network protocols specify how the network clients and servers communicate. They define the small "language" which both machines understand.

24.2.1 Hostnames

Most computers on a TCP/IP network are given a name, usually known as a host name (a computer can be known as a host). The hostname is usually a simple name used to uniquely identify a computer within a given site. A fully qualified Internet host name, also known as a fully qualified domain name (FQDN), uses the following format

hostname.site.domain.country

- Hostname

  A name by which the computer is known. This name must be unique to the site on which the machine is located.

- Site

  A short name given to the site (company, University, government department etc) on which the machine resides.

- Domain

  Each site belongs to a specific domain. A domain is used to group sites of similar purpose together. Table 24.2 provides an example of some domain names. Strictly speaking a domain name also includes the country.

Table 24.2 Example Internet domains.

Domain	Purpose
edu	Educational institution, university or school
com	Commercial company
gov	Government department
Net	Networking companies

- Country

  Specifies the actual country in which the machine resides. Table 24.3 provides an example of some country names. You can see a list of the country codes at http://www.bcpl.net/~jspath/isocodes.html

Table 24.3 Example Country Codes.

Country code	Country
nothing or us	United States
au	Australia
uk	United Kingdom
in	India
ca	Canada
fr	France

hostname

Under Linux, the hostname of a machine is set using the hostname command. Only the root user can set the hostname. Any other user can use the hostname command to view the machine's current name.

```
hostname
darkstar.org


To change hostname:
hostname fred
hostname
fred
```

Changes to the hostname performed using the hostname command will not apply after rebooting. The hostname is set during start-up from one of configuration files,

/etc/sysconfig/network. If we wish a change in hostname to be retained after you reboot, you will have to change this file.

A fully qualified name must be unique to the entire Internet, which implies every hostname on a site should be unique.

It is not always necessary to specify a fully qualified name; especially to refer to a machine in local LAN.

24.2.2 IP/Internet Addresses

Computers on the Internet communicate by exchanging packets of data, known as, IP packets. IP is the network protocol used to send information from one computer to another over the Internet. All computers in the Internet (by our definition in this book) communicate using IP. IP moves information contained in IP packets. The IP packets are routed via special routing algorithms from a source computer that sends the packets to a destination computer that receives them. The routing algorithms figure out the best way to send the packets from source to destination. In order for IP to send packets from a source computer to a destination computer, it must have some way of identifying these computers. All computers the Internet are identified using one or more IP addresses. A computer may have more than one IP address if it has more than one network interface to computers that are connected to the Internet.

Alpha-numeric names, like hostnames, cannot be handled efficiently by computers, at least not as efficiently as numbers. For this reason, hostnames are only used for the sake of humans. The computers and other equipment involved in TCP/IP networks use numbers to identify hosts on the Internet. These numbers are called IP addresses. This is because it is the Internet Protocol (IP) which provides the addressing scheme.

As such **IP addresses** are 32-bit numbers. They may be written in decimal, hexadecimal, or other formats, but the most common format is dotted decimal notation. This format breaks the 32-bit address up into four bytes and writes each byte of the address as unsigned decimal integers separated by dots. For example, one of my IP addresses is 0xccD499C1. Because 0xcc = 204, 0xD4 = 212, 0x99 = 153, and 0xC1 = 193, my address in dotted decimal form is 204.212.153.193.

IP addresses are currently 32 bit numbers (i.e.m in IPv4); IPv6 the next generation of IP which uses 128 bit address. IP addresses are usually written as four numbers separated by full stops (called dotted decimal form) e.g.m 132.22.42.1. Since IP addresses are 32 bit numbers, each of the numbers in the dotted decimal form are restricted to between 0-255 (32 bits divide by 4 numbers gives 8 bits per number and 255 is the biggest number you can represent using 8 bits). This means that 257.33.33.22 is an invalid address.

Dotted Quad to Binary

The address 132.22.42.1 in dotted decimal form is actually stored on the computer as 10000100 00010110 00101010 00000001. Each of the four decimal numbers represent one byte of the final binary number

- 132 = 10000100
- 22 = 00010110
- 42 = 00101010
- 1 = 00000001

Also, IP address is further divided as network address and host address. Machines in a network (LAN) will be having same network address while their host addresses will be differring. In order to route a packet to any machine in a network, the network address is needed. While delivering packet to a machine, we need its last address. With network address with nerwork address only packet will be routed to the destinations machine's LAN. After that, host address is needed.

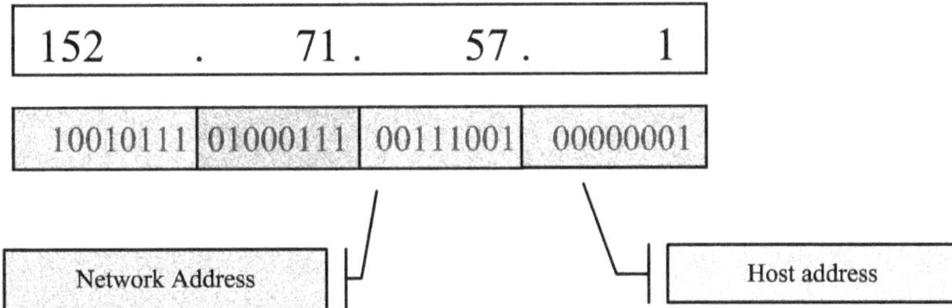

Networks and hosts

An IP address actually consists of two parts

• a network portion

This is used to identify the network that the machine belongs to. Hosts on the same network will have this portion of the IP address in common. This is one of the reasons why IP masquerading is required for mobile computers (e.g. laptops). If you move a computer to a different network you must give it a different IP address which includes the network address of the new network it is connected to.

• the host portion

This is the part which uniquely identifies the host on the network.

The network portion of the address forms the high part of the address (the bit that appears on the left hand side of the number). **The size of the network and host**

portions of an IP address is specified by another 32 bit number called the netmask (also known as the subnet mask).

To calculate which part of an IP address is the network and which the host the IP address and the subnet mask are treated as binary numbers (see diagram above). Each bit of the subnet mask and the IP address are compared and

- if the bit is set in both the IP address and the subnet mask then the bit is set in the network address,

- if the bit is set in the IP address but **not** set in the subnet mask then the bit is set in the host address.

For example

IP address	138.77.37.21	10001010	01001101	00100101	00010101
Netmask	255.255.255.0	11111111	11111111	11111111	00000000
network address	138.77.37.0	10001010	01001101	00100101	00000000
host address	0.0.0.21	00000000	00000000	00000000	00010101

The Internet is a network of networks

The structure of IP addresses can give you some idea of how the Internet works. It is a network of networks. We start with a collection of machines all connected via the same networking hardware, a local area network. All the machines on this local area network will have the same network address, each machine also has a unique host address.

The Internet is formed by connecting a lot of local area networks together. Usually, in a LAN one machine is called as router. Actually, all these routers are connected with some hierarchy involving MAN's, WAN's. These WAN's are connected; forming Internet. While connecting LAN's, MAN's and WAN's, we use variety of intermediate units known as repeaters, bridges, routers and gateways.

Network Classes

During the development of the TCP/IP protocol stack IP addresses were divided into classes. There are three main address classes, A, B and C. Table 24.4 summarizes the differences between the three classes. The class of an IP address can be deduced by the value of the first byte of the address.

Table 24.4 Network classes.

Class	First byte value	Netmask	Number of hosts
A	1 to 126	255.0.0.0	16 million
B	128 to 191	255.255.0.0	64,000
C	192 to 223	255.255.255.0	254
Multicast	224 – 239	240.0.0.0	

If you plan on setting up a network that is connected to the Internet, the addresses for your network must be allocated to you by central controlling organization. You can't just choose any set of addresses you wish, chances are they are already taken by some other site.

If your network will not be connected to the Internet, you can choose from a range of addresses which have been set aside for this purpose. These addresses are shown in Table 24.5

Table 24.5 Networks reserved for private networks.

Network class	Addresses
A	10.0.0.0 to 10.255.255.255
B	172.16.0.0 to 172.31.255.255
C	192.168.0.0 to 192.168.255.255

The addresses 127.0.0.X are special IP addresses. It refers to the local host. The local host allows software to address the local machine in exactly the same way it would address a remote machine. Usually these addresses are used to test network SW's developed.

Assigning IP addresses in a LAN: A example from Class C Networks

Some IP addresses are reserved for specific purposes and you should not assign these addresses to a machine. Table 24.6 lists some of these addresses

Table 24.6 Reserved IP addresses.

Address	Purpose
xx.xx.xx.0	Network address
xx.xx.xx.1	Gateway address *
xx.xx.xx.255	broadcast address
127.0.0.1	loopback address

* this is not a set standard

Gateways and routers are able to distribute data from one network to another because they are actually physically connected to two or more networks through a number of network interfaces.

As mentioned earlier the network address is the IP address with a host address part as all 0's. The network address is used to identify a network. The broadcast address is the IP address with the host address set to all 1's and is used to send information to all the computers on a network, typically used for routing and error information.

It is easier to remember i.e., pc12.doc.ntu.ac.uk compared to the related 32 bit IP number. This type of names are called domain names. This then requires some form of name lookup service to translate from the more understandable English like form back into an Internet address. Name lookup is performed by a **naming service,** some examples are

NIS (Network information Service)
DNS(Domain Naming Service)

Network naming is based upon the idea of organizing groups of machines and giving them a common name called a **domain** name (Figure 24.4). These domains are in turn themselves organized into other groups or domains hierarchically until at the top of the hierarchy there is a single domain name. A machine called a domain controller manages each domain in the hierarchy. This controller holds only the mapping between names and IP addresses for the machines in its domain.

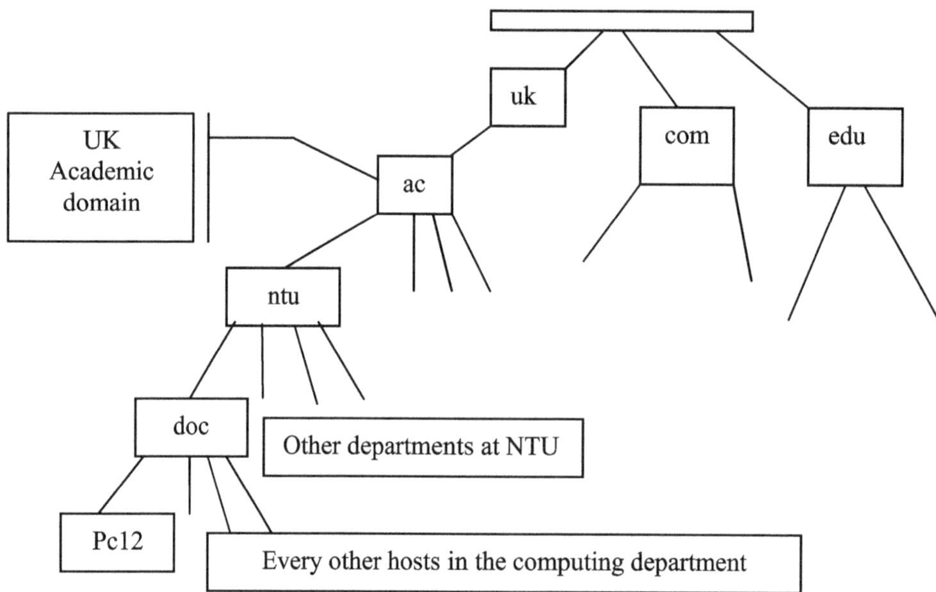

Fig. 24.4 Network Naming.

IP addresses are not easy to remember, even using dotted decimal notation. The Internet has adopted a mechanism, referred to as the ***Domain Name System*** **(DNS)**, whereby computer names can be associated with IP addresses. These computer names are referred to as *domain names*. The DNS has several rules that determine how domain names are constructed and how they relate to one another. For the purposes of this chapter, it is sufficient to know that domain names are computer names and that they are mapped to IP addresses. The mapping of domain names to IP addresses is maintained by a system of *domain name servers*. These servers are able to look up the IP address corresponding to a domain name. They also provide the capability to look up the domain name associated with a particular IP address, if one exists.

IP enables communication between computers on the Internet by routing data from a source computer to a destination computer. However, computer-to-computer communication only solves half of the network communication problem. In order for an application program, such as a mail program, to communicate with another application, such as a mail server, there needs to be a way to send data to specific programs within a computer. We will be knowing how this is solved as we progress further in this chapter.

24.2.3　Name resolution

The process of taking a hostname and finding the IP address is called **name resolution**. This is very much needed as computers works on the basis of numbers, i.e. addresses; whereas humans finds comfort dealing with symbolic things, i.e. names.

Methods of name resolution

There are two methods that can be used to perform name resolution

- `the /etc/hosts file, and`
- `the Domain Name Service.`

`Use of /etc/hosts`

One way of performing name resolution is to maintain a file that contains a list of hostnames and their equivalent IP addresses. When we want to know a machine's IP address, we look up the file. If any network SW needs IP address, it will check in this file. Under UNIX/Linux the file is /etc/hosts. /etc/hosts is a text file with one line per host. Each line has the format

IP_address hostname

or

IP_address hostname alias

Comments can be indicated by using the hash # symbol. Aliases are used to indicate shorter names or other names used to refer to the same host.

Problems with /etc/hosts

With over 3 million machines on the Internet it should be obvious that this is not a smart solution as the file size increases and lookup operation takes more time. Also, updating this file is not easy task.

Domain name system (DNS)

The Internet Domain Name System (DNS) was developed as a distributed database to solve this problem. Its primary goal is to allow the allocation of host names to be distributed amongst multiple naming authorities, rather than centralized at a single point.

DNS structure

The DNS is arranged as a hierarchy, both from the perspective of the structure of the names maintained within the DNS, and in terms of the delegation of naming authorities. At the top of the hierarchy is the root domain "." which is administered by the Internet Assigned Numbers Authority (IANA). Administration of the root domain gives the IANA the authority to allocate domains beneath the root.

The process of assigning a domain to an organizational entity is called delegating, and involves the administrator of a domain creating a sub-domain and assigning the authority for allocating sub-domains of the new domain; the sub domain's administrative entity.

Even though the DNS supports many levels of sub-domains, delegations should only be made where there is a requirement for an organization or organizational sub-division to manage their own name space. Any sub-domain administrator must also demonstrate they have the technical competence to operate a domain name server, or arrange for another organization to do so on their behalf.

Domain Name Servers

The DNS is implemented as collection of inter-communicating name servers. At any given level of the DNS hierarchy, a name server for a domain has knowledge of all the immediate sub-domains of that domain.

For each domain there is a primary name server, which contains authoritative information regarding Internet entities within that domain. In addition Secondary name servers can be configured, which periodically download authoritative data from the primary server. Secondary name servers provide backup to the primary name server when it is not operational, and further improve the overall performance of the DNS, since the name servers of a domain that respond to queries most quickly are used in preference to any others.

`Use of /etc/resolv.conf`

When performing a name resolution most UNIX machines will check their /etc/hosts first and then check with their name server. How does the machine know where its domain name server is. The answer is in the /etc/resolv.conf file.

resolv.conf is a text file with three main types of entries

- # comments

  Anything after a # is a comment and ignored.

- domain *name*

  Defines the default domain. This default domain will be appended to any hostname that does not contain a dot.

- name server *address*

This defines the IP address of the machines domain name server. It is possible to have multiple name servers defined and they will be queried in order (useful if one goes down).

For example

The /etc/resolv.conf file from my machine is listed below.

```
domain cqu.edu.au
nameserver 138.77.5.6
nameserver 138.77.1.1
```

24.2.4 Routing

So far we've looked at names and addresses that specify the location of a host on the Internet. We now move onto routing. Routing is the act of deciding how each individual datagram (packet) finds its way through the multiple different paths to its destination.

Simple routing

For most UNIX/Linux computers the routing decisions they must make are simple. If the datagram is for a host on the local network then the data is placed on the local network and delivered to the destination host. If the destination host is on a remote network then the datagram will be forwarded to the local gateway. The local gateway will then pass it on further.

Routing tables

Routing is concerned with finding the right **network** for a datagram. Once the right network has been found the datagram can be delivered to the host.

Most hosts (and gateways) on the Internet maintain a routing table. The entries in the routing table contain the information to know where to send datagrams for a particular network.

Constructing the routing table:

The routing table can be constructed in one of the two ways

- constructed by the Systems Administrator, sometimes referred to as static routes,
- dynamically created by a number of different available routing protocols

The dynamic table creation by routing protocols is complex and beyond the scope of this subject.

Making the connections Physically

ifconfig

Network interfaces are configured using the ifconfig command and has the standard format for turning a device on

ifconfig *device_name IP_address* netmask *netmask* up

For example

- ifconfig eth0 138.77.37.26 netmask 255.255.255.0 up

  Configures the first Ethernet address with the IP address of 138.77.37.26 and the netmask of 255.255.255.0.

- ifconfig lo 127.0.0.1

  Configures the loopback address appropriately.

  Other parameters for the ifconfig command include

  - up and down

    These parameters are used to take the device up and down (turn it on and off). ifconfig eth0 down will disable the eth0 interface and will require an ifconfig command like the first example above to turn it back on.

  - -arp

    Will turn on/off the address resolution protocol for the specified interface.

  - -pointtopoint *addr*

    Used to specify the IP address (*addr*) of the computer at the far end of a point to point link.

Configuring the name resolver

Once the device/interface is configured you can start using the network. However, you'll only be able to use IP addresses. At this stage, the networking system on your computer will not know how to resolve hostnames (convert hostnames into IP addresses).

This is where the name resolver and its associated configuration files enter into the picture. In particular, the three files we'll be looking at are:

- **/etc/resolv.conf**

  Specifies where the main domain name server is located for your machine.

- **/etc/hosts.conf**

  Allows you to specify how the name resolver will operate. For example, will it ask the domain name server first or look at a local file.

- **/etc/hosts**

  A local file which specifies the IP/hostname association between common or local computers.

/etc/resolv.conf

The /etc/resolv.conf is the main configuration file for the name resolver code. Its format is quite simple. It is a text file with one keyword per line. There are three keywords typically used, they are:

- Domain this keyword specifies the local domain name.
- search this keyword specifies a list of alternate domain names to search for a hostname
- nameserver this keyword, which may be used many times, specifies an IP address of a domain name server to query when resolving names

An example /etc/resolv.conf might look something like:

```
domain maths.wu.edu.au
search maths.wu.edu.au wu.edu.au
nameserver 192.168.10.1
nameserver 192.168.12.1
```

This example specifies that the default domain name to append to unqualified names (i.e., hostnames supplied without a domain) is maths.wu.edu.au and that if the host is not found in that domain too also, try in the wu.edu.au domain directly. Two name servers entry are supplied, each of which may be called upon by the name resolver code to resolve the name.

/etc/host.conf

The /etc/host.conf file is where you configure some items that govern the behavior of the name resolver code.

The format of this file is described in detail in the resolv+ man page. In nearly all circumstances the following example will work for you:

```
order hosts,bind
multi on
```

This configuration tells the name resolver to check the /etc/hosts file before attempting to query a name server and to return all valid addresses for a host found in the /etc/hosts file instead of just the first.

/etc/hosts

We have already discussed about this file in previous sections. In a well managed system the only hostnames that usually appear in this file are an entry for the loopback interface and the local hosts name such as the following.

/etc/hosts

```
localhost loopback
192.168.0.1 this.host.name
```

Configuring routing

Routing is a huge and complex topic. It is not possible to provide a detailed introduction in the confines of this text. Each host keeps a special list of routing rules, called a routing table. This table contains rows which typically contain at least three fields, the first is a destination address, the second is the name of the interface to which the datagram is to be routed and the third is optionally the IP address of another machine which will carry the datagram on its next step through the network.

In Linux, you can see this table by using the following command:

cat /proc/net/route
or by using either of the following commands:

/sbin/route -n

/bin/netstat -r

The routing process is fairly simple: an incoming datagram is received, the destination address (who it is for) is examined and compared with each entry in the table. The entry that best matches that address is selected and the datagram is forwarded to the specified interface. If the gateway field is filled then the datagram is forwarded to that host via the specified interface, otherwise the destination address is assumed to be on the network supported by the interface.

To manipulate this table a special command is used. This command takes command line arguments and converts them into kernel system calls that request the kernel to add, delete or modify entries in the routing table. The command is called 'route'.

A simple example. Imagine we have an Ethernet network. We have been told it is a class-C network with an address of 192.168.1.0. You've been supplied with an IP address of 192.168.1.10 for our use and have been told that 192.168.1.1 is a router connected to the Internet.

The first step is to configure the interface as described earlier. We would use a command like:

 # ifconfig eth0 192.168.1.10 netmask 255.255.255.0 up

We now need to add an entry into the routing table to tell the kernel that datagrams for all hosts with addresses that match 192.168.1.* should be sent to the Ethernet device. We would use a command similar to:

 # route add -net 192.168.1.0 netmask 255.255.255.0 eth0

Note the use of the `-net' argument to tell the route program that this entry is a network route. Your other choice here is a `-host' route which is a route that is specific to one IP address.

This route will enable you to establish IP connections with all of the hosts on your Ethernet segment. But what about all of the IP hosts that aren't on your Ethernet segment ?

It would be a very difficult job to have to add routes to every possible destination network, so there is a special trick that is used to simplify this task. The trick is called the `default' route. The default route matches every possible destination, but poorly, so that if any other entry exists that matches the required address it will be used instead of the default route. The idea of the default route is simply to enable you to say "and everything else should go here". In the example we have contrived you would use an entry like:

 # route add default gw 192.168.1.1 eth0

The `gw' argument tells the route command that the next argument is the IP address, or name, of a gateway or router machine which all datagrams matching this entry should be directed to for further routing.

So, your complete configuration would look like:

 # ifconfig eth0 192.168.1.10 netmask 255.255.255.0 up

 # route add -net 192.168.1.0 netmask 255.255.255.0 eth0

 # route add default gw 192.168.1.1 eth0

These steps are actually performed automatically by the startup files on a properly configured Linux box.

Startup files

In the previous section we've looked at the individual steps used to configuring networking on a simple Linux machine. On a normal Linux machine these steps are performed automatically in the system startup files. While the commands introduced in the previous section are standard Linux/UNIX commands, the startup and associated configuration files used by different distributions. This section briefly summarizes the startup files which are used on a Redhat 5.0 machine.

The files used include

- **/etc/sysconfig/network**

  A text file which defines shell variables for hostname, domain, gateway and gateway device.

- **/etc/sysconfig/network-scripts**

  A collection of scripts used to perform common tasks including bringing network interfaces up and down.

- **/etc/rc.d/init.d/network**

  A shell script which actually brings up the networking on start-up. Linked to from a number of scripts in the rcX.d directories.

24.2.5   Network Management Tools

nslookup

The nslookup command is used to query a name server and is supplied as a debugging tool. It is generally used to determine if the name server is working correctly and for querying information from remote servers. The nslookup can be used from either the command line or interactively. Giving nslookup a hostname will result in it asking the current domain name server for the IP address of that machine. The nslookup also has an ls command that can be used to view the entire records of the current domain name server.

For example

nslookup rambo

```
Server    : circus.cqu.edu.au

Address   : 138.77.5.6

Name      : jasper.cqu.edu.au

Address   : 138.77.1.1
```

netstat

The netstat command is used to display the status of network connections to a UNIX machine. One of the functions it can be used for is to display the contents of the kernel routing table by using the -r switch.

For example

The following examples are from two machines

netstat -rn

```
Kernel routing table
```

Destination	Gateway	Genmask	Flags	Metric	Ref	Use	Iface
138.77.37.0	0.0.0.0	255.255.255.	0	U	0	0	109130eth0
127.0.0.0	0.0.0.0	255.0.0.0	U	0	0	9206	lo
0.0.0.0	138.77.37.1	0.0.0.0	UG	0	0	2546951	eth0

netstat -rn

```
Routing tables

    Destination     Gateway          Flags      Refcnt       Use          Interface

    127.0.0.1       127.0.0.1        UH         56           7804440      lo0

    Default         138.77.1.11      UG         23           1595585      ln0

    138.77.32       138.77.1.11      UG         0            19621        ln0

    138.77.16       138.77.1.11      UG         0            555          ln0

    138.77.8        138.77.1.11      UG         0            385345       ln0

    138.77.80       138.77.1.11      UG         0            0            ln0

    138.77.72       138.77.1.11      UG         0            0            ln0

    138.77.64       138.77.1.11      UG         0            0            ln0

    138.77.41       138.77.1.11      UG         0            0            ln0
```

traceroute

For some reason or another, users on one machine cannot connect to another machine or if they can any information transfer between the two machines is either slow or plagued by errors. What do you do?

The traceroute command provides a way of discovering the path taken by information as it goes from one machine to another and can be used to identify where problems might be occurring. On the Internet, that path may not always be the same.

traceroute knuth

traceroute to knuth.cqu.edu.au (138.77.36.20), 30 hops max, 40 byte packets
1 knuth.cqu.EDU.AU (138.77.36.20) 2 ms 2 ms 2 ms

jasper is one network away from aldur

traceroute jasper

traceroute to jasper.cqu.edu.au (138.77.1.1), 30 hops max, 40 byte packets
1. centaurus.cqu.EDU.AU (138.77.36.1) 1 ms 1 ms 1 ms
2. jasper.cqu.EDU.AU (138.77.1.1) 2 ms 1 ms 1 ms

A machine still on the CQU site but a little further away

traceroute jade

traceroute to jade.cqu.edu.au (138.77.7.2), 30 hops max, 40 byte packets
1. centaurus.cqu.EDU.AU (138.77.36.1) 1 ms 1 ms 1 ms
2. hercules.cqu.EDU.AU (138.77.5.3) 4 ms 2 ms 12 ms
3. jade.cqu.EDU.AU (138.77.7.2) 3 ms 13 ms 3 ms

24.1.6 Ports

Generally speaking, a computer has a single physical connection to the network via its network card or DSL modem. All data destined for a particular computer arrives through that connection. However, the data may be intended for different applications running on the computer. So how does the computer know to which application to forward the data? Through the use of *ports*. Data transmitted over the Internet is accompanied by addressing information that identifies the computer and the port for which it is destined. The computer is identified by its 32-bit IP address (currently migration is taking place from IPv4 to IPv6 which uses 128 bit addresses), which IP uses to deliver data to the right computer on the network. Ports are identified by a 16-bit number, which TCP and UDP use to deliver the data to the right application.

In connection-based communication such as TCP, a server application binds a socket to a specific port number. This has the effect of registering the server with the system to receive all data destined for that port. A client can then rendezvous with the server at the server's port, as illustrated here:

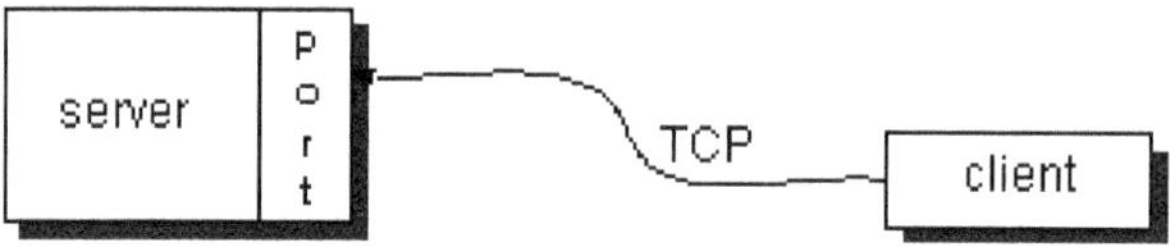

Definition: The TCP and UDP protocols use ports to map incoming data to a particular process running on a computer.

In datagram-based communication such as UDP, the datagram packet contains the port number of its destination and UDP routes the packet to the appropriate application, as illustrated in Fig. 24.5:

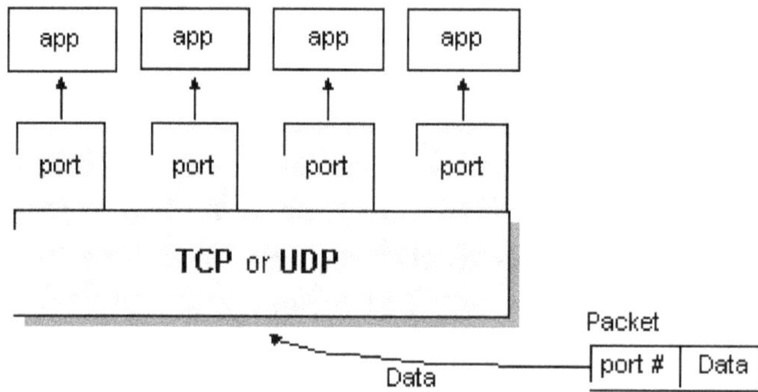

Fig. 24.5 Packet structure

Thus, each process accessing the network using the TCP/IP protocol is allocated a unique address comprising of two components

- The Internet address of the host machine.
- A port number to identify the process.

Let us assume that we have a host on which processes A, B, C and D are running which are looking at ports 172, 1050, 3670, and 64400. For example, when a packet arrives at this machine with port number 3670 then the OS (kernel) decides to handover the same to the process C which is looking at port 3670. Similarly, packets will be delivered to processes A, B, and C based on the port number in the incoming packet.

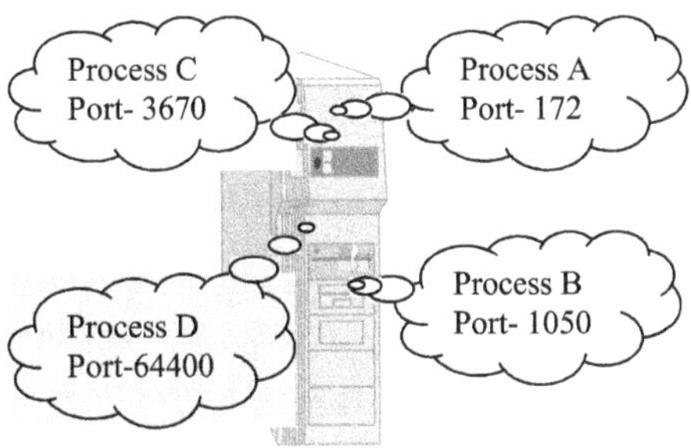

Consider the Fig. 24.6 which contains a server with IP address 128.2.194.242 and two server processes web server (looking at port 80) and an echo server (looking at port 7). If a packets arrives from a client with port 80, it will be handovered to web server process on the host 128.2.194.242. If the arrived packet contains port 7, then the same is handovered to echo server. Thus, port number is used to decide to which of the processes the packet has to be handovered.

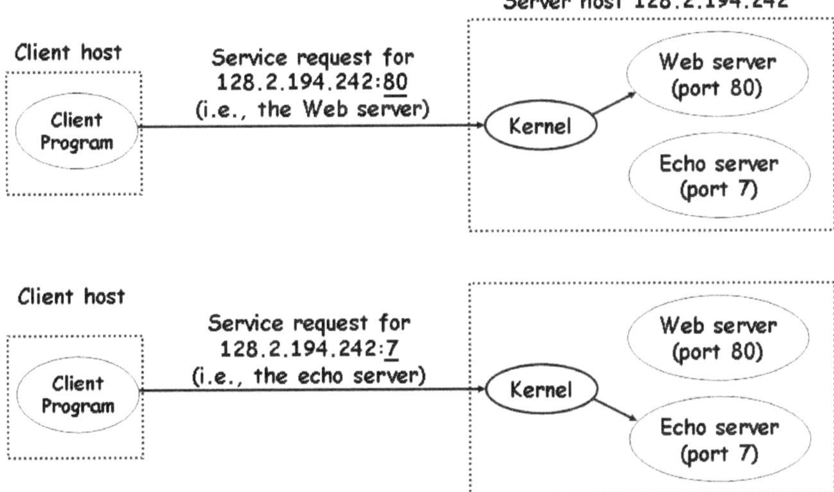

Fig. 24.6 Use of port number

All network protocols, including, http, ftp, SMTP, use either TCP or UDP to deliver information. Every TCP or UDP header contains two 16 bit numbers that are used to identify the source port (the port through which the information was sent) and the destination port (the port through which the information must be delivered.) Similarly, the IP header also contains numbers which describe the IP addresses of the computers which are sending and receiving the current packet.

Port numbers range from 0 to 65,535 because ports are represented by 16-bit numbers. The port numbers ranging from 0 - 1023 are restricted; they are reserved for use by well-known services such as HTTP, FTP and other system services (see Table 24.7). These ports are called *well-known ports*. The ports 0-256 are used by the network servers for well known Internet services (e.g. telnet, FTP, SMTP). Ports in the range from 256-1024 are used for network services that were originally UNIX specific. Network client programs and other programs should use ports above 1024. Our applications should not attempt to bind to well known ports. Here are a few example applications and related port numbers.

Table 24.7 Reserved Ports.

Port number	Purpose
20	ftp-data
21	ftp
23	telnet
25	SMTP (mail)
80	http (WWW)
119	nntp (network news)
110	Post office protocol

This means that when you look at a TCP/UDP packet and see that it is addressed to port 25 then you can be sure that it is part of an email message being sent to a SMTP server. A packet destined for port 80 is likely to be a request to a Web server.

Reserved ports

So how does the computer know which ports are reserved for special services? On a UNIX computer this is specified by the file /etc/services. Each line in the services file is of the format

Service-name port/protocol aliases

Where service-name is the official name for the service, port is the port number that it listens on, protocol is the transport protocol it uses and aliases is a list of alternate names.

The following is an extract from an example **/etc/services** file. Most /etc/services files will be the same, or at least very similar.

```
echo 7/tcp
echo 7/udp
discard 9/tcp sink null
discard 9/udp sink null
systat 11/tcp users
daytime 13/tcp
daytime 13/udp
ftp-data 20/tcp
ftp 21/tcp
telnet 23/tcp
smtp 25/tcp mail
nntp 119/tcp usenet # Network News Transfer
ntp 123/tcp # Network Time Protocol
```

We should be able to match some of the entries in the above example, or in the /etc/services file on your computer, with the entries in Table 24.1.

The **netstat** command can be used for a number of purposes including looking at all of the current active network connections. The following is an example of the output of netstat (it's been edited to reduce the size).

netstat -a

```
active Internet connections (including servers)
proto   Recv-Q Send-Q Local Address        Foreign Address        (State) User
root
tcp    1    7246 cq-pan.cqu.edu.au:www lore.cs.purdue.e:42468 CLOSING root
tcp    0    0 cq-pan.cqu.edu.au:www sdlab142.syd.cqu.:1449 CLOSE root
tcp    0    0 cq-pan.cqu.edu.au:www dialup102-4-9.swi:1498 FIN_WAIT2 root
tcp    0    22528 cq-pan.cqu.edu.au:www 205.216.78.103:3058 CLOSE root
tcp    1    22528 cq-pan.cqu.edu.au:www barney.poly.edu:47547 CLOSE root
tcp    0    0 cq-pan.cqu.edu.au:www eda.mdc.net:2395 CLOSE    root
tcp    0    22528 cq-pan.cqu.edu.au:www  eda.mdc.net:2397 CLOSE    root
tcp    0    0 cq-pan.cqu.edu.au:www  cphppp134.cyberne:1657 FIN_WAIT2 root
tcp    0    22528 cq-pan.cqu.edu.au:www  port3.southwind.c:1080 CLOSE root
tcp    0    9 cq-pan.cqu.edu.:telnet dinbig.cqu.edu.au:1107 ESTABLISHED root
tcp    0    0 cq-pan.cqu.edu.au:ftp  ppp2-24.INRE.ASU.:1718 FIN_WAIT2 root
```

Explanation

Table 24.8 explains each column of the output. Taking the column descriptions from the table, it is possible to make some observations

- All of the entries, but the last two, are for people accessing this machine's (cq-pan.cqu.edu.au) World-Wide Web server. You can say this because of cq-pan.cqu.edu.au:www. This tells us that the port on the local machine is the www port (port 80).

- In the second last entry, we are telneting to cq-pan from my machine at home. At that stage our machine at home was called dinbig.cqu.edu.au. The telnet client is using port 1107 on dinbig to talk to the telnet daemon.

- The last entry is someone connecting to CQ-PAN's ftp server,

- The connection for the first entry is shut down but not all the data has been sent (this is what the CLOSING state means). This entry, from a machine from Purdue University in the United States, still has 7246 bytes still to be acknowledged

Table 24.8 Columns for netstat.

Column name	Explanation
Proto	the name of the transport protocol (TCP or UDP) being used
Recv-Q	the number of bytes not copied to the receiving process
Send-Q	the number of bytes not yet acknowledged by the remote host
Local Address	the local hostname (or IP address) and port of the connection
Foreign Address	the remote hostname (or IP address) and remote port
State	the state of the connection (only used for TCP because UDP doesn't establish a connection), the values are described in the man page
User	some systems display the user that owns the local program serving the connection

24.2.7 Network servers

The **/etc/services** file specifies which port a particular protocol will listen on. For example SMTP (Simple Mail Transfer Protocol, the protocol used to transfer mail between different machines on a TCP/IP network) uses port 25. This means that there is a network server that listens for SMTP connections on port 25.

This begs some questions

- How do we know which program acts as the network server for which protocol?

- How is that program started?

How network servers start

There are two methods by which network servers are started

- executed as a normal program (usually in the start-up files)

  Servers started in this manner will show up in a **ps** list of all the current running processes. These servers are always running, waiting for a connection on the specified port. This means that the server is using up system resources (RAM etc.,) because it is always in existence but it also means that it is very quick to respond when requests arrive for their services.

- by the **inetd daemon**

  The **inetd** daemon listens at a number of ports and when information arrives, it starts the appropriate network server for that port. Which server, for which port, is specified in the configuration file **/etc/inetd.conf.**

Starting a network server via inetd is usually done when there aren't many connections for that server. If a network server is likely to get a large number of connections (a busy mail or WWW server for example) the daemon for that service should be started in the system startup files and always listen on the port.

The reason for this is overhead. Using inetd takes longer.

The **/etc/inetd.conf** file specifies the network servers that the inetd daemon should execute. The **inetd.conf** file consists of one line for each network service using the following format (Table 24.9 explains the purpose of each field).

service-name socket-type protocol flags user server_program args

Table 24.9 Fields of /etc/inetd.conf file

etd.conf **Field**	**Purpose**
service-name	The service name, the same as that listed in /etc/services
socket-type	The type of data delivery services used (we don't cover this). Values are generally stream for TCP, datagram for UDP and raw for direct IP
protocol	the transport protocol used, the name matches that in the /etc/protocols file
flags	how inetd is to behave with regards this service (not explained any further)
user	the username to run the server as, usually root but there are some exceptions, generally for security reasons
server_program	the full path to the program to run as the server
args	command line arguments to pass to the server program

How it works

Whenever the machine receives a request on a port (on which the **inetd** daemon is listening on), the **inetd** daemon decides which program to execute on the basis of the /etc/inetd.conf file.

Network clients

A network client is simply a program (whether it is text based or a GUI program) that knows how to connect to a network server, pass requests to the server and then receive replies.

By default when you use the command **telnet jasper**, the **telnet** client program will attempt to connect to port 23 of the host jasper (23 is the telnet port as listed in **/etc/services**).

It is possible to use the telnet client program to connect to other ports. For example the command telnet jasper 25 will connect to port 25 of the machine jasper.

Network protocols

Each network service generally uses its own network protocol that specifies the services it offers, how those services are requested and how they are supplied. For example, the ftp protocol defines the commands that can be used to move files from machine to machine. When you use a command line ftp client, the commands you use are part of the ftp protocol.

Request for comment (RFCs)

For protocols to be useful, both the client and server must agree on using the same protocol. If they talk different protocols then no communication can occur. The standards used on the Internet, including those for protocols, are commonly specified in documents called Request for Comments (RFCs). (Not all RFCs are standards). Someone proposing a new Internet standard will write and submit an RFC. The RFC will be distributed to the Internet community who will comment on it and may suggest changes. The standard proposed by the RFC will be adopted as a standard if the community is happy with it.

Table 24.10 RFCs for Protocols.

Protocol	RFC
FTP	959
Telnet	854
SMTP	821
DNS	1035
TCP	793
UDP	768

Table 24.10 lists some of the RFC numbers which describe particular protocols. RFCs can and often are very technical and hard to understand unless you are familiar with the area (the RFC for ftp is about 80 pages long).

Text based protocols

Some of these protocols such as smtp, ftp, nntp, http, are text based. They make use of simple text-based commands to perform their duty. Table 24.11 contains a list of the commands that smtp understands. The smtp (simple mail transfer protocol) is used to transport mail messages across a TCP/IP network.

Table 24.11 SMTP commands.

Command	Purpose
HELO *hostname*	start-up and give your hostname
MAIL FROM: *sender-address*	mail is coming from this address
TO: *recipient-address*	please send it to this address
VRFY *address*	does this address actually exist (verify)
EXPN *address*	expand this address
DATA	I'm about to start giving you the body of the mail message
RSET	oops, reset the state and drop the current mail message
NOOP	do nothing
DEBUG [*level*]	set debugging level
HELP	give me some help please
QUIT	close this connection

How it works

When transferring a mail message a client (such as Eudora) will connect to the SMTP server (on port 25). The client will then carry out a conversation with the server using the commands from Table 24.11. Since these commands are just straight text you can use telnet to simulate the actions of an email client.

Doing this actually has some real use. We often use this ability to check on a mail address or to expand a mail alias. The following shows an example of how we might do this.

The text in bold is what we have typed in. The text in italics are comments we have added after the fact.

telnet localhost 25

Trying 127.0.0.1...

Connected to localhost.

Escape character is '^]'.

220-beldin.cqu.edu.au Sendmail 8.6.12/8.6.9 ready at Wed, 1 May 1996 13:20:10 +1 000

220 ESMTP spoken here

vrfy david *check the address david*

250 David Jones <david@beldin.cqu.edu.au

vrfy joe *check the address joe*

550 joe... User unknown

vrfy postmaster *check the address postmaster*

250 <postmaster@beldin.cqu.edu.au

expn postmaster *postmaster is usually an alias, who is it really??*

250 root <postmaster@beldin.cqu.edu.au

24.1.8. Working with URLs

All of us certainly use URL's to access HTML pages. For example, to connect to google we might have typed www.google.com in our favorite browser. URL is the acronym for Uniform Resource Locator. It is a reference (an address) to a resource on the Internet. It's often easiest, although not entirely accurate, to think of a URL as the name of a file on the World Wide Web; because most URLs refer to a file on some machine on the network. However, remember that URLs also can point to other resources on the network, such as database queries and command output. We provide URLs to our favorite Web browser so that it can locate files on the Internet in the same way that we provide addresses on letters so that the post office can locate your correspondents.

The following is an example of a URL which addresses the Java Web site hosted by Sun Microsystems:

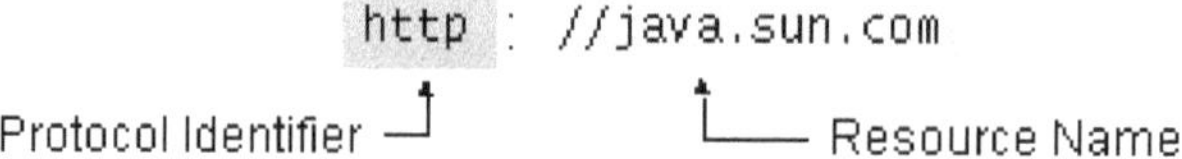

As in the above diagram, a URL has two main components:

Protocol identifier

Resource name

Note that the protocol identifier and the resource name are separated by a colon and two forward slashes. The protocol identifier indicates the name of the protocol to be used to fetch the resource. The example uses the Hypertext Transfer Protocol (HTTP), which is typically used to serve up hypertext documents. HTTP is just one of many different protocols used to access different types of resources on the net. Other protocols include File Transfer Protocol (FTP), Gopher, File, and News.

The resource name is the complete address to the resource. The format of the resource name depends entirely on the protocol used, but for many protocols, including HTTP, the resource name contains one or more of the components listed in the following table:

Host Name	The name of the machine on which the resource lives.
Filename	The pathname to the file on the machine.
Port Number	The port number to which to connect (typically optional).
Reference	A reference to a named anchor within a resource that usually identifies a specific location within a file (typically optional).

The same can be represented pictorially as:

Protocol	Server Address	Port Number	Target Source
http	://www.example.com	80	:/zyx/rao/abc.html

For many protocols, the host name and the filename are required, while the port number and reference are optional. For example, the resource name for an HTTP URL must specify a server on the network (Host Name) and the path to the document on that machine (Filename); it also can specify a port number and a reference. In the URL for the Java Web site java.sun.com is the host name and the trailing slash is shorthand for the file named /index.html.

24.1.9 What is WWW

A technical definition of the World Wide Web is: all the resources and users on the Internet that are using the Hypertext Transfer Protocol (HTTP). A broader definition is: " The World Wide Web is the universe of network-accessible information, an embodiment of human knowledge." Actually, *World Wide Web* is a distributed information system of Internet servers that support specially formatted documents. The documents are formatted in a markup language called HTML (*HyperText Markup Language*) that supports links to other documents, as well as <u>graphics</u>, audio, and video <u>files</u>. This means we can jump from one document to another simply by <u>clicking</u> on <u>hot spots</u>. Not all Internet servers are part of the World Wide Web. *World Wide Web* is **not** synonymous with *the Internet*!. There are several <u>applications</u> called <u>Web browsers</u> that make it easy to <u>access</u> the World Wide Web; two of the most popular being <u>Netscape Navigator</u> (Mozilla) and <u>Microsoft's Internet Explorer</u>.

24.3. The Client/Server Computing Model and the Internet

The Internet provides a variety of services that contribute to its appeal. These services include e-mail, newsgroups, file transfer, remote login, and the Web. Internet services are organized according to a client/server architecture. Client programs, such as Web browsers and file transfer programs, create connections to servers, such as Web and FTP servers. The clients make requests of the server, and the server responds to the requests by providing the service requested by the client. The Web provides a good example of client/server computing. Web browsers are the clients and Web servers are the servers. Browsers request HTML files from Web servers on your behalf by establishing a connection with a Web server and submitting file requests to the server. The server receives the file requests, retrieves the files, and sends them to the browser over the established connection. The browser receives the files and displays them to our browser window.

24.3.1 Sockets and Client/Server Communication

Clients and servers establish connections and communicate via *sockets*. Connections are communication links that are created over the Internet using TCP. Some client/server applications are also built around the connectionless UDP. These applications also use sockets to communicate. Sockets are the endpoints of Internet communication. Sockets can be idealised as streams or stream points. Clients create client sockets and connect them to server sockets. Sockets are associated with a host address and a port address. The host address is the IP address of the host where the client or server program is located. The port address is the communication port used by the client or server program. Server programs use the well-known port number associated with their application protocol. A client communicates with a server by establishing a connection to the socket of the server. The client and server then exchange data over the connection. Connection-oriented communication is more reliable than connectionless communication because the underlying TCP provides message-acknowledgment, error-detection, and error-recovery services. When a connectionless protocol is used, the client and server communicate by sending datagrams to each other's socket. The UDP is used for connectionless protocols. It does not support reliable communication like TCP.

22.3.2 *Sockets*

The *socket* is the software abstraction used to represent the "terminals" of a connection between two machines. For a given connection, there's a socket on each machine, and we can imagine a hypothetical "cable" running between the two machines with each end of the "cable" plugged into a socket. Of course, the physical hardware and cabling between machines is completely unknown. The whole point of the abstraction is that we don't have to know more than is necessary.

`Stream sockets are the end points of a communications link between two processes (see left Figure). The streams connecting the two sockets are bi-directional perfect error free communication streams. The lower level TCP protocol performs all error recovery.

Sockets are appropriate for applications that require guaranteed delivery of information.

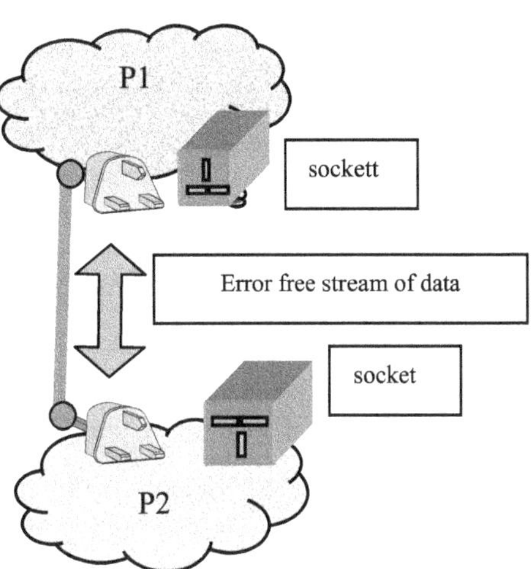

- Terminal sessions
- Remote login
- File Transfer applications
- Mail applications
- Hypertext applications.

Stream sockets are slower than datagram sockets because each packet from the sender must be confirmed as arriving at the receiver as error free and in the correct sequence, otherwise the sender will re-transmit the packet. There is also an initiation phase where the connection is established so that communication cannot start immediately.

If two processes wish to communicate they must each create a socket. Once created the socket must then be bound to a specific network address. One process must initiate the connection (This process is called the client). The other process must wait for a connection request (This process is the server). This delegation of responsibilities is highlighted in the diagrams below.

The client starts by trying to establish a connection with the listening socket at a server. If the server accepts the communication request then the connection is established and communication can start. If a connection cannot be established then the client process must recover from this situation. It can do this either by trying to re-connect to the same server or by choosing to connect to a different server that offers the same services.

Once communication has ended the sockets must be closed.

Class
       Server
	Collaborators
	  • Client
		Class
		       Client
			Collaborators
			  • Server

Responsibility
  • Implement a task
  • Waits for connection from another process.
  • Receives messages from other process
  • Sends messages to other process
		Responsibility
		  • Implements a task
		  • Requests connection from other process.
		  • Sends message to other process
		  • Receives messages from other process	

The client process needs to know the Internet address and the port number of the server process in order to initiate the connection. If the client simply knows the servers Internet address as a string such as "ducati.doc.ntu.ac.uk" then it must first use a lookup service to obtain the true 32 bit internet address of the server. When the client knows the server's real address, it sends a connection request packet containing its own Internet address and port number to the server process.

If the server process accepts the connection request from the client, it creates a new socket bound to a new port number for use by the client and sends this information back to the client as an acknowledgement.

Once the client receives a positive acknowledgment from the server, it re-bind its socket to the new port number supplied by the server and at this point a connection has been established. Both processes now know the Internet address and port number of the process at the other end of the connection and therefore communication can begin.

For example, in the fig. 24.7, we are having a server process B on one host and client process A on another host. First, server process (B) creates a socket (say 12) and calls accept connection which puts server process to go for infinite waiting loop for clients requests. Process A creates a socket (say 25) and calls connect call with HostB and 12 as its packet content; which process B (server) accepts and creates a new socket say 36 via which server (B) will communicate with client (A). Here, socket 12 is used for listening while other sockets are used for data communication. This is the typical activity in a connection based client server communication.

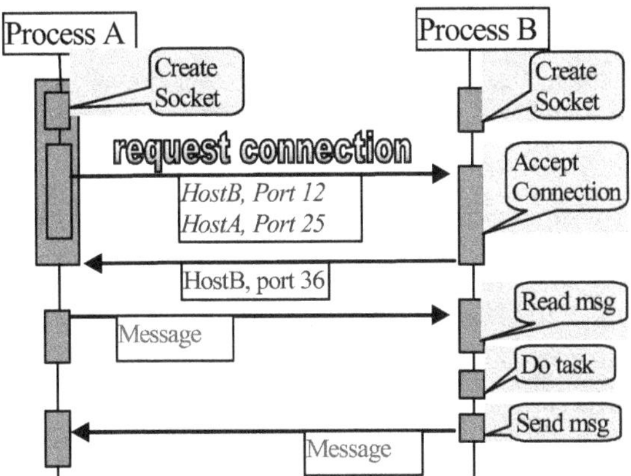

24.4 Useful Unix System Calls

24.4.1 The accept system call

The syntax of the accept system call is given below. This call returns the newly connected socket descriptor, or –1 on error, with *errno* set appropriately.

int accept(int *s*, struct sockaddr **addr*, socklen_t **addrlen*);

This is called by server side programs to welcome clients. Once we have gone through the trouble of getting a SOCK_STREAM socket and setting it up for incoming connections with **listen()**, then we call this **accept()** to actually get yourself a new socket descriptor to use for subsequent communication with the newly connected client.

The old socket that we are using for listening is still there, and will be used for further **accept()** calls as they come in.

s	The **listen()**ing socket descriptor.
Addr	This is filled in with the address of the site that's connecting to you.
addrlen	This is filled in with the **sizeof()** the structure returned in the *addr* parameter. You can safely ignore it if you assume you're getting a struct sockaddr_in back, which you know you are, because that's the type you passed in for *addr*.

`accept()` will normally block, and we can use **select()** to peek on the listening socket descriptor ahead of time to see if it's "ready to read". If so, then there's a new connection waiting to be **accept()**ed!. Alternatively, we can set the O_NONBLOCK flag on the listening socket using **fcntl()**, and then it will never block, choosing instead to return –1 with *errno* set to EWOULDBLOCK.

The socket descriptor returned by **accept()** is a bona fide socket descriptor, open and connected to the remote host. We have to **close()** it when it is no longer needed.

24.4.2 The bind system call

Main objective of this system call is to associate a socket with an IP address and port number. It returns zero on success, or –1 on error (and **errno** will be set accordingly). Its syntax is given as follows:

int bind(int *sockfd*, struct sockaddr **my_addr*, socklen_t *addrlen*);

Evidently, when bind system call is called, kernel registers IP address, port number along with the process. When a remote machine wants to connect to our server program, it needs two pieces of information: the IP address and the port number. When a packet arrives from a remote machine with server machines IP address and port number, kernel decides to which server program the packet to be handovered with the previously registered knowledge through **bind()** call.

24.4.3 The connect system call

This call is used to connect to a server. This is usually invoked by a client side program. This function returns zero on success, or –1 on error (and **errno** will be set accordingly.)

```
int   connect(int   sockfd,   const   struct   sockaddr   *serv   addr,
socklen_t addrlen);
```

Once we have built a socket descriptor (in client applications) with the **socket()** call, we can **connect()** that socket to a remote server using the well-named **connect()** system call. All we need to do is pass it the socket descriptor and the address of the server we are interested in getting to know better.

Usually this information comes along as the result of a call to **getaddrinfo()**, but we can fill out our own struct sockaddr if we want to.

If we haven't yet called **bind()** on the socket descriptor, it is automatically bound to our IP address and a random local port. This is usually just fine with us if we are not a server, since we really don't care what is our local port is; we only care what the remote port is so we can put it in the *serv_addr* parameter. We *can* call **bind()** if we really want our client socket to be on a specific IP address and port, but this is pretty rare.

Once the socket is **connect()**ed, we are free to **send()** and **recv()** data. If we **connect()** a SOCK_DGRAM UDP socket to a remote host, we can use **send()** and **recv()** as well as **sendto()** and **recvfrom()**.

24.4.4 The close() system call

To close a socket descriptor, we have to use close system call. This function also returns zero on success, or –1 on error (and **errno** will be set accordingly.) Its prototype is given as:

int close(int s);

After we have finished using the socket and we don't want to **send()** or **recv()** or, indeed, do *anything else* at all with the socket, we can call **close()** to close it, and it'll be freed up, never can be used again.

The remote side can tell if this happens one of two ways.

One: if the remote side calls **recv()**, it will return 0.

Two: if the remote side calls **send()**, it'll receive a signal SIGPIPE and send() will return −1 and *errno* will be set to EPIPE.

24.4.5 The getaddrinfo(), freeaddrinfo(), gai_strerror() system calls

Get information about a host name and/or service and load up a struct sockaddr with the result.

```
int getaddrinfo(const char *nodename, const char *servname,
const struct addrinfo *hints, struct addrinfo **res);
void freeaddrinfo(struct addrinfo *ai);
const char *gai_strerror(int ecode);
struct addrinfo {
  int    ai_flags;            // AI_PASSIVE, AI_CANONNAME, ...
  int    ai_family;           // AF_xxx
  int    ai_socktype;         // SOCK_xxx
  int    ai_protocol;         // 0(auto)or IPPROTO_TCP,IPPROTO_UDP
  socklen_t  ai_addrlen;      // length of ai_addr
  char  *ai_canonname;        // canonical name for nodename
  structsockaddr  *ai_addr;   // binary address
  struct addrinfo  *ai_next;  // next structure in linked list
};
```

getaddrinfo() is an excellent function that will return information on a particular host name (such as its IP address) and load up a struct sockaddr for us. It takes care of the gritty details (like if it's IPv4 or IPv6.) and replaces the old functions **gethostbyname()** and **getservbyname()**. The description, below, contains a lot of information that might be a little daunting, but actual usage is pretty simple. It might be worth it to check out the examples first.

The host name that we are interested in goes in the *nodename* parameter. The address can be either a host name, like "www.example.com", or an IPv4 or IPv6 address (passed as a string). This parameter can also be NULL if you're using the AI_PASSIVE flag (see below.)

The *servname* parameter is basically the port number. It can be a port number (passed as a string, like "80"), or it can be a service name, like "http" or "tftp" or "smtp" or "pop", etc. Well-known service names can be found in the our `/etc/services` `file`.

Lastly, for input parameters, we have *hints*. This is really where you get to define what the **getaddinfo()** function is going to do. Zero the whole structure before use with **memset()**. Let's take a look at the fields we need to set up before use.

The *ai_flags* can be set to a variety of things, but here are a couple important ones. (Multiple flags can be specified by bitwise-ORing them together with the | operator).

`AI_CANONNAME` causes the *ai_canonname* of the result to the filled out with the host's canonical (real) name. `AI_PASSIVE` causes the result's IP address to be filled out with `INADDR_ANY` (IPv4)or *in6addr_any* (IPv6); this causes a subsequent call to **bind()** to auto-fill the IP address of the `struct sockaddr` with the address of the current host. That's excellent for setting up a server when we don't want to hardcode the address.

If we use the `AI_PASSIVE`, flag, then we can pass `NULL` in the *nodename* (since **bind()** will fill it in for you later.)

Continuing on with the input parameters, you'll likely want to set *ai_family* to `AF_UNSPEC` which tells **getaddrinfo()** to look for both IPv4 and IPv6 addresses. You can also restrict yourself to one or the other with `AF_INET` or `AF_INET6`.

Next, the *socktype* field should be set to `SOCK_STREAM` or `SOCK_DGRAM`, depending on which type of socket you want.

Finally, just leave *ai_protocol* at 0 to automatically choose your protocol type.

Now, after you get all that stuff in there, you can *finally* make the call to **getaddrinfo()**!

Of course, this is where the fun begins. The *res* will now point to a linked list of `struct addrinfos`, and you can go through this list to get all the addresses that match what you passed in with the hints.

Now, it's possible to get some addresses that don't work for one reason or another, so what the Linux man page does is loops through the list doing a call to **socket()** and **connect()** (or **bind()** if you're setting up a server with the AI_PASSIVE flag) until it succeeds.

Finally, when we are done with the linked list, we need to call **freeaddrinfo()** to free up the memory (or it will be leaked, and Some People will get upset.)

This function returns zero on success, or nonzero on error. If it returns nonzero, we can use the function **gai_strerror()** to get a printable version of the error code in the return value.

24.4.6 The `gethostname()` system call

This method returns the name of the system. It returns zero on success, or -1 on error (and **errno** will be set accordingly.). It syntax is given as:

```
int gethostname(char *name, size_t len);
```

The parameter *name* should point to a buffer that will hold the host name, and *len* is the size of that buffer in bytes. **gethostname()** won't overwrite the end of the buffer (it might return an error, or it might just stop writing), and it will NUL-terminate the string if there's room for it in the buffer.

For instance, we can get our host name, and then call **gethostbyname()** to find out our machines IP address.

24.4.7 The `gethostbyname()`, `gethostbyaddr()` system calls

These functions can be used to get an IP address by giving hostname, and vice-versa. Syntax of these two functions are given as:

```
struct hostent *gethostbyname(const char *name);

struct hostent *gethostbyaddr(const char *addr, int len, int
type);
```

These two functions are superseded by *getaddrinfo()* and *getnameinfo()*. In particular, **gethostbyname()** doesn't work well with IPv6. These functions map back and forth between host names and IP addresses. For instance, if we have "www.ritchcenter.com", we can use **gethostbyname()** to get its IP address and store it in a `struct in_addr`.

Conversely, if you have a `struct in_addr` or a `struct in6_addr`, you can use **gethostbyaddr()** to get the hostname back. **gethostbyaddr()** is IPv6 compatible, but we should use the newer **getnameinfo()** instead.

If we have a string containing an IP address in dots-and-numbers format that we want to look up the hostname of, we would better use **getaddrinfo()** with the `AI_CANONNAME` flag.

gethostbyname() takes a string like "www.yahoo.com", and returns a `struct hostent` which contains tons of information, including the IP address. (Other information is the official host name, a list of aliases, the address type, the length of the addresses, and the list of addresses—it's a general-purpose structure that's pretty easy to use for our specific purposes once you see how.)

gethostbyaddr() takes a `struct in_addr` or `struct in6_addr` and brings you up a corresponding host name (if there is one), so it's sort of the reverse of **gethostbyname()**. As for parameters, even though *addr* is a `char*`, you actually want to pass in a pointer to a `struct in_addr`. *len* should be `sizeof(struct in_addr)`, and *type* should be `AF_INET`.

The `struct hostent` has a number of fields that contain information about the host in question.

`char *h_name`	The real canonical host name.
`char **h_aliases`	A list of aliases that can be accessed with arrays—the last element is NULL
`int h_addrtype`	The result's address type, which really should be AF_INET for our purposes.
`int length`	The length of the addresses in bytes, which is 4 for IP (version 4) addresses.
`char **h_addr_list`	A list of IP addresses for this host. Although this is a char**, it's really an array of struct in_addr*s in disguise. The last array element is NULL.
`h_addr`	A commonly defined alias for *h_addr_list[0]*. If you just want any old IP address for this host (yeah, they can have more than one) just use this field.

These functions return a pointer to a resultant `struct hostent` or success, or `NULL` on error.

Instead of the normal **perror()** and all that stuff we would normally use for error reporting, these functions have parallel results in the variable *h_errno*, which can be printed using the functions **herror()** or **hstrerror()**. These work just like the classic *errno*, **perror()**, and **strerror()** functions which one can use.

The following code snippets can be used to know the name if we know the IP address.

```
struct hostent *he;
struct in_addr ipv4addr;
struct in6_addr ipv6addr;
inet_pton(AF_INET, "192.0.2.34", &ipv4addr);
he = gethostbyaddr(&ipv4addr, sizeof ipv4addr, AF_INET);
printf("Host name: %s\n", he->h_name);
inet_pton(AF_INET6, "2001:db8:63b3:1::beef", &ipv6addr);
he = gethostbyaddr(&ipv6addr, sizeof ipv6addr, AF_INET6);
printf("Host name: %s\n", he->h_name);
```

24.4.8 The getipaddrs system call

The `getifaddrs` function stores a reference to a linked list of the network interfaces on the local machine in the memory referenced by *ifap*. The list consists of **ifaddrs** structures, as defined in the include file ifaddrs.h . The **ifaddrs** structure contains at least the following entries:

```
struct ifaddrs    *ifa_next;          /* Pointer to next struct */
char              *ifa_name;          /* Interface name */
u_int              ifa_flags;         /* Interface flags */
struct sockaddr   *ifa_addr;          /* Interface address */
struct sockaddr   *ifa_netmask;       /* Interface netmask */
struct sockaddr   *ifa_broadaddr;     /* Interface broadcast address */
struct sockaddr   *ifa_dstaddr;       /* P2P interface destination */
void              *ifa_data;          /* Address specific data */
```

The ifa_next field contains a pointer to the next structure on the list. This field is NULL in last structure on the list.

The ifa_name field contains the interface name.

The ifa_flags field contains the interface flags, as set by <u>ifconfig</u> (8) utility.

The ifa_addr field references either the address of the interface or the link level address of the interface, if one exists, otherwise it is NULL. (The sa_family field of the ifa_addr field should be consulted to determine the format of the ifa_addr address.)

The ifa_netmask field references the netmask associated with ifa_addr, if one is set, otherwise it is NULL.

The ifa_broadaddr field, which should only be referenced for non-P2P interfaces, references the broadcast address associated with ifa_addr, if one exists, otherwise it is NULL.

The ifa_dstaddr field references the destination address on a P2P interface, if one exists, otherwise it is NULL.

The ifa_data field references address family specific data. For AF_LINK addresses it contains a pointer to the *struct   if_data* (as defined in include file net/if.h) which contains various interface attributes and statistics. For all other address families, it contains a pointer to the *struct ifa_data* (as defined in include file net/if.h) which contains per-address interface statistics.

The data returned by `getifaddrs` is dynamically allocated and should be freed using `freeifaddrs` when no longer needed.

24.4.9 The `getnameinfo` system call

This function can be used to look up the host name and service name information for a given `struct sockaddr`. The syntax of this function is given as:

```
int getnameinfo(const struct sockaddr *sa, socklen_t salen,
                char *host, size_t hostlen,
                char *serv, size_t servlen, int flags);
```

This function is the opposite of **getaddrinfo()**, that is, this function takes an already loaded `struct sockaddr` and does a name and service name lookup on it. It replaces the old **gethostbyaddr()** and **getservbyport()** functions.

We have to pass in a pointer to a `struct sockaddr` (which in actuality is probably a `struct sockaddr_in` or `struct sockaddr_in6` that you've cast) in the *sa* parameter, and the length of that `struct` in the *salen*.

The resultant host name and service name will be written to the area pointed to by the *host* and *serv* parameters. Of course, you have to specify the max lengths of these buffers in *hostlen* and *servlen*.

Finally, there are several flags which we can pass, but here a couple good ones. `NI_NOFQDN` will cause the *host* to only contain the host name, not the whole domain name. `NI_NAMEREQD` will cause the function to fail if the name cannot be found with a DNS lookup (if we don't specify this flag and the name can't be found, **getnameinfo()** will put a string version of the IP address in *host* instead.)

This function returns zero on success, or non-zero on error. If the return value is non-zero, it can be passed to **gai_strerror()** to get a human-readable string.

24.4.10 The `getpeername` system call

It returns address info about the remote side of the connection once connection is established. This function returns zero on success, or -1 on error (and **errno** will be set accordingly). Its prototype looks like:

```
int getpeername(int s, struct sockaddr *addr, socklen_t *len);
```

This can be used by either server or client. Once we have either **accept()**ed a remote connection, or **connect()**ed to a server, we now have what is known as a *peer*; i.e., peer is simply the computer (process either server/client) we are connected to, identified by an IP address and a port.

The **getpeername()** simply returns a `struct sockaddr_in` filled with information about the machine we are connected to.

Although the function returns the size of the resultant address in `len`, we must preload `len` with the size of `addr`.

Example The following code snippet demonstrates how to use this method.

```
// assume s is a socket which is already connected to
server/client.
 socklen_t len;
struct sockaddr_storage addr;
char ipstr[INET6_ADDRSTRLEN];
int port;
len = sizeof addr;
getpeername(s, (struct sockaddr*)&addr, &len);
// deal with both IPv4 and IPv6:
if (addr.ss_family == AF_INET) {
    struct sockaddr_in *s = (struct sockaddr_in *)&addr;
    port = ntohs(s->sin_port);
    inet_ntop(AF_INET, &s->sin_addr, ipstr, sizeof ipstr);
} else { // AF_INET6
    struct sockaddr_in6 *s = (struct sockaddr_in6 *)&addr;
    port = ntohs(s->sin6_port);
    inet_ntop(AF_INET6,    &s->sin6_addr,    ipstr,    sizeof
ipstr);
}
printf("Peer IP address: %s\n", ipstr);
printf("Peer port     : %d\n", port);
```

24.4.11 The `fcntl` system call

Usually this function is typically used to do file locking and other file-oriented stuff, but it also has a couple socket-related functions that you might see or use from time to time. Syntax of the function for controlling socket descriptors is:

```
int fcntl(int s, int cmd, long arg);
```

Parameter s is the socket descriptor which we wish to operate on, cmd should be set to `F_SETFL`, and arg can be one of the following commands.

`O_NONBLOCK`	Set the socket to be non-blocking.
`O_ASYNC`	Set the socket to do asynchronous I/O. When data is ready to be **recv()**'d on the socket, the signal `SIGIO` will be raised. This is rare to see, and beyond the scope of the guide. It's only available on certain systems.

This function returns zero on success, or -1 on error (and **errno** will be set accordingly.)

24.4.12 Big-endian and Little-endian Machines

Different computers use different byte orderings internally for their multibyte integers (i.e. any integer that's larger than a `char`.). For example, Mac, Sun, Motorola follows big-endian style while Intel employs little endian style. That is, big-endian machines considers 00000000 as LSB (least significant byte) and 00000001 as MSB (most significant byte) in a 16 bit number 0000000000000001; while Intel sees 00000001 as LSB and 00000000 as MSB. Thus if we **send()** a two-byte `short int` (1) from an Intel box to a Mac, what Intel computer thinks is the number 1 (0000000000000001), the other (Mac) will think is the number 256 (0000000100000000), and vice-versa.

The way to get around this problem is for everyone to put aside their differences and agree that Motorola and IBM had it right, that is to convert our byte orderings to "big-endian" before sending them out. The following set of functions are used for this purpose. These functions convert from our native byte order to network byte order and back again.

This means on Intel these functions swap all the bytes around, and on PowerPC they do nothing because the bytes are already in Network Byte Order. But we should always use them in our code anyway, since someone might want to build it on an Intel machine and still have things work properly.

The `htons()`, `htonl()`, `ntohs()`, `ntohl()` system calls

These functions can be used to convert multi-byte integer types from host byte order to network byte order. Each function returns the converted value.

```
uint32_t htonl(uint32_t hostlong);
uint16_t htons(uint16_t hostshort);
uint32_t ntohl(uint32_t netlong);
uint16_t ntohs(uint16_t netshort);
```

The responsibility of these functions are given as:

`htons()`	host **to** network **short**
`htonl()`	host **to** network **long**
`ntohs()`	network **to** host **short**
`ntohl()`	network **to** host **long**

24.4.13 The `inet_ntoa, inet_aton, inet_addr system calls`

These functions are used to convert IP addresses from a dots-and-number string to a `struct in_addr` and back. However, these functions are deprecated as they can not support IPv6. We can as well use inet_pton(), inet_ntop().

```
char *inet_ntoa(struct in_addr in);

int inet_aton(const char *cp, struct in_addr *inp);

in_addr_t inet_addr(const char *cp);
```

All of these functions convert from a `struct in_addr` (part of your `struct sockaddr_in`, most likely) to a string in dots-and-numbers format (e.g. "192.168.5.10") and vice-versa. If we have an IP address passed on the command line or something, this is the easiest way to get a `struct in_addr` to **connect()** to, or whatever. If we need more power, try some of the DNS functions like **gethostbyname()**.

The function **inet_ntoa()** converts a network address in a `struct in_addr` to a dots-and-numbers format string. The "n" in "ntoa" stands for network, and the "a" stands for ASCII for historical reasons (so it's "Network To ASCII"—the "toa" suffix has an analogous friend in the C library called **atoi()** which converts an ASCII string to an integer.)

The function **inet_aton()** is the opposite, converting from a dots-and-numbers string into a `in_addr_t` (which is the type of the field `s_addr` in your `struct in_addr`.)

Finally, the function **inet_addr()** is an older function that does basically the same thing as **inet_aton()**. It's theoretically deprecated, but we can use it.

Return Values

inet_aton() returns non-zero if the address is a valid one, and it returns zero if the address is invalid.

inet_ntoa() returns the dots-and-numbers string in a static buffer that is overwritten with each call to the function.

inet_addr() returns the address as an `in_addr_t`, or −1 if there's an error. (That is the same result as if you tried to convert the string "255.255.255.255", which is a valid IP address. This is why **inet_aton()** is better.)

24.4.14 The `inet_ntop, inet_pton system calls`

These functions are up to date to convert IP addresses to human-readable form and back.

```
const  char  *inet_ntop(int  af,  const  void  *src,  char  *dst,
socklen_t size);
```

```
int inet_pton(int af, const char *src, void *dst);
```

These functions are for dealing with human-readable IP addresses and converting them to their binary representation for use with various functions and system calls. The "n" stands for "network", and "p" for "presentation". Or "text presentation". But we can think of it as "printable". "ntop" is "network to printable".

Sometimes we don't want to look at a pile of binary numbers when looking at an IP address. We want it in a nice printable form, like `192.0.2.180`, or `2001:db8:8714:3a90::12`. In that case, **inet_ntop()** is useful.

inet_ntop() takes the address family in the *af* parameter (either AF_INET or AF_INET6). The *src* parameter should be a pointer to either a `struct in_addr` or `struct in6_addr` containing the address we wish to convert to a string. Finally *dst* and *size* are the pointer to the destination string and the maximum length of that string.

What should the maximum length of the *dst* string be? What is the maximum length for IPv4 and IPv6 addresses? Fortunately there are a couple of macros to help us out. The maximum lengths are: INET_ADDRSTRLEN and INET6_ADDRSTRLEN.

Other times, we might have a string containing an IP address in readable form, and we want to pack it into a `struct sockaddr_in` or a `struct sockaddr_in6`. In that case, the opposite function **inet_pton()** is what you're after.

inet_pton() also takes an address family (either AF_INET or AF_INET6) in the *af* parameter. The *src* parameter is a pointer to a string containing the IP address in printable form. Lastly the *dst* parameter points to where the result should be stored, which is probably a `struct in_addr` or `struct in6_addr`.

Return Values

inet_ntop() returns the *dst* parameter on success, or NULL on failure (and *errno* is set).

inet_pton() returns 1 on success. It returns -1 if there was an error (*errno* is set), or 0 if the input isn't a valid IP address.

Example The following example demonstrates the use of inet_ntop() and inet_pton()

```
struct sockaddr_in sa;
char str[INET_ADDRSTRLEN];

// store this IP address in sa:
inet_pton(AF_INET, "192.0.2.33", &(sa.sin_addr));
```

```c
// now get it back and print it
inet_ntop(AF_INET, &(sa.sin_addr), str, INET_ADDRSTRLEN);


printf("%s\n", str); // prints "192.0.2.33"
// IPv6 demo of inet_ntop() and inet_pton()
// (basically the same except with a bunch of 6s thrown
around)

struct sockaddr_in6 sa;
char str[INET6_ADDRSTRLEN];

// store this IP address in sa:
inet_pton(AF_INET6,"2001:db8:8714:3a90::12", &(sa.sin6_addr));

// now get it back and print it
inet_ntop(AF_INET6, &(sa.sin6_addr), str, INET6_ADDRSTRLEN);

printf("%s\n", str); // prints "2001:db8:8714:3a90::12"
// Helper function you can use:

//Convert a struct sockaddr address to a string, IPv4 and
IPv6:

char *get_ip_str(const struct sockaddr *sa, char *s, size_t
maxlen)
{
    switch(sa->sa_family) {
        case AF_INET:
                inet_ntop(AF_INET, &(((struct sockaddr_in *)sa)-
                >sin_addr),
                    s, maxlen);
         break;

        case AF_INET6:
         inet_ntop(AF_INET6, &(((struct sockaddr_in6 *)sa)-
>sin6_addr),s, maxlen);
            break;

        default:
            strncpy(s, "Unknown AF", maxlen);
            return NULL;
    }
    return s;
}
```

24.4.15 The `listen` system call

This function is used to tell a socket to listen for incoming connections. Especially this used with socket which are created in server programs. This system call returns zero on success, or -1 on error (and **errno** will be set accordingly). The syntax of this system call is given as:

```
int listen(int s, int backlog);
```

This function takes two arguments, first one is a socket descriptor (s) and second parameter known as *backlog* parameter which can mean a couple different things depending on the system on which we are on, but loosely it is how many pending connections we can have before the kernel starts rejecting new ones. So as the new connections come in, we should be quick to **accept()** them so that the backlog doesn't fill. Try setting it to 10 or so, and if our clients start getting "Connection refused" under heavy load, set it higher.

Before calling **listen()**, our server should call **bind()** to attach itself to a specific port number. That port number (on the server's IP address) will be the one that clients connect to.

24.4.16 The `strerror` system call

This function prints an error as a human-readable string. Do remember about perror function which we have used earlier. This function can be used along with perror. This strerror takes errnum as argument and returns the pointer to the respective error message from the system level error table. Syntax of this system call is given as:

char * strerror(int errnum);

24.4.17 The `poll` system call

This function is used to test for events on multiple sockets simultaneously. The syntax of this method is given as:

```
int poll(struct pollfd *ufds, unsigned int nfds, int timeout);
```

This function is very similar to **select()** in that they both watch sets of file descriptors for events, such as incoming data ready to **recv()**, socket ready to **send()** data to, out-of-band data ready to **recv()**, errors, etc.

The basic idea is that we pass an array of *nfds* `struct pollfds` in *ufds*, along with a timeout in milliseconds (1000 milliseconds in a second.) The *timeout* can be negative if we want to wait forever. If no event happens on any of the socket descriptors by the timeout, **poll()** will return. Each element in the array of `struct pollfds` represents one socket descriptor, and contains the following fields:

```
struct pollfd {
    int fd;          // the socket descriptor
    short events;    // bitmap of events we're interested in
    short revents;   // when poll() returns, bitmap of events that
occurred
};
```

Before calling **poll()**, load fd with the socket descriptor (if we set fd to a negative number, this `struct pollfd` is ignored and its $revents$ field is set to zero) and then construct the $events$ field by bitwise-ORing the following macros:

POLLIN	Alert me when data is ready to **recv()** on this socket.
POLLOUT	Alert me when we can **send()** data to this socket without blocking.
POLLPRI	Alert me when out-of-band data is ready to **recv()** on this socket.

Once the **poll()** call returns, the $revents$ field will be constructed as a bitwise-OR of the above fields, telling you which descriptors actually have had that event occur. Additionally, these other fields might be present:

POLLERR	An error has occurred on this socket.
POLLHUP	The remote side of the connection hung up.
POLLNVAL	Something was wrong with the socket descriptor fd—maybe it's uninitialized?

This function returns the number of elements in the $ufds$ array that have had event occur on them; this can be zero if the timeout occurred. Also returns -1 on error (and **errno** will be set accordingly.)

Example 1 The following code snippet creates two sockets and tries to connect to a server. We are interested to find the arrival of normal or out-of-band (emergency or control) data (whose arrival raises SIGURG signal) using poll system call.

```
int s1, s2;
int rv;
char buf1[256], buf2[256];
struct pollfd ufds[2];

s1 = socket(PF_INET, SOCK_STREAM, 0);
s2 = socket(PF_INET, SOCK_STREAM, 0);

// pretend we've connected both to a server at this point
//connect(s1, ...)...
//connect(s2, ...)...
```

```
// set up the array of file descriptors.
//
// in this example, we want to know when there's normal or
out-of-band
// data ready to be recv()'d...

ufds[0].fd = s1;
ufds[0].events = POLLIN | POLLPRI;
// check for normal or out-of-band

ufds[1] = s2;
ufds[1].events = POLLIN; // check for just normal data

// wait for events on the sockets, 3.5 second timeout
rv = poll(ufds, 2, 3500);

if (rv == -1) {
    perror("poll"); // error occurred in poll()
} else if (rv == 0) {
    printf("Timeout   occurred!      No    data    after    3.5
seconds.\n");
} else {
    // check for events on s1:
    if (ufds[0].revents & POLLIN) {
        recv(s1, buf1, sizeof buf1, 0);
    // receive normal data
    }
    if (ufds[0].revents & POLLPRI) {
        recv(s1, buf1, sizeof buf1, MSG_OOB);
    // out-of-band data
    }

    // check for events on s2:
    if (ufds[1].revents & POLLIN) {
        recv(s1, buf2, sizeof buf2, 0);
    }
}
```

24.4.18 The `recv, recvfrom` system calls

In order to receive data on a socket, we use the following functions whose syntaxes are given below.

```
ssize_t recv(int s, void *buf, size_t len, int flags);
   ssize_t recvfrom(int s, void *buf, size_t len, int flags,
                    struct     sockaddr    *from,    socklen_t
   *fromlen);
```

Once a socket is up and connected, we can read incoming data from the remote side using the **recv()** (for TCP `SOCK_STREAM` sockets) and **recvfrom()** (for UDP `SOCK_DGRAM` sockets).

Both functions take the socket descriptor `s`, a pointer to the buffer `buf`, the size (in bytes) of the buffer `len`, and a set of `flags` that control how the functions work.

Additionally, the **recvfrom()** takes a `struct sockaddr*`, `from` that will tell you where the data came from, and will fill in `fromlen` with the size of `struct sockaddr`. (You must also initialize `fromlen` to be the size of `from` or `struct sockaddr`.)

The following flags can be used with recv function. We can bitwise-or these together, or just set `flags` to 0 if we want it to be a regular vanilla **recv()**.

`MSG_OOB`	Receive Out of Band data. This is how to get data that has been sent to you with the `MSG_OOB` flag in **send()**. As the receiving side, you will have had signal `SIGURG` raised telling you there is urgent data. In your handler for that signal, you could call **recv()** with this `MSG_OOB` flag.
`MSG_PEEK`	If you want to call **recv()** "just for pretend", you can call it with this flag. This will tell you what's waiting in the buffer for when you call **recv()** "for real" (i.e. *without* the `MSG_PEEK` flag. It's like a sneak preview into the next **recv()** call.
`MSG_WAITALL`	Tell **recv()** to not return until all the data you specified in the `len` parameter. It will ignore your wishes in extreme circumstances, however, like if a signal interrupts the call or if some error occurs or if the remote side closes the connection, etc. Don't be mad with it.

When we call **recv()**, it will block until there is some data to read. If we want, not to block, set the socket to non-blocking or check with **select()** or **poll()** to see if there is incoming data before calling **recv()** or **recvfrom()**.

These functions returns the number of bytes actually received (which might be less than we have requested in the `len` parameter), or -1 on error (and **errno** will be set accordingly.) If the remote side has closed the connection, **recv()** will return 0. This is the normal method for determining if the remote side has closed the connection. Normality is good, rebel!

24.4.19 The `select` system call

This function helps us to check simultaneously whether a set of sockets (descriptors) are ready to read/write. The following macros also required to be used with this system call.

```
FD_SET(int fd, fd_set *set);  // to add a descriptor to a
fd_set

FD_CLR(int fd, fd_set *set);  // to revive a descriptor from
a fd_set

FD_ISSET(int fd, fd_set *set);  // to checj a descriptor in
a fd_set

FD_ZERO(fd_set *set);  // to create an empty  fd_set
```

The syntax of this system call is given as:

```
int select(int n, fd_set *readfds, fd_set *writefds, fd_set
*exceptfds,

                struct timeval *timeout);
```

Before using this system call select, we have to use a fd_set type of structure. With the help of FD_ZERO, we have to make a fd_set as an empty set. Then, we may populate our set of socket descriptors using the macros, like **FD_SET()**, above. Once we have the set, we pass it into the function as one of the following parameters: *readfds* if we want to know when any of the sockets in the set is ready to **recv()** data, *writefds* if any of the sockets is ready to **send()** data to, and/or *exceptfds* if we need to know when an exception (error) occurs on any of the sockets. Any or all of these parameters can be NULL if we are not interested in those types of events. After **select()** returns, the values in the sets will be changed to show which are ready for reading or writing, and which have exceptions.

The first parameter, *n* is the highest-numbered socket descriptor (they're just `ints`, remember?) plus one.

Lastly, the `struct timeval`, *timeout*, at the end—this lets you tell **select()** how long to check these sets for. It'll return after the timeout, or when an event occurs, whichever is first. The `struct timeval` has two fields: *tv_sec* is the number of seconds, to which is added *tv_usec*, the number of microseconds (1,000,000 microseconds in a second.)

This function, returns the number of descriptors in the set on success, 0 if the timeout was reached, or −1 on error (and **errno** will be set accordingly.) Also, the sets are modified to show which sockets are ready.

Example 2 The following code snippet explains how to use system call select.

```
int s1, s2, n;
fd_set readfds;
struct timeval tv;
char buf1[256], buf2[256];

// pretend we've connected both to a server at this point
//s1 = socket(...);
//s2 = socket(...);
//connect(s1, ...)...
//connect(s2, ...)...

// clear the set ahead of time
FD_ZERO(&readfds);

// add our descriptors to the set
FD_SET(s1, &readfds);
FD_SET(s2, &readfds);

// since we got s2 second, it's the "greater", so we use
//that for
// the n param in select()
n = s2 + 1;

// wait until either socket has data ready to be recv()d
//(timeout 10.5 secs)
tv.tv_sec = 10;
tv.tv_usec = 500000;
rv = select(n, &readfds, NULL, NULL, &tv);

if (rv == -1) {
    perror("select"); // error occurred in select()
} else if (rv == 0) {
    printf("Timeout    occurred!      No    data    after    10.5
seconds.\n");
```

```
} else {
    // one or both of the descriptors have data
    if (FD_ISSET(s1, &readfds)) {
        recv(s1, buf1, sizeof buf1, 0);
    }
    if (FD_ISSET(s2, &readfds)) {
        recv(s1, buf2, sizeof buf2, 0);
    }
}
```

24.4.20 The `setsockopt, getsockopt` system calls

With the help of these functions we can set various options for a socket which is created.

```
int getsockopt(int s, int level, int optname, void *optval,
socklen_t *optlen);

int setsockopt(int s, int level, int optname, const void
*optval,socklen_t optlen);
```

Here, `s` is the socket we are talking about, level should be set to SOL_SOCKET. Then we set the `optname` to the name we are interested in. Some of the options and their use are given below.

SO_BINDTODEVICE	Bind this socket to a symbolic device name like eth0 instead of using **bind()** to bind it to an IP address. Type the command **ifconfig** under Unix to see the device names.
SO_REUSEADDR	Allows other sockets to **bind()** to this port, unless there is an active listening socket bound to the port already. This enables you to get around those "Address already in use" error messages when you try to restart your server after a crash.
SO_BROADCAST	Allows UDP datagram (SOCK_DGRAM) sockets to send and receive packets sent to and from the broadcast address.

As for the parameter `optval`, it's usually a pointer to an `int` indicating the value in question. For Booleans, zero is false, and non-zero is true. And that's an absolute fact, unless it's different on your system. If there is no parameter to be passed, `optval` can be NULL.

The final parameter, *optlen*, is filled out for you by **getsockopt()** and you have to specify it for **setsockopt()**, where it will probably be sizeof(int).

> **Warning**: on some systems (notably Sun and Windows), the option can be a char instead of an int, and is set to, for example, a character value of '1' instead of an int value of 1.

24.4.21 The send, sendto system calls

These functions can be used to send data out over a socket. Their prototypes are given as:

```
ssize_t send(int s, const void *buf, size_t len, int flags);
ssize_t sendto(int s, const void *buf, size_t len,
               int flags, const struct sockaddr *to,
socklen_t tolen);
```

The **send()** is used for TCP SOCK_STREAM connected sockets, and **sendto()** is used for UDP SOCK_DGRAM unconnected datagram sockets. With both **send()** and **sendto()**, the parameter *s* is the socket, *buf* is a pointer to the data you want to send, *len* is the number of bytes you want to send, and *flags* allows us to specify more information about how the data is to be sent. Set *flags* to zero if you want it to be "normal" data. Here are some of the commonly used flags, but check your local **send()** man pages for more details:

MSG_OOB	Send as "out of band" data. TCP supports this, and it's a way to tell the receiving system that this data has a higher priority than the normal data. The receiver will receive the signal SIGURG and it can then receive this data without first receiving all the rest of the normal data in the queue.
MSG_DONTROUTE	Don't send this data over a router, just keep it local.
MSG_DONTWAIT	If **send()** would block because outbound traffic is clogged, have it return EAGAIN. This is like a "enable non-blocking just for this send." See the section on <u>blocking</u> for more details.
MSG_NOSIGNAL	If you **send()** to a remote host which is no longer **recv()**ing, you'll typically get the signal SIGPIPE. Adding this flag prevents that signal from being raised.

The send function returns the number of bytes actually sent, or −1 on error (and **errno** will be set accordingly.) Note that the number of bytes actually sent might be less than the number you asked it to send! Also, if the socket has been closed by either side, the process calling **send()** will get the signal SIGPIPE. (Unless **send()** was called with the MSG_NOSIGNAL flag.)

24.4.22 The `shutdown` system call

This function call stops further sends and receives on a socket. The syntax of this function is given as:

int shutdown(int s, int how);

Once we call this function with a socket s, no more **send()**s are allowed on this socket, but we can still call **recv() function** to receive data on it and vice-versal!. If how is sent as zero, no more data can be received while how is sent as 1 then we can not sent any more data; is how is sent as 2 then neither we can send nor receive data on the socket s. Rather, we can use symbolic constants such as SHUT_RD to prevent further **recv()**s, SHUT_WR to prohibit further **send()**s, or SHUT_RDWR to do both.

When you **close()** a socket descriptor, it closes both sides of the socket for reading and writing, and frees the socket descriptor. If we just want to close one side or the other, we can use this **shutdown()** call.

As usual, this function returns zero on success, or -1 on error (and **errno** will be set accordingly.)

24.4.23 The `struct sockaddr`

In practice we need to use variety of structures for handling internet addresses which are given as:

```
include <netinet/in.h>


// All pointers to socket address structures are often cast
to pointers
// to this type before use in various functions and system
calls:


struct sockaddr {
    unsigned  short       sa_family;       // address  family,
AF_xxx
    char                  sa_data[14];   // 14 bytes of protocol
address
};
```

```c
// IPv4 AF_INET sockets:

struct sockaddr_in {
short               sin_family;    // e.g. AF_INET, AF_INET6
unsigned short      sin_port;      // e.g. htons(3490)
struct in_addr      sin_addr;      // see struct in_addr, below
char                sin_zero[8];   // zero this if you want to
};


struct in_addr {
    unsigned long s_addr;          // load with inet_pton()
};



// IPv6 AF_INET6 sockets:

struct sockaddr_in6 {
    u_int16_t       sin6_family;
// address family, AF_INET6
    u_int16_t        sin6_port;       // port number, Network
Byte Order
    u_int32_t        sin6_flowinfo; // IPv6 flow information
    struct in6_addr sin6_addr;       // IPv6 address
    u_int32_t        sin6_scope_id; // Scope ID
};


struct in6_addr {
    unsigned char  s6_addr[16];    // load with inet_pton()
};



// General socket address holding structure, big enough to
//hold either
// struct sockaddr_in or struct sockaddr_in6 data:
```

```
struct sockaddr_storage {
    sa_family_t  ss_family;      // address family

    // all this is padding, implementation specific, ignore
//it:
    char        __ss_pad1[_SS_PAD1SIZE];
    int64_t     __ss_align;
    char        __ss_pad2[_SS_PAD2SIZE];
};
```

These are the basic structures for all syscalls and functions that deal with internet addresses. Often we will use **getaddinfo()** to fill these structures out, and then will read them when we have to.

In memory, the `struct sockaddr_in` and `struct sockaddr_in6` share the same beginning structure as `struct sockaddr`, and you can freely cast the pointer of one type to the other without any harm, except the possible end of the universe.

Remember that whenever a function says it takes a `struct sockaddr*` you can cast your `struct sockaddr_in*`, `struct sockaddr_in6*`, or `struct sockadd_storage*` to that type with ease and safety.

`struct sockaddr_in` is the structure used with IPv4 addresses (e.g. "192.0.2.10"). It holds an address family (`AF_INET`), a port in `sin_port`, and an IPv4 address in `sin_addr`.

There's also this `sin_zero` field in `struct sockaddr_in` which some people claim must be set to zero. Other people don't claim anything about it (the Linux documentation doesn't even mention it at all), and setting it to zero doesn't seem to be actually necessary. So, if you feel like it, set it to zero using **memset()**.

Now, that `struct in_addr` is a weird beast on different systems. Sometimes it's a crazy `union` with all kinds of `#define`s and other nonsense. But what we should do is only use the `s_addr` field in this structure, because many systems only implement that one.

`struct sockadd_in6` and `struct in6_addr` are very similar, except they're used for IPv6.

`struct sockaddr_storage` is a struct you can pass to **accept()** or **recvfrom()** when you're trying to write IP version-agnostic code and you don't know if the new address is going to be IPv4 or IPv6. The `struct sockaddr_storage` structure is large enough to hold both types, unlike the original small `struct sockaddr`.

Example 3 The following code fragment demonstrates how to use addresses while working with sockets.

```
// IPv4:

struct sockaddr_in ip4addr;
int s;

ip4addr.sin_family = AF_INET;
ip4addr.sin_port = htons(3490);
inet_pton(AF_INET, "10.0.0.1", &ip4addr.sin_addr);

s = socket(PF_INET, SOCK_STREAM, 0);
bind(s, (struct sockaddr*)&ip4addr, sizeof ip4addr);
// IPv6:

struct sockaddr_in6 ip6addr;
int s;

ip6addr.sin6_family = AF_INET6;
ip6addr.sin6_port = htons(4950);
inet_pton(AF_INET6,                    "2001:db8:8714:3a90::12",
&ip6addr.sin6_addr);

s = socket(PF_INET6, SOCK_STREAM, 0);
bind(s, (struct sockaddr*)&ip6addr, sizeof ip6addr);
```

24.4.24 Socket System Call

The `socket` system call creates an endpoint for communication and returns a descriptor. The mechanism that application programs use to communicate on a network is the *socket*. Sockets were first introduced in Unix BSD 4.1 (1982), and the popularity of this operating system among academics made the TCP/IP Internet protocol a standard (although the socket interface can handle other protocols as well). There is a series of

Unix system calls that deal with sockets. The Win32 APIs for sockets are very similar. The syntax of the system call is given as:

```
int socket(int domain, int type, int protocol);
```

domain	*domain* describes what kind of socket you're interested in. This can, believe me, be a wide variety of things, but since this is a socket guide, it's going to be PF_INET for IPv4, and PF_INET6 for IPv6.
type	Also, the *type* parameter can be a number of things, but you'll probably be setting it to either SOCK_STREAM for reliable TCP sockets (**send()**, **recv()**) or SOCK_DGRAM for unreliable fast UDP sockets (**sendto()**, **recvfrom()**.) (Another interesting socket type is SOCK_RAW which can be used to construct packets by hand.)
protocol	Finally, the *protocol* parameter tells which protocol to use with a certain socket type. For instance, SOCK_STREAM uses TCP. Fortunately for you, when using SOCK_STREAM or SOCK_DGRAM, you can just set the protocol to 0, and it'll use the proper protocol automatically. Otherwise, you can use **getprotobyname()** to look up the proper protocol number.

The socket system call returns a socket (new), this new socket descriptor to be used in subsequent calls, or -1 on error (and **errno** will be set accordingly.)

As mentioned earlier in the table, the *domain* argument specifies a communications domain within which communication will take place; this selects the protocol family which should be used. These families are defined in the include file sys/socket.h . The currently understood formats are:

```
PF_LOCAL          Host-internal    protocols,    formerly    called
PF_UNIX,
PF_UNIX           Host-internal    protocols,    deprecated,    use
PF_LOCAL,
PF_INET           Internet version 4 protocols,
PF_PUP            PUP protocols, like BSP,
PF_APPLETALK      AppleTalk protocols,
PF_ROUTE          Internal Routing protocol,
PF_LINK           Link layer interface,
PF_IPX            Novell Internet Packet eXchange protocol,
PF_RTIP           Help Identify RTIP packets,
PF_PIP            Help Identify PIP packets,
PF_ISDN           Integrated Services Digital Network,
PF_KEY            Internal key-management function,
PF_INET6          Internet version 6 protocols,
```

```
PF_NATM              Native ATM access,
PF_ATM               ATM,
PF_NETGRAPH          Netgraph sockets
```

The socket has the indicated *type*, which specifies the semantics of communication. Currently defined types are:

```
SOCK_STREAM          Stream socket,

SOCK_DGRAM           Datagram socket,

SOCK_RAW             Raw-protocol interface,

SOCK_RDM             Reliably-delivered packet,

SOCK_SEQPACKET       Sequenced packet stream
```

A `SOCK_STREAM` type provides sequenced, reliable, two-way connection based byte streams. An out-of-band data transmission mechanism may be supported. A `SOCK_DGRAM` socket supports datagrams (connectionless, unreliable messages of a fixed (typically small) maximum length). A `SOCK_SEQPACKET` socket may provide a sequenced, reliable, two-way connection-based data transmission path for datagrams of fixed maximum length; a consumer may be required to read an entire packet with each read system call. This facility is protocol specific, and presently unimplemented. `SOCK_RAW` sockets provide access to internal network protocols and interfaces. The types `SOCK_RAW`, which is available only to the super-user, and `SOCK_RDM`, which is planned, but not yet implemented, are not described here.

The *protocol* argument specifies a particular protocol to be used with the socket. Normally only a single protocol exists to support a particular socket type within a given protocol family. However, it is possible that many protocols may exist, in which case a particular protocol must be specified in this manner. The protocol number to use is particular to the "communication domain" in which communication is to take place.

Sockets of type `SOCK_STREAM` are full-duplex byte streams, similar to pipes. A stream socket must be in a *connected* state before any data may be sent or received on it. A connection to another socket is created with a <u>connect</u> system call. Once connected, data may be transferred using <u>read</u> and <u>write</u> calls or some variant of the <u>send</u> and <u>recv</u> functions. (Some protocol families, such as the intel family, support the notion of an "implied connect", which permits data to be sent piggybacked onto a connect operation by using the <u>sendto</u> system call.) When a session has been completed a <u>close</u> may be performed. Out-of-band data may also be transmitted as described in <u>send</u>(2) and received as described in <u>recv</u>.

The communications protocols used to implement a `SOCK_STREAM` insure that data is not lost or duplicated. If a piece of data for which the peer protocol has buffer space cannot be successfully transmitted within a reasonable length of time, then the connection is considered broken and calls will indicate an error with −1 returns and with

ETIMEDOUT as the specific code in the global variable *errno*. The protocols optionally keep sockets "warm" by forcing transmissions roughly every minute in the absence of other activity. An error is then indicated if no response can be elicited on an otherwise idle connection for an extended period (e.g. 5 minutes). A SIGPIPE signal is raised if a process sends on a broken stream; this causes naive processes, which do not handle the signal, to exit.

SOCK_SEQPACKET sockets employ the same system calls as SOCK_STREAM sockets. The only difference is that <u>read</u> calls will return only the amount of data requested, and any remaining in the arriving packet will be discarded.

SOCK_DGRAM and SOCK_RAW sockets allow sending of datagrams to correspondents named in <u>send</u> calls. Datagrams are generally received with <u>recvfrom</u>, which returns the next datagram with its return address.

An <u>fcntl</u> system call can be used to specify a process group to receive a SIGURG signal when the out-of-band data arrives. It may also enable non-blocking I/O and asynchronous notification of I/O events via SIGIO.

ERRORS

The socket system call fails if:

[EPROTONOSUPPORT] The protocol type or the specified protocol is not supported within this domain.
[EMFILE] The per-process descriptor table is full.
[ENFILE] The system file table is full.
[EACCES] Permission to create a socket of the specified type and/or protocol is denied.
[ENOBUFS] Insufficient buffer space is available. The socket cannot be created until sufficient resources are freed.

Example 4 The following code snippet demonstrates how to call socket system call.

```
struct addrinfo hints, *res;
int sockfd;
// first, load up address structs with getaddrinfo():

memset(&hints, 0, sizeof hints);
hints.ai_family = AF_UNSPEC;          // AF_INET, AF_INET6, or
AF_UNSPEC
hints.ai_socktype   =   SOCK_STREAM;   //   SOCK_STREAM   or
SOCK_DGRAM

getaddrinfo("www.example.com", "3490", &hints, &res);
```

```
//  make  a  socket  using  the  information  got  from
getaddrinfo():
sockfd  =  socket(res->ai_family,  res->ai_socktype,  res-
>ai_protocol);
```

For an Internet socket the first argument, the domain, should be `PF_INET`, although the older form, `AF_INET` should also work. These two strings are defined as 2 in the header file `sys/socket.h`. The socket call returns a file descriptor if successful, and a negative number on failure. Failure is unlikely if our arguments are correct. Both client processes and server processes use sockets and the socket system call, but the sequence of system calls after creating the socket is different for clients and for servers.

Example 5: The following example takes a hostname along the command line and displays its IP address.

```
#include <sys/types.h>

#include <sys/socket.h>

#include <netinet/in.h>

#include <netdb.h>

#include <stdio.h>

#include <unistd.h>

#include <stdlib.h>

#include<string.h>

int main(int argc, char *argv[]){


    struct hostent *hp;


    if (argc != 2) {
            printf("Usage: %s machinename\n", argv[0]);
            exit(1);
    }
    hp = gethostbyname(argv[1]);
    if (hp==NULL) {
perror("Unknown host");
exit(-1);
    }
```

```
printf("%s\n", inet_ntoa(*((struct in_addr*)hp->h_addr)));

return 0;

}
```

A snap shot of the above program is given below. We assume that the program name is ipaddress.c.

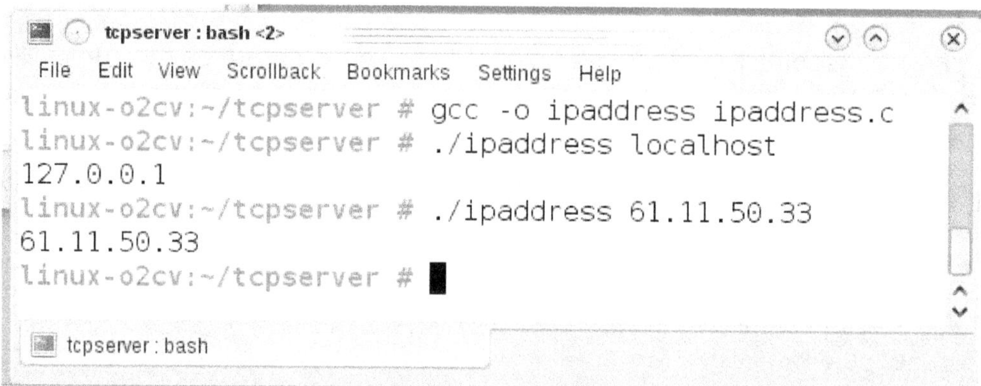

Example 6 The following program lists IP address of a given domain name. Main difference between this and the above one is that it traverses all the entries of addr_list array of hostent structure.

```
#include <stdio.h>
#include <errno.h>
#include <netdb.h>
#include <sys/types.h>
#include <sys/socket.h>
#include <netinet/in.h>
#include <arpa/inet.h>

int main(int argc, char *argv[]){
    int i;
    struct hostent *he;
    struct in_addr **addr_list;

    if (argc != 2) {
        fprintf(stderr,"usage: ghbn hostname\n");
        return 1;
    }
```

```c
    if ((he = gethostbyname(argv[1])) == NULL) {
    // get the host info
        herror("gethostbyname");
        return 2;
    }

    // print information about this host:
    printf("Official name is: %s\n", he->h_name);
    printf("    IP addresses: ");
    addr_list = (struct in_addr **)he->h_addr_list;
    for(i = 0; addr_list[i] != NULL; i++) {
        printf("%s ", inet_ntoa(*addr_list[i]));
    }
    printf("\n");

    return 0;
}
```

Example 7: The following example also demonstrates the IP address of a host given its name along the command line.

```c
/*
** showip.c -- show IP addresses for a host given on the
command line
*/

#include <stdio.h>
#include <string.h>
#include <sys/types.h>
#include <sys/socket.h>
#include <netdb.h>
#include <arpa/inet.h>

int main(int argc, char *argv[])
{
    struct addrinfo hints, *res, *p;
    int status;
    char ipstr[INET6_ADDRSTRLEN];
```

```c
if (argc != 2) {
    fprintf(stderr,"usage: showip hostname\n");
    return 1;
}


memset(&hints, 0, sizeof hints);
hints.ai_family = AF_UNSPEC; // AF_INET or AF_INET6 to
force version
hints.ai_socktype = SOCK_STREAM;


if ((status = getaddrinfo(argv[1], NULL, &hints, &res))
!= 0) {
    fprintf(stderr,            "getaddrinfo:         %s\n",
gai_strerror(status));
    return 2;
}


printf("IP addresses for %s:\n\n", argv[1]);


for(p = res;p != NULL; p = p->ai_next) {
    void *addr;
    char *ipver;


    // get the pointer to the address itself,
    // different fields in IPv4 and IPv6:
    if (p->ai_family == AF_INET) { // IPv4
        struct    sockaddr_in    *ipv4    =    (struct
sockaddr_in *)p->ai_addr;
        addr = &(ipv4->sin_addr);
        ipver = "IPv4";
    } else { // IPv6
        struct    sockaddr_in6    *ipv6    =    (struct
sockaddr_in6 *)p->ai_addr;
        addr = &(ipv6->sin6_addr);
        ipver = "IPv6";
    }
```

```c
        // convert the IP to a string and print it:
        inet_ntop(p->ai_family, addr, ipstr, sizeof ipstr);
        printf("  %s: %s\n", ipver, ipstr);
    }


    freeaddrinfo(res); // free the linked list


    return 0;
}
```

Example 8 The following example also displays the IP address of a machine whose name is given along the command line.

```c
#include <stdio.h>
#include <stdlib.h>
#include <sys/types.h>
#include <sys/socket.h>
#include <netinet/in.h>
#include <arpa/inet.h>
#include <net/if.h>
#include <ifaddrs.h>
#include <errno.h>

int main(int argc, char *argv[])
{
    struct ifaddrs *myaddrs, *ifa;
    void *in_addr;
    char buf[64];

    if(getifaddrs(&myaddrs) != 0)
    {
        perror("getifaddrs");
        exit(1);
    }

    for (ifa = myaddrs; ifa != NULL; ifa = ifa->ifa_next)
    {
        if (ifa->ifa_addr == NULL)
```

```c
            continue;
        if (!(ifa->ifa_flags & IFF_UP))
            continue;

        switch (ifa->ifa_addr->sa_family)
        {
            case AF_INET:
            {
struct sockaddr_in *s4 = (struct sockaddr_in *)ifa->ifa_addr;
                in_addr = &s4->sin_addr;
                break;
            }

            case AF_INET6:
            {
struct sockaddr_in6 *s6 = (struct sockaddr_in6 *)ifa->ifa_addr;
                in_addr = &s6->sin6_addr;
                break;
            }

            default:
                continue;
        }

if (!inet_ntop(ifa->ifa_addr->sa_family, in_addr, buf, sizeof(buf)))
        {
            printf("%s: inet_ntop failed!\n", ifa->ifa_name);
        }
        else
        {
            printf("%s: %s\n", ifa->ifa_name, buf);
        }
    }
```

```
        freeifaddrs(myaddrs);
        return 0;
    }
```

Example 9 A simple Connection Oriented Server and Client

1. A server process first creates a socket using the socket system call. To do this, we may employ the following statements.

```
int sock;

unsigned short port;

port = (unsigned short) 8080;

sock=socket(AF_INET, SOCK_STREAM, 0);

if (sock < 0) error("Opening socket");
```

2. It is required to *bound* this program to this address by calling bind system call as shown below. To do this, we have to fill details of sock_addr_in type of variable as shown below.

int len, retval;

```
    struct sock_addr_in server;

    server.sin_family=AF_INET;

    server.sin_addr.s_addr=INADDR_ANY;

    server.sin_port=htons(port);

    len=sizeof(server);

    retval = bind(sock, (struct sockaddr *)&server, len);

    if (retval < 0) error("binding");
```

The symbolic constant INADDR_ANY is used to refer to the internet address of the machine on which the process is running.

The function `htons()` function takes a short int (16 bit) as an argument, (which of course is in host byte order) and returns the value in network byte order. We have already explained about this function already.

3. Once a socket is created and bound to an address, a server socket has to listen for connections. The system call for this is `listen` which takes two arguments. The first is a socket which is bound to an address, the second is the length of the backlog queue; note that this is not the number of connections that can be accepted, this is the number of connections that can be waiting to be accepted.

4. Once a server is listening, it should enter an infinite loop to wait for clients to connect. The first (or at least one of the first) statements in this loop is a call to accept. As explained earlier,

The accept system call takes three arguments. The first is the socket, the second is a pointer to a struct sockaddr, and the third is the size of a struct sockaddr. A call to accept will block until a client connects to the server. This will wake up the server. Accept returns an int, which is another socket. This is confusing, because the server listens on one socket, but when a connection from a client is established, all of the communication is on a different socket, the value of which is returned by accept. The second argument to accept will be set to the address of the client so that the server can know to whom it is talking to.

5. Once a connection has been accepted, both sides can communicate on the new socket (the engineering term for this is full duplex). We can use read() and write() if we wish, but the preferred system calls are recv() for reading and send() for writing.

Here is a complete program for a very simple Connection Oriented server which accepts a connection request from client and displays a message.

```
/*   server.c   -   creates   a   connection   oriented   (stream)
Internet server
    for the Unix Operating system. Port is passed in as an
argument
    To compile
    gcc -o server server.c */


#include <sys/types.h>
#include <sys/socket.h>
#include <netinet/in.h>
#include <stdio.h>
#include <unistd.h>
#include <stdlib.h>
#include <arpa/inet.h>
#include <string.h>
#define BUFSIZE 1024
extern int errno;
void error(char *msg){
    perror(msg);
    exit(0);
}
```

```c
int main(int argc, char *argv[]){
    int sock, newsock, len, fromlen, n;
    unsigned short port;
    struct sockaddr_in server, from;
    char buffer[BUFSIZE];
    char *msg = "I Got your message";

    if (argc < 2) {
        fprintf(stderr,"usage %s portnumber\n",argv[0]);
        exit(0);
    }
    port = (unsigned short) atoi(argv[1]);
    sock=socket(AF_INET, SOCK_STREAM, 0);
    if (sock < 0) error("Opening socket");
    server.sin_family=AF_INET;
    server.sin_addr.s_addr=INADDR_ANY;
    server.sin_port=htons(port);
    len=sizeof(server);
    if (bind(sock, (struct sockaddr *)&server, len) < 0)
         error("binding socket");
    fromlen=sizeof(from);
    if (listen(sock,5) < 0)
         error("listening");
    while (1) {
        newsock=accept(sock,   (struct   sockaddr   *)&from,
&fromlen);
        if (newsock < 0) error("Accepting");
        printf("A connection has been accepted from %s\n",
              inet_ntoa((struct in_addr)from.sin_addr));
        n = recv(newsock,buffer,BUFSIZE-1,0);
        if (n < 1) {
      error("Reading");
        }
        else {
          buffer[n]='\0';
          printf("Message from client is: %s\n",buffer);
          len = strlen(msg);
          n = send(newsock,msg,len,0);
```

```
        if (n < len) error("Error writing");
        if (close(newsock) < 0) error("closing");
    }
    }
    return 0; // we never get here
}
```

This program creates a TCP socket in the Internet domain. It takes one argument, the port number that the server should be bound to. It binds the socket to that port on the local host (i.e. the machine that it is running on), listens for connections, and then enters an infinite loop. Whenever it accepts a new connection from a client, it reads a message from the client and displays it on the screen, sends a message back to the client, and closes the socket,

The only new function call in this program is `inet_ntoa` which takes one argument, an in_addr, (which is just a 32 bit unsigned int) and returns a string which is the IP address of its argument in dotted decimal form.

The Client Side Program

The client creates a socket just like the server. However, instead of binding to an address, it called the connect system call, which establishes a connection to a server. We assume our client program takes hostname along the command line. However, we need to fill in the port number and the IP address of the server for establishing connection and communication. Thus, we use the system call gethostbyname(). This takes one argument, a character string which is the name of the machine on which the server is running, and it returns a pointer to a **struct hostent**. This has a field , char *h_addr, which is the IP address and the size of this is in the field h_length. We use this information for connecting via connect system call. Do remember our client program needs port number also along the command line.

```
/* client.c      Creates Internet stream client for a Unix
platform.
    The name and port number of the server are passed in as
arguments.
    To compile
    gcc -o client client.c
    To run
    client servermachinename portnumber
*/

#include <sys/types.h>
```

```c
#include <sys/socket.h>
#include <netinet/in.h>
#include <netdb.h>
#include <stdio.h>
#include <unistd.h>
#include <stdlib.h>
#include <string.h>
char *msg = "Hello Venkat";
void error(char *msg){
    perror(msg);
    exit(0);
}

int main(int argc, char *argv[]){
    int sock, n;
    unsigned short port;
    struct sockaddr_in server;
    struct hostent *hp;
    char buffer[1024];

    if (argc != 3) {
        printf("Usage: %s server port\n", argv[0]);
        exit(1);
    }
    sock= socket(AF_INET, SOCK_STREAM, 0);
    if (sock < 0) error("Opening socket");

    server.sin_family = AF_INET;
    hp = gethostbyname(argv[1]);
    if (hp==NULL) error("Unknown host");
    memcpy((char *)&server.sin_addr,(char *)hp->h_addr, hp->h_length);
    port = (unsigned short)atoi(argv[2]);
    server.sin_port = htons(port);
    if (connect(sock, (struct sockaddr *)&server, sizeof server) < 0)
```

```
            error("Connecting");
n = send(sock, msg, strlen(msg),0);
if (n < strlen(msg))
            error("Writing to socket");
n = recv(sock, buffer, 1023,0);
if (n < 1) error("reading from socket");
buffer[n]='\0';
printf("The message from the server is %s\n",buffer);
if (close(sock) < 0) error("closing");
printf("Client terminating\n");
return 0;
}
```

Steps involved in this connection oriented client server program can be represented as in the Fig. 24.7.

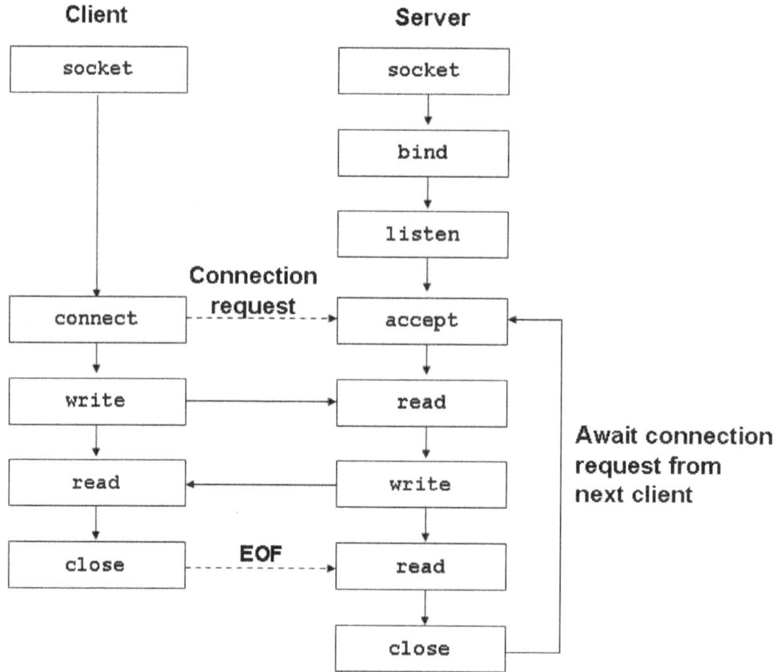

Fig. 24.7 Connection Oriented Client-Server Communication.

Also, the following figure demonstrates the snap shot of our working on our machine.

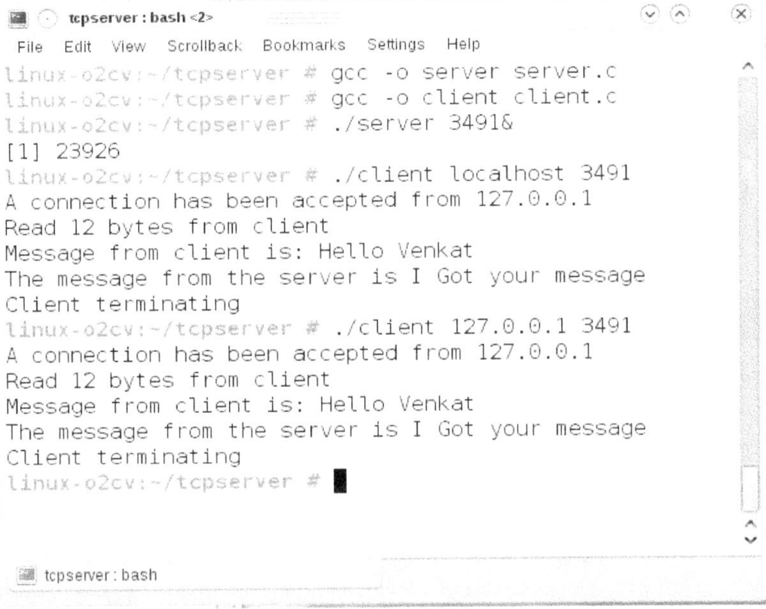

Exampe 10 A Simple Program To Transfer a Text file to a Machine

In this problem also, we will be having server and client machines. The server creates a socket and what ever it receives from client from read's will be written into a file 'Test'. The client program can be started with hostname, port number and file name to be transferred along the command line. The client program, as usual creates a socket and calls connect system call. After that it reads the opened file whose name is given along the command line using fgets and sends those strings to server using send system call till the end of the file is encountered. This is how we propose to transfer a text file. Of course, we accept this is little buggy program.

File Server1.c
```
/* server1.c - creates a connection oriented (stream) Internet
server
      for the Unix Operating system. Port is passed in as an
   argument
      To compile
      gcc -o server1 server1.c */

#include <sys/types.h>
#include <sys/socket.h>
#include <netinet/in.h>
```

```c
#include <stdio.h>
#include <unistd.h>
#include <stdlib.h>
#include <arpa/inet.h>
#include<string.h>

#define BUFSIZE 4096
extern int errno;
void error(char *msg)
{
    perror(msg);
    exit(0);
}


int main(int argc, char *argv[])
{
    int sock, newsock, len, fromlen, n;
    unsigned short port;
    struct sockaddr_in server, from;
    char buffer[BUFSIZE];
    char msg[1024];
    FILE *op;
    op=fopen("Test", "w");

    if (argc < 2) {
        fprintf(stderr,"usage %s portnumber\n",argv[0]);
        exit(0);
    }
    port = (unsigned short) atoi(argv[1]);
    sock=socket(AF_INET, SOCK_STREAM, 0);
    if (sock < 0) error("Opening socket");
    server.sin_family=AF_INET;
    server.sin_addr.s_addr=INADDR_ANY;
    server.sin_port=htons(port);
    len=sizeof(server);
    if (bind(sock, (struct sockaddr *)&server, len) < 0)
        error("binding socket");
    fromlen=sizeof(from);
```

```c
    if (listen(sock,5) < 0)
        error("listening");
    while (1) {
        newsock=accept(sock,    (struct    sockaddr    *)&from,
&fromlen);
        if (newsock < 0) error("Accepting");
        printf("Transferring file from  %s\n",
               inet_ntoa((struct in_addr)from.sin_addr));
      do{
       n = recv(newsock,buffer,BUFSIZE-1,0);
       printf("Read %d bytes from client\n",n);
       if (n < 1) {
    error("Reading");
         close(newsock);
         break;
       }
       else {
         buffer[n]='\0';
        fprintf(op,"%s\n", buffer);
   }
     }while(n);
  }

    return 0; // we never get here
}
```

File Client1.c
```c
/* client1.c     Creates Internet stream client for a Unix
platform.
   The name and port number of the server are passed in as
arguments.
   To compile
   gcc -o client1 client1.c
   To run
   client1 servermachiname portnumber filename
*/
#include <sys/types.h>
#include <sys/socket.h>
#include <netinet/in.h>
#include <netdb.h>
```

```c
#include <stdio.h>
#include <unistd.h>
#include <stdlib.h> /* for atoi */
#include<string.h>
void error(char *msg)
{
    perror(msg);
    exit(0);
}


int main(int argc, char *argv[])
{
    int sock, n;
    unsigned short port;
    struct sockaddr_in server;
    struct hostent *hp;
    char buffer[1024], msg[1024];
    FILE *IP;

    if (argc != 4) {
        printf("Usage:   %s   server   port   filename\n",
argv[0]);
        exit(1);
    }

  IP=fopen(argv[3], "r");

  sock= socket(AF_INET, SOCK_STREAM, 0);
  if (sock < 0) error("Opening socket");

  server.sin_family = AF_INET;
  hp = gethostbyname(argv[1]);
  if (hp==NULL) error("Unknown host");
```

```
memcpy((char *)&server.sin_addr,(char *)hp->h_addr,
        hp->h_length);
port = (unsigned short)atoi(argv[2]);
server.sin_port = htons(port);
if (connect(sock,  (struct  sockaddr  *)&server,  sizeof
server) < 0)
          error("Connecting");
while(!feof(IP)){
fgets( msg, 1024, IP);
 n = send(sock, msg, strlen(msg),0);
 if (n < strlen(msg))
          error("Writing to socket");
 }
 return 0;
}
```

The following snapshot shows our working with the this problem.

```
tcpserver : bash
File  Edit  View  Scrollback  Bookmarks  Settings  Help
linux-o2cv: /tcpserver # cat Test
linux-o2cv: /tcpserver # gcc -o server1 server1.c
linux-o2cv: /tcpserver # gcc -o client1 client1.c
linux-o2cv: /tcpserver # ./server1 2335&
[2] 3863
linux-o2cv: /tcpserver # cat nbv
I guess it will work
I hope so
Bye
linux-o2cv: /tcpserver # ./client1 localhost 2335 nbv
Transferring file from  127.0.0.1
Read 39 bytes from client
Read 0 bytes from client
Reading: Success
[2]+  Done                    ./server1 2335
linux-o2cv: /tcpserver # cat Test
I guess it will work
I hope so
Bye
Bye

linux-o2cv: /tcpserver #
```

tcpserver : bash

Exercise: Modify the above program such the server creates the file with the actual file name appended with the machine name from which it has arrived. Also, explore while the resulting file is showing last line two times.

Example 11: Another Version of Client & Server Pair which uses getaddrinfo system call. Here, by calling getaddrinfo system call we fill up the address related structures. Read showip program which is given earlier. Here, also we are calling listen system call in the server program to wait for client requests. We have written few lines to take care of dead processes. Then, the server program goes into infinite loop waiting for connection requests. One such a thing arrives, fork is called to create new process in which sockfd is closed as child is no longer interested to listen; rather it is interested to serve via new port returned from accept system call (Do remember that file descriptors are inherited to child processes). Via this new descriptor child process will use send and recv method to communicate with the client.

File Server.c

```
/*
** server.c -- a stream socket server demo
*/

#include <stdio.h>
#include <stdlib.h>
#include <unistd.h>
#include <errno.h>
#include <string.h>
#include <sys/types.h>
#include <sys/socket.h>
#include <netinet/in.h>
#include <netdb.h>
#include <arpa/inet.h>
#include <sys/wait.h>
#include <signal.h>

#define PORT "3490"   // the port users will be connecting
to

#define BACKLOG 10    // how many pending connections queue
will hold

void sigchld_handler(int s){
```

```c
        while(waitpid(-1, NULL, WNOHANG) > 0);
}

// get sockaddr, IPv4 or IPv6:
void *get_in_addr(struct sockaddr *sa){
   if (sa->sa_family == AF_INET) {
        return &(((struct sockaddr_in*)sa)->sin_addr);
   }

   return &(((struct sockaddr_in6*)sa)->sin6_addr);
}

int main(void){
   int sockfd, new_fd;  // listen on sock_fd, new connection
on new_fd
   struct addrinfo hints, *servinfo, *p;
   struct   sockaddr_storage   their_addr;   //   connector's
address information
   socklen_t sin_size;
   struct sigaction sa;
   int yes=1;
   char s[INET6_ADDRSTRLEN];
   int rv;

   memset(&hints, 0, sizeof hints);
   hints.ai_family = AF_UNSPEC;
   hints.ai_socktype = SOCK_STREAM;
   hints.ai_flags = AI_PASSIVE; // use my IP

   if ((rv = getaddrinfo(NULL, PORT, &hints, &servinfo)) !=
0) {
        fprintf(stderr,        "getaddrinfo:        %s\n",
gai_strerror(rv));
        return 1;
   }

   // loop through all the results and bind to the first we
can
   for(p = servinfo; p != NULL; p = p->ai_next) {
```

```
        if ((sockfd = socket(p->ai_family, p->ai_socktype,
                p->ai_protocol)) == -1) {
            perror("server: socket");
            continue;
        }

        if (setsockopt(sockfd, SOL_SOCKET, SO_REUSEADDR, &yes,
                sizeof(int)) == -1) {
            perror("setsockopt");
            exit(1);
        }

        if (bind(sockfd, p->ai_addr, p->ai_addrlen) == -1) {
            close(sockfd);
            perror("server: bind");
            continue;
        }

        break;
    }

    if (p == NULL)  {
        fprintf(stderr, "server: failed to bind\n");
        return 2;
    }

    freeaddrinfo(servinfo); // all done with this structure

    if (listen(sockfd, BACKLOG) == -1) {
        perror("listen");
        exit(1);
    }

    sa.sa_handler = sigchld_handler; // reap all dead processes
```

```
sigemptyset(&sa.sa_mask);
sa.sa_flags = SA_RESTART;
if (sigaction(SIGCHLD, &sa, NULL) == -1) {
     perror("sigaction");
     exit(1);
}

printf("server: waiting for connections...\n");

while(1) {  // main accept() loop
     sin_size = sizeof their_addr;
     new_fd   =   accept(sockfd,    (struct    sockaddr
*)&their_addr, &sin_size);
     if (new_fd == -1) {
          perror("accept");
          continue;
     }

     inet_ntop(their_addr.ss_family,
          get_in_addr((struct sockaddr *)&their_addr),
          s, sizeof s);
     printf("server: got connection from %s\n", s);

     if (!fork()) { // this is the child process
          close(sockfd);  //  child  doesn't  need  the
listener
          if (send(new_fd, "Hello, world!", 13, 0) == -
1)
               perror("send");
          close(new_fd);
          exit(0);
     }
     close(new_fd);  // parent doesn't need this
}

return 0;
}
```

The client process as usual creates a new socket and calls connect request. Then it uses send and recv system calls to communicate with the server.

File Client.c

```
/*
** client.c -- a stream socket client demo
*/

#include <stdio.h>
#include <stdlib.h>
#include <unistd.h>
#include <errno.h>
#include <string.h>
#include <netdb.h>
#include <sys/types.h>
#include <netinet/in.h>
#include <sys/socket.h>

#include <arpa/inet.h>

#define PORT "3490" // the port client will be connecting
to

#define MAXDATASIZE 100 // max number of bytes we can get
at once

// get sockaddr, IPv4 or IPv6:
void *get_in_addr(struct sockaddr *sa)
{
   if (sa->sa_family == AF_INET) {
        return &(((struct sockaddr_in*)sa)->sin_addr);
   }

   return &(((struct sockaddr_in6*)sa)->sin6_addr);
}

int main(int argc, char *argv[])
{
   int sockfd, numbytes;
```

```c
char buf[MAXDATASIZE];
struct addrinfo hints, *servinfo, *p;
int rv;
char s[INET6_ADDRSTRLEN];

if (argc != 2) {
    fprintf(stderr,"usage: client hostname\n");
    exit(1);
}


memset(&hints, 0, sizeof hints);
hints.ai_family = AF_UNSPEC;
hints.ai_socktype = SOCK_STREAM;

if ((rv = getaddrinfo(argv[1], PORT, &hints, &servinfo))
!= 0) {
        fprintf(stderr,          "getaddrinfo:          %s\n",
gai_strerror(rv));
        return 1;
}


// loop through all the results and connect to the first
we can
    for(p = servinfo; p != NULL; p = p->ai_next) {
        if ((sockfd = socket(p->ai_family, p->ai_socktype,
                p->ai_protocol)) == -1) {
            perror("client: socket");
            continue;
        }

        if (connect(sockfd, p->ai_addr, p->ai_addrlen) == -
1) {
            close(sockfd);
            perror("client: connect");
            continue;
        }

        break;
    }
```

```
    if (p == NULL) {
        fprintf(stderr, "client: failed to connect\n");
        return 2;
    }


    inet_ntop(p->ai_family, get_in_addr((struct sockaddr *)p-
>ai_addr),
                s, sizeof s);
    printf("client: connecting to %s\n", s);


    freeaddrinfo(servinfo); // all done with this structure


    if ((numbytes = recv(sockfd, buf, MAXDATASIZE-1, 0)) == -
1) {
        perror("recv");
        exit(1);
    }


    buf[numbytes] = '\0';


    printf("client: received '%s'\n",buf);


    close(sockfd);


    return 0;
}
```

Example 12 A threaded server

In the above program, we have made our server to create a new child process by calling fork and then allowed to communicate with the client. Already we know process creating is little demanding one. If the server is going to do anything more complicated than sending a string back to the client, it should handle each connection in a separate thread instead of a separate process. In general, thread is less demanding one compared to a process. In the following example, we are directly using a thread without going into the details of the same. Readers advised to refer books on operating systems. Evidently, every thread will be having an associated function which is known as thread function. When a thread is created this function will be executed like signal handler.

Here is a server which creates a new thread for each connection

```c
/* serverwiththread.c - creates a connection oriented (stream)
    socket  in  the  Internet  domain  for  the  Unix  Operating
   system
    Each connection is handled in a separate thread
    To compile
    gcc -o serverwiththread serverwiththread.c  -lpthread
*/
#include <sys/types.h>
#include <sys/socket.h>
#include <netinet/in.h>
#include <stdio.h>
#include <unistd.h>
#include <stdlib.h>
#include <arpa/inet.h>
#include <pthread.h>

#define BUFSIZE 1024

extern int errno;
void error(char *msg){
    perror(msg);
    exit(0);
}

int main(int argc, char *argv[]){
    int sock, *newsock, len, fromlen, retval;
    unsigned short port;
    struct sockaddr_in server;
    struct sockaddr_in from;
    pthread_t tid;
    void *ConnectionThread(void *); //function prototype
```

```c
    if (argc < 2) {
        fprintf(stderr,"usage %s portnumber\n",argv[0]);
        exit(0);
    }
    port = (unsigned short) atoi(argv[1]);
    sock=socket(AF_INET, SOCK_STREAM, 0);
    if (sock < 0) error("Opening socket");
    server.sin_family=AF_INET;
    server.sin_addr.s_addr=INADDR_ANY;
    server.sin_port=htons(port);
    len=sizeof(server);
    if (bind(sock, (struct sockaddr *)&server, len) < 0)
        error("binding socket");
    fromlen=sizeof(from);
    if (listen(sock,5) < 0)
        error("listening");;
    while (1) {
        newsock = (int *)malloc(sizeof (int));
        if (newsock == NULL) error("malloc");
        *newsock=accept(sock,   (struct   sockaddr   *)&from,
&fromlen);
        if (*newsock < 0) error("Accepting");
        printf("A connection has been accepted from %s\n",
                inet_ntoa((struct in_addr)from.sin_addr));
retval = pthread_create(&tid, NULL, ConnectionThread, (void
*)newsock);
        if (retval != 0)   {
            error("Error, could not create thread");
        }
    }
    return 0; // we never get here
}
```

```c
/****** ConnectionThread **********/
void *ConnectionThread(void *arg)
{
    int sock, n, len;
    char buffer[BUFSIZE];
    char *msg = "Got your message";

    sock = *(int *)arg;
    len  = strlen(msg);
    n = read(sock,buffer,BUFSIZE-1);
    while (n > 0) {
        buffer[n]='\0';
        printf("Message is %s\n",buffer);
        n = write(sock,msg,len);
        if (n < len) error("Error writing");
        n = read(sock,buffer,BUFSIZE-1);
        if (n < 0) error("Error reading");
    }
    if (close(sock) < 0) error("closing");
    pthread_exit(NULL);
    return NULL;
}
```

The function pthread_create creates a new thread. This requires address of an integer, name of the thread function (in this case it is ConnectionThread) and address of the arguments of this thread function. We want the resulting thread to use the socket returned from accept call to be used to communicate with the client. Thus, we are sending its address to the thread function.

24.4.25 Datagram sockets

There are two widely used protocols for the transport layer TCP and UDP. Stream sockets as described above use TCP; the connection is established prior to any data being transmitted, and the TCP software assures that the bytes are reliably delivered to the process in a stream in the order that they were sent. When speed is more important than reliability, a program should use the UDP protocol instead.

A socket which uses UDP is called a datagram socket. A datagram is connectionless and unreliable. It is simply a packet sent over the Internet on a best effort basis, with no acknowledgements or other reliability checks. The advantage of UDP is that it is much more efficient, and so for short requests, a time of day server for example, UDP is often used. UDP is also used for distributed file system requests which are typically on a LAN with very high reliability, and where performance is extremely important.

A server for UDP sockets uses the same system calls as the TCP server with the following differences.

- When calling `socket`, the second argument should be SOCK_DGRAM, not SOCK_STREAM.
  ```
  int socket(AF_INET, SOCK_DGRAM, 0);
  ```

- Do not use the `listen` or `accept` calls.

- To read a datagram use `recvfrom`. Here is the function prototype.
  ```
  ssize_t  recvfrom(int  s,  void  *buf,  size_t   len,   int flags,
  struct sockaddr *from, int *fromlen);
  ```

- This performs both the accept and the recv functions. It blocks until a datagram is received from a client, at which point it is awakened and returns. The message is in `buf`. The fourth argument, `from` is set to the IP address of the client, and it returns the number of bytes in the message.

- To send a datagram, use the `sendto` call.
  ```
  ssize_t sendto(int s,  const  void  *msg,  size_t  len,

  int flags, const struct sockaddr *to, int  tolen);
  ```

Example 13   Here is a complete program which creates a UDP server. It listens on port51717.

```
/* This program creates a datagram server process
   in the internet domain.  it listens on port
   51717.   To compile
   gcc -o udpserver udpserver.c */
#include<sys/types.h>
#include<sys/socket.h>
#include<netinet/in.h>
#include<netdb.h>
#include<stdio.h>
```

```c
#include<strings.h>
#include<arpa/inet.h>
#include<string.h>
#include<stdlib.h>

#define BUFSIZE 1024

void error(char *);
int main()
{
    int sock, length, fromlen, n;
    struct sockaddr_in server;
    struct sockaddr_in from;
    char buf[BUFSIZE];

    sock=socket(AF_INET, SOCK_DGRAM, 0);
    if (sock < 0)
        error("Opening socket");
    length = sizeof(server);
    bzero(&server,length);
    server.sin_family=AF_INET;
    server.sin_addr.s_addr=INADDR_ANY;
    server.sin_port=htonl(51717);
    if (bind(sock,(struct sockaddr *)&server,length)<0)
        error("binding");
    while (1) {
     n   =    recvfrom(sock,buf,BUFSIZE,0,(struct     sockaddr
*)&from,&fromlen);
        if (n < 0) error("recvfrom");
        buf[n]='\0';
        printf("The message from %s is %s\n",
            inet_ntoa((struct in_addr)from.sin_addr), buf);
     n   =    sendto(sock,"Got    your    message",16,0,(struct
sockaddr *)&from,fromlen);
```

```c
        if (n < 0) error("sendto");
    }
    return 0;
 }


void error(char *msg)
{
    perror(msg);
    exit(0);
}
```

A udp client is given below which needs server name and port numbers as command line arguments.

```c
/* Datagram client in the internet domain */
#include<sys/types.h>
#include<sys/socket.h>
#include<netinet/in.h>
#include<arpa/inet.h>
#include<netdb.h>
#include<stdio.h>
#include<strings.h>
#include<stdlib.h>
#include<string.h>
#include<stdlib.h>
#define DATA "I love India ..."
#define BUFSIZE 1024

void error(char *);
int main(int argc, char *argv[]){
    int sock, length, n;
    struct in_addr *hostaddr;
    struct sockaddr_in server;
    struct hostent *hp, *gethostbyname();
    char buf[BUFSIZE];
```

```c
    if (argc != 3) {
        printf("Usage: server port\n");
        exit(1);
    }
    sock= socket(AF_INET, SOCK_DGRAM, 0);
    if (sock < 0) error("socket");


    server.sin_family = AF_INET;


    hp = gethostbyname(argv[1]);
    if (hp==0) error("Unknown host");


    hostaddr =(struct in_addr *) hp->h_addr;
    bcopy((char *)hostaddr,
        (char *)&server.sin_addr,
         hp->h_length);
    server.sin_port = htonl(atoi(argv[2]));
    length=sizeof(struct sockaddr_in);
    n=sendto(sock,DATA,30,0,(struct                      sockaddr
*)&server,length);
    if (n < 0) perror("Sendto");
    n  =  recvfrom(sock,buf,BUFSIZE,0,(struct   sockaddr   *)
&server,&length);
    if (n < 0) error ("recvfrom");
    buf[n]='\0';
    printf("The return message was %s\n",buf);
    return 0;
}


void error(char *msg){
    perror(msg);
    exit(0);
}
```

A snap shot of our work on console is given below.

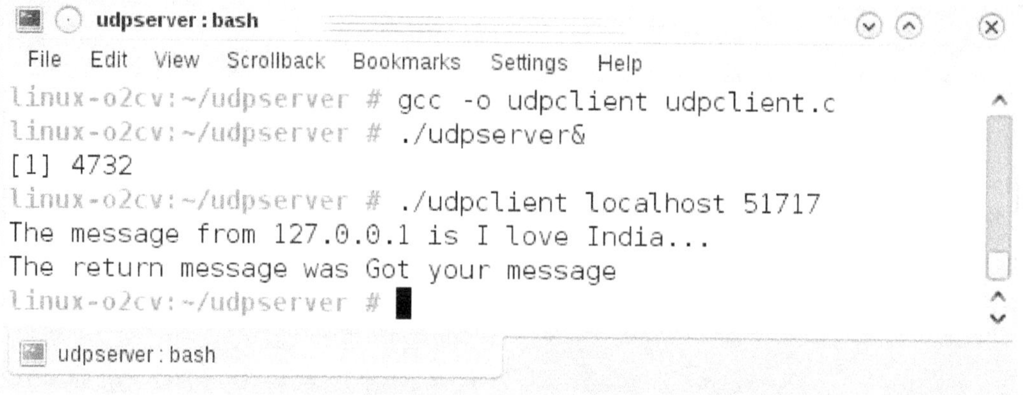

24.4.26 *Serving multiple clients*

The server code then simply waits for connections and spawns threads to handle client communication many involve the following steps.

1. create a server socket

2. Enter a loop which

   1. accepts calls on the ServerSocket.

   2. Creates a new socket whose port number is returned to client.

   3. Starts a new thread to handle the communication

   4. return back to listening on the ServerSocket.

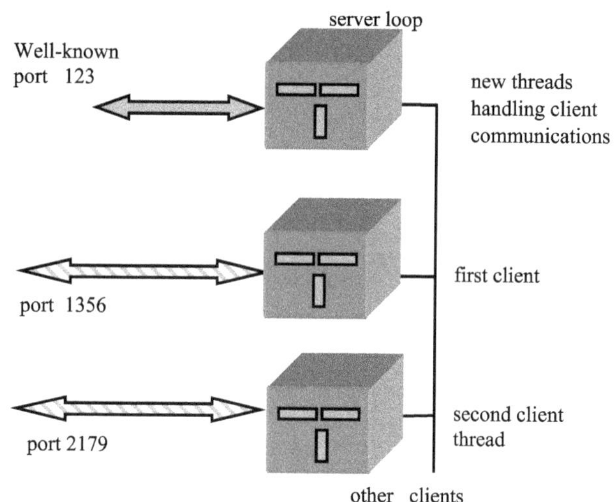

A client can connect to a ServerSocket once its **accept()** function has been called. This function returns the new Socket as its result. A ServerSocket cannot accept another connection until the **accept()** function is called again. The time that accept waits for a connection is infinite by default but can be set by calling the sockets **setSoTimeout(int time_in_milleseconds)** method.

Because it is possible to have several pending connections when the server is first started the programmer can specify the number of pending requests to queue once the main ServerSocket is created.

Example 14: The following example demonstrates the use of select system call to know which of the sockets are ready with data and how to deal with them.

File SelectServer.c

```c
/*
** selectserver.c -- a simple multiperson chat server
*/

#include <stdio.h>
#include <stdlib.h>
#include <string.h>
#include <unistd.h>
#include <sys/types.h>
#include <sys/socket.h>
#include <netinet/in.h>
#include <arpa/inet.h>
#include <netdb.h>

#define PORT "9034"   // port we're listening on

// get sockaddr, IPv4 or IPv6:
void *get_in_addr(struct sockaddr *sa){
  if (sa->sa_family == AF_INET) {
        return &(((struct sockaddr_in*)sa)->sin_addr);
  }

  return &(((struct sockaddr_in6*)sa)->sin6_addr);
}


int main(void){
    fd_set master;      // master file descriptor list
    fd_set read_fds;  // temp file descriptor list for select()
    int fdmax;          // maximum file descriptor number
```

```c
    int listener;      // listening socket descriptor
    int newfd;         // newly accept()ed socket descriptor
    struct sockaddr_storage remoteaddr; // client address
    socklen_t addrlen;

    char buf[256];     // buffer for client data
    int nbytes;

char remoteIP[INET6_ADDRSTRLEN];

    int yes=1;         // for setsockopt() SO_REUSEADDR, below
    int i, j, rv;

struct addrinfo hints, *ai, *p;

    FD_ZERO(&master);     // clear the master and temp sets
    FD_ZERO(&read_fds);

// get us a socket and bind it
memset(&hints, 0, sizeof hints);
hints.ai_family = AF_UNSPEC;
hints.ai_socktype = SOCK_STREAM;
hints.ai_flags = AI_PASSIVE;
if ((rv = getaddrinfo(NULL, PORT, &hints, &ai)) != 0) {
  fprintf(stderr, "selectserver: %s\n", gai_strerror(rv));
      exit(1);
}

for(p = ai; p != NULL; p = p->ai_next) {
    listener  =  socket(p->ai_family,  p->ai_socktype,  p-
>ai_protocol);
      if (listener < 0) {
            continue;
        }

        // lose the pesky "address already in use" error
message
```

```c
setsockopt(listener,    SOL_SOCKET,    SO_REUSEADDR,    &yes,
sizeof(int));

        if (bind(listener, p->ai_addr, p->ai_addrlen) < 0)
{
            close(listener);
            continue;
        }

        break;
    }

    // if we got here, it means we didn't get bound
    if (p == NULL) {
        fprintf(stderr, "selectserver: failed to bind\n");
        exit(2);
    }

    freeaddrinfo(ai); // all done with this

    // listen
    if (listen(listener, 10) == -1) {
        perror("listen");
        exit(3);
    }

    // add the listener to the master set
    FD_SET(listener, &master);

    // keep track of the biggest file descriptor
    fdmax = listener; // so far, it's this one

    // main loop
    for(;;) {
        read_fds = master; // copy it
    if (select(fdmax+1, &read_fds, NULL, NULL, NULL) == -1) {
            perror("select");
```

```c
                exit(4);
        }


        // run through the existing connections looking for
data to read
        for(i = 0; i <= fdmax; i++) {
            if (FD_ISSET(i, &read_fds)) { // we got one!!
                if (i == listener) {
                    // handle new connections
                    addrlen = sizeof remoteaddr;
                        newfd = accept(listener,
                            (struct sockaddr *)&remoteaddr,
                                &addrlen);

                        if (newfd == -1) {
                        perror("accept");
                    } else {
                FD_SET(newfd, &master); // add to master set
                if (newfd > fdmax) {    // keep track of the max
                            fdmax = newfd;
                        }
                    printf("selectserver: new connection from %s on "
                            "socket %d\n",

    inet_ntop(remoteaddr.ss_family,
get_in_addr((struct sockaddr*)&remoteaddr),
remoteIP, INET6_ADDRSTRLEN), newfd);
                    }
                } else {
                // handle data from a client
                if ((nbytes = recv(i, buf, sizeof buf, 0)) <= 0) {
                // got error or connection closed by client
                        if (nbytes == 0) {
                        // connection closed
printf("selectserver: socket %d hung up\n", i);
                        } else {
                            perror("recv");
```

```
                                   }
                               close(i); // bye!
                  FD_CLR(i, &master); // remove from master set
                       } else {
                           // we got some data from a client
                           for(j = 0; j <= fdmax; j++) {
                               // send to everyone!
                               if (FD_ISSET(j, &master)) {
                                   // except the listener and
ourselves
                               if (j != listener && j != i) {
                               if (send(j, buf, nbytes, 0) == -1) {
                                           perror("send");
                                       }
                                   }
                               }
                           }
                       }
                   } // END handle data from client
               } // END got new incoming connection
           } // END looping through file descriptors
       } // END for(;;)--and you thought it would never end!


       return 0;
   }
```

24.4.27 *Accessing shared resources in a concurrent Server*

Normally servers provide some constant functionality to their clients, which requires that the client-handling threads have access to some resource such as a data base or some such other data repository (file, array, table list etc). In a concurrent server this often entails several client-threads concurrently accessing the common shared resource. The problems of concurrent processes accessing a shared resource are well documented and we often have an example of the readers and writers problem.

As an example consider a retailing company with several production subsidiaries and many retailing outlets. The company keeps a central stock server accessible by both subsidiaries (who add stock to the company and therefore must be able to read and write to the stock database) and retailers who sell stock and also must be able to read and write to the stock database.

If we model the stock database as an object in the server then this object will be concurrently accessed by many client processes who may be readers who just look up information in the database and writers who change the information stored in the database.

It is well known that if we wish to keep our database consistent we must arrange that access is mutually exclusive. If we channel database access through a programming interface consisting of two functions *remove()* and *add()* our problem is then that of ensuring mutually exclusive access to these two functions.

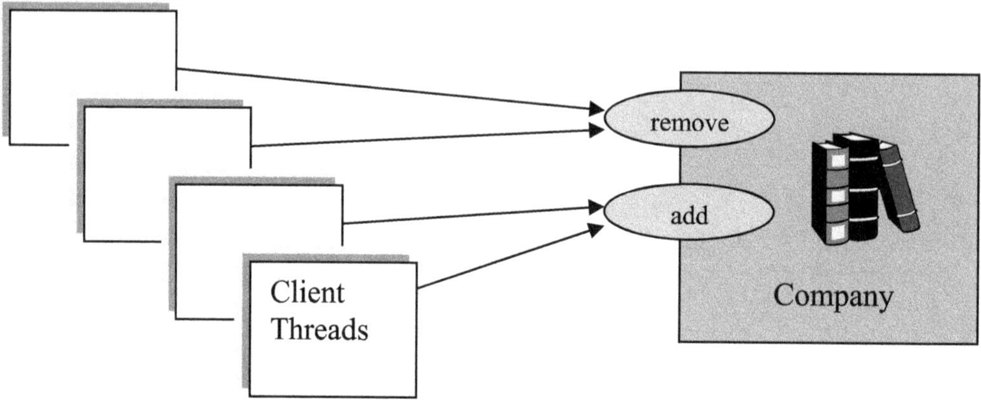

The solution to the mutual exclusion problem is to declare the two functions read and write to be **synchronized** when this is done Java automatically allocates a monitor to ensure mutual exclusion.

As an implementation note we must remember that the ClientThread is a separate class from the main server and thus by default is not able to directly access the company data object held in the server. We must therefore provide an access path. We have a choice of two methods

1. To place the Server class and the ClientThread class in the same package thus ensuring that each can access the others private variables.
2. To include a reference variable to the data object in the ClientThread class definition. Then to initialize this variable by passing a reference to the data object using the ClientThread constructor function.

24.5 Conclusions

This chapter gives essential foundations for network programming under Unix/Linux operating system. It details the theoretical background behind internet, TCP/IP, client-server computing. It then explains the most widely used Unix system calls for network programming. Live examples are included to demonstrate the concepts in a lucid manner.

Bibliography

1. Advanced Unix – A Programmer's Guide, Stephen Prata, BPB Publ, First Ed, 1986.

2. Advanced Programming in the Unix Environment, W. R. Stevens, AWL, First ISE, 1998.

3. The Design of Unix Opertaing System, M.J, Bach, Prentice Hall, Englkewood Cliffs, N.J, 1986.

4. AT&T Unix System V Release 4 Programmers Guide, STREAMS, PH, Englewood Cliffs, 1990.

5. MAGNIX Manuals, HCL India.

6. Modern Operating Systems, A.S. Tenenbaum, PHI, 1986.

7. Linux Kernel Development, Robert Love, Peasron Education, 2004.

8. B. Kernighan and D. Ritchie, The C Programming Language, PH, 1988.

9. Unix Internals: The New Frontiers, Uresh Vahalia, Pearson, 2001.